NURSING AND GLOBALIZATION IN THE AMERICAS: A CRITICAL PERSPECTIVE

Edited by
Karen Lucas Breda
University of Hartford, Connecticut

Critical Approaches in the Health Social Sciences Series
Series Editor: RAY H. ELLING

Baywood Publishing Company, Inc.
AMITYVILLE, NEW YORK

Baywood Publishing Company, Inc.
26 Austin Avenue
P.O. Box 337
Amityville, NY 11701
(800) 638-7819
E-mail: baywood@baywood.com
Web site: baywood.com

Library of Congress Catalog Number: 2009015604
ISBN: 978-0-89503-388-8 (Cloth)
ISBN: 978-0-89503-353-6 (Paper)

Library of Congress Cataloging-in-Publication Data

Nursing and globalization in the Americas : a critical perspective / edited by Karen Lucas Breda.
      p. ; cm. -- (Critical approaches in the health social sciences series)
   Includes bibliographical references and index.
   ISBN 978-0-89503-388-8 (cloth : alk. paper) -- ISBN 978-0-89503-353-6 (pbk. : alk. paper)
 1. Nursing--America. 2. Globalization--America. I. Breda, Karen Lucas, 1952-II. Series: Critical approaches in the health social sciences series.
   [DNLM: 1. Nursing--trends--North America--Case Reports. 2. Nursing--trends--South America--Case Reports. 3. Internationality--North America--Case Reports. 4. Internationality--South America--Case Reports. 5. Politics--North America--Case Reports. 6. Politics--South America--Case Reports. 7. Socioeconomic Factors--North America--Case Reports. 8. Socioeconomic Factors--South America--Case Reports. WY 16 N973387 2009]
   RT4 . N815 2009
   362.17'3021--dc22

                                2009015604

John Nordyke, designer (book cover)
Lanny Nagler, photographer (cover photo)

Daileann L. Hemmings, R.N., B.S.N. (nurse in photo)
Brandon J. Ricketts (baby in photo)

Dedication

To my father Emilio D. Breda
"Leo"
who taught me the importance of knowledge
and to all nurses who advocate for the rights of people every day.

Table of Contents

SECTION TWO

APPENDICES

Foreword

Nursing is vital to millions of people worldwide. This book details the ebb and flow of its fascinating history and politics through case studies from Brazil, Argentina, Chile, Colombia, Mexico, Canada, and the United States. Authors from across the Americas shared findings and explored new thinking about Western hemispheric-specific issues that affect nursing and health care. Using economic globalization as an overarching framework these cross-national case studies show the strengths and contradictions in nursing, elucidating common themes and examining successes. The partnership of authors shapes a collective understanding of nursing in the Americas and forms a basis for enduring hemispheric-wide academic exchange. Thus, the book offers a new platform for understanding the struggles and obstacles of nursing in a climate of globalization, as well as for understanding nursing's richness and accomplishments. Because politics, economics, health and nursing are inextricably linked, this volume critically explores the intersections among political economies and nursing and health care systems. The historical and con-textual background allows readers to make sense of how and why nursing in the Americas has taken on its present form.

Preface

Merrill Singer

This book is exceptional in a number of different ways. Nurses are the largest group of health care providers within the broad domain of biomedicine and one that is absolutely vital to its functioning locally, regionally, and globally. Nursing immediately impacts people's lives by shaping the quality of health care that patients receive. As anyone who has ever been in hospital or been the recipient of home care knows from personal experience, in response to the uncertainty of illness and the fear and vulnerability that it invokes for patients and their families, the role played by nurses in both recovery and coping with chronic symptoms is profound. Yet, as Karen Breda, a leader in the social science of nursing, aptly comments in the opening chapter of this edited volume, although much ink is spilled in the analysis of biomedicine—concerning its nature, function, impact, and social position—with only a relatively small number of exceptions, "nursing as a discrete entity is rarely [a] topic of study" (p. 5). Most books about nursing are by nurses and they are for nurses. Many are practical, some explore the underlying philosophy of nursing, most have an educational mission, but few are theoretically driven analyses of the practice of nursing in varied social contexts. This book is an exception to this pattern. The analytic perspective that the authors bring to their task is critical political economic theory, the framework historically derived from the work of Marx and Engels that draws attention to the fundamental importance of the exercise of power and structures of inequality in social process. More precisely, the book is framed by and its chapters organized around the perspective of world systems theory, as informed by anthropological attention to on-the-ground local diversity. This provides the book with a balanced approach that draws attention to the unique aspects and histories of local social worlds while attending to the ways cross-cutting forces like commodification, the global market and profit-seeking, the neoliberal restructuring policies pushed by international lending and governing institutions (e.g., privatization of health care), and strategies of capitalist labor control transcend separable national cases. In other words, this book brings social science insight to understanding the intricacies of unique local histories and social configurations of nursing in the countries of Colombia, Chile, Argentina, Brazil, Mexico, Canada, and the United States, while never losing sight of the fact that nursing in all of these places is impacted by common global changes and social and economic processes.

Notably, physicians don't write books about nursing. They do, however, write volumes about the nature of doctoring and the experience of being a physician. While the authors of such books may seek to address and influence those in the process of becoming doctors, many physicians who write books about doctoring have a broader audience in mind than just those relatively small number of individuals who will ever have M.D. inscribed after their names. What doctors know and experience, it is assumed, is of interest to everyone. This is not generally assumed about nursing. A purpose of this book, and a second way in which it is exceptional, is that it seeks to speak to a broad audience—one that includes but extends beyond those directly involved in the discipline—about the nature of nursing, as a domain of work that has struggled in multiple local contexts to overcome common structural challenges, including subordinate social status within an evolving and globalizing biomedical health care system, underpayment for increasingly professional labor, and poor and increasingly deteriorating working conditions. In this, an aim of this book is to make nursing an essential arena for understanding our changing world.

Like physicians, health and other social scientists (except those who are themselves nurses) also infrequently write books about nurses. They do, however, routinely write books about physicians and about other kinds of healers. Herein lies the dilemma of nursing from a scholarly perspective. While, as noted, nurses are undeniably central to the functioning of Biomedicine everywhere (a day without nurses would be a day without Biomedicine), at least within the bibliography of the social science of health, they are somewhat invisible. Like those who fill other social roles that are vital but which we take for granted, they are hidden in plain sight. To the degree that nursing has come to the attention of social scientists, there has been, as the book stresses, a tendency to under analyze it by narrowly viewing nurses relative to their subordination to doctors (often seen as a playing out of more general gender inequalities) and nursing as a field as a compliant handmaiden to biomedical hegemony. Avoiding this kind of reductionism too is a final way in which *Nursing and Globalization in the Americas: A Critical Perspective* is an exceptional book. Its focus is the critical social scientific analysis of nursing as a type of labor in cross-cultural and historic contexts. Its intention is to significantly expand social science understanding of nursing, but, also, the nature of Biomedicine generally by "unhiding" nursing. The book's focus, as its title indicates, is only on a part of the wide world of nursing, the Americas, the sector of the world system that is most immediately under the political, economic, and medical influence of the United States. The reason for this narrowing of the investigative lens is to increase analytic precision, while facilitating communication among the book's contributors, and avoiding some of the complexities and page length needed for a volume that was fully global in its scope. As a result, the book elevates to a historically appropriate level a vast, complex, and intriguing region that often, relative to the Unites States, has been as obscured as nurses have been to doctors.

While the explanations might differ, there is a broad agreement that health care is in crises. Most notably, even in the wealthiest country in the Americas, the United States (but not, by contrast, in Canada), a huge percentage of the population, most notably the poor and working classes, lack health insurance and hence good access to quality health care. In many of the countries of Latin America, economic inequality and structural adjustment policies have combined to make health care a consequential arena of social disparity. Moreover, health care costs have increased dramatically, further distancing the poor and working people from the kinds of health care available to wealthier social strata within and across countries. Further, nursing shortages have become common in many countries. Simmi Singh, a well-known health care information specialist, has written of a nurse friend who likes to joke that there are no Irish nurses left in Dublin because they are all in Boston, and no Filipino nurses left in Manila because they are all in Dublin. Labor pools within the healthcare professions, including nursing, have become global in nature, with a medical brain (and skill) drain producing a diaspora of health care professionals. In this light, a final message of this book concerns the future of nursing and the role of nurses in creating and improving the future of health care in the Americas. Simply put, to borrow an old saw about generals and war, health care is far too important to be left to economists, private insurance companies, the pharmaceutical industry, hospitals, or even doctors to decide. Moving quality health care from a privilege of the few to the right of all will require the participation of nurses within the communities they serve.

Acknowledgments

I am indebted to Series Editor Ray Elling who saw the need for a book on the political economy of nursing. He persisted in his vision for the book even when it looked like it was not possible. I send my heartfelt thanks to all of the co-authors who contributed to the case study chapters and without whom the book would not have been possible. Moreover, I thank the same co-authors for their patience with the long process of publication and for their responses to my many questions to them in the revision process. It has been a wonderful partnership for all of us. I applaud Ernesto Guttierez-Miravete for his translation work and all of the *Writing Warriors* who kept me on task. Last but not least, I thank Chopeta Lyons for her careful copyediting of the manuscript. Her expertise has allowed the many voices in the chapters to flow together in unison.

With great sadness we inform the readers that Dr. Maria Cecilia Puntel de Almeida passed away on February 15th, 2009. No words in Portugese or in English can translate how much she and her work will be missed–she truly was an admirable nurse scientist and a person who enriched the minds and lives of those she met. We were privileged to have had the opportunity to work with her in this endeavor and to share with you some of this experience.

The Authors

CHAPTER 1

The Context of Nursing and Globalization

Karen Lucas Breda

The practice of nursing is an ancient *art* and a modern *science*. Historically, the craft of nursing was passed on from one generation to the next by hands-on learning and informal apprenticeships. From its early origins, nursing was shaped not only by the individual needs of the sick and their surroundings, but by the collective needs of their society.

The birth of modern nursing occurred during the late 19th and early 20th centuries when a number of formal hospitals were created in urban centers throughout the Western hemisphere. The development of modern nursing throughout the Americas paralleled that of health care institutions, particularly hospitals, because nurses prepared to function in an organized way were needed to care for the increasing number of hospitalized patients.

Christian religious organizations played a pivotal role in the early development of modern nursing in the Americas, in part because religious groups possessed the infrastructure and the hierarchy needed to govern and they had the moral sanction of society to lead such an effort. Wartime and the military also influenced the evolution of modern nursing in that the large numbers of sick and injured soldiers during times of war required the presence of capable nurses at or near the battlefields. Nevertheless, the advancement of capitalism—including industrialization, technology and the growth of consolidated markets—had the most pervasive influence in shaping the institution of modern nursing in the Americas.

While *lay* nurses had functioned in the role of nurse caregiver and healer for centuries, their role was an informal one, locally-driven and bound by the constraints of culture, geography, politics and economy. Within the context of an increasingly industrialized, turn-of-the-20th-century society, the creation of formal schools of nursing garnered the potential labor of nurses and organized and standardized the care offered.

1

Throughout the Americas, rather than be free-standing schools of nursing, schools of nursing aligned themselves with existing hospital facilities and infra-structures. Hospitals needed a source of competent nurses who would not unduly drain economic resources and who would be socialized to the standards and prac-tices of the hospital setting. Also, the early schools of nursing were considered *safe havens* for the primarily female students who were required to live in the residences of the hospital-affiliated schools. The Victorian era conditions promoted the role of female nurses as caregivers attached to authoritarian hospital institutions and schools of nursing.

Religious organizations adhered to clear ideologies and doctrines for its members. While some geographical crossover existed for the major religions, South America and Mexico *primarily* followed Roman Catholic traditions while North America *primarily* followed Protestant traditions. When nursing was carried out in conjunction with religious groups, no monetary value could be placed on a nurse's time because nursing duties were carried out for the love of God and for humankind. Even when nursing grew into a more secular occupation within the Nightingale tradition, hospitals and nursing schools continued to combine religious values with the nursing role. Modern nursing effectively blended the "Catholic mystique of charitable care for the poor and the disabled with the Protestant ethic and the notion of work as a virtue and source of personal satisfaction" (Barrera & DeSouza, 2000, p. 2). This relationship between religion and nursing and its link to charity, piety and altruism continued in a symbolic form even after nursing's transition into a more secular and scientific era.

Whether connected to religious or non-religious hospitals and schools of nursing, nurses in the modern period were expected to follow prescribed norms for behavior and attitude. Conformity to rules and standards of practice, resignation to the authority of others, meekness, docility, and subservience were valued and rewarded within nursing and hospital hierarchies. Strict discipline, untenable schedules and low wages were possible to impose in a nursing culture that ostracized confrontation, belligerence and antagonism in the name of caring for the sick. Even today nursing theories privilege the concept of caring as a central tenet of nursing.

THE CREATION OF MODERN MEDICINE

The late 19th and early 20th centuries in the Americas were periods of intense competition among health care providers, particularly among those vying for dominance in a burgeoning health care market. While 19th century health care can be described as unquestionably pluralistic, with an array of recognized and established health care providers (homeopathic, osteopathic and allopathic physi-cians, as well as nurses, midwives, apothecaries, indigenous practitioners and healers, Shamans *(Chamanes), Curanderos* and *Machis* to name a few), the 20th century brought some oversight and regulation of health services and the increased dominance and legitimization of Western *allopathic* medicine (Baer, 2001; Ehrenreich & English, 1970).

During the early decades of the 20th century, Western *allopathic* physicians—what we know today as *conventional* or *regular* medical doctors (MDs)—gained political power and authority over other health care practitioners of the day, including nurses. At the same time throughout the Americas, certain prestigious schools of medicine were supported by corporate sponsors and the State, while other medical colleges (e.g., small allopathic medical colleges as well as homeopathic and osteopathic medical colleges) became increasingly marginalized and under-funded. In some cases, allopathic physicians emigrated from Europe to care for the upper classes. Over the course of the next several decades even though non-allopathic medicine continued to be practiced, allopathic medicine increasingly gained a foothold as the standard form of medical education in the Americas.

Indeed, during this time allopathic medicine transformed itself into what we know today as Western *biomedicine or biomedical science.* Western biomedicine adheres to a biological or biomedical model, that is, one that focuses on cell biology, human pathology and pathophysiology to find the origin or etiology of disease. Coincidentally, the 20th century introduction of the germ theory and its eventual acceptance added to the credibility of empirical science and the biological model during a time when biomedicine was in its infancy and needed a substantial evidence base.

The "biomedical" or "medial" model relies exclusively on cell biology for its fundamental premises; no mechanism exists in the biomedical model to address the social, political or environmental factors influencing disease and illness. Consequently, biomedical practitioners typically did not account for social and political concerns which affected the health and wellbeing of societies. In the case where a connection is made between a social condition (e.g., poverty) and illness, a biomedical practitioner would conceptualize the event as an "individual" biologically-determined pathology devoid of any social context (Baer, Singer, & Susser, 2003).

In the early 20th century, a climate of discontent and labor unrest permeated workers and the poor throughout the Americas. In light of growing dissatisfaction with government and the upper classes, biomedicine effectively "medicalized" social ills, thus taking attention off the social origin of disease and illness and focusing it instead on the new "scientific" biologically-driven medical view. Still, in Latin America, population-focused *socialized* medicine and public health established a strong foothold and effectively competed with private health care in philosophy and practice (Waitzkin, Iriart, Estrada, & Lamadrid, 2001). Alternatively, in Canada, population-focused health care evolved under the publicly funded public health services and the publicly funded and administered national health insurance program for hospital and medical care, along with an overlay of an individual-focused private system in that physicians, hospitals and other services are private entrepreneurs and institutions. However, in the United States, individual-focused, "privatized" health care centered on illness care and high technology emerged as the dominant form of health care (Castro & Singer, 2004; Elling, 1980; Navarro, 1979; Singer, 1995). As documented in the case studies in this text, (notwithstanding country-specific preferences for varying degrees of socialized or privatized medicine), a biomedical orientation to health care services gained influence in varying degrees throughout the

20th century. Over time, and as a result of its link to powerful stakeholders in the free enterprise system, biomedicine slowly but effectively secured more authority, legitimacy, and funding for its educational and clinical endeavors. Consequently, non-biomedical practitioners—indigenous and lay healers, nurses and midwives—found themselves in marginal and secondary positions vis-à-vis biomedical doctors. Undoubtedly, key events such as the release of the famous corporate-sponsored Flexner Report in 1910 fueled biomedicine's ascent to power and dominance. The Flexner Report gave exclusive credibility to biomedical education and essentially de-legitimized other forms of medical education systems (Baer, 2001; Ehrenreich & English, 1970).

Medical education programs that survived the aftermath of the Flexner Report were almost all biomedical programs affiliated with prestigious universities and colleges catering to wealthy and socially positioned male students. In this trans-formation, not only did biomedicine become the dominant model of medical education, but also biomedical education became the domain of the wealthy and the powerful, thus marginalizing those who lacked access to these privileged academic institutions (Ehrenreich & English, 1970).

By collaborating with private and public institutions, biomedical practitioners were able to find sponsors for new scientific education and research centers. This sponsorship was possible, in part because of biomedicine's close ties with elite members of private philanthropic organizations, and in part because of its align-ment with stakeholders in State and government hierarchies. During the decades following the release of the Flexner Report, biomedicine and biomedical physicians slowly but successfully edged out competitive health care systems and providers for both funding and power bases (Baer, 2001).

Accordingly, in the early part of the 20th century, women—as well as other groups such as middle class and poor men, people of color and indigenous peoples—were effectively barred from this new era of elite biomedical education. While nearly all women were essentially denied access to education in biomedical schools of medicine, they (at least White women of "good" backgrounds) were welcomed into the nursing schools created alongside hospitals catering to biomedical health care. An efficient way to staff the hospitals was to prepare as many nurses as possible to care for the new "customers." Whether religious or lay institutions, these organizations needed to attract people who could pay for the services of the new self-proclaimed *scientific* or *modern* biomedicine (Melosh, 1982; Reverby, 1987).

Early nursing care in this new system of health care was based on routine, tradition and established practice. Authors in this volume attest to the fact that throughout the Americas, the hospital system was ruled-driven and patriarchal. Nurses were expected to acquiesce to the wishes of others while keeping operations running smoothly. Hospitals could compete in the health care market by paying nurses little or no salary. So nursing students and religious sisters staffed many of the hospitals. Due to their low status and lack of power as well as their vows of humility and charity (in the case of religious sisters), they expected little in return for their services (Ashley, 1976; Melosh, 1982; Reverby, 1987).

SCOPE OF THE BOOK

This book explores the field of modern nursing in the Americas with particular emphasis on seven cross-national case study country sites. Our intent is to understand the trajectory of modern nursing in the Americas by analyzing the interrelationships of the political economy, globalization, health care delivery, and nursing educational systems. The basic issues addressed in the book are: What is the complexion of modern nursing in selected case study sites in the Americas and how are national realities in nursing shaped by the larger hemispheric and ultimately global political economy?

To provide context for the volume we address four questions in this introduction: Why focus on nursing? Why focus on the Americas? Why target a broad audience? And finally, why focus on globalization, neoliberalism, and nursing?

Why Focus on Nursing?

Nurses make up the "largest group of healthcare providers worldwide" (Falk-Rafael, 2006, p. 13). As such, nurses provide an incalculable service to the health and wellbeing of people everywhere. The adequate supply and the quality of nursing professionals are vital and crucial to the function of effective health care systems. The supply of this critical labor force worldwide is subject to repeated and unexpected fluctuations and dramatic cyclic shortages that are related more to the dynamics of the global political economy than to any single cultural or social cause.

Ideally, investing in the development of sound educational systems for nursing is a logical way to enhance the quality of the nursing labor force. Still, nursing in the examples from across the Americas recounted in this volume, is rampant with multiple, sometimes unrelated and noncontiguous, levels of educational preparation for nurses. As a result, contradictions inevitably abound among the levels and in the ultimate functions and responsibilities of nurses in practice. Additionally, a historic disjoint exists throughout the Americas between educational institutions and health care industry concerning the expectations for the education and qualifications for nurses. This discrepancy between the workplace and educational environments has a negative impact on the quality, status and trajectory of nursing.

These and other contradictions in nursing coupled with the unique position of nursing in the health care hierarchy make the field a ripe topic for socio-political analysis. Yet, when compared to the plethora of social science studies on physicians, similar studies on nurses are relatively few in number (Brannon, 1996, 1994, 1990; Coburn, 1988; Ehrenreich & English, 1970; Haywood & Fee, 1992; Melosh, 1982; Reverby, 1987; Rispel & Schneider, 1991; Sacks, 1988; Wagner, 1980; Wolf, 1988; Zadoroznyj, 1990). With only some exceptions, nursing as a discrete entity is rarely the topic of study. This rarity is the case even though nurses are intricately enmeshed in the political economy of health and nursing services themselves are vital to the functioning of health care systems and general health care promotion globally. Certainly, social scientists can benefit from focusing specifically on nursing as a distinct unit and as a form of social labor. This volume hopes to begin that dialogue.

Why Focus on the Americas?

To understand the dynamics of nursing globally, it is imperative to move beyond single country analyses and to examine multiple country examples. Doing so helps bring to light a variety of dimensions of nursing. Comparing and contrasting nursing among various nation states allow us to uncover parallels and contradictions in systems and to better link local realities and issues to the broad macro or global context.

While considering nursing worldwide would prove laudable and certainly enlightening, it is not feasible to complete a detailed analysis of nursing worldwide within the confines of one volume. As a data set, the territory of "the Americas," also known by the geopolitical term "Western Hemisphere," albeit not the entire world, is already vast and represents an acceptable unit of analysis. Cross-national selections of countries within the Western Hemisphere give ample examples of diversity and allow for rich comparisons. The levels of development and industrialization as well as the idiosyncrasies in the histories of nursing in the nation states selected for this volume give the reader the opportunity to visualize the range of challenges and contradictions modern nursing faces both as an occupational category and as an evolving discipline.

Unfortunately, it was not possible to capture samples from the entire Western Hemisphere in this current volume. For example, the islands of the West Indies, including Cuba and the territories in the extreme geographical periphery like Greenland are not represented. Nevertheless, the country case study sites that are included in this volume reflect important and diverse representations of nursing educational and health care systems, political and historical systems, socio-cultural realities and geographical areas. And, the level of economic development in the countries selected for case study analysis reflects a good mix of developed and underdeveloped nation states (Malvarez & Castrillón, 2005).

In addition to many differences, the Americas include some similarities. Old World powers colonized large areas of the Americas and their populations reflect the heterogeneity of various immigrant and native groups. Indeed, the aftereffects of colonization and slavery pervade many parts of the Americas. In terms of health and health care, the timeline for the development of modern nursing is also similar in many parts of the Western Hemisphere. Along the same lines, Western (allopathic) biomedicine emerged as the dominant form of medicine during the early 20th century. With it, hospitals and health care systems developed to accommodate Western biomedicine. Certainly, nursing care and nursing education programs across the Americas followed the trajectory of hospitals and Western biomedicine in general.

Finally, the relative geographical proximity of countries in the Americas and the similar time zones makes it feasible for social scientists and nurses to collaborate in completing more in-depth cross-national comparisons. This volume engages academics in social science and nursing from across the Americas in productive, collaborative analysis.

Why Target a Broad Audience?

To a large extent, nursing studies adopt a nursing perspective and social science studies adopt a social science perspective. Both disciplines target distinct audiences within their respective fields. This narrow focus limits dialogue and discourse and restricts the potential for exchange among paradigms and disciplines. Instead, then, this volume targets a broad audience of both nurses and social scientists throughout the Americas. The intent is to use the disciplinary logic and matrixes of both nursing and social science to produce a trans-disciplinary analysis that adopts conceptualizations from both fields. The hope is to expand the boundaries of the subject matter and intellectualization on the topic while opening up lines of discourse among the fields.

Why Focus on Globalization, Neoliberalism, and Nursing?

Globalization is an ambiguous concept used to refer to a variety of forces. While generically it means increased communication and ease of cultural exchange worldwide, specifically, it refers to economic globalization of finance within an increasingly powerful capitalist or free market system. As such, globalization is intricately connected to the development of market power and to the consolidation of economic institutions worldwide.

The concept of globalization is complex, multidimensional and highly politicized. Analysts who use the term are increasingly split into two camps: a pro-globalization camp which views the positive economic, social and cultural consequences of globalization and pro-social justice camp which views economic globalization as privileging the wealthy and creating devastating inequities for working people and a growing number of poor people worldwide.

Globalization is often linked to "neoliberal" ideology or thought. Neoliberal principles based on:

1. individualism;
2. free market through privatization and deregulation; and
3. decentralization, have permeated social, political as well as economic policy worldwide (McGregor, 2001).

In a neoliberal ideology, free market (capitalist) enterprises are privileged over public social welfare systems (McGregor, 2000; McGregor, Doull, & Fish, 2003).

Commonly referred to as neoliberalism, neoliberal reform seeks to restructure the economic and political segments of society within a free market environment. Neoliberalism privileges the private sector, fosters market forces and promotes deregulation (Lyon-Callo, 2004). It is a movement toward increased privatization and a "lean economy" that necessities work intensification and downsizing. In actuality, neoliberalism is a "theory of political economic practices" fostering individual business autonomy and lack of restrictions. At heart, it is known for its protection of "strong private property rights, free markets, and free trade" (Harvey,

2005, p. 2). Under neoliberalism, the role of the state is to protect neoliberal economic practices and to promote the expansion of the free market, while not interfering with or curtailing it in any way (Harvey, 2005).

Globalization, often referred to in connection with neoliberalism, is a broad and confusing term that has potentially contradictory meanings. While it may seem so, globalization is not a neutral concept. Different camps, usually conservative in nature, use the term globalization to put forth its own ideas and view of the world. Commonly, globalization is thought of as an increased connection between and among countries of the world. Enhanced communication and ease of travel, exchange and linkages instigated a movement toward a global worldview and a financial consolidation of world markets. It has been called both a "process" that includes events that take place on the ground and a "paradigm" or way of seeing and thinking about the world. Also, it is thought of as more than just a set of strategies. It is considered by some to be a theory or conceptual model.

Clearly, for conservative scholars, globalization is a mechanism for expanding free market capitalism and it is inextricably linked to neoliberalism. The logic of pro-globalization is the logic of free markets and the rules of supply and demand related to capitalism. Conversely, for critical theorists, globalization is associated with imperialism and increased social class inequities. For these critics, enhanced globalization means the "increased globalization of capitalist production" (Lyon-Callo, 2004, p. 11).

Hence, in thinking of globalization as a paradigm or worldview that informs practice and praxis (action that is informed and linked to certain values), globalization has different implications for different groups of people. Critical political economists see the economic processes liberally permitted under uncontrolled capitalism as producing great social and economic inequities in societies worldwide. While globalization can produce phenomenal wealth for capitalist enterprises (corporate stock holders and the owners of the means of production), it is "an economic nightmare for the poor" spawning great inequities and suffering for growing numbers of poor people worldwide (One World, 2004, p. 1).

Health care systems are not immune to the influence of globalization policies, nor are they immune to the neoliberal restructuring of economic and political institutions. Indeed, neoliberal policies have come to influence every segment of society, including health and social services. Some countries in Latin America embraced neoliberalism readily, while others had it thrust upon them by the World Bank, the IMF or another financial institution (Iriart, Waitzkin, & Merhy, in Fort, Mercer, & Gish, 2004). Yet, in the end, neoliberalism came to drive the logic of health care economics in much of Latin America and Canada, as well as in the United States. By the 1990s economic globalization and neoliberal reforms had infiltrated health care systems throughout the Americas and reshaped the nature of health care and educational systems in core nations as well as in the periphery.

This infiltration means that a thrust toward the privatization of services, the minimization of the role for government, and the deregulation of industry had infused national, regional and local health services. This was possible, in part, because within today's global context health care services designed specifically for core industrial nations (e.g., United States) were readily transplanted into the under-developed world (e.g., Latin America). Moreover, the transplanting of health care services occurred whether or not the services were appropriate for the recipient country. For better or for worse, in recent years, many countries in the Americas have used neoliberal reforms to transform their health care systems shifting their national health care systems from publicly funded universal health care systems to free market, for-profit systems where access to services is determined partly by one's ability to pay for it.

Within the context of globalization and neoliberal economic reforms, health care is viewed as a commodity and pro-social groups worldwide have opposed the "commodification" or "marketization" of health care services for decades. Commodities are goods or services to be bought and sold within a free market environment. The goal of commodity exchange is to realize a profit. Within a private, fee for service health care environment, the value of health care services is reduced to their profitability.

From a free market perspective, the introduction of neoliberal economic reforms and their companion "structural adjustment programs" (SAPs) were intended (ostensibly) to improve health services and health service financing throughout the Americas. The fostering of free trade, the privatization of previously nationalized health and social services, as well as the shrinking of health and welfare entitle-ments and services were all meant to cut government spending and to "kick-start" national economies. Yet it is clear that the consequences of neoliberal reforms on health services and on health outcomes in peripheral as well as in core countries in the Americas are not positive. The aftereffects of the reforms are particularly devastating for the poor of the countries involved (Fort et al., 2004).

Nursing and the quality of nursing care are also directly affected by neoliberal economic reforms in health care financing and in the health care delivery system. Driven by tenets of neoliberalism, private market health services focus on cost cutting to increase profit margins, on competitiveness and on downsizing. Under the premise that private markets are more cost effective and leaner, private health care is gradually replacing national publicly-funded health services and social (ancillary) programs throughout the Americas. Staffing ratios, as well as labor conditions and contracts for nurses and other health workers have also been directly and negatively affected by neoliberal reforms.

Educational systems, including programs that prepare nurses, were also subject to neoliberal reforms over the last decades. The number of private educational institutions that prepare nurses is on the rise, particularly, but not only, in peripheral, underdeveloped countries such as Chile. The entrepreneurial nature of the new institutions has turned education into a commodity for sale in the free market. Health care and educational changes in the Americas have closely followed these global neoliberal trends; consequently, nursing is directly affected by these developments.

While resistance to neoliberalism and new efforts to promote social justice are brewing in some of the case study sites explored, progress in shifting health care policy to a social justice model is difficult in light of the globalization of capital and the imbeddedness of neoliberalism (Drake, in Hershberg & Rosen, 2006).

In sum, globalization and neoliberal economic reforms have provided the logic of health care economics throughout the Americas since the 1980s. The movement toward private and corporate health services, and away from public services, has resulted in an exaggerated market-driven approach to care, with the subsequent gutting of many collective health provisions, particularly in countries with strong publicly funded programs. Health care workers, particularly nurses and other mid-level staff, are being caught in the crossfire of country-specific austerity programs. As a result, nurses and others have suffered work intensification, fragmentation of duties and increasingly poor working conditions.

This book examines the case of nursing internationally using data from Latin America, Canada and the United States. The analysis demonstrates how neoliberal economic reform focused on *profit* can erode solid national health plans as well as the health care labor process. The broad lens of critical social science is used to show how health care professionals, social scientists and other engaged scholars may contribute to the discourse and create a more humane and just society under contemporary globalization.

Organization of the Book

It is our intent that this book be used as a teaching text for graduate and under-graduate students in nursing and other health professions, as well as in the fields of the health social sciences, health policy and public health. For this reason, each chapter is designed both to stand alone as a country-specific case study and to be read together with other chapters to expose cross-national differences and similarities. As a result, readers will gain an incisive look at nursing in the Western hemisphere. The study questions at the end of the book are intended to provoke discussion and be used as points of departure to guide thinking on the topic and ultimately to help inform policy, intervention and practice changes. Additionally, the text is meant to help non-academics (especially health professionals and health social scientists) comprehend how political economy and history have shaped nursing cross-nationally.

The complexity of the topic we undertook forced us to make decisions about the main thrust of the text. Hence, we intentionally focused on the intersection of macro- and micro-level phenomena and in explaining the power relationships in health care systems and in the educational institutions that prepare nurses. Conversely, we eliminated some topics (such as the first-hand accounts of nurses and patients in the system) which would have been illuminating, had there been more space.

Structure of the Book

The book presents a series of seven cross-national case studies in nursing from the Western Hemisphere. The case studies are divided into two sections with the first section focusing on a selection of Latin American counties including Argentina, Brazil, Chile, Colombia, and Mexico. The second section focuses on the non-Latin American countries of Canada and the United States.

The case studies treat historical points in nursing, the evolution of nursing education programs, as well as nursing labor and race issues and place them within the context of the political economy specific to the country. In each case example, the historical role of biomedicine and patriarchy in health care systems are considered in relationship to nursing. The more contemporary influences of market forces, globalization and neoliberalism are considered as well. Each chapter articulates how local culture and social contradictions imbedded in the political economy helped to shape nursing's path and to explain both nursing's submissiveness and resistance to power.

The nursing case study of Colombia in South America is the lead chapter of Section One in the book. In it, authors Duque-Paramo and Lopez-Maldonado pay particular attention to Colombian nurses' increasing autonomy, independence and political participation over time. The authors show the impact of Law 100 (which instituted health and social service reform) and of Law 80 (which instituted higher education reform) on nursing and how public health and higher education policy, models of medical education, and developments in the nursing discipline influenced nursing in Colombia on the whole. The chapter elucidates the damaging effects of international and national neoliberal economic reforms on nursing and how Colombian nurses struggle to sustain a model of social justice over that of market forces in both higher education and practice.

The chapter on Chile is the second Latin American nursing case study in the book. Authors Jara Concha, Behn Theune, Ortiz Rebolledo and Valenzuela Suazo explain the unique course of Chilean nursing from its early connection to biomedicine at the Universidad de Chile in 1906. The authors discuss incongruous recent events such as the acclaimed insertion of nursing into the Chilean national public health code which enhanced nursing's autonomy and recognition as well as the alarming and detrimental changes in legislation on higher education that allowed a flourishing of unregulated, substandard nursing programs based in private colleges.

The chapter chronicles Chile's peripheral status in the capitalist world system along with its historically strong cultural preference for left-of-center wing populist governments with companion social health service structures that were in place from the early decades of the 20th century through the Allende socialist period of the early 1970s. Details of how the 1973 bloody military *junta* headed by Pinochet broke the historical precedent for socialism and abruptly reversed people's health programs are revealing. The authors' thorough examination of these events help readers to understand the subsequent facile institution of austere privatization strategies in Chile based on neoliberal economic reforms. The parallel evolution of nursing in this historical political economic environment explains current contradictions and dilemmas in Chilean nursing.

Argentina provides the third nursing case study example from Latin America. The chapter describes the role of the World Health Organization, the Pan American Health Organization and other international health organizations as well as private philanthropic organizations, particularly the Kellogg and Rockefeller Foundations on the evolution of nursing in Argentina. Chervo, Arzani and Micozzi closely analyze the transformation of Argentina from a pro-social welfare state following a

Keynesian philosophy (pre-1976), to a military dictatorship (1976-1983) that killed thousands and instituted the shift to neoliberal economic policies consistent with the macroeconomic theories of the "Chicago School." The authors explicate the ramifications these policies and styles of government had on the Argentinean health care system and on nursing. Also, the role of nursing unions and professional organizations are explored in light of the nursing labor market, nursing workforce and education needs now and in the future.

Brazil, the fourth nursing case study and the largest of the Latin American countries is considered a semi-peripheral nation in the capitalist world system. The chapter details the events that preceded the twenty-two year military dictatorship (1964-1985) during which time the so-called Brazilian economic miracle of the 1970s occurred. Brazilian authors Wright, Puntel de Almeida, Padilha, David, Albuquerque, and Da Silva explain how health and social conditions as well as working conditions for Brazilian workers in general, including nurses deteriorated during this period. Authors reveal the politically active role Brazilian nurses took during the dictatorship, how some of them were imprisoned during that period and their subsequent participation in Brazil's broad and encompassing people's movement. The authors describe Brazilian nursing's leadership position in Latin American in recent decades, Brazil's hosting of foreign students in nursing graduate programs and its spearheading of nursing research projects.

Authors Becerril, Gandara, Mejia, and Gomez contribute to the fifth nursing case study on Mexico, the volume's final Latin American case. The chapter analyses the socialization of Mexican nurses, focusing on how embedded social relations in health care institutions and schools of nursing reinforce social class and gender divisions. Particular attention is given to the present-day disjoint between the academic preparation of nurses and the actual work nurses carry out in health care institutions. The influence of nurses from other North American countries (United States and Canada), the growth in graduate nursing programs in Mexico and the social recognition of nursing in social and professional contexts and as a legitimate academic discipline come to bear on the analysis.

Section Two of the volume opens with a nursing case study of Canada as the first non-Latin American site represented in the book. Also, it is one of only two core capitalist nations represented in the volume, the United States being the other one. In the chapter on Canada, French and Emed thoroughly portray the rich diversity of the country and its evolution through the phases of competitive to monopoly to global capitalism. The authors artfully unveil the roots of Canada's coveted Medicare program and the development of its national health insurance system. Geographically located just to the north of the United States, Canada is directly and strongly influenced by the contrasting political economic and health policies of the country with which it shares a vast common border.

The authors detail philosophical as well as educational idiosyncrasies in Canadian nursing; its close ties to collectivism and labor activism; and its recent struggles with the segmentation of the nursing workforce after the introduction of neoliberal economic reforms in the country. Additionally, they describe the value of landmark health care initiatives such as "Health Canada" and the role of Canadian nurses in such endeavors.

The second nursing case study chapter in Section II and the last of seven case studies in the book is that of a core capitalist nation, the United States of America. Breda, Barbee, and Zadoroznyj explore the U.S. historical political economy in a fiercely market-driven economic system and show how U.S. nursing in that context grew in tandem with capitalist development. From the origins of modern nursing in hospital "diploma" school settings to the sophisticated doctoral-level specialization programs in elite universities, the authors illustrate how nursing evolved.

Accordingly, the U.S. chapter treats the role of the leadership as well as the evolution of educational systems, unions and professional organizations in nursing. Also, the authors examine how the broad biomedical industrial complex, biomedical physicians, health administrators, and health systems influenced nursing's direction. Last, they take into account how issues of social class, race and gender intersect with each other, the current crisis in the supply of nurses and the implications for the future of nursing.

Purpose of the Book

Despite our assumed knowledge of the origins of nursing and our alleged understanding of its development, comprehension of the real complexity of nursing as a form of social labor is lacking. For many health social scientists and health professionals alike, the crux of modern nursing is an enigma. The tendency to reduce the politics of nursing to a common denominator (e.g., nursing is the handmaiden of medicine or nursing is a gendered occupation) ignores the detail and the interplay among its many intricate dimensions. In short, only a detailed and critical analysis of the historical political economic and socio-cultural dimensions can reveal the numerous contradictions and realities present in the occupation of nursing.

Part of the rationale for using multiple country case study examples is to illustrate the breadth of nursing in the Western hemisphere. Also, it is meant to demonstrate that while nations develop within their own social contexts, they are influenced by the larger global environment and the capitalist world system. A selection of core (or central) and peripheral (or satellite) as well as semi-peripheral nations are used as case study examples. In each case in point, capitalism and biomedicine as well as power and ideology had a major role in shaping the trajectory of nursing and nursing education systems.

Nursing Supply

Some readers may wonder why the topic of nurse migration and the supply of nurses (also called the *nursing shortage*) are not treated in more depth in this volume. It is sufficient to say that the recurring cyclic shortages in the supply of nurses and the promotion of nurse migration are best understood as a product of the capitalist world system. Core or central capitalist nations particularly those with weak labor laws such as the United States, have historically sought out cheap labor in the form of nurses from peripheral or satellite countries.[1] Typically, nurses who migrate offer industry a relatively docile workforce willing to work for inferior wages and hesitant to resist exploitative labor practices.

While issues of nursing supply are not new to nursing and in fact, have plagued organized nursing for its entire history, the most recent "shortage" of nurses was triggered during the 1980s when the nursing workforce was significantly downsized. In the Western Hemisphere this downsizing was particularly strong in the United States. During this time, professional nurses were replaced by less educated workers and unlicensed personnel. Simultaneously, other efforts at cost containment produced greatly increased workloads and arduous working conditions for nurses. Acuity levels in health care facilities rose due to decreased lengths of stay. Professional nurses were described by the Joint Commission on Accreditation of Healthcare Organizations as:

> . . . "canaries in the coal mine." Many have been sacrificed before the now widespread realization that there is something wrong with the work environment. Nurses leave hospitals because they are overworked and overburdened, often with tasks that were once the responsibilities of less skilled workers. They similarly have neither the managerial support not the control over their environment—through delegated authority—to marshal and deploy scarce resources in order to manage the often challenging, and sometimes critical patient care situation which they may face at any hour of the day or night. (Kingma, 2006, p. 33)

As a result of these local political economic issues, nurses in industrialized countries left the profession in record numbers and enrollment rates in nursing programs plummeted. At the same time, some peripheral nations could not fully employ the nurses they prepared as they had produced an overabundance of nurses for their labor needs (as some of these nations were also undergoing downsizing) and some of their nurses were eager to migrate. This eagerness was fueled because economic reforms throughout the 1990s in all areas including the health care industry caused significant downsizing of the workforces in peripheral nations, particularly the nursing workforce (Kingma, 2006).

Today, part-time employment, contract work and temporary work arrangement have become commonplace employment practices for nurses throughout the Western hemisphere. Paradoxically, while nurses complain that they do not have sufficient staff to provide safe nursing care services, health care administrators,

---

[1] This term is taken from the "development of underdevelopment" thesis of Andre Gunder Frank (1967). Andre Gunder Frank sees underdevelopment "not as a precursor to development, but as a consequence of its power imbalance with a developed area" (Breda, 1992, p. 25), such as Latin America vis-à-vis the United States. The developed country actively extracts surplus wealth from underdeveloped areas thus promoting more underdevelopment. This phenomenon is best understood as the result of "an ongoing and active strategy of exploitation adopted by the developed area" (Breda, 1992, p. 25).

increasingly tying to contain costs in a private health care environment, declare that all the positions they have allocated for nurses are filled (Kingma, 2006).

While market forces drive the migration of many nurses worldwide, reports show that foreign nurses can be paid significantly less than domestic nurses when employed in the same capacity; that foreign nurses are offered jobs not wanted by other nurses in less than ideal settings; and that foreign nurses are sometimes placed in capacities beneath their qualifications, that is, forced to work as nursing auxiliaries despite their qualifications as professional or registered nurses (Kline, 2003, pp. 107-111). While these ethical concerns are commonplace within the global market economy and difficult to monitor, probably the most troubling ethical issue tied to nurse migration is the draining of experienced and skilled nurses from poor nations. The migration of skilled nurses from underdeveloped, peripheral countries to core capitalist countries can be so dramatic in some cases that it causes significant human resource losses and negative ramifications for the donor country (Kline, 2003). The International Council of Nurses (ICN) and its companion foundation, the Florence Nightingale International Foundation as well as other international health and pro-social justice groups have taken strong positions against these ethical issues pertaining to the global nursing shortage and nurse migration and funded important research to address it (ICN, 2006a, 2006b).

Free Markets and the World System

The spread of free market capitalism from the busiest urban center to the most remote rural village has made it an intensely contested economic form. While capitalism has been around in some form or another for nearly five centuries, the most recent of which is called global capitalism, it has been able to inundate every corner of the world. Some analysts posit that it is precisely the pervasive characteristic of capitalism that "has made *globalism* a more popular or precise concept then capitalism because it implies a new epoch of free trade, industrial restructuring, and greater ease of transfer of finance capital across international borders (Collins, in Collins & Wingard, 2000, p. 1).

The concept of a "world system" provides a basic framework for understanding the growth of free market capitalism and for understanding the movement of goods and services globally (Wallerstein, 1983). It explains in part why, historically, the free market system has produced such great wealth and "success" in some sectors of the population, while it has produced unparalleled inequities and suffering in other sectors of the population. In this volume, the concept of the world systems is adopted as a part of the context for understanding globalization.

The world system's perspective sees the elements of the system as interdependent parts of the whole. These parts continually interact with each other to form a whole that is greater than the sum of the parts. The world system's schema considers the entire world as its "target" system or unit of analysis. It is a holistic way of looking at relationships among countries and it offers a way to explain movement and change among countries rather than simply within countries (Frank, 1967).

World system's approach assumes that a market-driven system is the rationale for economic relationships worldwide and that countries obey the logic of the market. It categorizes countries on a continuum of core, periphery and semi-periphery in size and function. It focuses on the movement of goods and products among countries. Because the unit of analysis is the entire world system and not individual countries, the focus can be put on such factors as the distribution of wealth and poverty worldwide. Within a capitalist world system, surplus goods and profits are shifted from the periphery into the core and semi-periphery. Similarly, skilled labor, such as skilled nursing personnel, also follows the same movement from periphery to the core.

The world system is a dynamic model in which all of the elements of the system are constantly changing and evolving. In nursing, the concept of the world system can be used to make sense out of who benefits and who loses, as well as issues such as how nursing labor is organized, particularly the supply of and the demand for nurses cross-nationally, and the migration of nurses (from the periphery and semi-periphery into the core.)

RE-CONCEPTUALIZING NURSING IN THE AMERICAS

The co-authors of this volume shared analytical perspectives to attain a common understanding of the topic at hand. The orthodox or hegemonic view deems knowledge as moving from core (or Andre Gunder Frank's notion of *developed*) into peripheral (or Frank's notion of *underdeveloped*) nations. Conversely, the counter-hegemonic view regards knowledge as emanating from both the core and the periphery while privileging local, collective knowledge. Indeed, it was Latin America contributors to this volume who helped the rest view globalization from a neoliberal perspective. Prashad (2006) corroborates this view when he states . . . "[t]hat we now use the word "neoliberalism" (*neoliberalismo*) to describe the phase of capitalism to which we are opposed is a testament to the organizational and ideological preparation of the movements in Latin America" (p. 18). He continues by verifying that it was groups from the South that "took the lead in providing a framework for understanding globalization" (p. 18). Similarly, while the generation of formal knowledge in the discipline of nursing has been dominated by hegemonic U.S. values and political economy (Lutzen, 2000), the authors of this volume intentionally give voice and legitimacy to locally-generated knowledge and pro-social justice values.

Our hope is that this critical methodology will bring into being an illuminating analysis of nursing in the Americas. Our intent is that it will produce knowledge that is useful and pragmatic and that it will sow the seeds of social change.

REFERENCES

Ashley, J. (1976). *Hospitals, paternalism & the role of the nurse*. New York: Teachers College Press.
Baer, H. (2001). *Biomedicine and alternative healing systems in America: Issues of class, race, ethnicity and gender*. Madison, WI: University of Wisconsin Press.

Baer, H., Singer, M., & Susser, I. (2003). *Medical anthropology and the world system* (2nd ed.). Westport, CT: Praeger.

Barreira, I. E., & De Souza, B. S. (2000). *A pesquisa e a documentacao en história de enfermagem no Brasil* [Nursing research and history in Brazil]. Ponencia presentada en el I Coloquio Latinoamericano de Historia de la Enfermería. Río de Janeiro, Brasil, 28-31 de agosto.

Brannon, R. (1990). The reorganization of the nursing labor process: From team to primary nursing. *International Journal of Health Services, 20*(3), 511-524.

Brannon, R. (1994). *Intensifying care: The hospital industry, professionalization, and the reorganization of the nursing labor process.* Amityville, NY: Baywood.

Brannon, R. (1996). Restructuring hospital nursing: Reversing the trend toward a professional work force. *International Journal of Health Services, 26*(4), 643-654.

Breda, K. M. (1992). *Politics, culture and Gramscian hegemony in the Italian health service: A comparison of USLs.* Unpublished doctoral dissertation, University of Connecticut, Storrs.

Castro, A., & Singer, M. (Eds.). (2004). *Unhealthy health policy: A critical anthropological examination.* Walnut Creek, CA: Altamira Press.

Coburn, D. (1988). The development of Canadian nursing: Professionalization and prole-tarianization. *International Journal of Health Services, 18*(3), 437-456.

Collins, T., & Wingard, J. (2000). *Communities and capital: Local struggles against corporate power and privatization.* Athens, GA: University of Georgia Press.

Drake, P. (2006). The hegemony of U.S. economic doctrines in Latin America. In E. Hershberg, E., & Rosen, F. (Eds.). (2006). *Latin America after neoliberalism: Turning the tide in the 21st century?* (pp. 26-48). Amityville, NY: Baywood.

Ehrenreich, B. & English, D. (1970). *Witches, midwives, and nurses: A history of women Healers.* New York: The Feminist Press at the City University of New York.

Elling, R. (1980). *Cross-national study of health systems: Political economies and health care.* New Brunswick, NJ: Transaction Press.

Falk-Rafael, A. (2006). Globalization and global health: Toward nursing praxis in the global community. *Advances in Nursing Science, 29*(1), 2-14.

Fort, M., Mercer, M., & Gish, O. (Eds.). (2004). *Sickness and wealth: The corporate assault on global health.* Cambridge, MA: South End Press.

Frank, A. G. (1967). *Capitalism and underdevelopment in Latin America.* New York: Monthly Review Press.

Harvey, D. (2005). *A brief history of neoliberalism.* New York: Oxford.

Haywood, S., & Fee, E. (1992). More in sorrow than in anger: The British nurses strike of 1988 *International Journal of Health Services, 22*(3), 397-415.

Hershberg, E., & Rosen, F. (Eds.). (2006). *Latin America after neoliberalism: Turning the tide in the 21st century?* New York: The New Press.

Iriart, C., Waitzkin, H. & Merhy, E. (2004). HMO's abroad: Managed care in Latin America. In M. Fort, M. A. Mercer, & O. Gish (Eds.), *Sickness and wealth: The corporate assault on global health* (pp. 69-78). Cambridge, MA: South End Press.

International Council of Nurses [ICN]. (2006a). *The global nursing review initiative: Policy options and solutions.* Retrieved June 15, 2006, from www.icn.ch/global/

International Council of Nurses [ICN]. (2006b). *The global nursing shortage: Priority areas for intervention.* Retrieved July 6, 2006, from www.icn.ch/global/report2006.pdf

Kingma, M. (2006). *Nurse on the move: Migration and the global health care economy.* Ithica, NY: Cornell University Press.

Kline, D. (2003). Push and pull factors in international nurse migration. *Journal of Nursing Scholarship, 35*(2), 107-111.

Lutzen, K. (2000). A global perspective on domestic and international tensions in knowledge development. *Journal of Nursing Scholarship 32*(4), 335-337.

Lyon-Callo, V. (2004). *Inequality, poverty, and neoliberal governance: Activist ethnography in the homeless sheltering industry*. Orchard Park, NY: Broadview Press.

Malvarez, S., & Castrillón, C. (2005). *Overview of the nursing workforce in Latin America*. Washington, DC: Pan American Health Organization. Retrieved June 15, 2006, from http://www.icn.ch/global/Issue6LatinAmerica/pdf

McGregor, S. (2000). Globalization, capitalism, neoliberalism and social Darwinism, University of Manitoba, Human Ecology, Family Studies. Retrieved June 17, 2006, from www.consultmcgregor.com/PDF/research/globalization

McGregor, S. (2001). Neoliberalism and health care: *International Journal of Consumer Studies. Special Edition on "Consumers and Health," 25*(2): 82-89. Retrieved June 16, 2006, from www.consultmcgregor.com/PDFs/research/neoliberalism.pdf

McGregor, S., Doull, J., & Fisk, L. (2003). *Neoliberalism, microbes, and peace: A human ecological perspective*. Retrieved June 17, 2006, from http://www.kon.org/archives/forum/14-1/McGregor.html

Melosh, B. (1982). *The physician's hand: Work culture & conflict in American nursing*. Philadelphia, PA: Temple University Press.

Navarro, V. (Ed.). (1979). *Imperialism, health and medicine*. Amityville, NY: Baywood.

One World. (2004). Globalization. Retrieved January 1, 2004 from www.oneworld.org/guides/globalization/index.html

Prashad, V. (2006). They rise from the earth: The promise of Latin America. In V. Prashad & T. Ballve (Eds.), *Dispatches from Latin America: On the frontlines against neoliberalism* (pp. 13-20). Boston, MA: South End Press.

Reverby, S. (1987). *Ordered to care: The dilemma of American nursing 1850-1945*. Cambridge, MA: Cambridge University Press.

Rispel, L., & Schneider, H. (1991). Professionalization of South African nursing: Who benefits? *International Journal of Health Services, 21*(1), 109-126.

Sacks, K. B. (1988). *Caring by the hour: Women, work, and organizing at Duke Medical Center*. Urbana & Chicago, IL: University of Illinois Press.

Singer, M., & Baer, H. (1995). *Critical medical anthropology*. Amityville, NY: Baywood.

Wagner, D. (1980). The proletarianization of nursing in the United States, 1932-1946. *International Journal of Health Services, 10*(2), 271-290.

Waitzkin, H., Iriart, C., Estrada, A., & Lamadrid, S. (2001). Social medicine then and now: Lessons from Latin America. *American Journal of Public Health, 91*(10), 1592-1601.

Wallerstein, I. (1983). *Historical capitalism*. London: Verso.

Wolf, Z. R. (1988). *Nurses' work, the sacred and the profane*. Philadelphia, PA: University of Pennsylvania Press.

Zadoroznyj, M. (1990). *Paths of professionalization and unionization: The collective mobility projects of U.S. registered nurses, 1965-85*. Unpublished doctoral dissertation, University of Wisconsin–Madison.

SECTION ONE

CHAPTER 2

Nursing in Colombia

María Claudia Duque-Páramo and
Martha Cecilia López-Maldonado

Since the second half of the 20th century, Colombian professional nurses have steadily worked to transform a practice considered a subordinate discipline, characterized by low status, low wages, and poor working conditions. Starting in the 1970s, Colombian professional nurses have become more independent, achieved recognition as equals among the health professionals, and steadily earned—in some areas[1]—better wages and working conditions. Nursing higher education played a critical part in producing these changes through such diverse strategies as basing curricula on the health profile of the population; developing research strategies and graduate programs; implementing nursing care process, theories and models; creating an association of schools of nursing; and developing theories based on the Colombian nursing practice.

However, since the mid-1990s, health care in Colombia has experienced yet another major shift in its focus and ideology. This shift is partly due to a health care reform characterized by three measures: the decentralizing the state's responsibilities in providing health services, the privatizing health services, and the focusing of state subsidies on the poorest of the poor. As a result, Colombian professional nurses now face deteriorating working conditions while at the same time, the nursing higher education programs strive to improve the nursing practice, moving to new conceptual and theoretical frameworks for nursing knowledge. Thus two divergent views of nursing—the market-driven practice versus the social justice ideology of higher education—conflict with and contradict each other.

---

[1] Nurses working in education, particularly those laboring in universities, usually have higher status and higher salaries than nurses working in hospitals and clinics.

Colombian nurses occupy several different levels within two main groups: vocational and professional. The vocational group includes primarily the nursing auxiliary, a certified nurse who studies one year in a hospital or in a non-university school. The professional group includes the nursing technician (a titled nurse that studies two or three years, similar to the same position in the United States); the nursing professional or "nurse" (a titled nurse who studies four or five years in a university, similar to the Bachelors of Science in Nursing (BSN) in the United States (*Iniciativa Trilateral para la Enfermería en Norteamérica,* 1996); and graduate level nurses (nursing specialists in clinical areas and nurses with master's degrees[2]). This chapter focuses on the professional level.[3]

Our first of three purposes in this chapter is to explore and discuss how several social, economic and cultural factors have shaped the present realities of nursing higher education programs. Our second purpose is to illustrate how the interactions between national and international political and economic forces have determined policies for health services and public health, as well as the current nursing practice in Colombia. Our third purpose is to discuss the history of changes to nursing in Colombia and identify the current contradictions between the goals of nursing practice and those of nursing higher education.

Thus, this chapter is in three main parts. In the first part, we focus on the Colombian environment, describing "neoliberal" economic and social policies. We present an overview of the status of Colombians' health and describe the 1993 health reform law as well as the national and international factors that shaped the health reform and the current health policies. We conclude this section by discussing some of the effects of main health reform on the national public health system.

In the second part, we examine the influences on Colombia's university level programs in nursing health care, reviewing specifically the four factors by which Colombian education programs in nursing have historically been shaped:

1. public health policies;
2. models of medical education;
3. higher education policies; and
4. developments of the nursing discipline itself.

We also discuss the roles national and international forces—especially political and economic—have played in defining university nursing education policies and programs. Doing so provides a context for the current inequities and inconsistencies between Colombian nursing education and its practice. One of the major forces shaping nursing higher education, of course, is that for the better part of the 20th century, medical school professors and national health policy makers had more

---

[2] Both specialization and master's are graduate programs which are equivalent to master programs in the United States.

[3] Higher education and vocational education are two different and independent subsystems of nursing education in Colombia.

power than nursing professors in determining the curricula for nursing education programs. Since the 1970s, however, nurses have increased their role in nursing policy making. Additionally, they have gained increasing autonomy in shaping education programs and policies, as well as improving the quality of education in order to ensure high standards.

We continue our discussion of the international forces shaping nursing education programs, both directly, such as North American forces (United States and Canada), and indirectly, such as the North American and French medical disciplines and the health policies by international organizations such as the Pan American Health Organization (PAHO). Also, we review relevant topics in nursing higher education through three time periods: before the 1970s, the 1970s-1980s, and the 1990s-2000s. Finally at the end of the second part, we analyze gender, age, and socioeconomic status of students enrolled in higher education programs.

In the third and last part of this chapter, we look to the future based on our past and present achievements, issues, and challenges.

THE COLOMBIAN CONTEXT

Located in the north west corner of South America, Colombia has five geographically diverse regions: the Caribbean region on the north coast; the Andean region in the central part of the country; the Pacific region on the west coast; the West Plains region; and the Amazonas to the south. The 2005 population is estimated at 46,039,144 inhabitants (*Departamento Administrativo Nacional de Estadistica* [DANE; National Administrative Department of Statistics], 2005) with 1.7% annual growth rate (*Organización Panamericana de la Salud* [OPS/OMS], 2002). As a result of national and international economic policies during the second half of the 20th century promoting the industrialization of the large cities, Colombians are more urban and modern. As just one example of the shift, in 1930, 70% of the population lived in rural areas and 30% in urban areas, but by the end of the 1980s, this ratio was completely reversed: 70% were living in urban areas (Oróstegui, 1990). However, modernization has not decreased poverty for the majority, nor has it reduced the huge inequalities among the different Colombian social classes and socioeconomic strata.

Colombia is often described as having a centralist government where Spanish is the primary language. In reality, since the days of colonization, most Colombians have lived in the Andean Region, a varied geographic zone that includes warm valleys, mild regions, cold savannahs, and snowy mountains. And, although it is true that most of the population speaks Spanish, 80 indigenous ethnic groups speak around seventy different languages (Arango & Sánchez, 1998).

The Andean Region is central both geographically and in the concentration of political and economic powers, as legislated by the 1886 Constitution. The centralization of power, however, caused unequal national development, the unequal regional distribution of resources, and the unequal concentration of nurses in the Andean region and the large industrial cities rather than in the outlying regions and small towns.

An important internal conflict, sometimes referred to as a "Civil War" has existed in Colombia since the end of the 1940s. Spurred by poverty and social class inequities, large right and left wing militant groups have gained an inordinate amount of power in Colombian society. The production of cocaine and subsequent drug-trafficking has come to define much of this conflict. By 2007, the main actors of this conflict were the left wing groups particularly the Farc (Revolutionary Armed Forces of Colombia) and the smaller ELN (National Liberation Army), the Colombian army and the right-wing paramilitaries primarily the AUC (United Self Defense Forces of Colombia).

While the conflict is complex and multi-faceted with many permutations over the years, ongoing U.S. subsidies and their involvement in the recent aggressive Plan Colombia have, in the minds of many, fueled the conflict and exacerbated the situation. The toll on human life over the decades is enormous with a conservative estimated 3,000 civilian deaths each year in addition to thousands more who die from urban street violence. Additionally, the recent mass eradication of coca crops via aerial spraying of herbicides pose significant negative heath consequences for local populations (BBC News, 2005).

Civilians are the main victims of the conflict. Colombia is a nation where "the presence of the state has always been weak, the result is a grinding war with multiple fronts, in which the civilian population is caught in the crossfire and often deliberately targeted for 'collaborating'" (BBC, 2005). Besides the thousands killed each year—including trade unionists, women, social leaders, political activists, university teachers, human right campaigners, indigenous peoples, children and journalists, more than 3.8 million people out of the country's 40 million people have been internally displaced during the last 20 years (*Consultoria para los Derechos Humanos y el Desplazamiento* [CODHES; Consulting for Human Rights and Displacement], 2006, p. 3). These internally displaced people often are forced to live in the shanty towns around the cities where they lack employment and have little or no access to health and educational services.

In 1991, the democratically elected representatives of the *Asamblea Nacional Constituyente* (National Constituent Assembly) ratified a new Constitution that, for the first time, recognized the great ethnic and cultural diversity of Colombians. As part of that recognition, the 1991 Constitution promoted autonomy for the regions and decentralization of the national state. The 1991 Constitution was the result of internal political forces—striving for democratic participation in policy making—and international forces—pushing Latin American countries to reform and adjust their policies. To illustrate the conflux of these two influences, the 1991 Constitution's political and administrative decentralization of the Colombian government answered the clamor for autonomy from people living in regions outside of the capital city of *Bogotá*). At the same time, it fulfilled the international banks' strategy for reducing the size of government. For advocates of regional autonomy, decentralization meant having the democratic power to choose their regional rulers and to manage their regional resources. For the advocates of the international banks, decentralization was a necessary step in implementing neoliberal policies, which reduced the government's responsibility to decrease social disparities through the redistribution of wealth. The international banks—World Bank (WB), the International Monetary Fund (the IMF) and the Inter-American Development Bank (IADB)—made loans to indebted countries, such as Colombia, contingent to upon social and economic reforms, including those known as neoliberal policies.

Neoliberalism inflames the passions of both its defenders and its enemies. According to Bejarano (2004), classic economic liberalism, which advocates for the personal and economic freedom as well as for free market economy, languished at the end of the 19th century. Particularly in the United States and the United Kingdom, the term "liberal" came to connote an interventionist or social liberalism (Centre for Public Policy and Management. The Robert Gordon University, 2005). In these two countries to this day, liberal in the political sense refers to those who support the intervention of the state to correct social injustices.

In present Colombian economic policies, the term "neoliberal" means the complete opposite. The concept of the "Welfare State" shaped the social and economic policies of many Western countries. Bejarano (2004) defines the Welfare State as "a complex of public actions that intend to warrant to every citizen access to a minimum of services to improve his/her living conditions."[4] Welfare State economics aim to provide employment, to stimulate economic growth, and to provide low-income populations access to health services, education, housing, and retirement. After World War II, the Welfare State model shaped the economic and social policies of North America and many European countries, encouraging the growth of a large middle class. However, in Colombia, as in most Latin American countries, the Welfare State was not consistent. There were significant improvements during the second half of the 20th century such as lowered infant mortality rates and increased educational levels. Yet, despite these improvements, most Colombians never gained access to full public health services, education, or retirement.

Partly caused by the economic crisis of 1970s, the State had a reduced role in controlling economic policies and social functions. No longer seen as a solution to economic problems (as it is in a Welfare State), the State was viewed as the cause of unemployment, inflation, and stagnant economic growth. State intervention and bureaucratization were seen as responsible for economic problems. With the advent of the 1980s Reagan era, economic policies aimed to reduce the state controls were seen to be interfering with the free-market. Thus "neoliberalism" meant the liberation of the markets from state controls and regulations. As Bejarano postulates:

> According neoliberal principles, the main purpose of economic policy is to favor market flexibility by eliminating all the obstacles to free competition. Neoliberalism proposes exposing the national economy to international competition, adopting flexibility to change types and ultimately, removing all protections, stimuli and aids to the producers. (Bejarano, 2004)

In brief, from the late 1980s to the beginning of the 1990s, political and economic reforms characterized as neoliberal were adopted by practically all the Latin America

---

[4] Liberal translation in this case and whenever the original is in Spanish.

countries including Colombia (Ahumada, 1996). These policies included opening the national economies "to the markets and the international capital, cutting expenditure for public services and eliminating of the state subsidies, privatization of public companies and social services and, in general, the establishment of the most propitious climate for foreign investment" (Ahumada, 1998, p. 9). Martinez and García (2000) emphasize, however, that the nations implementing these reforms saw such consequences as wage reduction, the elimination of workers' rights, benefitting from government subsidies and tax breaks providing windfalls for businesses but cutting expenditures for social services such as education and health; reduction of government regulations such as job safety and environmental protections; privatization of state-owned enterprises such as banks, hospitals, or public service companies, resulting in greater concentration of wealth in the hands of a few; and the elimination of the concept of public good, replacing it with the notion of individual responsibility. Martinez and Garcia note that the reality of the neoliberal policies is the "pressuring the poorest people in a society to find individual solutions to their lack of health care, education and social security—then labeling them as 'lazy' if they fail in their efforts" (Martinez & García, 2000).

In accordance with the IMF and WB prescribed social and economic neoliberal policies, the Colombian government instituted a series of structural reforms aimed at opening the Colombian markets to international investors. Some Colombian economists note that the neoliberal policies have helped moderate the excesses of state interventionism, but they also acknowledge the neoliberal model "has contributed to debilitate the social policies, the access of low income groups to basic services and have concentrated the benefits of the market in a few groups" (Bejarano, 2004).

In Colombia, this neoliberalism shaped the health care reform and the current health model. Indeed, the health care reform's central three strategies are identical to the social policies of decentralization, privatization, and focalization (focusing) of subsidies on only the poorest of the poor as recommended by the multilateral agencies represented by the IMF, the WB and the IADB (Ahumada, 1996).

The Colombian Health Situation

Over the last few decades, there have been key changes in the Colombian epidemiologic profile. In the 1960s, the major causes of diseases and death were the infectious and nutritional diseases. Since the late 1980s, the epidemiologic profile still indicates infectious diseases but there is also an increase in injury and death rates caused by chronic diseases, accidents, and violence. The Colombian profile is determined by geographic and biological diversity as well as by great social disparities. An analysis published by PAHO in 1998 serves to identify determinants and trends for the health of Colombians:

1. *Migration.* By 1997, one of every four Colombians lived outside his or her native region. Internal migration flows mainly toward the Andean region. External migration flows primarily to Ecuador, the United States of America,

Venezuela, and Spain. Since 1995, as the result of the economic crisis and internal violence, there has been a significant increase in all migration. The violence of both left- and right-wing groups caused alarming numbers of internal displacement: Between 2000 and 2004 the *Red de Solidaridad Social* (Social Solidarity Web) reported 1,512,194 people were displaced from their rural homes to the municipalities (OPS/OMS, 2004). Thousands of peasants, forced to suddenly abandon their homes, have fled to urban areas. Displaced peasants have overloaded the health services of the municipalities where they have sought refuge. A humanitarian disaster, there is a marked deterioration in the living conditions and health of millions of Colombian men, women and children.

2. *Cultural and ethnic diversity.* Colombia is multicultural and multiethnic. Along with whites and mixed population, there are 80 indigenous groups who represent 1.75% of the total population (Arango & Sánchez, 1998) and a sizable population of African Colombians (25%). There are also Gypsies living in family groups scattered throughout the Andean region and *Raizales,* people of African ancestry who live in the Caribbean archipelago of *San Andrés*, *Providencia* and *Santa Catalina* (Fundación Hemera, 2004). Cultural diversity is widespread throughout the geographic regions and there is also diversity of health care knowledge and practices.

3. *Developmental indicators.* General improvement in developmental indicators exist side-by-side with huge disparities based on region, on whether a Colombian is urban or rural, and on his or her social class. For example, between 1960 and 1996 the Infant Mortality Rate (IMR) decreased from 82 to 26 per 1,000 live births. The Under-Five Mortality Rate (the probability of dying between birth and exactly 5 years of age, expressed per 1,000 live births) decreased from 130 in 1960 to 31 in 1996 (The United Nations Children's Fund [UNICEF], 1998). However, upon closer inspection, the data shows much higher IMR and Under-Five Mortality Rates for those living in rural areas, marginal areas of cities, or in regions such as the Pacific or the *Amazonas.* The PAHOs (1998) report about Colombia states the problem clearly:

> [Diversity in Colombia] produces not only cultural differences but also wide variations in living conditions and hence different types of diseases. In general, the demographic indicators show steady improvement from 1970–1975 to 1990–1995. However, the statistics for the country as a whole obscures large differences among regions, between urban and rural areas, and among social levels. For example, in the period 1990–1995 the Pacific region, where the Colombian population of African ancestry predominates, had the worst indicators. . . . There were also differences between the urban and rural populations: in the former, the overall fertility rate was 2.65 children per woman, whereas in the latter it was 4.41 children per woman. Mortality from communicable diseases was three times greater for the population with an index of unmet basic needs between 90 and 100 than for those with an index lower than 20. The improvement of living conditions for

the general population in the municipal seats (urban areas) has apparently had a positive influence on the demographic indicators. However, despite the encouraging trend observed between 1973 and 1993, the poverty gap between the municipal seats and the rest of the municipalities actually widened. (p. 181)

4. *Education deficits.* Despite the government's efforts and the recognition of the importance of an educated populace for development, the deficiencies in education are still immense.

> In 1994, 2 of every 10 children between the ages of 6 and 11 were not attending primary school, and 5 of every 10 youths 12 to 17 years of age were not in secondary school. Of every 100 children enrolled in primary school, only 30 completed the ninth grade and only 7 managed to reach that level without having to repeat a year. In urban as well as rural areas, poor people receive the least education. In 1973, illiteracy in rural areas (22.8%) was more than three times higher than in urban areas (6.0%). As for number of years of schooling, in the urban population the figure (7 years) was double that in the rural population (3.2 years). In 1993 the rates of school attendance according to educational level were 36.9% at the preschool level (children aged 3 to 5 years), 79.1% at the primary school level (6 to 11 years old), and 54.1% at the secondary school level (12 to 17 years old); 8.7% of 18- to 24-year-olds pursued a higher education. (PAHO, 1998, p. 181)

5. *Disparities in basic household services.* Even though the number of households having of basic household services increased significantly between 1985 and 1993 (from 70.5% to 82.1% in water supply and from 59.4% to 69% for sewer connections), there are still between 6 and 10 million people who lack one of these services. In rural areas, between 5 and 8 million people lack at least one of these services. In fact, only 62% of the urban population receives water that is fit for human consumption, and the situation is worse for the rural population, where only 10% receives good quality water.

6. *Effects of the neoliberal model on the economy.* A look at the economic indicators from the 1960s to the 1990s validates that the Colombian economy experienced growth and diversification. Nevertheless, the neoliberal reforms of 1990s have not sustained long-term progress. Instead, the external debt has increased; the Gross Domestic Product (GDP) has diminished, and many companies ceased operations, causing massive layoffs. Over all, there has been a deterioration of the urban labor market.

These trends have a direct relationship on most Colombians' health. Although over time one sees an improvement in the general health indicators of the total population, there are also noticeable social disparities that the neoliberal policies magnify.

History of 1990s Health Reform

To step back, in the 1990s, it was clear that some sort of legislation was needed to fix health care. Certainly the National Health System based on a model of Primary Health Care, operating since the end of the 1970s, had failed to reduce disparities in health as well as to achieve health for all. Instead of one system, three independent systems provided health services: the Ministry of Health (health posts, clinics and hospitals) provided health services to underserved populations; the Social Security Institute (clinics and hospitals) provided health services to the labor force; and private services (private professionals and private hospitals) provided health services to those who could afford them: "(a)ctually it was not a system but a group of disperse and inefficient institutions, lacking coherent policies, inequitable, with major quality problems and which spent 7% of the Gross National Product" (Castrillón, Agudelo, Orrego Sierra, Pérez Peláez, Ceballos, Elena, & Arenas Cadarid, 1998, p. 27).

Additionally, the old national public health system, based on government assistance, had several problems: (a) its vertical organization was deficient in coverage (around 50% of the total population) with huge regional disparities; (b) it was inefficient; and (c) its financial system, based on institutional demands and subsidies to health providers, actually further resulted in deep regional disparities. Concurrently, the *Instituto del Seguro Social* (Social Security Institute) covered only 15% of the general population, one of the lowest coverage rates in Latin America. An additional 5% of the population had access to special health insurance and 10% could afford private health care. The remaining 20% did not have access to health insurance nor to governmental assistance (Salud Colombia, 2000). In brief, by the early 1990s, most health providers and policy makers agreed that the old health system had several problems related to quality, coverage, management, finances, and efficiency.

The encounter between internal forces striving to transform the health system and international forces, pushing to adjust economic policies, engendered the health care reform. It was widely accepted that the old 1886 centrist Constitution was obsolete and had helped create the marked social classes and regional disparities underpinning the social conflict and violence from which the country still suffers.

To address these problems, the 1991 Constitution defined health and social security as public services as well as duties of the national state, and made it responsible for directing, coordinating and controlling an efficient social security system for all Colombians (Jaramillo Pérez, 1995; Sarmiento Anzola, 1991). In other words, the 1991 Constitution forced the State to provide universal access to uniform health care services in order to minimize social disparities in health based on socio-economic standing as well as to reduce the social inequalities in social security. Additionally, the 1991 Constitution sought to ensure state control in the redistribution of wealth.

Although it appeared as if the Colombian Constitution and the international banks' neoliberal policies shared common principles, such as efficiency and decentralization, the two views conflicted. The 1991 Constitution assumed a strong State to control policies and resources; the international banks' policies sought a small, weak State with little or no social responsibility. Even though the written law mixed principles from both sides, unfortunately for health care, the neoliberal policies dominated in the actual implementation of the Colombian health reform.

In December 1993, Law 100 was established to reform the National Health Care System and the Social Security Institute by creating a unified General Social Security System on Health Care. Over a 10-year period, Law 100 sought to reach 100% health insurance coverage for Colombians. By 2004, at the 10-year mark, however, this goal was far from being achieved.

The 1993 Law 100 is both "contributory" and "subsidized" and is based on the following principles of universality, equity, solidarity, integrality, freedom, quality, social participation, and efficiency.

- *Universality* means 100% of coverage.
- *Equity* means that everyone pays proportional to his or her economic situation.
- *Solidarity* means that those with financial resources help subsidize those who lack them. Thus, the "contributory regimen" targets those who can afford contributing to the social security system through their wages or their independent income. The "subsidized regimen" targets those who cannot afford to contribute and who must be subsidized for the obligatory insurance. And in fact, this policy of financing the most impoverished citizens has earned international recognition for the Colombian social security system.
- *Integrality* means that the system integrates the several health and social security institutions into one single social security system which includes health services, professional risks, and retirement.
- *Freedom* means the client has the ability to select health insurance and the health providers of his or her own choice.
- *Social participation* means that clients elect their own representatives to legally represent them at the different levels throughout the system. Furthermore, Law 100 established a market-driven ideology where traditional state public health institutions, such as hospitals, clinics and health posts, must compete with private health providers.
- *Quality* refers to the high quality of health care the market driven competition would theoretically produce.

Given this background, under Law 100, previous public health institutions were no longer state subsidized. The subsidies were to be transferred to those poor who required health services. The new social security system was to be based on insurance and on competition both between private and public insurance administrators and between private and public health care providers. Hospitals and clinics that were previously part of the national public health system were now required to be fiscally efficient and competitive. They were converted into *Empresas Sociales del Estado*–ESE (State's Social Enterprises) in order to reach their profit goals by selling health services. Unfortunately, the survival of public hospitals and their staff became too dependant on their competitive ability, not on the breadth or quality of their care. This change was catastrophic for the public hospitals that served the poorest population. Several had to close their doors. The biggest and most prestigious pediatric national hospital in *Bogotá–Hospital Infantil Lorencita Villegas de Santos*—was closed in the late 1990s.

Today, critics of the health reform are divided. While some believe the problems stem from the poor implementation of a good law during the 1990s economic crisis, others believe that the reform, rather than solving the problems of the former national health system, created even larger health disparities and greater health problems because of its neoliberal market-driven ideology.

We concur that Law 100 changed the public health system as well as contributed to the deterioration of the population's health. The law also has had an impact on both nursing practice and nursing higher education.

Effects of the Reform on the National Public Health System

Overall, the 1990s health reform negatively affected the public health programs which had provided health services to underserved populations since the 1970s, resulting in a crisis of the public health system and the deterioration of the health status of the poorest (Duque-Páramo, 2001). Before 1993, the poor had free access to health services through governmental public health institutions. As prescribed by international policies (stated in the Declaration of Alma Ata) from the 1970s through the 1990s, prevention and health promotion were integrated public health services as part of Primary Health Care (PHC). Most public health providers viewed public health as a public value. However, the 1990s health reform separated prevention from health promotion[5], thus undermining the accumulated social acceptance of the public health sector and throwing the public health programs into a state of confusion, characterized by a lack of accountability at all levels. Indeed, a study conducted in Bogotá (Duque-Páramo, 2001; Sánchez & Ahumada, 2004) showed that the implementation of the health reform had the worst impact among the poorest who depend on the public health system the most.

The new private enterprises, created by the 1993 Law 100 and driven by profit motives and market-driven principles, disregarded public health philosophy. Law 100 explicitly states that private enterprises are responsible for implementing preventive approaches. Yet, during the first five years after the law was enacted, the private enterprises focused only on curative health services. Furthermore, these enterprises also demonstrated a lack of knowledge about health promotion and prevention. Also, because the private health enterprises focused on economic profit, they created barriers to access. For example, to reduce costs, they limited hours for preventive services, such as vaccination programs, (before reform, these

---

[5] Within the Law 100 framework, private health enterprises are responsible of individual preventive actions, while majors and local government are responsible of collective actions of health promotion and prevention.

services were free and widely-available) and served only people who had health insurance coverage.

In the same research study conducted in *Bogotá* and cited above (Duque-Páramo, 2001; Sánchez & Ahumada, 2004), we interviewed officials of PAHO, the Ministry of Health, and the Secretary of Health of *Bogotá*. Talking about the private health enterprises, a PAHO functionary pointed out:

> [With the health reform] new organizations sprang up in the health sector. These newly-minted organizations are unfamiliar with the concept of public health, and instead based their services on marketing concepts. They are mainly interested on profit and in providing curative services such as medical consultations and hospitalizations. They don't have well-defined health promotion and prevention policies. (Duque-Páramo, 2001, p. 14)

Meanwhile, in the public sector, the Ministry of Health lost control over national public health policies, programs and services. Primary Health Care teams disappeared. Such teams, comprising health professional and technicians, were built through a tremendous and ongoing effort beginning in the 1970s. Indeed, these teams had been the basic underpinnings of the national public health system, which had made significant strides throughout the country in reducing morbidity and mortality caused by infectious diseases. Other effects of the 1990s reforms on public health care were disparities for the various economic and ethnic groups:

- By 2000, the mortality rate caused by diarrhea was double in poorest municipalities what it was in wealthy ones.
- Mortality related to undernourishment was four times higher in the poorest populations than it was in wealthy municipalities.

The Infant Mortality Rate (IMR) in *Bogotá* also showed inequities (Duque-Páramo, 2001). *Santafe* where 95.5% of the population is from the lowest economic stratums[6] reported an IMR of 21.6 per 1,000 live births. Yet, in *Teusaquillo,* where 81.8% of the population is from the highest stratums, the IMR was just 11.4.

Another effect in public health is in prevention. Since 1995, vaccination coverage has decreased dramatically across the whole country. With data from *Bogotá* (Table 1) showing more than 10 years of data for all the vaccines coverage, we can see that DPT (Diphtheria, Pertussis, and Tetanus vaccine) coverage in children less than 1 year old was 64.2% in 1986, 95.3% in 1996, but by 2000 it had dropped back to 64.7%. OPV (Oral Polio Vaccine) coverage was 66.9% in 1986, 95% in 1996, but decreased to below 1986 levels to 64.7% in 2000. Measles vaccination

---

[6] The socioeconomic stratification is a technical tool based on the evaluation of housing and its environment to classify Colombian population and municipalities. It is used mainly to pay different utility rates, so those who can afford pay more and subsidize those who cannot afford. It is accepted that stratums 1 and 2 are lower classes, 3 and 4 middle classes, and 5 and 6 upper classes.

Table 1. Vaccination Coverage of Children Less than 1 Year Old
in Bogotá 1986–2000

	Less than 1 year old					
Year	Polio	DPT	Measles	BCG	Haemo-philus	Hepatitis B
1986	66.9	64.2	52.8	97		
1988	72.9	61.7	58	98.9		
1990	87.6	81.8	72.5	100		
1992	78.4	75	71.6	86.5		
1994	90.8	83.7	85.8	100		
1996	95	95.3	70.8	100		100
1998	79	76.7	100	100	69.8	84.4
2000	66.6	64.7	65.7	75.2	65.9	64.3

Source: Secretaría Distrital de Salud (2001).

coverage was 52.8% in 1986, 70.8% in 1996, but decreased to 65.7% in 2000. BCG (Bacille Calmet-Guerin) vaccination coverage was 97% in 1986, 100% in 1996, but decreased dramatically to 75.2% in 2000 (Duque-Páramo, 2001).

Also, communicable diseases reemerged. While the national cholera incidence in 1993 was 2 per 100,000 inhabitants, in 2000 that number increased to 3.9 per 100,000 inhabitants. During the same period, the mortality rate by cholera increased seven times, from 0.1 to 0.7. The under-five years old mortality caused by acute diarrhea, increased from 0.04 per 100.000 inhabitants in 1996 to 7.7 per 100.000 inhabitants in 1997. Similarly, the incidences of acute respiratory infectious and HIV/AIDS increased after the health reform. There have also been new outbreaks of forgotten diseases such as yellow fever, which are once again making headlines in local papers (*El Espectador,* 2004). The backsliding of these and other epidemiological indicators indicates the holes in prevention and health promotion programs dug by having a market-driven ideology direct the health sector.

To summarize, the economic, social and health reforms of the 90s have turned the clock back on the health status of the population. Public health was no longer an integral responsibility of the state but rather was a responsibility scattered among public and private enterprises that handled, in their own separate ways, the needs of the population. Ironically, the *public* in public health was deeply diminished or even absent.

Nursing Higher Education: A Perspective through Time

From the onset of formal nursing education in the 19th century up until the 1960s, physicians modeled curricula for Colombian nursing education on the physicians medical education. The nursing profession was understood to be both "caring for illness" in hospitals and an "instrument of the physician for medical treatment." Nursing care took place in hospitals and depended on physicians' orders. The few nurses who worked in ambulatory clinics lacked professional autonomy and also were under the physicians' authority. However, since the 1960s, nursing has gained both autonomy and independence.

The Models of Medical Education

During the 19th century and at the beginning of the 20th century, the French clinical model dominated the curriculum of medical schools in Colombia. The French model focused on "semiology" which studies the signs and symptoms of disease "symptomatology." In this model, diagnosis and treatment of disease are carried out in hospitals at the "patients' bedside." This model remains the preferred version in Colombia. Despite the influence of the North American emphasis on sanitation, the French clinical model continued, at least until the end of World War II, framing the medical education in Colombian hospitals and in clinic settings.

Yet by the end of World War II, with the expansion of the Marshall Plan into Latin America, the United States exerted even more influence over Colombian medical education. As a result of the visits of two North American missions in 1948 and 1953, Colombian medical educators enacted major changes based on the Flexner model[7] that sought not only to regulate medical education in Colombian universities but also to modernize medical practice. These changes included: reorganizing the administration of the schools of medicine; creating departments in each of the medical fields; training young physicians in foreign universities, mainly in the United States and Europe; importing foreign professors; creating and regulating graduate programs; strengthening education in the basic sciences such as anatomy, physiology, and pathology; and reforming hospitals and hospital teaching.

Even the introduction of the Flexner principles did not completely replace the French model. What emerged over time was a blend of U.S. and French models with some unique Colombian characteristics mixed in. So from the 19th century until the 1960s, nursing education in Colombia closely followed the pattern of medical (physician) education by adapting the French and the U.S. models.

---

[7] "The Flexner Report of 1910 was a Carnegie-sponsored study of the state of the medical profession in the United States that revealed a wide array of unregulated and competing schools of medicine. The report led to the enforcement of much higher standards, coupled with substantial funding, for allopathic medical school and physicians and to the closing of homeopathic and other 'irregular' medical schools, many of which had admitted blacks and women. Thus, the Flexner Report was instrumental in cementing the cultural dominance of 'regular' (allopathic) medicine and ensuring that the vast majority of American physicians would be white, middle-class and upper-class, and male" (Jordan, 1997, p. 75).

The Early U.S. Influence on Colombian
Public Health Policies

As alluded to in the first part of this chapter, during the early 20th century, Colombian public health policies were framed by the mandates of the politically centrist 1886 Constitution, which defined public health as "a function of the national state." Public health policies, centered on hygiene, focused on:

1. control of epidemic diseases;
2. environmental sanitation; and
3. control of the ports (Quevedo, Hernández, Miranda, Mariño, Cárdenas, & Wiesner, 1990a[8]).

Yet, with scarce resources, following international political agreements, and pushed by the international markets, the Colombian state did little to create an effective national public health system.

Then, around 1910, the national economic policies focused on creating a modern and capitalist state, developing a national market, and consolidating coffee bean production as the first export crop. Subsequently, coffee as a cash crop became the basis for Colombian economic development. After 1923, large international loans were awarded to the government for building roads to connect different regions and support developing a national market. Thus, foreign creditors began influencing all aspects of life in Colombia, including the national health policies. In this environment, the United States began its remarkable influence on Colombian economic policies, as well as in other social and cultural areas from as early as 1920 on.

Throughout the 20th century, the United States gradually increased its influence worldwide. Because of its geographic proximity, the U.S. economic policies had a significant impact on all aspects of life in Central and South America. In Colombia, U.S. influence on public health policies occurred primarily through international agencies such as PAHO[9] and private philanthropic foundations such as the Rockefeller Foundation.

Since its inception, PAHO has played a central role in shaping national health policies in Colombia, including everything from the control of transmissible diseases; policies developed for commerce and international maritime communications in the 1920s and 1930s; the definition of national public health programs focused on children and mothers; to the control of infectious disease during the 1970s and 1980s.

---

[8] The discussion on public health policies and medical models is based mainly on the socio-historical analysis of the public health in Colombia. Such work directed by Emilio Quevedo (Quevedo et al., 1990a, 1990b, 1998) was first published in 1990 as part of the National Study of Health (Yepes, 1990).

[9] On December 2, 1902, at the First International Sanitary Convention of the Americas in Washington, DC, 11 nations joined to form the International Sanitary Bureau for the Americas, later it was transformed in the Pan American Sanitary Bureau and in 1946 became the Pan American Health Organization.

As one example of the U.S.'s influence, the Rockefeller Foundation funded in 1901 the *Instituto Rockefeller de Investigaciones* (Rockefeller Institute of Research) which focused on prevention and control of tropical diseases. For decades, the Rockefeller Foundation funded research in Colombia to eradicate tropical diseases such as uncinariasis and yellow fever, while also working as an advisor to develop national public health policies and exercising influence on medical and public health education.

During the 1920s and the 1930s, along with the increased economic influence of the United States and the increased Colombian dependence on U.S. loans, North American sanitary policies were systematically introduced. Through the Good Neighbor Policy[10] promoted by F. D. Roosevelt (Houghton, 2005), in the 1940s the *Servicio Cooperativo Interamericano de Salud Pública*–SCISP (International Bureau of Public Health) was created in the Ministry of Labor, Hygiene and Social Security. In September 1942, at the invitation of the Colombian government, Nelson Rockefeller visited Colombia as a representative of the Coordinator of the Office of Inter-American Relations. Based on this visit, the Colombian Minister of Labor, Hygiene and Social Security defined the following as the public health priorities: nutrition, malaria, rickettsia infections, bartonellosis, and ports sanitation. This visit, along with another 1 month later, from other officials from the North American Institute of Inter-American Relations, defined the creation of SCISP. Thus, from the 1940s until the end of the 1950s, SCISP was the central technical guide for the Minister of Labor, Hygiene and Social Security as well as the driver of the modernization processes. In fact, the creation of SCISP marked the beginning of several decades of U.S. intervention that shaped Colombian public health policies and the education of health care professionals and technicians, including nurses (Quevedo et al., 1990a).

Nursing Higher Education Before the 1970s

The first nursing education program in Colombia began in 1826 at the Santa Clara Hospital in the city of *Cartagena de Indias*. In 1903 the program was absorbed by *Universidad de Cartagena* (Cartagena University) which granted the 3-year graduates the title of Nurse and Midwife. Until the 1940s, there was no state regulation of educational programs in nursing. Most nursing schools were affiliated with hospitals and followed the French model of medical education where nurses cared for the sick in hospitals. All teaching (as well as care) took place at the *patient's bedside* and was directed by physicians and senior nurses. The different hospital schools had their own length of coursework and nursing titles such as Nurse Midwife or Hospital Nurse.

The American educational model slowly replaced the French model. In the 1930s, training moved from the hospitals to formalized education in universities. The American educational model slowly replaced the French model. In the 1930s,

---

[10] The Good Neighbor policy refers to the Hoover-Roosevelt policy of refraining from armed intervention in Latin America.

training moved from the hospitals to formalized education in universities. First nursing schools were directed by physicians. In 1937 the *Escuela Nacional de Enfermeras* (National School of Nurses) was created. It was directed by a Colombian woman who studied nursing in the United States. Nursing education was organized in two phases, preclinical and clinical (Velandia Mora, 1995).

During the 1940s and the 1950s the Colombian state began regulating the increasing number of nursing programs. Higher education nursing programs were standardized to a 3-year course of study with graduates earning a common title of *General Nurse*. Additionally, the Flexner model also shaped nursing higher education curricula. According to Velandia Mora (1995), the model, based on allopathic medicine, was criticized because its positivistic approach with a mechanistic perspective that views the individual in isolation from his or her environment. The model also generates an elitist and socially uprooted medical and nursing practice, divorced from the population it serves.

During the early 1960s, the Ministry of Social Protection conducted a study which concluded that nursing programs should be 4 years (instead of 3) of study. The study revealed weaknesses of professional nurses in three areas and recommended strengthening education to prepare graduating nurses for the demands of the market. The Ministry of Health and the schools of nursing concurred that health services and the nursing profession required competent professionals for these three areas: the administration of nursing services; education of the new generations of nurses; and guidance of research projects to promote the theoretical and practical development of the profession as well as to help solve the health problems of Colombians (Velandia Mora, 2006). Based on the study's findings and recommendations, the *licentiate* (bachelor) nursing programs were created. The first licentiate program started at the *Universidad Nacional de Colombia* (Colombian National University) in 1961. Velandia Mora (2006, p. 30) points out that apparently this program (along with the program at the school Anna Nery of the Federal University of Rio de Janeiro in Brazil) was the first licentiate nursing program in Latin America. By 1967, the *Pontificia Universidad Javeriana* also revamped its General Nurse degree into a licentiate program. The U.S. influence on licentiate programs in Colombia is noteworthy. The director of the school of nursing of the *Universidad Nacional de Colombia* studied in a U.S. bachelors program in nursing and the dean of the school of nursing of the Pontificia Universidad Javeriana from 1964 to 1967 was an American nurse. Additionally, through an agreement between the *Universidad Nacional de Colombia* and the Catholic University in Washington, professors of the licentiate program were first trained in the United States.

The *Licenciado* programs marked the real beginnings of Colombian nursing as an autonomous discipline and represented a major shift in the principles guiding both nursing higher education and the professional practice. Instead of focusing solely on medical treatment, the licentiate programs incorporated key disciplines: nursing care, health education, administration of the health services, and the health profile of the population. These disciplines related to the emergence of new roles such as the nurse administrator of health services and the nurse educator. Thus, nursing higher education schools expanded beyond medical knowledge as the sole criteria for their curricula and began exploring nursing knowledge and the practice itself.

The 1970s and the 1980s

A national study of nursing (*Ministerio de Salud Pública,* 1972)—jointly conducted by nurses from the Ministry of Health and nurse educators from several schools of nursing—analyzed the nursing situation in Colombia as groundwork for designing nursing practice policies which would contribute to national health plan goals. The study emphasized coordinating the efforts between the nursing schools and health services. The study also focused on nursing education's need to be based on the epidemiological profile of the population. Nurses would no longer be just medical helpers, assisting physicians, but independent resources, within the public health system, for improving the health of all Colombians.

This 1972 study identified three main problems: (a) a scarcity of professional nurses (0.9 per 10.000 habitants in 1972); (b) the unequal distribution of nurses;[11] and (c) the high concentration of nursing schools in *Bogotá*. Together, these three factors translated to a high concentration of nurses in large urban hospitals which coupled with the lack of nurses in rural areas, did not meet the heath needs of the overall population. Interestingly, the same study also highlighted the increase of nurse students in baccalaureate programs.[12]

In 1970s, nurses emerged with a new role in the Colombian society: providers of solutions to the population's health problems. Nurses with the *Licenciado*, because of their new training in administration, education and research, became chiefs in charge of general and auxiliary nurses and leaders of "health teams" for achieving the national health plan.

In sum, to support nursing's new role in the national health plan, nursing higher education was transformed. Curricula were reshaped based on the national epidemiological profile which, by the 1970s, was characterized by high mortality and morbidity due primarily to infectious and nutritional diseases and secondarily to chronic diseases. The "new" administration courses included theoretical approaches and models of administration of health services and also internships in hospitals and ambulatory services where students played a role as directors of nursing services. Over time physicians stopped being seen as the chiefs and supervisors of the nurses and licentiate nurses began to be recognized as professionals and partners, instead of assistants and medical auxiliaries. Courses in education enabled licentiate nurses to practice as health educators at the same time that they trained newcomers for teaching at the schools of nursing. Some teachers enrolled in graduate programs in administration and education. After decades of dependency on physician-led medical education, Colombian nurses steadily began to educate

---

[11] The unequal distribution of nurses was geographically and within type of health institutions. By 1970, 67% of nurses worked in *Bogotá, Cali,* and *Medellín* (the three major cities) and 80% worked in hospitals.

[12] From 1970 to 1971 the number of students increased by 49.4%.

their own students. Thus, over the course of a couple of decades, nurses began determining their own curricula for undergraduate and graduate programs. Autonomy and independence in nursing education was steadily achieved. Research became a tool for planning local health programs, and the nursing care process became a means for designing nursing care programs and developing the discipline.

Primary Health Care and the Role of PAHO

In 1978, the World Health Organization (WHO) and the United Nations Children's Fund (UNICEF) held the world's first International Conference on Primary Health Care in Alma Ata, Kazakhstan (WHO, 1978) with the goal of "Health for all by the year 2000." The Colombian government adhered to the concepts and strategies proposed in the Declaration of Alma Ata and adopted Primary Health Care (PHC) as a main strategy to improve Colombians' health status as well as to reduce inequalities in the coverage and access to health services.

In accordance with these national and international social justice ideals, nursing schools of higher education embraced PHCs principles and strategies and combined them with Colombian social theories and the community experiences with health workers.[13] In the 1960s, Fals Borda (1962), a Colombian sociologist, theorized on the relationship between research and action on local and marginal communities. By the 1970s, his *Investigación Acción Participativa*–IAP (Participative Action Research PAR) was widely used in national public and private universities. By the 1980s, the individual was no longer the only subject of nursing care, and studies began to include courses on nursing care to communities and collectives. Several courses on anthropology, psychology and sociology[14] were added, as well as internships in hospitals and community settings in urban and rural areas.

The leadership role of professional nurses also evolved. In the mid-1970s, the national obligatory social service practicum previously required for physicians and dentists, became required for those professional nurses working in local hospitals in towns, small cities, and rural areas. As part of their obligatory social service practicum, professional nurses rotated through the institutions in leadership roles overseeing auxiliary nurses and community health workers. Yet, despite the lack of continuity in the leadership, professional nurses throughout the country, even in the most isolated jungle areas, emerged as a cornerstone supporting local hospitals and implementing the national Primary Health Care policies. As result, professional nurses earned widespread social recognition as health professionals.

Even though nurses continued to be subordinate to physicians in the hospitals, in Primary Health Care, nurses emerged not only as equals with other health

---

[13] One of the oldest world's documented experience of community health workers was conducted in the 1950s in Colombia (Sandoval & Muñoz, 1990).

[14] For example, the curricula of the Javeriana University includes as required courses: three courses on anthropology, one on sociology, and four courses on psychology (general, child, women, adult and elderly).

professionals such as physicians and dentists but sometimes as the coordinators or leaders of the PHC teams.

During the 1970s and the 1980s PAHO was central in shaping the national public health and Primary Health Care policies as well as contributing directly to the development of Colombian nursing. Together the PAHO, the Colombian Ministry of Health, and higher education schools of nursing created continuing education programs for nursing teachers and updated training on the national and international public health programs for vulnerable populations. The curricula included courses on the national system of health as well as on the public health programs such as those for vaccination, acute respiratory infections, maternal and child health programs, and other specific conditions such as high blood pressure.

PAHO also provided a vehicle for nursing teachers to keep abreast of new developments in anthropological, sociological, and epidemiological models of health and disease. Nursing schools built their curricula based on preventive and socio-epidemiological models such as the ecological model of diseases and a disease's natural history. Sociological and anthropological topics such as health systems, medical systems and life-courses infused nursing courses, practice, and research. Some schools integrated ideas of social justice that promoted health such as those proposed in the Ottawa Charter for Health Promotion (WHO, 1986) into the nursing higher education curricula.

By the end of the 1980s, nursing higher education curricula were firmly based on the national epidemiological profile. At many schools, there were equal numbers of theoretical and practical courses about conducting national public health programs in hospitals ambulatory and community settings. Nurses worked in hospitals providing nursing care and administrating hospital services. They worked in ambulatory health services managing the national public health programs. They also worked in community-based projects promoting community health and community development. Nursing higher education had transformed itself to contribute to the overall well-being and social development of Colombians.

Despite all the progress and the emphasis on achieving coverage for rural and urban marginal populations, the nursing national study conducted from 1985 to 1987[15] (*Ministerio de Salud* et al., 1989; Niño de Peña, Quintero, & de Villalobos, 1988) concluded that the goal of equal distribution of nurses across the nation was not reached. Nurses continued to be concentrated in the hospitals. The moderate gains in staffing at ambulatory clinics were due to the increase in the number of auxiliary nurses, not professional nurses. Further, few changes were actually achieved in the health services models themselves: instead of incorporating preventive and collective approaches, the curative and individualistic models continued to dominate. The study authors noted their concern that, despite the efforts made, Colombia had not achieved the international norm issued by PAHO in 1960 for the minimum number of nurses in ambulatory services. Based on its findings and recognizing the insufficient solutions to regional inequalities, the study

---

[15] This study was conducted by the Ministry of Health and ACOFAEN.

recommended changing nursing's function within the health system. Finally, the national study noted the lack of legal definitions and clear distinctions between the functions of professional nurses and auxiliary nurses. Still, it was not until years later, in 1996, that nurses' organizations promoted a national law for the professional practice.

Higher Education Policies and Nursing Education

In 1980, Law 80 reformed Colombia's entire higher education system. The national reform produced four changes in nursing education:

1. titles for the bachelors degrees changed from *Licenciado en Enfermeria* to just "Nurse";
2. the program name changed from *Licentiate* in Nursing to Nursing;
3. two kinds of undergraduate programs and degrees were defined: the 4-year bachelor program granted a nurse degree and the 3-year program granted a nurse technologist degree; and
4. three graduate programs were established: specialization in specific areas, masters, and doctorate.

Such changes were structural, but did not affect the role of the nurses or the actual curricula of the higher education programs.

The technological programs created by "Law 80" are an interesting example of how political forces affect nursing education. The technological nursing programs caused tensions among nurses, educators, regional politicians, private schools of nursing of the middle cities, and government institutes. In 1985, the *Instituto Colombiano para el Fomento de la Educación Superior*–ICFES (Colombian Institute for the Promotion of the Higher Education) along with the *Asociación Colombiana de Facultades de Enfermería*–ACOFAEN (Colombian Association of Schools of Nursing) and the *Consejo Nacional de Recursos Humanos* (National Council of Human Resources of the Ministry of Health), agreed that the two undergraduate levels (nurse and nurse technologist) overlapped and generated confusion in the actual day-to-day practice. At that time, the ICFES, as a governmental institute, was able to accredit every program of higher education and change national policies. So the ICFES, based on the recommendations of ACOFAEN and the National Council of Human Resources of the Ministry of Health, eliminated all the technological programs and directed them to transition to 4-year nursing programs. Within 6 years, however, three factors reversed this trend. The 1991 Constitution reduced state control; the 1992 Law 30 gave universities their autonomy; and local politicians (mainly in middle-size cities) applied pressure. So in 1992, the technological program in university institutions was reinstated. To this day, nursing higher education includes both the 2- to 3-year technological level and the 4- to 5-year baccalaureate level programs.

Additional major changes in higher education stemmed from the principle of university autonomy introduced by the 1992 Law 30. Promoted by large and traditional universities seeking to reduce state control and increase their own, the new policy of autonomy stimulated unexpected and massive creation of educational programs in several professions.[16] In a country such as Colombia, where higher education is a privilege for the few who can either afford the high costs of private universities or get into the highly competitive public universities, and where demand for higher education is great, the reduced state regulations provided a free market opportunity. Beginning in 1992, baccalaureate programs with low educational merit proliferated in many disciplines, including nursing. For example, while 1972, there were 11 baccalaureate programs (*Ministerio de Salud Pública,* 1972). By 1987, with deregulation, the number doubled to 22 (*Ministerio de Salud* et al., 1989), and by 2003, the number almost doubled again to 41. Also, in addition to these university programs, several technological nursing programs have opened or reopened. The unchecked proliferation prodded ACOFAEN to press for quality of nursing higher education by promoting such policies as the one establishing minimal requirements.

Note, however, that the rapid expansion of the number of higher degree granting institutions in conjunction with a decrease of the quality of education is not solely a Colombian issue, but a worldwide phenomenon. In 1960, worldwide, there were 13 million registered students; by 1995 there was an estimated 82 million (*Organización de las Naciones Unidas para la Educación, la Ciencia y la Cultura* [United Nations Educational, Scientific and Cultural Organization, UNESCO], 1998). In the World Declaration on Higher Education for the Twenty First Century (UNESCO, 1998), representatives of over 180 countries recognized that such expansion in the number of enrolled students during the second half of the 20th century was also marked by great stratification and represented:

> . . . the period which has seen the gap between industrially developed, the developing countries and in particular the least developed countries with regard to access and resources for higher learning and research, already enormous, becoming even wider. It has also been a period of increased socioeconomic stratification and greater difference in educational opportunity within countries, including in some of the most developed and wealthiest nations. (UNESCO, 1998)

The declaration highlights that the rapid growth in the number of institutions of higher education has negatively affected quality. And so, the UNESCO declaration recommends two main strategies to remedy the situation: accreditation based on self-evaluation and the establishment of quality standards.

To summarize, Colombian nursing higher education in the 1970s shifted from being guided by the hospitals' requirements to being guided by national public health policies—most policies internationally defined under the auspices of Primary Health Care. From the 1970s to the 1990s, PAHO had a central role in defining

---

[16] Since 1992 the offer of higher education programs increased in most professions, yet in health disciplines such as dentistry, medicine, and nursing the increments have been remarkable.

national public health policies as well as in supporting and training nurses. Colombian nursing teachers' own commitments and their desire to improve Colombians' health status, well-being, and quality of life were also important forces that transformed curricula and nursing practices.

The Colombian Association of Schools of Nursing–ACOFAEN

ACOFAEN, created in 1968, also played a key role in developing the professional nursing in Colombia, serving as well as a model for other Latin American countries. ACOFAEN is a national, private, nonprofit organization that links university institutions, schools, departments, and programs of professional nursing. ACOFAEN is dedicated to activities that contribute to the progress of the nursing education as well as to the health care of individuals and collectives. As such, ACOFAEN's mission is to consolidate and to maintain the nursing academic community and to promote the development of the nursing profession.

To fulfill these purposes, ACOFAEN focuses on research, teaching, evaluation, accreditation, consultation, coordination, and extension. ACOFAEN also helps define policies on the quality of nursing education, the levels of nursing education, and the processes of self-evaluation and accreditation. For example, in the 1980s, ACOFAEN was instrumental in transforming the technological programs to the 4- or 5-year professional nursing model. As recently as 1996, the Law 266 authorized ACOFAEN to accredit nursing university undergraduate and graduate programs[17] (the processes of accreditation and self-regulation were developed nationally and by consulting with other South American countries).

Since the early 1990s, ACOFAEN has been working jointly with representatives of the education, private business, and policy makers to define the nursing higher education policies in several areas: ethics and humanization; research; self-evaluation and accreditation; nursing guides of intervention based on scientific evidence; health promotion and prevention of the diseases; and management of nursing services.

Because of ACOFAEN's strengths and its willingness to cooperate nationally and internationally, it was designated a PAHO/WHO collaborative center in 1991, traditionally a designation reserved for schools of nursing. ACOFAEN is the only association with this designation. As a collaborative center, ACOFAEN works toward:

- continuous quality improvement of nursing education as well as promoting accreditation and support for the schools of nursing.
- strengthening and basing nursing on scientific evidence, a key to attaining quality nursing education and practice.

---

[17] However, the *Consejo Nacional de Acreditación* (Council of National Accreditation–CNA) is the organization that accredits all the higher education programs in Colombia.

- ACOFAEN's international cooperation produced joint projects and programs with international experts, creating international networks exchanging ideas for improving nursing education and the health services.

At the national level, ACOFAEN has joined with other organizations and professional associations to develop policies for improving health services, integrating schools and health services, and contributing to the well-being of communities. Policies have been developed for family health, nursing management, as well as organization and productivity of the health services. Also, ACOFAEN participated in and drove the following initiatives: protection for women and children; promotion of breastfeeding;[18] nursing practice based on scientific evidence; the Andean strand of the *Red de Enfermería de América Latina*–REAL (Latin American Web of Nursing); strengthening of graduate programs, and the creation of the doctorate of nursing in Colombia. Since the 1990s, the ACOFAEN sought to emphasize ethics in teaching and nursing practice. As a result, the code of ethics for nurses was established and formed the basis for the Law 266.

Research has been always a priority for ACOFAEN. In 1980, it initiated the national colloquiums of research. Besides being forums for professional and investigative development, such events have brought together well-known national and international nurses. From 1980 and 2003, there have been 15 colloquiums organized by universities such as *Universidad del Valle* (Valle University), *Universidad Industrial de Santander* (Santander Industrial University), *Universidad del Norte* (North University), *Universidad de Antioquia* (Antioquia University), *Universidad de Cartagena* (Cartagena University), *Universidad del Cauca* (Cauca University), *Universidad de Caldas* (Caldas University), *Pontificia Universidad Javeriana* (Pontifical Javeriana University), *Universidad Pedagógica y Tecnológica de Colombia* (Colombian Pedagogic and Technological University), and the *Universidad Nacional de Colombia* (Colombian National University). Central themes included: nursing and epidemiology; science and research in nursing; interdisciplinary work; communication and information; nursing practice; women and health; social research applied to health; developing lines of nursing research; and humanization of the health care.

Then again, with research as a key priority, in 1988, ACOFAEN led and developed the first Pan-American Colloquium of Nursing Research. Since then, the Pan-American colloquiums have been held every other year in different countries of Pan-America. In 2000, the association hosted the seventh Pan-American Colloquium of Nursing Research in cooperation with the University of Texas at Galveston and the University of California at San Francisco.

To summarize, ACOAFEN has been successful in meeting its goals of improving nursing higher education through teacher training and exchange; defining minimal requirements for national nursing programs; designing and implementing models of self-evaluation for accreditation; developing and strengthening nursing curricula

---

[18] ACOFAEN is member of the National Committee on Breastfeeding since 1991.

components such as ethics, research, and health promotion; and participating actively in developing strategies for a single type of baccalaureate of nursing. ACOAFEN also supported the work-study strategy developed to allow auxiliary nurses to study for the baccalaureate in universities.

The 1990s and the 2000s

Two seemingly complementary phenomena have characterized nursing higher education during this period: (a) the development of processes of theorization and conceptualization; and (b) the national health care reform. Yet, these two phenomena are actually creating contradictory effects and outcomes. During this period a strengthening and consolidation of undergraduate nursing programs occurred through processes of accreditation. The number of graduate programs—specialization and masters—has increased and in 2004 the *Universidad Nacional de Colombia* initiated the first nursing doctorate.

Two other developments are noteworthy. Early research titled *Modelo Pedagógico en Enfermería [Pedagogic Model in Nursing]* (Romero Ballén, 1992. concludes that nursing education in Colombia is still dominated by reliance on the teacher's medical knowledge but not on sound pedagogy of best instructional practices. The researchers point out that the students' abilities, interests, and desires are not taken into account in determining how best to educate them; instead, the teacher determines what the student should learn. The researchers conclude that nursing education is based on rote repetition, rather than on the students' cognitive transformation. Second, ACOFAEN and ICFES (Gómez Serrano, C. & Gómez Serrano, H., 1997) conducted a project on modernization and modernity of nursing curricula. The project's one national and three regional workshops were based on participatory methods. The workshops discussed two topics: (a) the characteristics of nursing higher education; and (b) a proposal to its change. The minutes of these workshops, published in 1997, included the following recommendations:

- Rather than focusing on curative actions, nurses should develop a theoretical framework focused on the social, biological, and cultural dimensions of health that promote well-being.
- Promoting nursing students as autonomous, respectful, and active actors in the promotion of social change; promoting them as individuals with critical thinking skills and commitment to the development and strengthening of the nursing profession.

Conceptual and Theoretical Models

To trace the development of conceptual and theoretical models, it's necessary to step back 40 years. With the initial baccalaureate nursing programs in the 1960s, "nursing care" was introduced in the curricula both as a fundamental basis of the nursing discipline as well as a pedagological tool. This North American nursing model, based on patients' needs and on a process of assessment, diagnosis, nursing plan, and evaluation, has been a central strategy of nursing education for generations of Colombian professional nurses. Indeed, this nursing process is a hallmark of professional nursing, separating it from vocational nursing.

The ongoing relationship with North American nursing through PAHO, nursing textbooks, and the training Colombian nurse educators received in the United States were the prime reasons the nursing models and theories were studied, discussed, and spread into traditional Colombia nursing higher education schools. Such schools led what has been called the "process of conceptualization." In some cases, North American conceptual models in nursing were adopted with just few adaptations. In other cases,[19] deeper epistemological discussions, based on phenomenological research, centered on the nature of nursing care in Colombian. Nursing scholars at a number of Colombian universities (the Colombian National University, the *Antioquia* University, The *Valle* University, the *Santander* Industrial University and the *Pontifical Javeriana* University) created nursing conceptual models specific to the Colombian reality.

Castrillón Agudelo (1999) notes that despite the interest in the conceptualization of the nursing practice, the reality is that nursing education still concentrates on mechanical techniques isolated from a comprehensive vision of nursing. Thus, groups developing nursing conceptualization have proposed "caring" as a means to structure instruction about the social purpose of nursing and the nurses' historical function. In contrast to the traditional medical models focusing on disease and a mechanical perspective of care, the proposed concept of nursing care is based on social interaction between nurses and the individuals or collectives for whom they are responsible. Nursing care means working within communities to address health needs and promote well-being, quality of life and social development in addition to the traditional focus on disease prevention, treatment and rehabilitation.

To further this initiative, Castrillón Agudelo from the *Universidad de Antioquia*, Sánchez from the *Universidad Nacional de Colombia*, and Duque-Páramo from the *Universidad Javeriana* have defined nursing and nursing care. Paraphrasing Castrillón Agudelo (1999), nursing practice aims at preserving life and improving health as well as satisfying the physical, social, emotional, and cultural needs of the patient. At the same time, nursing practice aims at providing comprehensive nursing care for health promotion as well as disease prevention, treatment, and rehabilitation. Sánchez (2000, p. 25) defines nursing care as "an act of human interaction, reciprocal and integral, that guides nursing knowledge and practice." Duque-Páramo (1999) defines nursing as a social practice based on the act of caring. Nursing care is an interaction between nurses and communities where the motives and goals are defined by both health and illness. Individual and population health and illness needs initiate the interaction; health promotion and illness management are the intermediate phases; and the wellbeing and improving of quality of life of individuals and populations are the ultimate goals of nursing care.

---

[19] Such is the case, for example, of the school of nursing of the *Pontificia Universidad Javeriana.*

These developments in nursing conceptual models paralleled the increase in graduate programs, which also integrated concepts such as social interactionism, communication, and the socio-cultural dimensions of the health-disease phenomenon, using student participation and dialog instructional methods. Indeed, many graduate and undergraduate curricula are being organized around this central professional concept: nursing care.

The nursing conceptual models also shaped national nursing legislation. Law 266, issued in 1996, defines nursing as "a liberal profession and a social discipline whose subject of attention is the person as an individual, social and spiritual being. The object of nursing is the person, family, and community's integral health care along the life-course within the health-disease spectrum."

Today, some schools of nursing believe that re-thinking and re-conceptualizing the Colombian nursing practice is key to improving the quality of nursing education programs and the nursing practice, in order to improve health services and to gain academic and social status.

Effects of the Health Care Reform on Nursing

The effects of the health reform on nursing higher education and practice range from the positive of adding new curricula content to the negative of adversely affecting labor conditions. Law 100 sees as a priority improving efficiency (particularly financial efficacy) management of health and nursing services. Thus, management, audit and quality control are now included on nursing higher education curricula.

However, Castrillón Agudelo et al. (1998) in their study of the health reform's impact on nursing practice, regulation and nursing education in Colombia,[20] document marked increases in the workloads for nurses and staff at different levels in both public and private health institutions. The increases have weakened working conditions and lowered the quality of nursing care. Nursing contracts without social security benefits and the increase in the number of short-term contracts also contribute to deteriorated working conditions. A scarcity of nursing supplies and high turnover in staff, resulting in little personal commitment to the institution, also contribute to a lowered quality of nursing care. Yet, "paradoxically, despite the need for more nurses, due to financial crisis, several institutions are firing staff and sub-employment has dominated Colombian nursing during the 1990s" (Castrillón Agudelo et al., 1998, p. 82).

Law 100 also stimulated cost controls and billing processes which generated greater bureaucratization of the nursing practice and the health services. Since survival depended on efficiency, nurses, physicians, and general health staff very quickly moved from their social ideology of Primary Health Care, toward a goal of

---

[20] This research was part of a multicentric study about the impact of health reforms in Latin American nursing conducted in five countries: Argentina, Brazil, Colombia, Mexico, and the United States.

billing in order to assure their jobs. Indeed, several nurses have changed their top priority from "caring for people" to becoming part of management and administration. In fact, new professional areas have emerged—health management, health marketing, institutional accreditation, audit, and quality control.

Even though the health reform has impaired labor conditions, it is important to note that low wages and work overload were already present before Law 100. And, with the law's focus on such policies as the minimal requirements for health and nursing services, and the quality of the health services, it is anticipated that Law 100 will overcome some of the negative conditions the health reform has caused.

Gender, Age, and Socioeconomic Stratification

Gender—As in most places, nursing in Colombia is a feminine profession. A research study conducted with students of the *Javeriana* University (López-Maldonado, Navarro Flórez, Delgado Arjona, & Sánchez Toro, 2000) reported only 8% male students. In 2003, of the 2,501 undergraduate students who took the first *Examen Nacional de Calidad de la Educación Superior en Enfermería*–ECAES (National Exam of the Nursing Higher Education Quality), 12% were male and 88% were female (López-Maldonado, 2004). Even though the previous national studies did not include gender, it is clear that the number of male students at the professional level has steadily increased since the beginning of the 1990s.

This increase may reflect an increased number of nursing auxiliaries "crossing over" and being admitted to the higher education programs. During the 1970s and the 1980s, there were few auxiliary nurses seeking professional degrees; this changed in the 1990s. During the 90s, work-study programs (which provide scheduling to facilitate students being able to study and work at the same time) made it easier for auxiliary nurses to be admitted and to finish their degrees.

Age—Work-study has also increased the number of students who are in the 30-40 years of age range. The same 2003 ECAES study shows that 20% of final semester students are over 30 years old.

Class—During the 1960s and the 1970s most nursing higher education students, particularly those in private universities, were from either the medium or upper social classes. However, with other social and economic changes during the 80s and 90s, women from these social classes were able to find other, better paying professions. As gender discrimination for other professions became less common, the number of nursing school applicants from the higher socioeconomic stratums (4, 5, and 6) decreased. The analysis of the 2003 ECAES indicates that 38% of the students are from the lowest socioeconomic stratums (1 and 2), while only 2.8% are from the highest stratums (5 and 6). Again, these percentages are influenced by the higher number of auxiliary nurses now entering the nursing higher education programs. Still, it is likely that low wages and difficult working conditions have made nursing unattractive to applicants from higher stratums. At the same time, for people from low stratums, a professional title in nursing still represents higher social standing and prestige.

Contradictions and Inequalities

Beginning in the 1960s, nurses in Colombia have been transforming nursing practice into an independent profession as well as contributing to developing the nursing discipline and to implementing national public health programs to improve the health of the population. Still, Colombian nursing higher education faces many contradictions and inequalities. Some, such as the unequal access to higher education, represent socio-economic barriers present since the inception of the Colombian nursing profession. Others, however, resulted from the health reform, the international adjustment policies, and the economic crisis.

Inequalities in the Access to Nursing Higher Education

To summarize, Colombia has been a society with marked social class inequalities and where higher education is a privilege of upper classes. Until the late 1970s, gender discrimination in other academic disciplines resulted in an overrepresentation of middle and upper class women in nursing. However, once Colombian upper class women gained equal access to male-dominated professions, nursing became a less attractive option. In the 1980s, there was a major decrease in applicants for both private and public schools of nursing, and from the mid-1990s on, there has been a marked increase in applicants from the lower classes, increasing demand for nursing education programs. Unfortunately, the increased demand for professional nursing has not changed the unequal geographical distribution of nurses. The concentration of schools of nursing and nurses in the main capital cities continues. Paradoxically, the increased demand has not driven down educational costs. Instead tuition fees have increased.

Professional nurses have access to graduate programs,[21] which sometimes can provide social mobility.[22] Yet, graduate studies did not result in better working conditions nor in social mobility for nurses working in health services, although it may provide nurses in academic settings better wages and improved working conditions. Again, although the health reform increased the popularity of graduate studies in the management of health services, there is presently no evidence that such programs have improved nurses' working conditions.

---

[21] Besides graduate programs in nursing in areas such as intensive care, maternal and child health, and surgery, nurses began to study graduate programs in other areas, such as occupational health and administration of health services which allowed them to migrate from the hospital and earn autonomy and in some cases better wages and working conditions.

[22] Many nurses, because of their skills and capabilities in administration and because they were tired of low wages, low autonomy, and poor working conditions in hospitals, have migrated to work as managers in other sectors, for example, in financial institutions.

The Social Purposes of the Profession versus the Demands of the Labor Market

The health reform represents a big challenge for nursing schools faced with the contradictions of the older ideology focused on social justice and the newer focus on a market-driven ideology. In fact, a recent study about Colombian health care human resources points out the gap between education and the work world reality among all disciplines (Ruiz et al., 2001). Nursing schools have recognized the importance of responding to the health system's demands for nurses with management training for the new administrative processes produced by the reform. Curricula now include courses on topics such as the finances of health services, audit of health services, and quality of health services. However, since many schools continue supporting ideals of social justice and health as central elements of human development, the basic contradiction between the two ideologies still exist.

Finally, while some schools of nursing maintain a curriculum based on an inter-active view of nursing where communication and social contexts are central, the state's the health services focus on reducing costs, efficiency, and standardizing care. As a strategy to reduce the gap between nursing education and nursing practice, some schools are integrating content about cost control, efficiency, and standardized care into content on communication, interaction, and humanized nursing care.

Weaving the Past with the Future

At the beginning of the 21st century, Colombian nursing higher education faces two critical challenges: (a) incongruity between a market-driven ideology in the health system and a social justice ideology in the curricula; and (b) inequality in access to higher education. Further complicating these challenges, a close analysis reveals the complex interaction of national and international political and economic factors in shaping professional development. The analysis also reveals the deterior-ation of labor conditions.

Since the 1970s, higher education nursing schools has been central in the shift away from a practice dependent on the physician to a more independent profes-sional practice. At the professional level, nursing schools have gained autonomy in defining their own curricula while also contributing to the development of national policies on nursing education and nursing practice.

Nurses themselves are helping to define the effects of the international policies and to improve the quality of the nursing education. Nurse researchers are con-tributing to the understanding of the adverse effects of the health reform on the health of the population (Duque-Páramo, 2001) and on the deterioration of the nurses' labor conditions (Castrillón Agudelo et al., 1998). Unfortunately, since nursing schools are now autonomous, without government regulation, many new schools with poor quality programs have sprung up.

Colombian nurses have also been central in promoting higher standards of nursing education. In accordance with international recommendations, (UNESCO, 1998), ACOFAEN and the Colombian government are promoting the accreditation of schools and the establishment of minimum quality standards. Accreditation, although voluntary, provides public recognition of high quality nursing higher education. Quality standards are obligatory for all unaccredited programs and they establish minimum requirements to guarantee, for students, the quality of the programs and, for society, the quality of the nursing professionals.

Further, despite the efforts of schools of nursing and the national government to reduce the unequal distribution of nurses, the unbalance still remains. Also, gaps still exist between what is taught in the schools and what is practiced in the work environment. In sum, research highlights three main conclusions:

1. the gap between nursing education and practice is related to a contradiction between education and work world realities;
2. the increases in higher education programs and enrollment have not changed regional inequalities, diluted the concentration of professionals in the large cities, improved access for low-income population or lowered costs of tuition; and
3. finally, there is often an overlap in the tasks performed among physicians, professional nurses and auxiliary nurses.

Certainly, our present is interwoven with our past. Our current reality is the result of the individual and collective nurses' struggles and achievements; national and international socioeconomic and public health policies; medical educational models; North American nurses' educational models; and a long history of political, economic, and scientific colonialism. Although professional nurses have helped to positively transform our own profession and the health of the population, many Colombian nursing professionals are still, at the beginning of the 21st century, facing deteriorated working conditions that are the result of the neoliberal policies directed by international banks.

REFERENCES

Asociación Colombiana de Facultades de Enfermería [ACOFAEN]. (2004). *Acofaen 35 años.* [Acofaen 35th anniversary]. Bogotá: Editorial Gente Nueva.

Arango, R., & Sánchez, E. (1998). *Los pueblos indígenas de Colombia 1997.* [The indigenous people of Colombia 1997]. Bogotá: Tercer Mundo Editores.

Ahumada, C. (1996). *El modelo neoliberal.* [The neoliberal model]. Bogotá: El Áncora Editores.

Ahumada, C. (1998). Política social y reforma de salud en Colombia. [Social policy and the healthcare reform in Colombia]. *Papel Político,* (7), 9-35.

BBC News. (2005, May 24). Q&A: *Colombia's civil conflict.* Retrieved October 13, 2007 from http://news.bbc.co.uk/1/hi/world/americas/1738963.stm

Bejarano, J. A. (2004). *Qué es neoliberalismo? Su significado en la historia de las ideas y de la economía.* [What is the neoliberalism? Its significance in the history of ideas and the economy]. Retrieved December 17, 2004, from http://www.banrep.gov.co/blaavirtual/credencial/9102.htm

Castrillón Agudelo, M. C. (1999). *La dimensión social de la práctica de enfermería.* [The social dimension of nursing practice]. Medellín: Universidad de Antioquia.

Castrillón Agudelo, M. C., Orrego Sierra, S., Pérez Peláez, L., Ceballos, V., María Elena, & Arenas Cadavid, G. S. (1998). *El impacto de la reforma del sector salud en la práctica, la regulación y la educación enfermería en Colombia. Estudio multicéntrico y coolaborativo.* [The impact of the healthcare reform on nursing practice, regulation, and education in Colombia]. Medellín: Universidad de Antioquia. Organización Panamericana de la Salud. Fundación W. K. Kellog. Asociación Colombiana de Facultades de Enfermería.

Centre for Public Policy and Management. The Robert Gordon University. *An introduction to social policy. The welfare state.* Retrieved March 17, 2005 from http://www2.rgu.ac.uk/publicpolicy/introduction/wstate.htm

Consultoria para los Derechos Humanos y el Desplazamiento [Consulting for Human Rights and Displacement; CODHES]. (2006). *Boletín de la consultoría para los derechos humanos y el desplazamiento.* [Newsletter of the Colombian human rights and displacement consulting group], No. 69. Retrieved October 29, 2007 from http://www.codhes.org/Info/Boletines/BOLETIN69DEFINITIVO.pdf

Departamento Administrativo Nacional de Estadistica [National Administrative Department of Statistics; DANE]. (2005). *Indicadores demográficos 1985–2015.* [Demographic indicators 1985-2015]. Retrieved December 9, 2005 from http://www.dane.gov.co/inf_est/series_proyecciones.htm

Duque-Páramo, M. C. (1999). *La dimensión cultural del cuidado de enfermería.* [The cultural dimension of nursing care]. In: XIV Coloquio Nacional de Investigación en Enfermería, Tunja, Colombia.

Duque-Páramo, M. C. (2001). *Indicadores de salud. La globalización y las reformas económicas y sociales de los noventas: Su impacto en las condiciones de salud en Colombia. Un estudio de caso sobre Bogotá.* [Health indicators. Globalization and economic and social reforms in the 90's: Its impact on healthcare conditions in Colombia. A case study of Bogota]. Bogotá: Pontificia Universidad Javeriana.

El Espectador. (2004, February 15). Editorial. La salud en problemas. [Healthcare problems].

Fals Borda, O. (1962). *Facts and theory of sociocultural change in a rural social system.* Bogotá: Universidad Nacional de Colombia.

Fundación Hemera. (2004). *Etnias de Colombia.* [Ethnic groups in Colombia]. Retrieved December 1, 2004, from http://www.etniasdecolombia.org

Gómez Serrano, C., & Gómez Serrano, H. (1997). *Modernización y modernidad de los programas de pregrado en enfermeria.* ACOFAEN ICFES, Bogotá: Unión Gráfica LTDA.

Houghton Mifflin. (2005). *Good neighbor policy.* The Reader's Companion to American History. Retrieved February 2, 2005, from http://college.hmco.com/history/readerscomp/rcah/html/ah_037500_goodneighbor.htm

Iniciativa Trilateral para la Enfermería en Norteamérica (Trilateral Initiative for North American Nursing). (1996). *Una evaluación de la enfermería en Norteamérica.* [An evaluation of the nursing in North America]. Philadelphia, PA: Comisión de Egresados de Facultades de Enfermería en el Extranjero (Comission of Graduates of Foreign Nursing Schools).

Jaramillo Pérez, I. (1995). *El futuro de la salud en Colombia.* [The future of healthcare in Colombia] (2nd ed.). Bogotá: Tercer Mundo Editores.

Jordan, B. (1997). Authoritative knowledge and its construction. In R. E. Davis-Floyd & C. F. Sargent (Eds.), *Childbirth and authoritative knowledge* (p. 57). Berkeley, CA: University of California Press.

López-Maldonado, M. C. (2004). *Informe de análisis de resultados. Exámenes de Calidad de la Educación Superior ECAES.* [Report on the analysis of findings: Higher education quality control tests ECAES]. (Report). Bogotá: Instituto Colombiano para la el Fomento de la Educación Superior ICFES, Asociación Colombiana de Facultades de Enfermería ACOFAEN.

López Maldonado, M. C., Navarro Flórez, P., Delgado Arjona, M., & Sánchez Toro, J. M., (2000). *Caracterización de los estudiantes de la carrera de enfermería.* [Characterization of nursing students]. (Report). Bogotá: Pontificia Universidad Javeriana.

Martinez, E., & García, A. (2000). *What is "neo-liberalism"? A brief definition.* Retrieved December 17, 2004, from http://www.doublestandards.org/martinezl.html

Ministerio de Salud Pública. Oficina de Administración de Recursos Humanos para la Salud. (1972). *Estudio nacional de la situación de enfermería en Colombia: Macrodiagnóstico de enfermería.* [National study on the nursing situation in Colombia: Nursing macro-diagnosis]. Bogotá: Ministerio de Salud Pública.

Ministerio de Salud. Organización Panamericana de la Salud OPS/OMS. Asociación Nacional de Enfermería de Colombia ANEC & Asociación Colombiana de Facultades y Escuelas de Enfermería ACOFAEN. (1989). *Estudio nacional de enfermería 1985–1987. Actualidad y Perspectiva.* [National Study on Nursing 1985-1987: Recent findings and perspectives]. Bogotá: Ministerio de Salud.

Niño de Peña, L., Quintero, S., & de Villalobos, M. M. (1988). *Estudio nacional de enfermería 1985-1987.* [National Study on Nursing 1985-1987]. Bogotá: Ministerio de Salud. República de Colombia. Asociación Colombiana de Facultades de Enfermería. Organización Panamericana de la Salud.

Oróstegui, M. (1990). Situación de salud. [The healthcare situation]. In F. Yepes (Ed.), *La salud en Colombia (Estudio sectorial de salud)* (Vol. 1, pp. 219-475). Bogotá: Ministerio de Salud, Departamento Nacional de Planeación.

Organización Panamericana de la Salud OPS/OMS. (1998). *Colombia health profile.* Retrieved December 11, 2003, from http://www.col.ops-oms.org/situacion/erfil.asp

Organización Panamericana de la Salud OPS/OMS. Representación Colombia. (2002). *Análisis de situación de salud y sus tendencias. Indicadores básicos de salud 2000-2002.* [Analysis of the healthcare situation and trends. Basic healthcare indicators 2000-2002]. Retrieved February 9, 2005, from http://www.col.ops-oms.org/sivigila/Indicadores/default.asp

Organización Panamericana de la Salud OPS/OMS. Representación Colombia. (2004). *Salud y desplazamiento. Cifras y estadísticas.* [Healthcare and displacement. Figures and Numbers]. Retrieved February 9, 2005, from http://www.disaster-info.net/desplazados/investigacion.htm

Quevedo, E., Hernández, M., Miranda, N., Mariño, C., Cárdenas, H., & Wiesner, C. (1990a). *La salud en Colombia. Análisis sociohistórico.* [Healthcare in Colombia. Socio-historical analysis—Part I]. Primera parte. Retrieved November 14, 2003, from http://www.saludcolombia.com/actual/salud54/informe.htm

Quevedo, E., Hernández, M., Miranda, N., Mariño, C., Cárdenas, H., & Wiesner, C. (1990b). *La salud en Colombia. Análisis sociohistórico. Segunda parte.* [Healthcare in Colombia. Socio-historical analysis—Part II]. Retrieved November 14, 2003, from http://www.saludcolombia.com/actual/salud55/informe.htm

Quevedo, E., Hernández, M., Miranda, N., Mariño, C., Cárdenas, H., & Wiesner, C. (1998). La salud y el desarrollo (1958-1974). [Healthcare and development]. *Papel Político, 7,* 37-67.

Romero Ballén, M. N. (1992). *Modelo pedagógico en enfermería.* [Pedagogical nursing model]. (Report) Tunja: Universidad Pedagógica y Tecnológica de Colombia.

Ruiz, F., Camacho, S., Jurado, C., Matallana, M., O'Meara, G., Eslava, J., et al. (2001). *Los Recursos Humanos de la salud en Colombia: balance, competencias, prospectiva.*

[Healthcare human resources in Colombia: Assessment, competency, perspective]. Bogotá: Fundación Cultural de Artes Gráficas, Javegraf. 417 p.

Salud Colombia. (2000). *The reform. The Colombian social security system on health care.* Retrieved 11-14-03, 2003, from http://www.saludcolombia.com/actual/reform.htm

Sandoval, R., & Muñoz, A. L. (1990). Atención primaria. [Primary healthcare]. In F. Yepes (Ed.), *La salud en Colombia (Estudio sectorial de salud)* (Vol. 2, pp. 419-470). Bogotá: Ministerio de Salud, Departamento Nacional de Planeación.

Secretaría de Salud de Bogotá. (2001). *Situación de salud en Bogotá. Indicadores básicos por localidad.* [The healthcare situation in Bogota: Basic indicators by geographic location]. Bogotá: Secretaría de Salud. Alcaldía Mayor de Bogotá.

Sánchez, B. (2000). *Cuidado y práctica de enfermería.* [Nursing care and practice]. Bogotá: Universidad Nacional.

Sánchez Segura, J., & Ahumada Beltrán, C. (2004). La globalización y las reformas de los noventa. Su impacto sobre la situación económica y social de Colombia: El caso de la salud en Bogotá. [Globalization and the Nineties' reform, its impact on economic and social conditions in Colombia: The case of healthcare in Bogotá.]. *Papel Político, 16,* 29-75.

Sarmiento Anzola, L. (1991). El desarrollo social en la antigua y nueva constitución. [Social development under the old and in the new Constitution]. *Revista Foro, 16,* 38-54.

The United Nations Children's Fund [UNICEF]. (1998). *Estado Mundial de la infancia 1998.* [The State of the World's Children 1998]. New York: UNICEF.

Velandia Mora, A. L. (1995). *Historia de la enfermería en Colombia.* [History of Nursing in Colombia]. Bogotá: Universidad Nacional de Colombia.

UNESCO (1998). *World declaration on higher education for the 21st century: Vision and action.* Retrieved February 9, 2005, from http://www.unesco.org/education/educprog/wche/declaration_eng.htm

Velandia Mora, A. L. (2006). *La facultad de enfermería de la Universidad Nacional de Colombia en el siglo XX.* [The School of Nursing at the Universidad Nacional de Colombia in the Twentieth Century]. Bogotá: Universidad Nacional de Colombia.

World Health Organization [WHO]. (1978). Primary health care report of the International Conference on Primary Health Care, Alma-Ata, USSR. September 6-12, Geneva, Author.

World Health Organization (WHO). (1986). Health and Welfare Canada and the Canadian Public Health Association (1986). *Ottawa charter for health promotion.* Ottawa, Ontario, Canada: Canadian Public Health Association.

Yepes, F. J. (Ed.). (1990). *La salud en Colombia. Estudio sectorial de salud.* [Healthcare in Colombia: A health sector study] (Vol. 1 & 2). Bogotá: Editorial Presencia.

CHAPTER 3

Nursing in Chile*

Patricia Jara Concha, Veronica Behn Theune, Nestor Ortiz Rebolledo and Sandra Valenzuela Suazo

Professional nursing in Chile has experienced, and continues to experience, significant changes related to the political, social and economic transformations taking place in the nation. As all aspects of Chilean society grapple with the worldwide process of globalization and free market economics, additional pressure is on the nursing profession to change and adapt. Further, the profession must accommodate various social group and epidemiological profiles. Finally, uneven income distribution contributes to inequalities in health care and access to heath care services. The disparity in income is often tied to geographic area, leading regions to make health care decisions based on local needs and resources. As a result, the central region of Chile, where most of the population is concentrated, has more varied health care service access than the rest of the country.

From its beginning, the nursing profession supported this regional nature of health care in Chile, while at the same time recognizing advances in health care occurring nationally. In fact, in its earliest manifestation, Chilean nursing was completely regional and made up of women from local communities. Nursing was not separate from medicine and was performed by *Machis*, traditional healers who used special rites and claimed the knowledge of the healing qualities of plants, water, the sun, and the moon.

Throughout the Spanish conquest, neither nurses nor physicians arrived from Spain to augment or supplement these indigenous health care providers. Even in 1556, as the first hospital in the city of Santiago opened its doors, nursing care was the responsibility of indigenous people and slaves. This hospital was a public

*All opinions expressed in this chapter are the exclusive responsibility of the authors and they do not represent a position of the organization or institution where they work nor its administration.

hospital that met the needs of the poor. Members of the wealthy classes were still taken care of at home by family members and servants.

The first formal nursing school was created within the Universidad de Chile in 1906 by physicians. Its curriculum followed the biomedical model and focused on curative health care. When the Sisters of Charity arrived in Chile from Spain, they disagreed with the nursing school curriculum that was designed by physicians and they were unsure of the quality of the academic preparation of these nursing school graduates. So, in 1926, they redesigned the nursing curriculum to include preventive health care oriented toward the family and the community.

With the expansion of hospital and health care services an increase in the demand for nursing services occurred between 1950 and 1960. To meet the need, both hospital and public health services incorporated nursing services within their organizations and they created the *Colegio de Enfermeras de Chile* (Chilean Nurses Association), the professional organization for nurses. The urgency of the need for nurses also allowed for the creation of nursing schools in several other cities in Chile to educate more nurses.

During the 1970s, the demand for nurses surfaced again. Since nurses worked mainly in hospitals, the biomedical model of illness influenced the public view of the nursing supply and the kind of preparation nurses were thought to need. Thus, the need for specialized nurses was seen to be in areas such as cardiology, nephrology, maternity and pediatrics, ophthalmology and other areas of clinical specialization that mirror medical specializations. To accommodate the need for specialized nursing practitioners, it was necessary to create graduate level education in nursing at Chilean universities. Additionally, by collaborating with international organizations such as the World Health Organization (WHO) and the Kellogg Foundation, significant numbers of Chilean nurses were educated abroad.

In this same time period, social and political changes also affected the profession. The *Colegio de Enfermeras* repeatedly and actively lobbied the government regarding the *Colegio*'s lack of participation in the restructuring of nursing services and the continuing lack of recognition of nurses as a valuable resource in community health care. During the 1980s, the new political Constitution of Chile and the 1981 Higher Education Reform Law effecting university education ended the exclusivity of public universities in the granting of nursing degrees. With the new legislation, private for-profit colleges were allowed to mount degree granting nursing programs. (Private colleges in Chile are considered grossly inferior to public universities.) Although Chile's nurses objected to this degree-granting by non-public university institutions, they have been unsuccessful in overturning the legislation.

In the 1990s, and aided by the start of democratic reorganization in the country, the nurses worked to strengthen the credentials for the nursing profession. The Chilean Society for Nursing Education (now named Chilean Association for Nursing Education) proposed a nursing curriculum leading to the degree of *"Nurse"* or *"Licenciado en Enfermeria"* (Licenciado in Nursing) through a course of study, lasting a full 10 semesters or 5 years, after completion of high school. The inclusion of the nursing profession in the national public health code, at the end of the 20th century, also helped to provide autonomy and recognition for the nursing field.

However, despite the fact that nursing is now included in the Chilean national public health code, the Chilean nursing profession is alarmed at recent changes in nursing education. Many private "for-profit" degree granting colleges were recently allowed to open nursing education programs preparing students for the *Licenciado* in Nursing. The trend is worrisome because the curriculum of these new private programs is considered inferior to that of the public universities that award the same degree. The for-profit motive in the private colleges places profit above the quality of the education. Additionally, they do not foster the professional growth of their nursing professors, treating them rather like hourly workers.

The nursing curriculum in the private colleges focuses heavily on the technical aspects of nursing preparation with little emphasis on the professional and analytical components. The fear is that the leadership skills and analytical thinking of future nurses will be diminished and nursing will be degraded to that of a technical occupation. A second fear is that future nurse educators who were prepared at the private colleges will be unprepared to guide and mentor new generations of Chilean nurses.

In part, the empowerment of nurses rests on their ability to perform autonomous functions. To empower students, Chilean nurse educators need a solid theoretical background in pedagogy as well as in the meaning of the discipline. They must be analytical and capable of critical thought so that they can contribute to new knowledge and discover new applications for both practice and the classroom. Educators are charged with the responsibility of preparing students to deliver health care based on scientific, ethical and humanistic principles that can address health care concerns of healthy people, sick people and persons at the end of life. The future of Chilean nursing requires the profession to foster transcendent, holistic changes that maintain and strengthen the position of academic nursing. Nursing will advance when nurse educators contribute through scientific research to the knowledge required to create these changes. They also must hold fast to their mission of educating future nurses to be agents of change, nurses who have solid personal and professional self-esteem as well as confidence about themselves and their role in the health care team. Nurse educators must do so without neglecting the development of nursing leaders, who are also much needed today and in the future.

In sum, nursing in Chile can benefit from a critical examination, starting with the issues of globalization and health care and continuing with discussions of gender, hegemony, subordination and submission of nurses and of health care itself. New generations of nurses are at a unique crossroads where they can, if properly educated, demonstrate autonomous performance in the various areas of professional practice. They can do so by recognizing the impact their nursing activities have on the health care of individuals, groups and communities.

CHILE AND GLOBALIZATION IN THE AMERICAS

Chile is considered a peripheral country in the world capitalist system. It is a land of diversity both for its geography and for its political economy. Geographically, it is a very long, narrow country nestled between the Andes Mountains on the east and the Pacific Ocean on the west; it shares common borders with Argentina, Bolivia, and Peru. Chile is home to majestic mountains in the east which make take up one-third of its territory, the Atacama Desert in the North classified as the "driest place on Earth," and a massive and fertile valley in the central part of the county. Rich in natural resources, it is known for its production and exportation of copper. In part because of its copper, Chile has one of the strongest economies in Latin America.

In terms of political economy Chile is capitalist, but it tends toward left-of-center wing populist ideology. In 1970 Socialist Salvador Allende was elected president. He made significant changes toward socialism in Chile including a socialist health care reform, an agrarian reform which expropriated land from wealthy landowners and nationalization of many private companies including some U.S.-owned companies. The threat of socialism beyond Chile and the boldness of Allende's social and economic reforms inspired a military *coupe d'etat* led by then Army Chief of Staff Augusto Pinochet who later became president. The military junta, covertly aided by the CIA of the United States, and the subsequent 17-year dictatorship resulted in an estimated 3,500 deaths or disappearances. Many of the health and social reforms initiated by Allende were quickly reversed by Pinochet who then implemented conservative neoliberal policies. In the year 2000 Chile reelected a socialist president who maintained more moderate principles than Allende. In 2006 Chile elected its first female president, Socialist Michelle Bachelet.

In Chile, globalization is viewed as the outcome of the need of developed countries to control the production and distribution of resources in developing countries. Many Chileans see globalization as a by-product of post World War II reconstruction and the so-called "European economic miracle" as well as the fear of dependency connected to the energy crisis of the 1970s. While developed (or core) countries make up only 20% of the world's population, they consume 80% of the energy resources, and contribute to environmental degradation in similar proportions. Ninety percent of exports from developing nations to core nations consist of raw materials. The core nations process the raw materials into goods and resell them to developing countries for a large value-added profit. In essence, rich developed nations extract raw materials from poorer developing countries, convert them into products and then resell them back to the developing country for a large profit. This further impoverishes the developing nation, adds to their level of underdevelopment and increases the debt burden of these countries. Even the United Nations Program for Development (UNPD, 2004) has acknowledged this fact.

Despite the fact that developed nations benefit enormously from all of this, they are not directly held responsible for the negative economic and social consequences of globalization. A greater contradiction exists in the role of transnational corporations within the global economy. The holdings and large profit margins of transnational corporations serve as an incentive for the governments of developed nations to continue to support these economic goals (Castells, 1999). For example, former U.S. President G. W. Bush's intimate relationship (and collusion) with international oil companies, his refusal to acknowledge the Kyoto protocol (regarding the emission of contaminants), and his "crusade against evil" and for the control of Middle East oil gave credence to the ways in which core nations support the efforts of multinational corporations to the detriment of poor developing countries and people worldwide.

The struggle of the Brazilian government with transnational pharmaceutical companies over the high cost of generic drugs for AIDS is an example of how multinational corporations work against peripheral nations (in this case Brazil and its people) and in favor of the core nations (pharmaceutical company headquarters are housed in the United States and Western Europe). World domination either through the appropriation of resources or through the imposition of friendly governments is gradually replaced by international laws regarding patents that have resulted in the appropriation of the products of research by international enterprises, especially in biotechnology. This means that international commerce centers can reap great profits by determining how much each country may produce and in what amount, without they themselves contributing any resources to the production process.

While economic globalization has certainly benefited many segments of society, it has enormous negative effects on the growing number of poor families and communities in the developing world. The negative health consequences on this segment of society are devastating. This places an undue burden on the health care systems of those countries and on nurses. Chilean nurses are directly influenced by the context in which they work and live. The need to provide health services to the growing number of sick and poor people takes a toll on the entire system. Nurses themselves struggle under increasingly difficult economic and working conditions. The creation of an efficient and economically viable health care system depends on the government's concept of life in society and on the social responsibility of the State in maintaining collective health. Health and welfare systems in Chile are highly politicized. Each political party takes an ideological position on the role of the State in the provision of services and on how programs are funded.

Historically, "solidarian financing" is the most popular type of health care finance system in Chile. Under solidarian financing, Chilean citizens contribute a set percentage of their salaries to the health care system (e.g., 7% of their salary). Fairness and equal access to services (without regard to class and based on individual need) is a priority of solidarian financing. In regard to health services, three main views represent the diversity of positions in the Chilean political spectrum. While solidarian financing for health care services is the norm, other perspectives are taking hold in Chile. A description of the three perspectives follows here:

1. *Neoliberal Perspective:* The neoliberal perspective maintains that the market must regulate the supply and demand of health care. Thus, care is regarded as a tradable good. The view is that the State should concern itself only with the health care of the most disadvantaged and should exert as little influence as possible in the regulation of the market.
2. *Moderate Perspective:* The moderate perspective maintains that countries need to have associations or mutuality's that protect people's health according

to their social stratus with particular attention to the production sector. In this case, members of social strata with more resources (the wealthy) arrange for their own protection (insurance) while the State is obligated to take care of the poorest. Also, the State is required to facilitate the development of associations for the protection of workers.

3. *Welfare State:* With a progressive Welfare State, the goal is a universal health care system where every one has their needs addressed regardless of social status and in which financing depends on the contributions of everyone according to their abilities. Here, the State assumes the main responsibility for management of the system. Oscillation between the position where the State has minimal intervention and favoring freedom of choice based on one's ability to pay and its resulting inequality and the position where the State owns and manages a hegemonic system of universal access was one of the great political discussion of the 20th century (Castells, 1999). This discussion brought the world into an ideological struggle between Marxism and neoliberalism. Through globalization, the 21st century has unwittingly inherited, as an unpredictable situation the two great rival ills of the previous century: hegemony and inequity.

Politics, Economics, and Health in Chile

The history of social security and public health in Chile began early. A law mandating Compulsory Workers Insurance, passed in 1924 made Chile the first Latin American country to adopt a farsighted, solidarian approach to occupational health. Compulsory Workers Insurance benefited those who suffered disability due to accidents, old age or illness. Workers paid for the insurance plan using the principles of solidarian financing. It did not cover all workers, as it was only a first attempt to create a public health policy in a solidaristic manner by the workers and also because it emerged in a society with "high class discrimination" (Rosselot, 1993).

In the political setting, Chilean public health originated with the 1925 Constitution that for the first time required the State to maintain a national public health service. However, the programs and institutions charged with providing health care were dispersed and did not interact with each other (Labra, 2002). An important advance took place in 1952 when the Chilean National Health Service (NHS) was created as an experience replicating the 1948 creation of the British National Health Service. In this way, Chile became the second non-socialist country adopting epidemiological and preventive health strategies on a national scale and through the action of government institutions that adopted political and technical roles. The Chilean National Health Service implemented a centralized planning system based on epidemiological evidence, including the national integration of all preventative and curative efforts and the evaluation of outcomes by means of epidemiological tracking.

Health care unions and professional organizations played a key role in the history of the Chilean health care system. Particularly striking is how the medical profession in Chile repeatedly used the *Colegio Medico de Chile* (Medical Association of Chile or Chilean Medical Association) which was founded in 1948 to enlarge physicians' sphere of influence, to protect physicians' private practice and fee for service and to maintain the status of the physician over and above the status of other health care workers. From its inception, the Chilean Medical Association received explicit differentiated treatment in the public administration code and maintained strong opposition to all health care reforms aimed at the creation of a system based on solidaristic financing and leading to a single, fair and accessible health care system.

An example of the above is the failure of the legislature in 1968 to pass a law creating a universal single payer system of health care, without distinction by social class and based on solidaristic financing. Nonetheless, such a system of universal health care was put into place, despite the opposition of the Chilean Medical Association, during the tenure of Socialist Party President Allende. Through powerful associations such as the Chilean Medical Association, physicians achieved preferential treatment within the public administration in the health care arena at the exclusion of other professionals who may have had stronger academic backgrounds in administration. A more recent example occurred in early 2004 when the Chilean Medical Association protested the appointment of two nurses as directors of two hospitals in Chile's Region Eight, despite the fact that the candidates' educational background and administrative experience prepared them well to assume the positions.

Continued development of Chilean public health service took place between 1952 and 1973 culminating with the implementation of a unified health care system during the Allende years, sometimes also called the Chilean socialist utopia or the *allendista* dream. The *allendista* dream, taken from Allende's name, consisted of a protective State providing free and equal access to health care and education. While this idea was very well received by Chile's popular classes it was not welcomed by members of the upper classes or by those who lost privileges during the socialist period. At the international level, the continuing polarity between the former Soviet Union and the United States made it impossible to implement any social and public health transformations without foreign interventions. This was the case also for the popular "Alliance for the Progress" *(Alianza para el Progreso)* implemented by President J. F. Kennedy as well as for the technical public health aid provided by foundations such as the Rockefeller Foundation or by governments such as that of the former Soviet Union.

In Chile, the ideological discussion about social prevention systems and their financing was passionate during the Allende years. Health and social services were considered basic rights for all (rather than privileges for the wealthy minority) and included the concept of citizen's participation in the development and institution of the services. Allende's socialist agenda included social educational and economic reforms.

Unfortunately, the September 11, 1973 military takeover dramatically changed the nature of social relations for Chileans. It had particularly devastating effects on the poor and the middle classes as many of the state-funded pubic health and social services they relied on for survival disappeared. The ideology of collective rights and citizen participation so much embraced during Allende's rule ended precipitously with the military take-over and subsequent 16-year-long dictatorship. The discussion in Chile about social prevention systems and their financing was abruptly interrupted by the 1973 military dictatorship that reversed the people's health service and converted health care financing to a market-driven system. The military prioritized macroeconomic development and the globalization of Chile at the expense of social programs. As this took place in the context of an international economic crisis, poverty in Chile increased by 44.6% (Labra, 2002), exacerbating differences among the social classes.

The social security of workers during the Chilean military regime was dealt with by creating two kinds of private enterprises of compulsory insurance (for profit): the Administrators of Pension Funds (AFP/*Administradora de Fondo de Pensiones*), charged with the administration of the funds each worker could assemble during his life with the purpose of financing his own retirement, and the Social Security Institutes (ISAPRE/*Institucion de Salud Previsional*) that in exchange for a monthly contribution from the worker participated partially in the payment for health care services. Due to inadequate State supervision of these bodies and the multiplicity of branches and subsidies, they showed constant structural surpluses that became deficits against the contributing workers and benefits for the transnational holdings that bought them. In this sense, Chile became the best laboratory for the neoliberal experiment in Latin America that in the process left behind poverty and a marked social inequality (Titelman, 2001). The result was the development of three strata of health care insurance in Chile:

1. Those with high socio-economic level were able to purchase excellent private health insurance from ISAPRES and represented 20% of the population.
2. The military, with health care benefits as good as the private ones (ISAPRES) that were financed by special autonomous resources from the national budget constituted a population no greater than 500,000 inhabitants.
3. The rest of the population depended on the State health system that at the time offered inferior care with inadequate resources. State health care employees were poorly paid and poorly motivated.

Moreover, primary health care suffered greatly when the responsibility for services was shifted to individual municipalities and its financing was subject to the existing inequalities between rich and poor municipalities.

Neoliberalism in Latin America

Internationally and specifically in Europe, the fall of the Berlin wall was the event that terminated the long process culminating in the Cold War and that ultimately triggered the movement toward the global hegemony of neoliberalism. In Latin America, the movement toward neoliberalism almost always happened through military takeovers. Many Latin American countries (including Chile) suddenly and violently changed paths when military dictators assumed power after a *coup d'etat*.

As revealed in recently declassified Chilean documents, the Chilean case was only one of several military dictatorships instigated by the United States Central Intelligence Agency (CIA).

Selected labor organizations and far right economic groups opposed to solidarism and equalitarian policies for the financing of health care and education spurred the destabilization of the Chilean socialist government of Salvador Allende thus triggering the military coup of September 11, 1973. The Chilean coup, intended as a short termed measure to enhance governability and restore democracy, lasted for more than 16 years. Military leaders chose to lengthen the coup for personal and professional gain. Ultimately, they left a trail of criminal acts and human rights violations for which they never assumed total responsibility.

The Chilean military government, driven by the economic and social principles of the Chicago School and its conservative principles, opened the way for Chile's inclusion into the global economy. Export diversification and the attraction of foreign capital allowed the total insertion of Chile in the developed world. This situation resulted in the deepening of inequality gaps such that, at the start of the 21st century, Chile became one of the countries with the highest scores from the International Monetary Fund (IMF). Paradoxically, Chile is one of the countries with the highest inequality in wealth distribution in the world (Titelman, 2001).

In 1989 when a democratic government took power, the fear of a new military uprising appeared. This concern was associated with the constitution that was shaped to perpetuate conservative power relations and ideology and to discourage citizen participation. The early "neo-democratic" governments continued the same economic development model, hoping that an increase in wealth would eliminate poverty, which still today has not happened. Even though in the year 2000 Chile succeeded in electing its first socialist president since Allende, Mr. Ricardo Lagos's administration was not able to sufficiently disengage from the neoliberal world economic model to begin the process of reversing social inequalities. Initiatives put forth by his socialist administration were limited and modified by a politically polarized parliament. In the health care arena, health care reform was initially blocked by neoliberals and later when the law passed, it was significantly influenced by ISAPRES and the Chilean Medical Association (*Colegio Medico*). A powerful neoliberal voice in parliament succeeded in dismissing two Ministers of Health and to institute a health care policy that was significantly more sympathetic toward market forces than the one originally proposed.

In summary, as a result of power struggles in the political, economic and labor organization spheres, the contemporary Chilean health care system can be categorized into three periods:

1. The "Public Health" period, from 1953 to 1973 that was marked by sustained development of public health that set an example for social and health security in the world.
2. The "Neoliberal Health" period, from 1974 to 1998 in which social and public health security were dismantled and became inserted in the international free market,

3. The "Global Health" period, from 1990 onward, in which using a mercantilist approach elements of justice and social integration have been slowly achieved.

Public Health Care (1953 to 1973)

In 1918, the first Public Health Code was consolidated and a network of public health organizations were created in different public health "zones" of the country. This organization is regarded as the precursor to the Chilean National Health Service (*Servicio Nacional de Salud*) created in 1952. The creation of the Chilean National Health Service is the result of bringing together several organizations responsible for the health of the country as follows:

1. Savings Bank for Workers Insurance (*Caja del Seguro Obrero*);
2. General Ministry for the Protection of Children and Teens (*Direccion General de Proteccion a la Infancia y Adolescencia*);
3. Medical Service for the Municipalities (*Servicio Medico para la Municipalidades*);
4. Section of Work Related Accidents from the Ministry of Labor (*Seccion de Accidentes del Trabajo del Ministerio del Trabajo*); and
5. the Bacteriological Institute (*Instituto Bacteriologico*).

Later on, the National Medical Service for Employees (*Servicio Medico Nacional de Empleados*–SERMENA) was created as a free choice system for current and retired public and private workers.

In Chile, the National Health Service implemented a regionalized approach to care that (a) blended preventive and curative aspects of care; (b) developed integrated care involving different health care team members; and (c) provided a continuity of care. In this way, a chain of health care providers offered health care services at clinics in local neighborhoods, in acute care settings, and in the home. The protection of the health of the population focused on environmental hygiene, food control and vaccinations. Also, social services were added to help families and communities. This regionalized approach had a great impact on infant mortality rates: while in 1930 there were 212 deaths per thousand live births, in 1960 the number was reduced by half.

The National Health Service was driven by administrative and health policies. The administrative structure was simplified by having a Senate-appointed General Health Director and a National Health Council made up of representatives from various sectors interested in population health. Between 1950 and 1968, the country was divided into 13 "health zones." Each "health zone" provided decentralized health care activities within areas covering a specific geographical territory. Priorities for health care policies were determined through epidemiological analyses of population-specific public health problems.

The National Health Service focused on primary, secondary and tertiary care. Home care and neighborhood services were coordinated by community health clinics (*Consultorios Externos*). The community health clinics offer team-based integrated health care. A combination of preventative services such as vaccinations and health education as well as medical treatments dramatically improved health indicators in Chile.

In 1958 the realization that serious problems existed in relation to workplace accidents and the lack of occupational health provisions for the protection of workers led to the creation of Mutual Aid Associations (*Mutualidades de Seguridad*). These were non-profit labor organizations created on the principle of solidarity. Protection against workplace risks were provided by means of an insurance policy. In 1968 an occupational health law was passed for health care workers that covered both work-related accidents and illness. By 1988, a total of 37,000 companies with 1,400,000 health workers were registered under the law (Jimenez, 1990).

Neoliberal Health Care (1974-1998)

Chileans embraced the primary health care philosophy of "Health for All by the Year 2000" put forth at Alma Ata in 1976. Both its philosophical under-pinnings and its practical aspects were incorporated into Chilean health care policies. In spite of the existence of already good health care coverage, Chile began a series of health care and pension system reforms in 1979. The functions of the Health Ministry including the Minister of Health were reformulated. Law No 2.763 created the National System of Health Care Services (*Sistema Nacional de Servicios de Salud*–SNSS). In this system employees are required to contribute a health tax (totaling 7% of annual income) to either the National Fund for Health Care (*Fondo Nacional de Salud*–FONASA) or the Institutions of Health Surveillance (*Instituciones de Salud Previsional*–ISAPRES). The latter (ISAPRES) are a series of private, for-profit or not-for profit entities with free choice systems that provide health care and other benefits to its affiliates (French-Davis, 2001).

Global Health Care (1990–Present)

As of June 2001 the population of Chile was 15.4 million with 80% of the people living in urban areas. Eight indigenous towns represented 10% of the total population: *Aymará, Atacameños, Quechua, Mapuche, Rapanui, Colla, Kawaskar,* and *Yámana.* The poverty rate of the indigenous populations living in these towns is higher than the average of those living in other geographic areas of the country. In fact, a high correlation exists between areas with high poverty and areas inhabited by indigenous peoples. Also, health statistics shows high infant mortality rates among indigenous groups. For instance, in the case of the *Atacamaños,* the infant mortality rate is 40 deaths per 1000 live births, well above the national average. The life expectancy is as much as 10 years less than the national average, as it in for the *Aymará.* Since indigenous native peoples have received unequal access to health care services and are members of discriminated groups, the current health reform focused on improving the quality of life in indigenous communities. It has become one of the most important priorities for policy development. Today, the 15 administrative "health zones" are the responsibility of the Regional Ministry Secretary that in turn is designated by the Ministry of Health following the report of the Regional Quartermaster. Each "health zone" is divided into "health care service" units that are functionally decentralized state organisms with judicial and fiscal autonomy. These organisms allow the fulfillment of demands for health promotion, protection, and recovery of health and the rehabilitation of the sick for the entire population.

The Health Ministry coordinates all the sectors of the health service, is responsible for formulating and establishing health policies and for issuing norms and general plans for the entire system. The ministry is also responsible for the supervision, control, and evaluation of services. The Health Ministry provides oversight to the following bodies: (a) Health Care Services, (b) the National Health Fund (FONASA), (c) the Superintendent of ISAPRE, (d) the Public Health Institute (ISP), and (e) the National Supply Center (CENABAST). Furthermore, (SESMA) health services are responsible for environmental control in the Metropolitan Region and the Institute for Public Health (ISP) regulates all drugs and medical consumables.

Health care is regulated by norms framed in Chile's "Health Care Plans" (*Programas de salud*) put forth by the Ministry of Health in the year 1952. These Plans define coverage, frequency, and periodicity of the contacts between users and health care providers as well as responsibilities by attention level in the system. Public health regulation of public and private health care establishments is the responsibility of the Health Services Head Offices for those establishments located within the jurisdiction of the respective Health Service. The basic programs of the Health Ministry (e.g., maternal child health, adult medicine, and dentistry) were structured with an integral approach designed to incorporate health promotion, prevention, cure, and rehabilitation. The Health Ministry developed numerous prevention programs targeting specific conditions among which the following are noteworthy: immunizations and vaccinations, complementary nutrition, winter campaign (control of respiratory problems), motor vehicle accident prevention, "red tide" control, and the eradication of Chagas' disease (a parasitic illness). Also, excellent programs for the detection of cervix-uterine and breast cancers have respective coverage of 60% and 30% of the targeted population.

From 1991 onward, the Health Ministry contributed to the prevention, treatment, and rehabilitation of alcoholism and drug addiction by maintaining 300 centers for prevention and rehabilitation of mental health issues and substance abuse. Concurrent with this, preventive programs have been put in place focusing on adolescents, based on research findings indicating the majority of drug abusers in Chile began use during their adolescence. Included among the protection factors promoted by these communication efforts are the values, interests, and dreams of the young such as freedom, love, communication, family, and self-esteem. Another example of a prevention program is the Special Program for Elder Care that was created in 1994. Its purpose is to improve access to health care services and the quality of life for those over 65 years of age. Since then, the elder population had benefited increasingly from the public system.

The public health care service network is composed of clinics and hospitals spanning the entire range of health care services. The clinics include urban and rural general medicine clinics, rural outposts, and medico-rural stations. According to the size of the population, this represents approximately one clinic for every 28.5 thousand inhabitants (1 for every 17,100 if one considers only the population that is affiliated to the FONASA). Also, a rural outpost is in place for every 1,900 inhabitants when one counts only those people living in the area (estimated at 14.6% of the total population). There are about 30,000 hospital beds, amounting to one bed for every 5,000 inhabitants.

Emergency health care is provided by the emergency services at hospitals and by the Primary Emergency Health Care Services (*Servicios de Atencion Primaria de Urgencia*–SAPU). The main private hospitals and clinics also offer emergency health care services. Auxiliary diagnostic and blood bank services are offered through both public and private affiliates. Within the public sector, these services are mainly located in hospitals, fulfilling not only the demand created there but also the demand generated by ambulatory care services. During the year 2000, external technical cooperation was focused on social themes, quality of life, mental health, epilepsy, health equality measures, and HIV/AIDS. There was a significant effort toward the establishment of a base line of social indicators with the objective of ordering and seeking work axes with increased sharing among the System of United Nations as well as between the latter and its national counterparts.

A new health reform was proposed for the period 2000-2006, with the goal of guaranteeing the right to health care for the entire population without discrimination of any kind. Other goals included the improvement in health status and the reduction in inequalities according to the socioeconomic conditions and geographical localization of the population. The short range goals of the Ministry (2000-2002) contained priorities regarding: access and opportunities for health care, citizen's rights to health care through the fulfillment of the Card of Patient's Rights and the creation of a program for the participation of users of the health care system. The basic guidelines of the reform established a Guaranteed Plan that commits the public insurer (FONASA) as well as the private insurers (ISAPRE) to establish guaranteed, efficient, and timely care for those with illnesses that are more frequent, more serious, and more costly. The priority was primary health care, strengthening the family and community health care teams. In structural terms, the reform pointed to the creation of a Solidarian Fund with contributions from the revenue authority and 3/7th of the compulsory health care contributions. This would provide the required financing of the Guaranteed Plan for those affiliated with FONASA and ISAPRE (Giaconi, 2005).

Currently in Chile the population profile is in a process of demographic and epidemiologic transition. During the last few decades there has been a reduction in both birth and death rates. In 1998, those younger than 15 years old constituted 28.8% of the population, those between 15 and 64 were 64% of the population and those over 65 were 7% of the population. The dependency ratio was 35.8% in 1998. Life expectancy at birth in the period 1995-2000 has been estimated at 75.2 years of age.

In 1999 the mortality rate was 510.7 for every 100,000 inhabitants; the stated causes corresponding to the adjusted mortality rates (for every 100,000 inhabitants) are the following: circulatory system diseases (150.3), malignant neoplasms (124.2), transmissible diseases (67.5), and external causes (57.6).

Concerning infant mortality, in 2002, there were 7.8 deaths for each 1000 live births. A decrease has been observed in three components: late infant death, neonatal mortality, and precocious neonatal mortality. The main causes of infant death are: prenatal infections, congenital anomalies, respiratory system diseases, trauma, and poisoning. Children between 5 and 9 years of age, concentrates 0.3% of all deaths and thus becomes the group with the smallest death rate. The group of adolescents between 10 and 19 years of age has a death rate of 0.37 for every 1000 inhabitants.

The population group between 20 and 60 years of age represents 53% of the total population of Chile. Adults between 20 and 44 have a death rate of 1.3 for every 1000 inhabitants. As in the adolescent group, the main causes of death are external. For the 45- and 59-year-old age group, mortality reaches 5.2 for every 1000 inhabitants. Deaths in this group are due mainly to tumors, constituting 30% of the total; in second place are circulatory system diseases with a 21%. Mortality for those between 65 and 79 years of age rises to 31.5 for every 1000 inhabitants. Tumors are still the first cause of death and are followed by circulatory and respiratory system diseases.

Ninety-nine percent of people living in urban areas in 2002 had access to clean drinking water available through public networks, 90% of them had access to sewage services and 4% had access to septic tanks and absorbent wells. As a result, vector transmission diseases are scarce in Chile. There are no cases of malaria or dengue fever and cases of Chagas disease are restricted to a geographic area with an approximate population of 850,000 inhabitants. Immuno-preventible diseases are controlled thanks to the coverage of 95% of the infant population; the last case of polio was diagnosed in 1975 and that of diphtheria in 1996. Measles has been diagnosed sporadically and in localized breakouts. Tetanus has also appeared sporadically and no neonatal tetanus has been registered since 1997. Parotidithis has decreased but German measles has increased somewhat during the last 5 years. Infectious intestinal diseases appeared during a cholera breakout in 1998 and there has been a marked reduction in typhoid fever since 1996. Tuberculosis has decreased markedly to 22 for every 100,000 inhabitants. Rabies has maintained its epidemiological pattern and trichinosis occurs with sporadic breakouts. Incidences of the human hidatidosis, a parasitic disease, have also dropped. Among emerging diseases one must note that the pulmonary syndrome due to Hantavirus Pulmonary Syndrome (HPS); meningococcical meningitis is endemic and HIV/AIDS continues to increase.

Diseases of the circulatory system continue occupying one-third of the causes of death and are the leading cause of death in Chile. Malignant neoplasms cause 22% of deaths while accidents and violence are the fourth cause of death.

The Evolution of Nursing in Chile

It is important to preface this section by noting that Chile suffers from a chronic lack of qualified nurses active in the profession and a comparative abundance of physicians. While 17,467 physicians practice in Chile, only about 8,000 of the 18,000 nurses are currently practicing as nurses.

To reconstruct the history of Nursing in Chile from a perspective of political and cultural hegemony, it is useful to present it as taking place in three stages: vocational, technical, and professional with the most emphasis placed on the latter, mainly because of the conception society has of health in each of the historical periods and because of its impact on the development of nursing (Collière, 1997).

To preface this section, here are a few key historical points. The Hospital *San Juan de Dios*, the first Chilean hospital, was opened in the city of Santiago by *Don Pedro de Valdivia* in 1552 during the Spanish conquest. There, rather than helping patients recover, the goal was to isolate those with infectious and contagious diseases. Subsequently, epidemics of typhus exantemathic and smallpox periodically decimated the population. Smallpox could only be managed when in 1805 mass vaccinations against smallpox were initiated.

At the time of Chilean independence from Spain in 1832, a number of uncoordinated and fragmented health care organizations existed: (a) the Committee Headquarters of Hospitals and the House of Foundlings of Santiago (*Junta Directora de Hospitales y Casa de Expositos de Santiago*), (b) the Committee of Charity (*Junta de Beneficencia*), (c) the General Committee of Public Health (*Junta General de Salubridad*), and (d) the Council for Public Health (*Consejo de Higiene Publica*) which was especially committed to the community public health of municipalities. The fragmentation of health services continued in Chile for many decades and the 19th century ended amidst a series of uncoordinated health care.

Vocational Nursing Period

The vocational stage of Chilean history is marked by the strong religious influence that followed the Spanish conquest. Its oldest reference goes back to the times of the Conquest and the Colony (1550s–1800s) when the first public health measures were the responsibility of the district councils created by the Spanish Crown. These measures had an embryonic level in regard to topics such as urban public health, the health inspection of food and drink, the provision of clean drinking water, and prophylactic and curative measures during epidemics.

The care of the poor and destitute became an important endeavor under *Don Pedro de Valdivia's* government in 1552. Thus, they founded in Santiago the first Chilean hospital with 50 beds. This hospital was later passed on to the Congregation *San Juan de Dios* and it adopted that name. This religious order, originally from Spain, was motivated not only to help, counsel, and serve fellow human beings, but also to find God in suffering and pain as a way to atone for sins and to make a divine offering.

The needs associated with the progress of the country led to the creation of the University of Chile, School of Medicine in 1842. By law, the following main functions were assigned to the School of Medicine: (a) to develop the discipline of medicine, (b) to study diseases endemic in Chile, and (c) to improve public and domestic health. The structure and role of the School of Medicine facilitated the emergence of the second phase of nursing, the technical phase. In this way, a method was established for the developing specialists and for the promotion of national research in the health disciplines.

The development of medical knowledge came about slowly and was focused on finding the causes and treatment for diseases. As the use of medical technology increased, it led to the use of increasingly complex instrumentation. The concentration of public health resources in hospitals was promoted so that these institutions became the only ones providing care. Technological complexity made it necessary to have personnel capable of carrying out some of the tasks physicians assumed, such as diagnostic tests and treatments. People who cared for the sick became known as "auxiliary personnel," a term descriptive of the tasks that physicians delegated to them and that they performed. The beginning of this stage coincides with the first course for nurses in 1902 in a wing of the Hospital *San Borja* in Santiago (Flores, 1965a, 1965b). This early 3-year education course for nurses focused on the curative aspects of disease. The program of this nursing "course" was strongly influenced by physicians who "contemplated the value of having someone help them carry out biomedical treatments" and it led to the early medicalization of nursing (Sanhueza, 1996).

The appearance of the role of "medical helper" allowed nursing to distance itself from its religious roots and to begin the makings of a profession. This stage did not manifest itself until 1906 when the State School of Nursing (*Escuela de Enfermeras del Estado*), the first government-sponsored nursing school, was created. The development of the state school was based on a request by the *Facultad de Medicina y Farmacia* (Departments of Medicine and Pharmacy) at the University of Chile Hospital San Vicente in Santiago (*Escuela de Enfermeria, Universidad de Chile*, 1942). The school was directed by physicians who were aided by Catholic nuns who supervised nursing practice. Teaching took place at Hospital San Vicente de Paul. The State School Nursing is considered to be the first School of Nursing in South America.

Technical Nursing Period

It was not until 20 years later in 1926, when the School of Public Health Nurses (*Escuela de Enfermeras Sanitarias*) was created, that the curative vision of these professionals broadened to integrate a preventive and community health role into their functions. The North American Public Health Model spurred an orientation toward family and community health care. Because this trend was only beginning in Latin America and Chile was on the forefront of the movement, Chile is considered a pioneer of this approach in Latin America (*Escuela de Enfermeria, Universidad de Chile*, 1942). This new community approach to care in Chile had many implications for the daily activities of nurses and it made it necessary to prepare professionals to function in this role. This was achieved through an improvement plan based on scholarship awards to nurses by organizations such as the World Health Organization, the Rockefeller Foundation, and the Kellogg Foundation, among others.

This period marking the technical stage in Chilean nursing history was characterized as a time when nurses began to differentiate their professional roles as they concentrated their efforts on acquiring specific nursing skills. Thus, some focused on teaching as their area of nursing expertise while others dedicated themselves to acquiring further technological skills to work in the clinical setting and others to improve their public health skills.

During the 1950s and 1960s, because of Chilean nurses' experience in teaching, hospital services and particularly in public health, a group of them were asked to serve as consultants to other Latin American countries. Also, Chile was selected as the country for the preparation and improvement of a group of Latin American nurses.

An increased demand for nursing services occurred between 1950 and 1960. It was exacerbated by the simultaneous migration of Chilean nurses to other countries and by a reduction in nursing positions with in the National Health Service. The paradox is that at a time when professional nursing positions were cut, the number of "nurse auxiliary" positions was maintained at a constant level. As a result of these changes, personnel needs in hospital and public health services were reorganized according to a nursing perspective. The structures became more organized and new norms were established to provide better nursing care. Moreover, in 1953, by Law 11,161, the Chilean Nurses Association was created as a "response to the continuous growth and self-improvement challenges of the profession." This new organization became a key for the expression of the sentiment of nursing professionals toward the forthcoming changes. That same year, during the Second National Congress, the "Project for the Structure of Nursing within the National Health Service" was released and the Chilean Nursing Association was incorporated to the International Nursing Council.

Professional Nursing Period

As a result of research findings from the "Study of Chilean Human Resources and Nursing Needs" conducted by Doris Krebs in 1960-1961, it became evident that it was urgent to increase the number of nurses (*Colegio de Enfermeras de Chile*, 1965a). As a response, representatives from Chile, the World Health Organization and UNICEF 3200 signed a three-party treaty called the "Program to Assist the Development of Nursing in Chile." This program proposed the creation of nursing schools at various places throughout the country (*Colegio de Enfermeras de Chile*, 1965b). Administratively, nursing schools reported to the National Health Service and academically, they reported to the University of Chile. During the university reform of 1968, Chilean nursing experienced a period of uncertainty. The new direction of the university system which aimed to have a better fit in the economic, social, and cultural development of the country, forced schools of nursing to improve their planning and administrative systems, and to articulate the concept of planning with the concept of autonomy.

This period is the onset of the professional stage in Chilean history and is characterized by the national movement to develop a professional body emphasizing nurses' commitment to establish themselves as a profession in the country.

During this time nurses sought to empower themselves through their professional association.

Health Care Programs of that time during the 1960s exhibited the typical characteristics of a developing country, where the socio-economic and environmental conditions determine the level of health. These programs focused on addressing those health problems that at the time were common in the country such as infections, diseases, malnourishment, infant and maternal mortality, among others. The trend of health care policies was to provide integral care to the population without neglecting the priorities of preventive care, particularly those relating to maternal child health. Nursing became an important participant in this trend.

The 1970s were marked by changes and confrontations that translated into social, political, and economic contrasts and contradictions in the health field. In a study on Chilean human health care resources, Meneses et al. (1995) found that in 1970 only 2,428 nurses were actively employed. Three-quarters of these nurses worked in clinics, hospitals, and community settings. The majority of these nurses carried out administrative activities. Over one-half of the nurses (52%) were located in Santiago or in towns with more than 20,000 inhabitants. Nine out of ten nurses worked in the public sector. In this study Meneses et al. identified some problems concerning the practice of the profession at the time: (a) a lack of opportunities for career development in nursing, (b) a lack of clarity regarding the nursing role in the health care team, and (c) a lack of knowledge among health administrators of the close relationships between human resources and health care resources to ensure quality of nursing services. Examples of these trends included: difficulties obtaining hourly extension and transportation for ambulatory care; funding approval for nurses' overtime; lack of motivation for public health work, especially in rural areas; a lack of opportunities for career development inside and outside health care institutions; and scarce economic incentives, in general.

These issues were so problematic that in the early 1970s, the Chilean Nurses Association proposed an Action Plan where they highlighted their main concerns for the nursing profession. This action plan included the following aspects:

1. With respect to professional practice and the laws of the profession (*Colegio de Enfermeras de Chile*, 1970, 1972), nurses advocated for the development of legal parameters to regulate professional practice through a proposed "Nursing Practice Act." They also demanded to be present every time there was an attempt to legislate about nursing in the Public Health Code. Nurses also demanded to actively participate with National Health Service authorities in the definition of policies regarding the administration of anesthesia by nurses.
2. Concerning education, in this Action Plan, nurses promoted and supported the creation of nursing specialties, joining forces with universities and the Chilean Nurses Association.
3. In regard to research, nurses proposed to promote nursing research with a view to generate evidence to improve nursing care. Nursing put forth this Action during Allende's government when a concern for social rights and egalitarian health services were a priority.

In 1972 during the Allende government, the 3rd Meeting of Health Ministers in the Americas (*III Reunión Especial de Ministros de Salud*) was held in Chile. The focus of the meeting was on creating a mechanism for providing universal health care services to all. The estimate at the time was that 40% of the population had no access to health care services and that 68% of all hospital expenditures involved patients with preventable illnesses or illnesses that could be treated in outpatient settings. In those years, nurses carried out most of their duties inside hospitals, were driven by the biomedical model and focused on the curative aspects of care. However, the new approaches that were generated during meetings such as the one indicated above made nurses question their practice of the profession and in turn propose new curricular approaches.

A critique of nursing from within the profession surfaced at about the same point in time. It included a critique of professional practice as well as the educational system used to prepare nurses. The critique focused on the chronic shortage of professional nurses and the fact that almost all nurses functioned in hospital settings with few of them in community settings. The critique focused on the necessity to create innovations in nursing practice as well as in the academic environment to better prepare nurses in basic community health theory. The innovations expanded the focus of nursing beyond administrative work (which constituted the major portion of nursing activities inside hospitals) and toward (community) health policy, program and organizational planning (*Colegio de Enfermeras de Chile*, 1977, 1978a). This was a movement by nurses for population-based care.

Aware of the growing importance of graduate studies, the *Pontificia Universidad Catolica de Chile* started a master's level degree program in community public health nursing with a focus on mental health and psychiatric nursing in 1972. Later on, specialization programs in cardiology, neurosurgery, neonatology, nephrology, and pediatrics were instituted. In papers published at the time, ways to introduce a new focus on the nurse's role became evident. The aim was to produce a professional better prepared in the strategies required for primary care and community participation. This was supported by the findings of a Committee of Nursing Experts, commissioned by the OPS branch of the World Health Organization in June 1974.

The Neoliberal Influence on Nursing (Pinochet Military Dictatorship)

Because of the persecution and killing of members of the ousted Socialist Allende regime, the 1973 Chilean *coup d'etat* by the military junta is known as one of the "bloodiest in the history of Latin America." The *coup d'etat* and the subsequent 17-year, right wing military dictatorship of General Augusto Pinochet ended in 1990 after an estimated 3,500 people died or "disappeared." The military *junta,* of which the United States played an active role in supporting, created a total "isolation" of the country not only from a political perspective due to the censorship expressed by democratic countries against it, but also from a cultural perspective since the *junta* occupied Chilean universities and closed down departments of journalism, history, and sociology. Chilean universities came under State control through *Rectores Delegados* and this situation continued until the end of the military government.

The Chilean military government tried to reduce inflationary anarchy through a liberalization of the economy and a reduction in the size of the State. The Pinochet administration intended to create the conditions for the development of a free market economy and the strengthening of private enterprise. They adopted a neoliberal economic model in 1974 while decentralizing and regionalizing the public administrative structure. Neoliberalism included an opening to foreign trade while the economy was subjected to the strategies of the so-called "Chicago School," derived from the theories of Milton Friedman and Von Hayek.

By the mid-1970s the process of "economic opening" characterized by a reduction in taxation and a lifting of all barriers to foreign trade was initiated. This unilateral process produced a slow stabilization of the economy. During this period international organizations especially the Kellogg Foundation, sponsored nursing professionals in graduate programs leading to a master's degree. Those studies which took place mainly in the United States focused on the sciences and education. They became the cornerstone for the formation of nursing graduate nursing programs in Chile.

But, in 1976, other problems associated with the poor participation of nursing in the planning, budgeting, and restructuring of nursing services provoked the Chilean Nurses Association (Colegio de Enfermeras) to issue a "Warning Call of Protest" *(Clarinada de Advertencia)* entitled the "scream of rage" (*grito di furia*) in *Enfermeria*, its official publication. This "Warning Call of Protest" complained about the lack of incentives for nurses, the difficulty in obtaining economic and wage improvements, the unrecognized expansion of the nurse's role, and the evolution of the nursing profession and other related problems. Also, the "Warning Call of Protest" argued that nurses as an important community health care resource were unrecognized and that the problems stated above worked against the image and status of the profession. Ultimately, this provoked frustration in nursing and caused large numbers of Chilean nurses to leave the profession.

Because the Chilean Nurses Association (*Colegio de Enfermeras de Chile*) functioned as the leading organization representing nursing labor, it was extremely important that they recognized, in a public fashion, deficits in the status, and recognition of Chilean nursing. The Chilean Nurses Association had representatives in national and international organizations including the Geneva-based International Council of Nurses; the Pan-American Federation of Nurses; the Confederation of Professional University Colleges of Chile and the Central Committee of the Chilean Red Cross. As a result, the outcry had great public resonance (*Colegio de Enfermeras de Chile*, 1976, 1978a, 1978b, 1978c).

The health status of the Chilean population showed that the country was under an "epidemiological transition" (Miranda & Vergara, 1993). The transition situation was the result of health problems characteristic of both a developed country, requiring a high level of technical complexity for their solution and those of a developing country requiring comprehensive coverage, but at a low level of technical sophistication. The solution had to be tackled through the creation of health policies that were constrained by scarce resources and slow economic growth. These constraints required clear criteria for setting priorities. According to government statistics from that period of time, Chile's mortality rates were "less than average for Latin America and each day more similar to the values encountered in Europe and the USA." However, the military government controlled, restricted, and centralized all statistical and journalistic information. Censorship existed with no freedom of expression. National resources were scarce during the years of the military dictatorship and a political economic adjustment produced large problems for those who were the least protected: the poor.

In the area of health care, contributions made by the Inter-American Development Bank (IDB) and the Pan-American Health Organization (*Organizacion Panamericana para la Salud*–OPS) were the most noticeable. A number of efforts were made by international banks to lend money to Chile to improve the health status of the population. However, the initiatives differed dramatically from the socialist-inspired initiatives. In 1976 the Inter-American Development Bank awarded a loan to provide drinking water and to improve the health of the poorest rural sectors of the country. These factors, by being so closely linked with the quality of life and health of the population, would reduce the mortality due to transmissible diseases by means of the construction of integrated systems for the capture, transport, storage, purification, and distribution of drinking water to individual households (Ministry of Health, Chile, 1977).

In 1978 the Inter-American Development Bank again supported Chile by awarding two loans to improve and expand health care services in the country's rural areas. This meant the initiation of a program of action that combined aspects of preventive and curative medicine with the construction and equipping of seven health centers capable of offering medical and hospital service. This also allowed the establishment of health posts providing elementary public health services to low income communities in five regions of the country (between *Coquimbo* in the north and *Puerto Mont* in the south) where 69% of the country's rural population lived. These rural areas had the highest infant mortality rate in the country and also had the least access to health care services. Moreover, the Pan-American Health Organization collaborated on 18 other health-related projects involving numbers of technical experts.

Technical cooperation also included scholarships for nurses and other health care professionals to study abroad, for courses, seminars, subsidies, books, and student supplies (*Colegio de Enfermeras de Chile*, 1978b, 1978e). Chilean nurses and the country, in general, embraced the goal of the 1978 Alma Ata Conference to achieve "Health for All by the Year 2000." Chileans attempted to devise a plan to provide primary health care services to the entire population and to improve the conditions of life in the forthcoming decades. However, nurses noted the limitations of the profession in transforming the stated strategies into practice: "one of the problems nursing confronts is the multiplicity of activities nurses are required to perform encompassing health prevention, illness treatment and rehabilitation amidst the climate of limited human resources. The latter is worsened by inadequate geographical distribution of nurses and the marked lack of proportion between helper to nurse and physician to nurse."

The Chilean National Health Service (*Sistema Nacional de Servicios de Salud–SNSS*) was created in 1979 with the passing of decree Law 2,763 that allowed the process of administrative decentralization and reorganization of the Ministry of Health. Both these changes were regarded as positive. However, there was no benefit for nursing, as the Chilean Nurses Association (*Colegio de Enfermeras*) points out that same year in an editorial for their magazine *Enfermeria* where it was noted that "the current situation of the profession, which has seen a decrease in participation in decision making and in the setting of direction for the discipline, is of concern not only to nurses themselves since it impacts the handling of nursing services, but also to the general population because it ultimately affects the quality of health care."

During the military dictatorship in the 1980s a new constitution replaced the one created in 1925. Also during the period of dictatorship, in 1981, Chile instituted major reforms on the system of higher education. The new law regarding university education (LOCE/*Ley Organica Constitucional de Enseñanza Superior*) included only 12 professions and excluded some professions, such as nursing. The reform on the system of higher education required professional nursing education to take place outside of the university setting, in so-called "professional institutes."

Chilean nurse educators considered the reform of higher education a great setback for nursing in Chile. The *Colegio* (Chilean Nurses Association) claimed that with this "the nursing professional became marginalized from the academic setting." The reformed structure for nursing education in Chile was not accepted then and has been rejected ever since by Chilean nurses to no avail (*Colegio de Enfermeras de Chile,* 1980).

Regardless of the state imposed reform of higher education, both nurses and nursing educators were aware of the need for improvement, diversification, and deepening of knowledge offered by specialization programs in nursing. In 1981 the University of *Concepción*, School of Nursing started a new educational program. This was a graduate level program with an international dimension leading to the master's degree in nursing with concentrations in medical-surgical nursing and community health nursing. A similar program was begun at the *Universidad Catolica* (Catholic University) 2 years earlier. With the higher education reform in 1981, universities became responsible for their own costs and university education was no longer free to students. Students were required to pay registration and tuition fees that were much higher than the modest university fees prior to 1981.

While Chile was instituting a new democratic government in 1990, it was still suffering from the consequences of an economic depression that affected the country one decade earlier. Between 1993 and 1995, the Chilean Society for Nursing Education developed a proposal to strengthen the profession. To begin this process, they established a 10-semester university-based "*Licenciatura*" program in nursing and began to standardize professional nursing education.

In the 1990s Chilean nursing scholars began submitting proposals to national and international organizations to fund research projects and scholarships for degree candidates to attend scientifically sound graduate programs outside of Chile.

Examples of success in this area are the Chilean nursing professionals who completed master's degrees, the Chilean nurse scholars who received national scholarships for doctoral studies, and the funding provided by the Kellogg Foundation and other organizations to support nursing research on health promotion, well-being, and development, thus enhancing the key role nursing professional play around the world.

Challenges for Chile's Health Care System

During the late 20th century, health conditions in Chile improved significantly, as a result of both changes in living conditions and the implementation of public health policies that had a great impact on the population. Chileans experienced a demographic transition characterized by a significant decrease in mortality rates for all age groups. Today, Chileans can expect to live on average 17 years longer than they did in 1965. A decrease in fertility rates also accompanied this demographic. While Chile's epidemiological profile for communicable diseases has greatly improved, the incidence of chronic illnesses such as cancer, cardiovascular diseases, accidents, new illnesses, and some diseases thought to be under control is greater. To confront the increase in chronic illnesses and to enhance the degree of success with communicable diseases achieved to date requires the participation of many sectors. Education, housing, public works, transportation, revenue collection, and social work can partner with nursing and other health professions. The health care system Chile, as in other Latin American countries, requires more reform to reach the World Health Organization's goal of Health Care for All. Nurses in Chile took on an important role in the health care reform that was led by an internal commission in the Chilean government's Ministry of Health.

The publication "Chilean Public Health Goals for 2000-2010" (published by the Health Ministry) outlines the country's four major public health challenges for the 21st century:

1. the progressive aging of the population with its increasing load of degenerative pathologies requiring expensive medical care;
2. health care inequalities that translates into a public health gap among groups from different socioeconomic levels in the population;
3. the need to appropriately respond to the legitimate expectations of the population in regard to the health care system, often pointed out as unsatisfactory by Chilean society; and
4. the solution of pending problems while maintaining the public health achievements obtained to date.

The strategy for addressing these four challenges are the same as the central objectives of the health care system, namely:

1. to improve the health of the population;
2. to lengthen life expectancy as well as the years of life free from illness; and

3. to reduce the inequalities in health care by improving health care to those groups in society who are most disadvantaged.

With the health of the population as a primary goal, professional nurses in Chile believe they need to provide holistic primary care in efficient multi-disciplinary teams. According to the CASEN survey (Feedback Consultores, 2000), the level of access to health care in Chile is high but inequalities associated with different socioeconomic levels exist. Middle class groups are most negatively affected by these health care system inequalities because they frequently have a higher cost burden for health care regardless of the system to which they are assigned.

Access to health care services is determined by income levels and by the probability that people may become ill. In this context, FONASA provides services to groups who represent the lowest economic level and the highest medical risk, while ISAPRE attracts people with high incomes and low medical risk. This tiered segmentation of the population, produced by the public-private mix in Chile has a negative impact on health care equity. Chile is challenged to create a system of solidarian financing that benefits everyone. FONASA incorporates financial mechanisms of income redistribution from those with higher income to those with smaller income and it also operates a health insurance system that goes from the healthy to the sick.

The quality of health care is the property of health care system products and services measured by the degree of satisfaction expressed by users when they compare what they get against their expectations. Research studies were carried out to investigate the perceptions and expectations of Chilean people regarding the health care system. Within the framework of the proposed reform, Feedback Consultores (2000) investigated the perceptions, expectations and attitudes of Chileans concerning the health care system. Feedback Consultores found that Chileans want (a) effective, complete, and timely health care systems; and (b) well-informed, dedicated, deferential, polite, and professional health care personnel. Also, Chileans value the right to be informed, the right to receive dignified treatment in a timely fashion. Other studies show that Chileans place a high value on the conditions of health care facilities and the knowledge and experience of nurses and physicians. They consider these dimensions necessary to a quality health care system. The speed at which care is provided is another, although less crucial component of the NHS.

The improvement of the quality of health care is a long-term objective of the Chilean health care system. The Health Ministry acknowledges that while it has established and carried out many activities aimed at evaluation and quality improvement, they are insufficient because (a) they are not sufficiently systematic and routine, (b) they fail to cover all health care processes, (c) they are not scientifically rigorous regarding the definition of health care standards, (d) they do not involve the structured supervision of processes, and (e) they do not sufficiently document client outcomes. The strategies the Health Ministry proposes to enhance quality improvement include:

1. To promote the permanent establishment of Quality Improvement Processes.
2. To strengthen and develop all programs related to quality.

3. To standardize requirements and processes for public health authorizations.
4. To establish accreditation systems.
5. To promote the use of evidence-based evaluation of public health technologies and medicine.

The system providing health care services in Chile is a mixed system. The National Health Fund (*Fondo Nacional de Salud*–FONASA) offers public health insurance and ISAPRES offers private health insurance. The provision of services is also mixed: the vast majority of top level establishments (Primary Health Care–*Atencion Primaria de Salud*–APS) depend on municipalities while hospitals are under the direction of Health Services. Between 1981 and 1987 health clinic oversight was transferred to municipalities. This was a process called "municipalization" of primary health care in which health care entities (units) continued to be a part of the National System of Health Care Services while municipalities took over the management and the provision of resources. The goal of "municipalization" was to provide more efficient care to local communities. This was true because the characteristics and needs of communities all over the country are different. Nevertheless, "municipalization" requires more effort due to the varying resources and economic status of different municipalities, as is amply demonstrated by the low number of nurses working in the community. All of the above offers an opportunity to show the impact nursing can have in community public health. More studies regarding the cost benefit and the cost effectiveness of nursing care in communities are still needed.

Today, the nursing community is satisfied because the structure of the profession of nursing was recognized in the public health authority law within the health care reform legislation (*ley central de la reforma de la salud*), in the exact terms that nursing requested. This achievement is the result of almost 3 decades of work and allowed for the insertion of nursing into the 1997 Public Health Code, thus making nursing an autonomous profession. This shows the importance of structuring nursing health care within the health care system of the country and it creates the much awaited opportunity for professional nurses to demonstrate more autonomy.

Nursing in the Context of Globalization in Chile

To understand the influence political economy has on the nursing workforce it is important to recognize that the socio-economic policies of a government are expressed in practice by the way they regulate the actions of citizens' daily lives. Therefore, the political approach of a government will determine the evolution and development of areas such as education, health and employment. Over the last 40 years Chile has experienced governments with very different sociopolitical orientations and it has also been immersed in the sociopolitical change imposed by globalization. Thus, the complex of problems facing the nursing workforce can be deduced from the reality of the country as well as that which Latin America as a whole has experienced.

Following World War II and the configuration of Eastern and Western blocks, the world became subjected to the capriciousness of the Cold War or the global reordering in favor of the interests of hegemonic powers, as exemplified by the fate of Yugoslavia or Czechoslovakia. On the American continent, the same struggle resulted in a number of socialist revolutions supported by the former Soviet Union (Nicaragua, Guatemala, and Chile). These revolutions were violently crushed by dictatorships supported by the United States. The dictatorships were led by high ranking military officers interested in gaining local power. The military dictators received illicit money and goods in exchange for maintaining the U.S. political economic model. Despite the presence of the dictators, the Soviet block aligned with Cuba while the rest of Latin America remained in the hands of North America. This happened by means of the effectiveness of negotiations of the "Plan for the Development of the Americas" originated by the Kennedy administration.

The fall of the socialist block created an overwhelming ripple effect for progressive governments in Latin America. At the time social concerns and health and welfare issues became secondary to the major economic and development issues. Probably the only advantage of the period following the Cold War in Latin America was the fact that the agreements and economic potential of the continent lessened the possibility of a military take-over or war by hegemonic powers such as the United States as had been the pattern throughout the Cold War and earlier as recognized by recently declassified CIA documents.

It became clear that international macroeconomic groups (banks and multinational corporations) reap more benefits from countries with democratic regimes and social stability than from countries functioning without a ruling government and those engaging in war and insurgence. These ideas were even acknowledged in the United Nations Development Program development objectives for the millennium (*Programa de las Naciones Unidas para el Desarrollo*–UNPD). As it was mentioned earlier in the chapter, Chile experienced three major governmental changes representing three difference political economic perspectives. Each time this happened, nursing had to renegotiate its participation in the government. This is due not only to the rapidly changing political economy in Chile, but also because of nursing's relative powerlessness within Chile's traditional paternalistic society and within an irrationally bio-medicalized health care system.

Prior to the 1973 coup, solidarian finance and the public health elements of health care in Chile solidly placed the State in the position of guardian of health, education and employment services. During that period, labor rights and stability were slowly consolidated in the form of health benefits, mainly within state institutions. The development difficulties nursing encountered during that period were influenced by the lack of inclusion of nursing in the public health code and the poor image nurses had as "handmaidens to the physician." Even prior to 1973 when the role of the community health nurse evolved and was strengthened by public health policies including a role for nurses, the image of nursing as dependent on the medical profession and lacking autonomy was difficult to change.

During the period of military dictatorship (1974 through the late 1980s) both the health sector and nurses work in Chile underwent major transformations. A neoliberal model of reform was imposed on the country under which health care and education were no longer considered "rights" for which the State was responsible.

Instead, both health care and education became "goods" or commodities for sale and available only if one had the means to purchase them. The Chilean State began to provide services on a limited basis (e.g., health and education for the poor).

The neoliberal reform dramatically reduced nursing positions in the public sector. Between 1965 and 1985 the number of nurses hired by the public sector grew from 1095 to 2800 nursing positions, but by the year 1988 the number of positions for nurses dropped to 2186. This decline in public sector nurses was caused by: (a) stagnation of social investment in health, and (b) migration of nurses to the private sector where they could obtain higher wages. It is important to note that the Chilean government instituted a number of emergency economic measures during this time, such as the "Economic Plan of Expansion" (instituted in 1979), which attempted to cover the economic deficits in the collapsed health care system. As part of the Plan of Expansion, nurses were hired for 36 hours weekly with wages amounting to only one-fourth that of the wages earned by other nurses and the new hires had no right to vacations, maternity leave, or other labor protection. Another fact that led to the loss of status for nursing at the time was the passing of the Higher Education Reform law, (*Ley Organica Contitucional de Enseñanza*) which excluded nursing from those professions requiring a university degree.

After the fall of the military dictatorship, political economic struggles among the various Chilean political parties focused a lot of attention on the amount of control the State had in the country's neoliberal reform within a globalized economy. While the post-dictatorship democratic government significantly increased its investment in health care services, positive outcomes for health indicators have not yet appeared and hence do not reflect the new government's concerted economic investment in health care. As we know, social and health status changes take time and results are not immediate.

Nursing care has become more complex and technologically more advanced. But, at the same time, compensation for nurses is still lower than for other male-dominated professions requiring the same number of years of study. Chilean women still receive wages that are 30% lower than those earned by men performing similar activities (CIE, 2004). Moreover, today one can anticipate an increase in competition in the nursing workforce (even for low paying nursing positions) as private universities begin to create degree programs in nursing and potentially glut the market. The Chilean Association for Nursing Education (*Associacion Chilena de Educacion en Enfermeria*–ACHIEEN) and the Chilean Nurses Association (*Colegio de Enfermeras de Chile*) follow these situations closely and lobby the government to maintain the high quality and standards that are characteristic of Chilean nursing.

Based on the realities of the nursing labor market, in 1976 the Chilean government initiated a two-way exchange program for new nurses from neighboring countries to Chile and for Chilean nurses seeking better career and living conditions to travel to developed countries. This migration of nurses will most likely affect the development of nursing in Latin America and must be noted here.

Until 1977 medical practice and the practice of some health professions was regulated by language in Chile's public health code, especially in article 112.

However, the code did not include language specifically for nurses in the same way that it did for physicians, psychologists, dentists, pharmaceutical-chemists, midwives, and others. Because of the absence of specific nursing language in the public health code, in hospital settings, nursing functions continued to be subordinated to that of physicians. In community settings within the public health code, nurses exercised more autonomy. Ultimately, through dedicated and continuous struggle, the Chilean Nursing Association (*Colegio de Enfermeras de Chile*) successfully lobbied to include language for nurses in the Chilean public health code thus determining the setting and the legal limits for professional nursing practice. The modification of the public health code was introduced in 1997 (article 113, item 4) and it established the legal framework for the practice of professional nursing. In this manner one can clearly appreciate the effects of different political and economic strategies on the nursing workforce as well as the projections that the profession can have in the immediate future.

Gender and Nursing

The practice of nursing is intimately connected to the history of women. The care of others is one of the basic components of women's make-up. Because nursing is socially recognized primarily as women's work, it suffers from the disadvantages associated with other female-dominated professions and occupations. Nursing as a female-dominated form of social labor is socially devalued as "feminine" labor with low pay and status. Thus, the mostly female nurses are forced to take on second jobs, "moonlighting" to make ends meet. They are subordinated to primarily male supervisors who reproduce autocratic power structures. Hierarchical work relations differ significantly from the collaborative team work that is talked about, but is rarely part of the real daily work life for nurses.

Over the decades Chilean nursing has had to face many crises: identity; professional autonomy; and social recognition among others. But, only part of the reason for these crises can be explained by the nature of the profession and its historical context. Nursing carries the burden of the problems associated with it being a "feminized" profession; from its early origin nursing has been invisible and its work has been devalued.

During the 1980s the new health care model associated with the military dictatorship and the transformation of the Chilean State involved a rapid movement toward a neoliberal political economic model. This had a great impact on nursing in Chile. In fact, a number of important reforms were put in place that directly affected both nursing and the health care sector. Specifically, a reduction in the allocation of funds to the national publicly-funded health and social security occurred when those systems were privatized. Also, the National Health Service, as it was known, was dismantled and replaced by an alternative (private) system consisting of 27 Health Care Services. The personnel and operating budget remained flat for 10 years following the creation of the 27 Health Care Services. Moreover, the process of "municipalization of primary care" was initiated and maintained for 10 years.

All of these factors connected to neoliberal reform had a major role in the disintegration and the displacement of a well-established Chilean public health system which had the positive characteristics of being (a) national, (b) unified, and (c) solidarian. The elimination of Chile's public National Health System also displaced and wreaked havoc in nursing services as it eliminated the structures for nursing services all over the country and left nursing services under the direction of medical services.

During the period of the neoliberal reform, nursing services lost whatever autonomy it had gained during the Allende socialist period. The other most important long-term consequence for nursing provoked by the change in health care structures is the significant shortage of nurses nationally with a particularly serious shortage in public sector nursing services. Both the severe deficit of nurses and the loss of structure for nursing services in practice settings are the result of the privatized neoliberal health care model put in place by the military dictatorship and still in place after several decades (Avendaño & Grau, 1997).

While nursing is a profession that improves the quality of life of others, it is not able to resolve problems affecting its own nursing workforce. Poor working conditions, workplace safety issues, job insecurity, on-the-job violence, exposure to illness and unhealthy working conditions are common (Borges, 1998; Letelier & Valenzuela, 2002). Despite the transformative, complex and multifaceted nature of the nurse's work acknowledged by society, and regardless of the progress achieved to date, Chilean nurses are not yet compensated or respected at a level that corresponds to the importance and the responsibility of the activities they perform while maintaining the health and well-being of the population. Nurse's work in hospitals is continuous, 365 days per year, 24 hours a day, including weekends and holidays. In hierarchical hospital institutions, men and women share space but they perform different activities based on socially-constructed attributes. It is primarily women who carry out nursing tasks related to care, cleaning, cooking, secretarial, and receptionist work. Men exercise power with greater levels of autonomy and decision-making power. Nursing activities are classified as being of "social usefulness." Regardless of its necessity, "socially useful" work has little social recognition and is devalued and invisible to other professionals in the health field and also to the clients seeking attention (Sánchez, Valenzuela, & Solares, 2002).

Nursing work is carried out uninterrupted, in alternating shifts with overtime and altering the biological rhythm of workers, thus exposing them to a variety of specific risks related to the organization and the environment of the workplace (Gestal, 1993). Nurses work most of the time on their feet with movements consisting of flexing and extending the vertebral column, intimately associated with the delivery of care, the movement and transport of patients, and thus create great physical demands that causes fatigue and weariness (Valenzuela et al., 2003). Travel from one room to another is routine and it is expected throughout the entire rotation or shift of work. Nursing activities include great responsibility for preventing death and the deterioration of conditions. Nurses' work requires a high level of attention and knowledge acquisition. Work relations are characterized by power and mediating relationships between physicians and patients (Avendaño et al., 1995).

Long-term night work can lead to family and interpersonal conflicts. The work hours also cause distancing from friends affecting social coexistence. Although nurses are expected to work at night, they are not exempt from working double duty: they take the children to school, go shopping, cook, clean, and prepare food for the following day. The overload of this double duty of home and work exacerbates problems and creates anxiety due to the difficulty in finding equilibrium among family, society, and workplace demands (Trucco, Valenzuela, & Trucco, 1999). Today, it is acknowledged that economies place little value in the service professions. Rather, society places value on those that produce a product. Nursing's products, such as restored health and well-being, are difficult to measure objectively. As a result of these dimensions, the responsibilities nurses assume easily escapes value and respect.

Nursing Higher Education in Chile

Chile has the distinction among countries of Latin America of an uninterrupted history of nursing education in institutions of higher education over the last 100 years. From the beginning, it has been distinctive in producing professionals who are able to call upon a broad body of knowledge, a range of technical and management abilities that have been used effectively in providing care at all levels, thus making an important contribution to the improvement of health. In spite of the contribution to health care made by nurses, there is now a shortage of nurses needed to maintain the availability of quality care.

The urgent need to create a place to educate nurses was recognized at the end of the 19th century in Santiago. The goal was then to produce skilled personnel for the care of the sick, either in hospitals or at home, and with a focus on curative aspects. Thus, based on observations made by a physician, Dr. Eduardo Moore, during a trip to Europe at the end of the 19th century, the Hospital San Borja, a tuition free nursing program, consisted of six semesters of study, was created in 1902. The first director was Dr. Moore, the greatest supporter of this initiative. To be admitted as a student, the person needed to meet the following requirements: "good home breeding, to have completed elementary education, unquestionable morality, good health, and being between 18 and 37 years old. Nursing courses were coordinated by Benigna Silva, one of the students of the first class, chosen by her own classmates. She also was responsible for offering the deontology course. The excellent results of this initiative showed that patients felt safer and showed quicker improvements having this young, distinguished, discrete, assertive, and healthy girl taking such good care of them. All this led to start the first non-hospital based school of nursing, by the Supreme Government of Chile in 1906. This was the first school of this kind, not only in Chile but in all South America. The school was part of the administrative structure of the School of Medicine and Pharmacy at the University of Chile.

The founders of the School of Nursing showed interest in being an integral part of the university as a means to have the necessary academic support for the education of professional nurses capable of taking full responsibility for the care of the sick (Flores, 1965a, 1965b). This provides clear evidence of the scientific character that the founders wanted to give to the profession so as to produce graduates with the ability and interest in continued learning and commitment to the perpetuation of the profession. The Council for Public Education in 1921 ratified a decree that the formation of nurses is the responsibility of the University. In 1924, another decree established the High Council for Nursing Service which was charged with over-seeing the education of nurses and placing them in position in accordance with their academic preparation.

Only 3 years later, in 1927, it became recognized that it was necessary also to have personnel qualified to guide public health aspects in the community with an emphasis on prevention and health promotion. The above led Dr. Cora Mayer, with the advice of a North American nurse Sara Adams, to create in Santiago the School for Public Health Nurses, as a part of the General Directorate of Public Health. In 1929 hospital and public health schools united to form the first program of the School of Nursing at the University of Chile. The plan of study required 4 years and a comprehensive final examination (*Colegio de Enfermeras de Chile,* 1965c, 1965d).

Stimulated by such development in nursing education, Don Carlos Van Buren provided financial support for the creation of a school of nursing in Valparaiso. This program started in 1933 with 16 students pursuing a 3-year program of study focused on hospital nursing and on preventive care at home. There was high attrition in this first class, only three graduated. A National Admission Test to the university became a requirement for admission to the school of nursing. This new admission requirement effectively reduced attrition. However, one of the three graduates of the first class in Valparaíso was Gladys Peake who eventually occupied important academic and management positions in professional organizations, served as the National Director of Nursing in Chile, culminating in a position within the International Council of Nurses in Geneva.

In 1941, following a visit to Chile by a representative of the Rockefeller Foundation of the United States and subsequent collaboration with Elizabeth Brackett, an American nurse, funding became available to create Public Health Units in Chile. These units became laboratories for the teaching of nursing and were funda-mental to induce interdisciplinary teamwork. In this era, schools of nursing were directed by nurses. Their preparation for the academic mission was supported eco-nomically by the Rockefeller Foundation, the Kellogg Foundation, Pan-American Health Organization (PAHO), and the Organization of American States (OAS). Scholarships were granted in agreement with the Supreme Government of Chile through the Ministry of Health and various universities. The educational and clinical experiences acquired by these nurses, mainly in Canada and the United States, enriched the curricula with courses such as public health nursing, public health education, sociology, pedagogy, and social medicine.

It was within this context that the First National Congress of Nurses in Chile, meeting in 1948, initiated a critical analysis of the curriculum. Based upon this analysis, it was decided to incorporate knowledge about preventive and social aspects from the very first year of nursing education. This feature is still main-tained with great emphasis along with increased emphasis on health promotion today in Chile.

In 1947 Gladys Peake was asked to develop a project to open a school of nursing in the south of Chile. The proposal materialized in *Concepción* with a program of study lasting 3 years, and 3 months, leading to the award of the title of Hospital and Public Health Nurse. The program was sponsored by the University of Chile, with initial economic and administrative support from the Director of Social or Public Welfare and later from the National Health Service. In 1953, the University of *Concepción* took academic responsibility for the courses and in 1970 it took complete responsibility for the nursing title in *Concepción*.

However, in 1950 the religious Congregation, called the *Esclavas del Corazon Misericordioso de Jesus y Maria, of the Instituto Cristo Rey* of the Catholic University of Chile, created the school *"Isidora Lyon Cousiño"* with the professional counsel of two nurses from the School of Social Welfare and under the direction of one of the religious members of the Congregation, Sister Paula Puelma. In the present it is the school of nursing at the Catholic University of Chile. Toward the 1970s, this School introduced curriculum changes that led to the option of obtaining the double title of nurse and midwife simultaneously (*Colegio Enfermeras de Chile*, 1965c, 1965d).

Following the First National Nursing Congress in 1948 in *Concepción* which included the presentation of 39 papers, the first four university schools of nursing initiated a struggle to begin their training in nursing research (Krebs, 1965a). As a result, the teaching of statistics and epidemiology was incorporated into the curriculum and the performance of a thesis or research project became a requirement in order to obtain the professional title as nurse.

From the recognition of the importance of professional development consistent with the health needs of the society, increasing interest developed in the creation of a professional nursing service organization concerned with nursing practice. The realization of national meetings in the various areas of professional practice, preparation for practice, professional ethics, and the administration of nursing and public health services, also increased (Krebs, 1965a). This led to the formation of the Chilean Nursing Association (*Colegio de Enfermeras de Chile*), a national entity established by law.

In subsequent scholarly meetings organized by the Chilean Nursing Association (*Colegio de Enfermeras*), the majority of the presentations were made by nurses from academic institutions and this motivated the realization in 1964 of the first Seminar of Nursing Education during which the then recently created Chilean Society for Nursing Education (*Sociedad Chilena de Educación de Enfermería*) was introduced. This is now called the Chilean Association for Nursing Education (*Asociación Chilena de Educación en Enfermería*–ACHIEEN). Subsequent seminars were responsible for the development of new curricular directions, they also provided recommendations for the education of academic personnel based on research results in that area and for development of guidelines for continuing education.

After earning the bachelors of science degree in 1959, Doris Krebs founded the Chilean Center for Nursing Research with the support of the Chilean government, WHO, and UNICEF 3200. The Center supported the development of nursing in

Chile. The Center focused on the determination of methods of nursing care and on the organization of Chilean nursing services. As a result of this effort, one of the most influential nursing research projects in the country emerged: "Nursing Resources and Needs in Chile" (Krebs, 1961, 1962). This work provided the foundation for the need to open new nursing programs at the universities in the north of Chile at *Antofagasta*, at *Santiago* in the north, south, and east sectors of the city, and in the south of Chile at *Temuco* (Flores, 1966).

The momentum for creating new schools of nursing continued and in 1962, as a result of a Bilateral Treaty between the National Health Service and the *Universidad Austral de Chile*, the *Valdivia* School of Nursing opened in 1963. A Counsel of Nursing Education expert, Mary X. Rogan, helped to create the curriculum oriented in maternal child health there, thus augmenting the generalist nursing program. Focus on maternal child health the school of nursing of the *Universidad Austral de Chile* at *Valdivia*, sought to improve maternal and infant mortality rates that were particularly high in the local region.

As leadership in nursing education expanded beyond the largest cities, it was possible to hold important national nursing meetings for the first time in the southern part of the country. In 1965 the Fourth National Nursing Congress was held in *Valdivia*. The goal of the congress was to define the functions of nursing in Chile. The lack of clarity in nursing functions had "negative consequences on the profession that amounted to: frustration, immigration, criticism, feelings of being misunderstood, low pay, and low acceptance due to the setting where nursing is carried out" (Krebs, 1965b). This assessment was reinforced by research studies presented the same year at the VIII Nursing Education Seminar held in *Concepción* which sought to define the boundaries of the nursing actions by analyzing the specific functions nurses performed. The nursing curriculum slowly began to separate from the hegemonic biomedical model and to give greater emphasis to health care based on the needs of persons as part of families and communities and to consider the person's biological, psychological, and social dimensions. The development of specific courses was the responsibility of nurse educators and only the basic scientific subjects were taught by other professionals. Clinical content constituted 70% of the curriculum; these courses were offered in large hospitals and in neighborhood clinics offering preventive population-based health care.

Nursing programs at *Chillan* and at *Magallanes* in the south of Chile were created in the early 1970s during the socialist government of President Salvador Allende. By 1972, 12 university-based nursing programs were open and producing about 290 new nurses each year. Yet, even with the new programs, the number of graduates in nursing was still, without a doubt, insufficient to satisfy the health care demands of the population.

Unfortunately, when the military regime took control of the government in 1973, the deficit of nurses was not acknowledged and there was subsequent failure to support the development of academic units responsible for the education of nurses. On the contrary, the regime permitted the continuation of only one of the three nursing programs at the University of Chile in *Santiago*. The years after 1973 were characterized by a series of changes and hostilities that translated into marked divides in social, political, economic, and health care realities. During the years of military rule, the growth of nursing education came to a halt as there were only nine schools open producing a number of graduates that were insufficient to satisfy the nursing needs of the population. Administration of universities was usurped by the military and remained under the control of the State through military-appointed directors. However, the qualitative development of nursing schools during that time allowed Chile to maintain nursing professionals with leadership qualities that were recognized both inside the country and abroad (Sanhueza, 1996).

A group of nursing academics concerned about the formal education of professors in the area of research design and research methodology continued their studies within universities, at masters programs in nursing in Boston, Massachusetts in the United States, and at the Catholic University of Chile. At the time of the military take-over, the latter had just started the first master's program in community health nursing with a concentration in psychiatric mental health nursing. This program functioned from 1973 to 1979. Later on, a course on research methods was incorporated to the undergraduate curriculum. The first national research projects in Chile focused on the study of the professional role of the nurse and led to the first research journals organized by the schools together with the Chilean Nurses Association (*Pontificia Universidad Católica de Chile,* 1990).

In 1972 Ebensperger, Gonzales, Jerez, Krebs, and Royo, in their article "Schema for Nursing Research," analyzed the growing awareness of professional nurses in regard to the importance of nursing research. They proposed four topic areas for nursing research: nursing heath care, nursing services, nursing education, and nursing in the social context. It soon became apparent that most of the research projects were focused on nursing education and that 90% of the articles in the journal *Revista del Colegio de Enfermeras* were written by nurses in academic institutions.

During that time, the nursing process was incorporated into the nursing curriculum and its importance was discussed during the VIIth National Nurses Congress held in October 1972 in Arica. (Ebensperger et al., 1972). Educational advances were created through the incorporation of new teaching methods and by encouraging independent learning through the use of self-teaching modules. Nursing curricula put particular focus on primary health care for childhood vaccinations, children's growth and development programs, to the feeding of children from birth to 6 years of age, and the care of pregnant mothers.

In 1976 the Chilean Society of Nursing Education identified the need to create specialization courses in nursing and detailed how the new specializations needed professional legitimacy and recognition. In response, some nursing programs initiated specialization programs in nursing of patients with chronic renal diseases, nursing in psychiatry and mental health, nursing of children, critical care nursing, and geriatric nursing care of patients with cancer or cardiac disease. The nurses who completed the specialization programs were not recognized in any way or compensated for their new knowledge. Patients were not referred to the new nurse specialists.

As noted earlier in this chapter and as a consequence of the higher education reform in the late 1980s, only 12 disciplines were included as professions in the university system. Even though nursing was not included in the group of professional disciplines at the university level, nursing continued to be offered only as a university-based program in the country, through a curriculum that led to the degree of *Licenciado en Enfermeria*. This was possible thanks to both the long history of nursing education at the university level and to the strong nurses' resistance to lowering down the quality of nursing education.

In 1980 the first master's of science degree program in nursing was initiated at the *Universidad de Concepción* with concentrations in medical surgical nursing and in community health nursing. Students in the program were primarily nurse educators from various Chilean schools of nursing. The new master degree programs allowed nurse scholars to raise the level of nursing research, to improve the pedagogy in undergraduate programs and to enhance the quality of nursing practice in clinical sites. Today, this program continues to attract nursing professionals from within the country and from abroad. It is highly rated and fully accredited by the Chilean National Commission for the Accreditation of Graduate Programs (*Comisión Nacional de Acreditación del Posgrado*–CONAP).

During the 1990s great emphasis was placed on the dissemination of new nursing knowledge generated through research. Peer-reviewed publications and scientific conference presentations were the preferred vehicles for dissemination. Three new peer reviewed nursing journals were created to validate the advances in scientific knowledge production in Chile. Chilean nurse researchers who complete methodologically rigorous research studies now had additional venues for international dissemination of their work. The new periodicals are: *Revista de Enfermería*, published by the Chilean Nurses Association (*Colegio de Enfermeras*); *Horizonte de Enfermería*, published by the *Pontificia Universidad Católica de Chile*; and *Revista Ciencia y Enfermería*, published by the *Universidad de Concepción* as Scientific Electronic Library (ScIELO).

In 1990 Maria Figueroa Figueroa became the first Nurse Emeritus Professor at the *Universidad de Concepción*. This was considered a great nursing achievement, especially given the long standing lack of recognition of nursing worldwide and in Chile. She deserved the honor based on her distinguished career in teaching and research. She was instrumental in developing university-based programs of study in nursing, in advancing the general level of education for nurses and in developing nursing research.

Beginning in 1992, 2 years after the reinstatement of a non-military government, new nursing degree programs were created throughout the country. Simultaneously, enrollment increased in all of the pre-existing schools. This explosion of student capacity in nursing was motivated by the increasing demand for professional nurses. University-based colleges of nursing began awarding the degree of *Licenciado* in nursing as well as the professional certification of *Nurse* following a 5-year program of study. Today, nursing curricula are examined and rigorously evaluated by the Curriculum Commission of the Chilean Association of Nursing Education (ACHIEEN). Designated programs are then incorporated as active members of this Association. After the changes detailed above, it was necessary to design a preliminary document detailing the requirements for "Accreditation of

Schools of Nursing." The preliminary document was used as basis for the expanded accreditation document put out by the Chilean Association of Nursing Education's Technical Committee on Nursing.

As a result of the 1997 reform of the Public Health Code, which recognized nursing as a profession, the discipline of nursing was strengthened as an autonomous practice at the baccalaureate level. As an outcome of the reform, other aspects of nursing were delineated including: the social commitment of the profession, the ability to think critically, the potential for transformative leadership, and the commitment of nurses to establish an autonomous professional identity. By the onset of the 21st century, Chilean nursing academics and researchers had developed the capacity to establish international relationships in Latin America, North America, Canada, and Spain. The main impetus for these relationships was to initiate academic collaboration agreements and to develop multi-centric research projects. One initiative that was very significant in supporting nursing education was the Pan-American Health Organization (PAHO) "Textbook Program." This program funded the translation of nursing textbooks into Spanish making them easily accessible to many students and nurses. Another key program was the Kellogg Foundation Scholarship Program which provided funding support for nursing graduate education and nursing participation in social development.

Since 1995 the Latin American Association of Schools and Faculties of Nursing (ALADEFE) has selected Chilean nurses to hold the positions of Vice-President of the South Cone and Chairperson of the Research and Education Committees. At the same time well-known nurse educators successfully completed doctoral studies in nursing at universities in Brazil, Spain, and Canada. Chilean pioneers in completing the doctorate in nursing include: Luz Angelica Muñoz, Alejandrina Arrate, Sandra Valenzuela, Olivia Sanhueza, Maria Soledad Rivera, Tatiana Paravic, Jasna Stiepovich, Rossina Cianelli, Eugenia Urra, Anna Santos, and Ana Maria Alarcón (PhD in medical anthropology). As of this writing, 10 Chilean nurses have pioneered in obtaining the doctoral degree. As a result of the academic level reached by these scholars, five of whom are members of the faculty at University of Concepción, a doctoral program in nursing began there in 2004. Ten doctoral students are currently enrolled in the program in *Concepción*, and 10 in *Santiago* at University *Andrés Bello*.

The International Center for Nursing Research of the Chilean Association of Nursing Education (ACHIEEN) was created in 2001 with the support of the Division of Nursing at New York University. As an important initiative for Latin America, the mission of the organization is to promote and encourage nursing research in Chile and to disseminate knowledge acquired through research. It is the hope of ACHIEEN that the "Center" will work collaboratively with other Latin American countries. To that end, in the last 2 years, Colombian and Mexican nurse researchers took part in workshops at the Center. The Center has become the most important Chilean institution offering support for the management of nursing research projects, education for nurse researchers, and consultation on nursing research initiatives.

Beginning in 2002, the creation of a system to insure high quality nursing education became a top priority. One of the motives for this initiative is to garner public approval for professional nursing. The Ministry of Education asked ACHIEEN to participate in a Technical Committee charged with the establishment of criteria for the accreditation of undergraduate programs in nursing. This committee established areas of general and specific competencies comprising knowledge as well as skills and abilities of the professionals in the area. The approval of this document allowed schools of nursing to begin "self-review" as a first step in preparation for the accreditation process and ultimately to achieve accreditation. Most of the 17 schools of nursing affiliated with ACHIEEN have begun to review their own programs in a process called "self-study," a prerequisite for accreditation. As of 2006, five schools were accredited while the remaining 12 programs in various stages of the accreditation process.

Given the large number of new nursing programs created primarily in private colleges over the last 10 years, it was necessary to find strategies to ensure the proper education of students. Many of the new programs, particularly those emanating from private universities, lacked clarity in their educational goals and lacked human or material resources for the educational process. A joint initiative developed by the Chilean Association of Nursing Education and the Chilean Nurses Association (*Colegio de Enfermeras*) created mechanisms to monitor quality and excellence in nursing education programs. This consists of the implementation of a national licensure, which must be taken by all graduates receiving the "*Licenciatura*" in nursing as well as by those nurses who graduated from foreign nursing schools and whose professional certification does not fulfill the current legal requirements. Work on this project began in 2004.

CHALLENGES FOR NURSING IN CHILE IN THE 21st CENTURY

Social versus Free Market Demands on Higher Education in Nursing

A dramatic need for nurses in Chile manifested itself at the onset of the new millennium. Young high school graduates are interested in studying nursing, in part, because they are able to find good jobs in the field after graduation. Each year for many years now, long lists of prospective students are denied admission to public university programs in nursing because the programs are filled to capacity. Because of the need for more nurses and the limited enrollment available in schools of nursing, the Chilean Department of Higher Education created a plan for increasing the number of students prepared in nursing programs (Urra, 2004).

As part of the plan to increase the number of nurses nationally, private colleges were allowed to open nursing programs. As a result, many of the new nursing programs are housed in private colleges. Unlike the previous nursing programs in public universities that were created under a standard curriculum and with regulations already in place, many of the nursing programs created at private colleges have less stringent criteria for: admission, hiring standards for faculty, infrastructure, and clinical placement opportunities.

The privatization in higher education for nursing programs in Chile produced a gradual loss of quality and accountability in what one understands as university-level education. Rather than high quality teaching-learning environments characterized by analysis and critical thinking, Chilean schools of nursing in private colleges (operating within a price competitive market place) are sometimes educational systems based on simple information transfer. Regrettably, higher education in the form of private colleges was transformed into a system that pushes academic institutions into competition in accordance with the laws of supply and demand.

Between 2002 and 2008 the total number of nursing schools in Chile reached 84, with more than 30 programs being of recent creation. This fact, while it could be considered an opportunity given the chronic shortage of professional nurses in the country, is instead a threat to the quality of nursing education. The new schools of nursing opened their doors with a minimum of academic resources both in terms of quality and suitability of faculty for academic work and often with precarious material conditions when compared to the criteria and parameters formulated by the National Commission for the Accreditation of Undergraduate Programs (CNAP).

In this context an urgent need exists to develop impartial mechanisms for overseeing the quality of nursing education. In 2002 the Ministry of Education, through CNAP, invited the Chilean Association of Nursing Education (ACHIEEN) to participate in a Technical Committee on Nursing, to prepare a document on the criteria required to accredit undergraduate programs in nursing. The Committee established areas of general and specific competencies in knowledge, skills, and abilities. The approval of this document allowed nursing programs with at least one class of graduates to begin a process of self-evaluation with the ultimate goal of achieving accreditation. The majority of the 17 schools of nursing affiliated with ACHIEEN initiated this self-evaluation process in 2002. By early 2006, 10 programs had been accredited while the rest were in the accreditation process.

In the near future we expect that graduates from nursing programs may choose to enroll in specialization and in graduate nursing programs (Master and Doctoral programs). This is to acquire specialized knowledge to improve the quality of care. Nurses choosing graduate studies in master and doctoral program will assume nursing leadership responsibilities, participate in health policy formulation and contribute new nursing knowledge through research development in priority areas: human health, health promotion, control of drug use, occupational health, and others.

Contradictions in the Global Market and the Impact on Nursing

Nursing today is confronted with flagrant contradictions that require awareness and responsible planning. While the new century brought great technological advances to society, it also revealed serious discrepancies in societal values, ethics, and mental health status. Anxiety and depression were predominant social pathologies of a 20th century culture that fostered repression and homogenization. Violence, inequality, and exclusion characterize early 21st century ethos. This is a distortion of societal values and models that are shaped, in part, by a hegemonic political economic power that lacks an ethical foundation.

Mental health and public health problems will be insurmountable obstacles for medicine and technology. In this context, addiction and personality disorders (mainly psychopathic types) are viewed as the result of a deficit created by post-modern culture. Macroeconomics and international policy that create economic success for small segments of society, breeds individualism and competitiveness and deters resolution of drug addiction at the macro level (Ortiz, 2005). It also explains the widespread increase in toxic personality traits in society in general and particularly among people occupying social positions considered "successful."

The paradox or duality of the effects of globalization and exclusion is predomi-nant in nursing work environments. International entities (such as the United Nations and the Organization of American States) that value participation and inclusion are directed by officials and financed by mechanisms that respond to political economic interests that contradict the official international organizations' mission and goals. Also, as a result of their ineffectiveness in dealing with recent international conflicts, peace keeping and health organizations have lost much of their credibility. For example, North America's failure to adhere to the United Nation's directives for disarmament in the conflict with Iraq is an example of North America's blatant disregard for the United Nations as an organization. From an international per-spective, this episode weakened the United Nations and reversed the progress made to date in multilateralism and international law.

The enhanced effectiveness of information technology systems helps to create a systematic body of knowledge for evidence-based health research. Yet at the same time, it is an important for nurses and other health professionals to objectively assess knowledge possessed by non-dominant cultures that differs from knowledge and assumptions held by the dominant one. This untapped knowledge may very well have answers to problems that conventional research methods have been unable to address. Using alternative research strategies involving international teams, nursing can be on the forefront of this type of research and knowledge generation.

The ease of migration for professionals from country to country means that health professionals, including nurses, can readily move from developing countries to developed countries. This phenomenon, colloquially called "brain drain," handi-caps the workforces of developing countries while giving the health care labor force of developed countries a great advantage. Since the career possibilities and working conditions in developed nations are often better and, as in the case of nursing, a great demand for services exits, nursing health professionals readily leave their nations of origin to work in the developed world.

Because of this mobility among nation states, the education of nurses is becom-ing more homogeneous and the criteria for the output of nursing programs are becoming more standardized. Chilean nurses are well connected to the international job market and the success of the new nursing schools will be determined by the ability of their graduates to find employment, as well as the quality of their educational preparation which, in grand part, will be measured through a rigorous accreditation process.

Professional nursing needs a plan to evaluate its outcomes in all settings where nursing is practiced (the micro context). But, it cannot do this without taking into account the political, economic, and social perspectives (the macro context) that in some way determines its possibilities for success and its effective positioning among the sciences and in society (Wright, 2000). Nursing is an important social force.

Because nursing provides a valuable service and because it is practiced primarily by women, nursing in Chile has taken great pains to achieve what it now has. Reproduction of methods used to date is not sufficient to overcome future challenges in healthcare and in nursing. Effective nurses will not only be prepared to influence the political decisions that structure the model of society, but also they will seek and avail themselves of the opportunity to strive for social change locally and nationally. The essence of nursing is made up of ethically-grounded health promotion activities as well as care of the sick. But, this requires translated into actions that are not simply palliative and uncritical (like trying to mop up all of the water in the sea with a handkerchief). Rather, international nursing praxis must commit to using all its potential in the construction of society.

A LOOK TO THE FUTURE OF NURSING IN CHILE

A critical analysis of the past and a reflection of the present allow the visualization of the future for nursing in Chile. Over the next decades nursing in Chile will confront the following challenges:

- Increasing specialization: the need for a high technical and analytical knowledge and specialty competence in nursing is associated with technological advances, prevention of disease and illness, diagnosis, and treatment. A great challenge in Chile is the education and creation of nurse specialists. Scientific knowledge increases logarithmically and the globalization of communications requires professional nurses to gain technical and computer sophistication and knowledge. Today, if nurses seek more specific knowledge about a problem, it is not possible to work in isolation. Rather, future nurses will learn to be a vital part of multidisciplinary research teams.
- To offset the shortage of nurses, an increase in nursing institutes for the preparation of nurse technicians is taking place. This increase of non-professional level nurses will promote the view of nursing as one made up of ancillary workers, especially if a clear mechanism for academic surveillance does not exist to assess of the quality of the education of students in these institutes. Nurses prepared in professional university education programs are fearful that the mere presence of this category of nursing worker will compromise the quality of health care. The Chilean Nurses Association and other organizations, nurse educators and researchers continue to strive for a clear professional identity and to increase the recognition of the nurse's work as an essential and basic activity in health care institutions.

- Nursing in Chile is expected to make adjustments in its educational programs to better respond to new and emerging health issues: particularly an investment in a new curriculum structure. Chilean nursing will evolve by searching for new health care models and the resolution of new ethical problems related to the progress of health care on topics such as: genetics, infertility, organ transplant, euthanasia, and assisted suicide.
- An increase in home care nursing and the expansion of the role of the nurse: Chilean society will benefit from population-based care. The nurse is ideally placed to fulfill that need. With current technology and virtual computer ability, nurses can create methods for reaching people in new and different ways, particularly regarding activities targeting health promotion and disease prevention.
- To create new programs of graduate study to increase the development of nursing knowledge. The participation of professionals in scientific and technological development is a responsibility of all disciplines, including nursing. Nursing can increase its participation in technological advancement by using research as a tool to better understand situations that may be harming the profession and also to seek solutions to the health problems suffered by individuals, families, and communities. National and international research groups can examine problems from different methodological perspectives. It is essential that researchers using quantitative and qualitative methodologies work together on the same problem using different approaches thus enriching, comparing, and verifying the results of their research. In this manner nursing will achieve more detailed knowledge to answer research questions and problems derived from practice. Through research, Chilean nurses can improve and transform reality based on the information obtained in our unique local settings.

Nursing in Chile faces many future challenges. The first steps are to enhance its own self-image, assume new roles and extend its domain. In that way Chilean nurses can frame better research proposals and obtain more funding from national and international organizations. This funding is necessary to carry out national and international research studies to enhance the discipline's solid scientific knowledge. Chilean nursing needs better formal preparation to carry out good research and to foster the development of new generations of researchers. More continuing and graduate education is necessary to accomplish this. Chilean nurses can no longer risk being unprepared as researchers. Rather, good researchers must be educated.

The application of observation, critical thinking and hands-on practical experience will allow nursing to actively integrate into multidisciplinary research projects. Knowledge production, generation, and application require the reorientation and systematization of the scientific process to better diffuse research findings. A clear discussion of the implications of research findings for practice is needed to optimize the health and well-being of people in Chile and beyond.

REFERENCES

Avendaño, C., & Grau, P. (1997). Salud de las enfermeras chilenas. Visibilizando riesgos [The health of Chilean nurses: Perceiving the risks]. *Cuadernos Mujer y Salud, 2,* 92-97.

Avendaño, C., Grau, P., & Yus, P. (1995). Riesgos para la salud de las enfermeras del sector público de Chile [Health risks for Chile's public sector nurses]. *Enfermería, 102,* 15-26.

Borges Romero, A. (1998). Personal de enfermería: Condiciones de trabajo de alto riesgo. Notas y reflexiones [Nursing staff: High risk working conditions: Notes and reflections]. *Salud de los trabajadores, 6*(2), 113-119.

Castells, M. (1999). *O poder da identidade* [The power of identity]. Sao Paulo: Paz e Terra.

Colegio de Enfermeras de Chile. (1965a). El centro de Experimentación en Enfermería apasiona a Doris Krebs [Doris Krebs's passion for the Nursing Testing Center]. *Enfermería, 1,* 8.

Colegio de Enfermeras de Chile. (1965b). Plan de Acción Organizadora [Organizational Action Plan]. *Enfermería, 2,* 18-20.

Colegio de Enfermeras de Chile. (1965c). Escuela de Enfermería "Isidora Lyon Cousiño" [Isidora Lyon Cousiño School of Nursing]. *Enfermería, 5,* 6-8.

Colegio de Enfermeras de Chile. (1965d). Escuela de Enfermería del S.N.S. [S.N.S. School of Nursing]. *Revista Enfermería, 5,* 9.

Colegio de Enfermeras de Chile. (1970). Conclusiones y Recomendaciones del VI Congreso Nacional de Enfermeras, 11-16 de octubre de 1970 [Conclusions and recommendations of the VI National Nursing Congress, October 11-16, 1970]. *Enfermería, 26,* 9-10.

Colegio de Enfermeras de Chile. (1972). XIX Asamblea General Ordinaria del Consejo General del Colegio de Enfermeras de Chile.-Periodo desde Abril de 1971 a Abril de 1972. Memoria Anual [Annual Report: Chilean Nurses Association XIX Ordinary General Assembly, General Council, April 1971 to April 1972]. *Enfermería, 32*(79), 27-32.

Colegio de Enfermeras de Chile. (1976). Análisis crítico del ejercicio professional [Critical analysis of professional work]. *Enfermería, 50*(11), 4-9.

Colegio de Enfermeras de Chile. (1977). Memoria Anual del Consejo General del Colegio de Enfermeras de Chile, Periodo Mayo 1976 a Abril de 1977 [Annual Report: Chilean Nurses Association General Council, May 1976 to April 1977]. *Enfermería, 51*(12), 33-44.

Colegio de Enfermeras de Chile. (1978a). Esfera de Acción de la Enfermera [Spectrum for nursing action]. *Enfermería, 55*(12), 7-11.

Colegio de Enfermeras de Chile. (1978b). Es hora de reconocer [It's time to recognize it]. *Enfermería, 55*(12), 3.

Colegio de Enfermeras de Chile. (1978c). Proposiciones para una política de Desarrollo de la Investigación de Enfermería [Proposals for nursing research policy development] Dpto. de Investigación Colegio de Enfermeras. *Enfermería, 56*(12), 4-7.

Colegio de Enfermeras de Chile. (1978d). Fundamentos para un nuevo enfoque de Enfermería en Salud Comunitaria [Fundamentals for a new nursing focus on community health]. *Enfermería, 56*(12), 12-16.

Colegio de Enfermeras de Chile. (1978e). Memoria Anual del Consejo General. Colegio de Enfermeras. Periodo 1° de Junio de 1977 a 31 de Mayo de 1978. [Annual Report: Chile Nurses Association General Council, June 1st, 1971 to May 31st, 1972]. *Enfermería, 58*(13), 31-40.

Colegio de Enfermeras de Chile. (1980). Discurso de la Presidenta del Colegio de Enf. Srta. Carmen Oye. IX Congreso Nacional de Enfermeras [Speech by the President of the Nurses Association, Ms. Carmen Oye. IX Nursing National Congress]. Viña del Mar, Octubre, 1980. *Enfermería, 66*(16), 4-6.

Collière, M. F. (1997). *Promover la Vida: de la práctica de las mujeres cuidadoras a los cuidados de enfermería* [Promoting life: From the practice of caring for women to nursing care]. España: McGraw Hill/Interamericana.

Ebensperger, C., González, A., Jerez, I., Krebs, D., & Royo, T. (1972). Esquema para la Investigación en Enfermería [Outline for nursing research]. *Enfermería, 31,* 13-19.

Escuela de Enfermeria. Universidad de Chile. (1942). *Primer Centenario (1942): Reseña Histórica de la profesión de enfermera en Chile* [First Century (1942): A historical account of Chile's nursing profession]. Prensas de la Universidad de Chile, Santiago.

Feedback Consultores. (2000). *Encuesta CASEN* [CASEN Survey]. Gobierno de Chile, Chile.

Flores, R. (1965a). Escuela de Enfermería de la Universidad de Chile [The University of Chile's Nursing School]. *Enfermería, 5,* 2-5.

Flores, R. (1965b). *Historia de la Enfermería en Chile. Síntesis de su evolución educacional, I Parte* [History of Chilean nursing: Synthesis of the educational evolution: Part I]. Documento Colegio de Enfermeras de Chile A. G.

Flores, R. (1966). Escasez de Enfermeras, un desafio para la educación y los servicios de salud [The nursing shortage: Education and health service challenges]. *Enfermería, 10,* 17-20.

French-Davis, R., & Stallings, B. (2001). *Reformas, crecimiento y políticas sociales en Chile desde 1973* [Reform, growth and social policy in Chile since 1973]. Naciones Unidas. Primera edición.

Giaconi, J., & Concha, M. (2005). El Sistema de Salud Chileno Reformado [Chilean healthcare system reform]. Serie Monografias Universidad Mayor, 226 pp.

Jiménez, J. (1990). *Subsistema de Mutuales de Seguridad* [Subsystems for work-related accident insurance]. Corporación de Promoción Universidaria, Santiago de Chile.

Krebs, D. (1961). *Necesidades y recursos de enfermería en Chile. Parte I* [A report of Chilean nursing needs and resources, Part I]. Imprenta de la central de talleres del S.N.S., Santiago, Chile.

Krebs, D. (1962). *Necesidades y recursos de enfermería en Chile. Parte II* [A report of Chilean nursing needs and resources, Part II]. Imprenta talleres del S.N.S., Santiago, Chile.

Krebs, D. (1965a). Una mirada al pasado para pensar en el futuro [Looking back so we can plan the future]. *Revista de Enfermería, 4,* 12-13.

Krebs, D. (1965b). Porqué estudiamos nuestras funciones [Why study our duties?]. *Revista de Enfermería, 4,* 14-15.

Labra, M. (2002). La reinvención neoliberal de la inequidad en Chile. El caso de la salud [Neoliberal redesign of inequity in Chile]. *Cadernos de Saúde Pública, 18*(4), 1041-1052.

Letelier, P., & Valenzuela, S. (2002). Violencia: Fenómeno relevante de estudio en campos clínicos intrahospitalarios de enfermería [Violence: Relevant study phenomena in hospital nursing clinics]. *Ciencia y Enfermería, 8*(2), 21-26.

Meneses, A., Prieto, A., Muñoz, Z., et al. (1995). *Estudio del Recurso de Enfermería Profesional en Chile* [Study of professional nursing resources in Chile]. Sociedad Chilena de Educación en Enfermería. Chile.

Ministry of Health, Chile [Ministerio de Salud de Chile]. (1977). *Políticas de Salud* [Health policy]. Lord Cochrane, S.A. Comunicaciones y Relaciones Públicas del Ministerio de Salud.

Ministerio de Salud de Chile. (2002). *Los Objetivos Sanitarios para la Década 2000-2010* [Healthcare objectives for the Decade 2000-2010]. Gobierno de Chile. Primera Edición.

MINSAL. (2000). *Situación de salud en Chile año 2000, Análisis Epidemiológico* [Chilean healthcare outcomes for the year 2000: An epidemiological analysis]. Ministerio de Salud de Chile. MINSAL: www.minsal.cl

Miranda, E., & Vergara, M. (1993). *Evolución y Estructura del Sector Salud en Chile* [Evolution and structure of the Chilean healthcare sector]. En: Cuaderno Técnico N° 36 OPS, Estructura y Comportamiento del Sector Salud en La Argentina, Chile y El Uruguay. OMS/OPS, Washington, E.U.A.

Ortiz, N., & Costa, M. (2005). Significados y Contradicciones del Fenómeno de las Drogas: Drogas Lícitas e Ilícitas en Chile [Meaning and contradictions of the drug phenomenon: Licit and illicit drugs in Chile]. *Revista Latino-Americana de Enfermagem, 13,* 903-911.

Pontificia Unversidad Católica de Chile. (1990). Cuarenta años de historia [Forty years of history]. *Horizonte de Enfermería, 1*(1), 3.

Rosselot, J. (1993). Reseña histórica de las instituciones de salud en Chile [An historic account of Chilean healthcare institutions]. *Cuadernos Médico-Sociales, 34*(1), 7-20.

Sánchez, R.,Valenzuela, S., & Solares, J. (2002). Percepción de violencia que afecta a los profesionales de enfermería [The perception of violence affecting nursing professionals]. *Enfermería, 120,* 10-14.

Sanhueza, O. (1996). *Década del 70: Docencia de Enfermería en Chile* [The decade of 1970's: Nursing education in Chile]. Seminario de Asignatura de Doctorado Escola de Enfermagem Ribeirão Preto, U.S.P. Brasil. Manuscrito no publicado.

Titelman, D. (2001). Capitulo 8: Las reformas del sistema de salud: desafíos pendientes [Chapter 8: Healthcare system reforms: Pending challenges]. In *French-Davis y Stallings: Reforma, crecimiento y política social en Chile desde 1973* (pp. 263-294). Santiago de Chile, LOM Ediciones.

Trucco, M., Valenzuela, P., & Trucco, D. (1999). Estrés ocupacional en personal de salud. [Occupation stress in health professionals]. *Revista Médica de Chile, 127,* 1453- 1461.

United Nations Program for Development [UNPD]. (2004). En el documento Exportaciones crecientes, menor crecimiento económico y mayor desigualdad [Documenting increased exports, diminished economic growth and growing inequality]. html://www.undp.org/rblac/finaldrafsts/sp/Capitulo1-Introduccion.pdf

Urra, E. (2004). *Struggling to achieve professional recognition: A case study of nursing in Chile.* Dissertation doctoral program, University of Alberta, Canada.

Valenzuela, S., Sanhueza, O., Riquelme, N., et al. (2003). Salud laboral: Situación de los accidentes de trabajo en el equipo de enfermería [Workplace health: Conditions of work-related accidents in the nursing team]. *Enfermería Clínica, 13*(2), 94-102.

Wright, M. G. M. (2000). A critical-holistic paradigm for a interdependent world. *American Behavior Scientist, 43*(5), 808-832.

CHAPTER 4

Nursing in Argentina

Maria Alejandra Chervo, Eduardo Miguel Arzani, and Teresa Isabel Micozzi

Nursing in Argentina evolved within a national health care system that grew to strength in the mid-20th century, coinciding with the emergence of nursing as a profession. Prior to that time, nursing work was regarded as simple and manual, as an extension of women's domestic duties, and not something requiring formal education. It was a form of work that depended completely on physician direction.

During the 1960s, a socio-economic development model based on fiscal and economic efficiency infused all segments of Argentinean society. It significantly influenced the development of the nursing profession. International agencies such as the Pan American Health Organization (PAHO) and the World Health Organization (WHO) offered recommendations to increase the quantity and the quality of nurses. As a result, the course of nursing in Argentina was irrevocably changed through such agents as the introduction of university-affiliated programs of nursing education which granted a *Licenciado en Enfermería*. Also playing its part was a law regulating the curriculum of nursing education, including non-university affiliated nursing education programs and the technical programs of study for nurses. To be recognized by the Argentinean Ministry of Education, all nursing education programs were required to follow a common curriculum.

Other changes included the creation of 9-month-long programs for "nursing auxiliaries" to alleviate the nursing shortage. These nursing auxiliary programs were open to graduates of middle school, who upon completion were awarded a certificate as a "nurse auxiliary" roughly equivalent to an LPN in the United States. Over the subsequent decades, large numbers of nursing auxiliaries were quickly prepared and hired by hospitals and clinics.

Unfortunately, the creation of the nursing auxiliary program delayed the development of professional nursing. First, the new category of "auxiliary" segmented the nursing workforce by creating another category of nurse. Second, because the nursing auxiliary position was not part of a strategic plan for workforce develop-ment, no provisions were made for career advancement for nursing auxiliaries. Third, all members of the nursing staff, regardless of their educational level, were grouped into the same category of health care workers and classified as "non-professional." Finally, because nursing auxiliaries also provided community health nursing care in communities, it was difficult for the average citizen to understand how university-educated nurses differed and could provide higher quality care.

This chapter offers a historical and political economic look at Argentinean nurs-ing within the national health and educational systems in four parts. Part one introduces Argentina's history from a political economic and social perspective. Changes made since 1970 are particularly significant, including the transformation of Argentina from a *welfare system* to a *neo-liberal system*. Part two outlines the structure and function of the health care system and explains the socio-historical conditions at the national and international "macro" level as well as at the local "micro" level. Parts three and four describe the problems of the labor market for nursing education.

PART ONE: ARGENTINA IN THE CONTEXT OF GLOBALIZATION IN THE AMERICAS

"Globalization" is the expansion of the market and goods both locally and globally (Ferrer, 1996), and it coexists with the local culture, markets, and resources. In fact, the connection of the local to the broader national and global contexts deter-mines, to a certain extent, a country's level of development. To understand Argen-tinean nursing specifically and the Argentinean health care system in general, we must examine how globalization shapes local conditions.

Historical Considerations

Colonial Period—Pre-Industrialization in Argentina

Historically, the people living in Argentina were in diverse and fragmented groups, geographically isolated from each other. Most of the population lived far from the powerful Incas, located in the north. Only tribes and clans living close to the Incas were linked politically and administratively to them. Later, when the Incas themselves succumbed to the Spaniards during the Spanish Conquest, all of the Argentinean territory became a Spanish colony and soon became dependent on Spain for much of its economic livelihood. The young Argentina was a weak, peripheral power especially when compared to larger Atlantic powers and to Spain.

After the conquest, Argentinean leather and wool products were fostered first, followed by the export of agricultural and livestock products (Areces, 1999; Ferrer, 1996). Because of its excellent conditions for shipping, Argentina's "Rio de la Plata" harbor was transformed into an important urban center. Most of Argentina's eco-nomic and trade relations were with Europe, particularly with Spain and France, and not with North America, Asia, or Africa. Consequently, the political leadership for the Rio de la Plata came from Europe, which planned Argentinean national

political, economic, and social organization. Naturally, European models of education, politics and culture—the revolutionary bourgeoisie mixed with the strong
influence of Roman Catholicism (the latter was not simply a religious practice)—
were major influences in shaping all aspects of Argentinean society.

Agricultural Export Model (Argentina 1862-1930)

Argentina admired the old continent and adopted the European model. When
the nation state of Argentina emerged and the republic was consolidated (between
1863 and 1880), there was a "homogeneity of the dominant [European] power:
[that is] a bourgeoisie class composed of landlords alternating with men of liberal
professions educated in Europe and sharing the same origins" (Romero, 2002,
p. 98). The government policies created during that period aimed at increasing
the population and implementing a national education program designed to teach
the peasants and working classes how to read and write, or, in other words "to
educate the sovereign" (Romero, 2002, p. 105).

Immigration, particularly European migration, was strongly promoted. At the
turn of the 20th century, the census showed that 25% of the Argentinean population
included immigrants; a few years later, the census of 1914 showed 30%. The
majority of the immigrants were Spanish and Italian with smaller numbers of
Syrians, Lebanese, Germans, and Swiss. However, there was no clear immigration
policy and the immigrant distribution throughout Argentina was uneven. In some
areas of the country such as in the desirable ". . . Eastern regions of the country, the
fertile plains near to the harbors witnessed more than a seventy percent increase
in population . . ." and no clear criteria existed for the assignment of land (Romero,
2002, pp. 104, 113, 114). To implement the second aim of a national education
program, an educational policy was put in place to promote secular education,
compulsory elementary school, and the education of teachers (Romero, 2002,
pp. 105, 117).

During the second phase of the capitalistic industrial revolution, the country
was a supplier of raw materials. Even though the number of companies had increased
and the technological facilities and methods had improved, the mightiest sector
of the economy was the indispensable extractive and manufacturing activities,
tied to farming production or to the industries meeting the most elementary
necessities of the population: "As far as industrial development, companies that sur-
passed artisan production were few. Those of the food industry stood out . . . especially refrigeration, factories of *quebracho* extract, some textile and metallurgical
factories, and the sector of construction" (Rapoport, 2006, p. 68). Still, as a result
of this industrialization, a new upwardly mobile middle class with a higher
social status emerged and formed a liberal political party to compete with the
existing conservative party. During this time, a significant union movement also
took hold, led by immigrants who had been involved with unions in their countries of origin.

Thus, at the beginning of 20th century, Argentina already had high levels of
education and good social development. However, the development was fragmented

and uneven. In the interior of the country and in rural areas, land and business ownership was concentrated in the hands of a few wealthy families. This concentration produced an "oligarchy," a condition whereby local landlords concentrated economic and political power (Luna, 1996). The unevenness affected the entire country because, while pockets of advanced democratic development existed, most of the country was characterized by oligarchy and limited democracy.

In brief, during this period the conditions for the modern Argentina were established: strengthened institutions, creation of a national identity (with education as the main tool), increase in the population, modernization, and urbanization. As Kosacoff notes (1995, p. 98), several factors determined that Argentina "was developing into the most outstanding industrial structure of the region" with competitive goods from the primary sector (refrigerating, tannin, leather, wool, flours, etc.); the European migratory wave with expertise in those industries; the early development of education as well as technical and professional specialization; and the growth of the internal market.

Import Substitution Period—Argentina 1930-1945

> The exhaustion of the expansion of the farming border, along with the international crisis of 1929 and the conflicting triangular relations between Argentina, Great Britain and the United States, ended the operation of the agricultural export model. (Kosacoff, 1995, p. 98)

Impelled by the diminishing importance of foreign trade in the Gross Internal Product (GIP), and supported by the previous industrialization, a process of "import substitution" in the "easy sections" of the manufacturing production began. "The producing industries of consumer goods (foods, textile industry, and the apparel industry), home appliances, simple machineries, metallurgy and the construction industry were the most dynamic activities" (Kosacoff, 1995, p. 98).

As Rapoport points out (2006, pp. 242-243), the *Confederación General del Trabajo (CGT)* (General Confederation of Labor) in 1930, displaced "both the anarchists, who had been the motor for organizing the workers and along with them, their democratic forms of decision making." Bureaucracy prevailed and, stoked by new political power, increased in the following period, coming to characterize the CGT in later years. The CGT was divided between the "Unionists," who rejected the identification of the labor movement with a political party and the "Socialists" who aspired for just such identification.

In 1936, a third communist fraction was incorporated in the CGT. Together with the Socialists, they spearheaded the branch form (industry specific) of unions to replace the old unionism by office. Although the traditional unions (bonded to the economy based on agricultural exports as well as the transport and services sectors) still maintained the greatest presence, workers from new branches of industry were incorporated within the unions. Nevertheless, there was a low union affiliation: whereas "the number of industrial workers reached 534,000 and the agriculturists reached 800,000, the number of workers affiliated with the CGT was only 232,000" (Rapoport, 2006, p. 243).

Unions, during the period 1930-1945, incorporated the health benefits for workers and their families, and initiated coverage for industrial accidents. Thus, the unions continued the tradition that the early *mutuales* (collectives) had initiated which later provided them the right to manage the funds for the workers' health coverage through *Obras Sociales* (Social Works).

Argentina 1945-1970

By 1945, a Keynesian-style populist government came to power in Argentina. The new government promoted the State's intervention in the economy and the expansion of its role in social functions. During this period, a strong Argentinean workers' movement thrived, and sweeping legislation recognizing workers' work rights, was passed. These events helped shape the future of Argentina's political scene, especially the development and evolution of the health care sector: Unionism, which had been born in the previous period, acquired political power as "the spine" of the Peron government's party.

As it will be discussed in detail later, nursing was included in the nonprofessional workers category of the health care sector, thus becoming part of the "Health Union." Thus, nurses were not able to differentiate themselves from the other workers. However, this Union movement helped nationalize the railroad industry and public services as well as industrialize the country, a process that became most visible toward the end of the 1950s and the beginning of the 1960s. During this period "the input of foreign capital, especially North American capital . . . allowed the development of basic industries such as petrochemical, iron and steelmaking and automotive industries" (Romero, 2002, p. 170).

The doctrine known as "Alliance for Progress," created by U.S. President John F. Kennedy, encouraged economic development throughout the world. Latin America "agreed to carry out a series of reforms, among them agrarian reform, in exchange for a series of economic aid and new U.S. investment" (Larrouse, 1997, p. 256). Also instrumental in encouraging economic growth, the United Nations created the "United Nations Program for Development." Through these economic policies, the primary concern of the powerful core capitalist nations was to provide external aid for the development of countries on the periphery. This period is known as the "decade of development" (Araújo de Mattos, 2002, p. 82).

This influence of international development policies was very strong in Argentina. Development theory (Raúl Previch, 1949) envisioned an enhanced, efficient technology sector with efficiency infiltrating all aspects of social life, particularly the fields of health care and education. This vision was maintained regardless of the political climate, through periods where democratically elected governments strongly controlled by political parties alternated with military dictatorships.

This vision also had a direct impact on nursing. In education, a study of existing schools was conducted. The study reported two great sources of degreed professionals: private schools, grouped in the SNEP (*Superintendencia Nacional de*

Enseñanza Privada–National Supervision of Private Education), and public schools from the Provincial Ministries and the Universities (between 1960-1970 when the first four universities began in Argentina). The initial purpose of unifying titles was specified in a Decree Law (35/69) that defined the curriculum for the education of nurses. Even today, applicants who aspire to achieve the second level of nursing degree (Licensed in Nursing) must have a certificate that says specifically that they have completed the first level—"in agreement with Decreto-Ley 36/79."

In health services, a Ministry of Health study executed with the technical advice of the PAHO, revealed both a quantitative and a qualitative deficit of nurses. It also revealed an absence of structures of nursing. Thus, the study's recommendations gave priority to education of nurses and to the formation of nursing departments in hospitals.

Generally, developmental projects defined Argentina as "underdeveloped" and supposed industrialization would provide the country basic industries in steel, petrochemicals, metallurgy, machinery, and the generation of energy (Rapoport, 2006, p. 456). Although economic development was limited by the political crisis that characterized the decade, it continued through the 1960s, and its repercussions continue today.

Argentina 1970-1990

The 1970s began with great hope for democracy and for political and economic independence. These dreams quickly collapsed in March of 1976 when a terrorizing military dictatorship took power and remained in control until 1983. During this period, human rights abuses soared, but also Argentina entered a period of economic decline, and its external debt grew enormously. The reasons for this were related to the 1978 "National Reorganization Project" which was presented as the foundation for a new Argentina (Belmartino, 1991, p. 22). The project proposed to reform social relationships both in the economic as well as in the political arenas through the eradication of "anti-establishment" forces. The National Reorganization Project sought Argentina's emergence into the world market through a neoliberal economic model which promoted a free market economy with a deregulation of prices and a reduction in economic protectionism, thus dismantling national industries. In essence, the National Reorganization Project maintained the three principles of neoliberalism: individualism, privatization and deregulation.

The new economic policies allowed the survival of only those activities that provided comparative advantages in the world market. The National Reorganization Project was supported by powerful sectors that controlled the most dynamic branches of the economic production sector (big businesses, industry, and agricultural and cattle sectors). These sectors were the same ones that later provided capital for financial business. During this period, the State:

> . . . refused to regulate financial activities leading to the proliferation of private financial entities launched to seize people's savings. During those moments when the rise in the international price of oil created a rush of capital-seeking

quick earnings, the financial opening allowed the rapid entrance of this capital into the country thus feeding speculation and creating the basis for an external debt that subsequently became the strongest conditioner of the local economy. (Romero, 2002, pp. 189-190)

The authoritarian National Reorganization Project depoliticized Argentinean society and liberated the economy. In 1983, with the end of the military dictatorship and the beginning of a "democratic recovery," the new government attempted to end financial speculation, stimulate production and improve the income of the working class. But the initial popular enthusiasm for the new movement hid the magnitude of Argentina's political and economic problems as well as the limits of the government's power, and so the traditional corporate sectors survived. As one example, the attempt to democratize the unions resulted in a clear confrontation between unionists and government (Belmartino, 1991, p. 28; Romero, 2002, pp. 194-195) because of the financial management of the *Obras Sociales* (Social Works). Still, all Argentinean society gave importance to *democracy* as a way of life—demanding it as a central "value" in all the institutions producing meaningful changes. So, for example, at the University, professors who had been exiled during the dictatorship were able to return to their re-opened positions. In the case of the School of Nursing of the *Universidad del Rosario* (University of Rosario), 14 positions were filled, which also increased the prestige of the institution.

Rupture of the Welfare State

By the end of the 1980s, hyperinflationary conditions erupted leading to drastic economic measures during the 1990s. These measures returned Argentina to neo-liberal principles and included a reduction in the fiscal spending budget, a privatization of state enterprises (accepting as partial payment certificates of external debt) and strong links with those international economic groups that benefited the most from the privatizations, North American and European (mainly Spanish, French, and British) capital (Romero, 2002, pp. 201-202). In April 1991, the Argentinean national "Law of Convertibility" established even more dramatic neoliberal reforms, including broad and sweeping structural changes that once again focused on the neoliberal principles of privatization, deregulation, and individualism. The premises imbedded in the new legislation stood in stark contrast to Argentina's earlier provisions favoring collective, public rights and services. Pautassi elaborates here on the Law of Convertibility.

(It) had a stabilizing impact that together with a favorable international context and the support of multilateral credit institutions, facilitated a series of economic reforms . . . I) all public enterprises became private, ii) the domestic economy became open to the free movement of foreign capital, iii) import duties diminished . . . at the same time there were advances in commercial accords . . . (Mercosur); iv) the foreign debt was renegotiated . . . and new and greater indebtedness was acquired; v) labor law was modified so as to reduce the stability of employment, wage costs and severance pay thus reducing the employer's responsibilities; vi) deep changes in public management; vii) the internal revenue system was modified and traditional sources of financing of social policies were reduced, maintaining greater relative weight of indirect tax loads. (Pautassi, 2002, p. 11)

Despite these widespread economic reforms during the early 1990s, Argentina still suffered a devastating economic blow a few years later. In 1996 "a strong fluctuation in international financial markets led to the withdrawal of flight-prone capital (*capitales golondrinas*) and submerged the Argentinean economy into a deep economic depression. Unemployment rates skyrocketed and symptoms of social tension appeared" (Romero, 2002, p. 203). The events detailed above, together with the discovery of corruption never before publicly known, awakened the dormant and depoliticized middle class. This revitalized middle class began a search that continues today for new, acceptable political economic models, especially since "unemployment and other social conditions decimated the historically large middle class (in 1980 the middle class made up 74% of the Argentinean population)" (Belmartino, 1991, p. 28). This recent shrinking of the working and middle classes led to the "new poor."

PART 2: NEOLIBERAL GLOBALIZATION IN ARGENTINA

The literature tends to use the term globalization to designate those processes that have taken place over the last 2 decades driven primarily by the economy, and is characterized by the "growing integration of diverse economies and societies as a consequence of greater fluxes of goods, capital, people and ideas" (Collier & Dollar, 2002). But, even those authors who emphasize the benefits of globalization cannot deny that it is a "process by which national and international leaders promote national deregulation and external liberalization" (Tobar, Garraza, Monsalvo, & Falbo, 2002, p. 20).

Certainly, our world is constantly becoming more complex and incomprehensible. Pondering sociopolitical forces helps us understand the evolution of Argentinean nursing and the health care system in which it exists, both in regard to its educational aspects as well as its role in the workforce. We use the term globalization to refer to "neoliberal globalization" (Araújo de Mattos, 2002, p. 78), "that takes into account the prevailing ideology" in the Western world and its implementation in Argentina.

The economic measures adopted since the Law of Convertibility was passed in 1991 made Argentina's economy dependent on external forces. Pautassi explains that "when the opening of the economy and the mobility of foreign capital are implemented, those traditionally external variables such as the international interest rate and capital fluctuation become elements that are external to the domestic economy" (Pautassi, 2002, p. 11). Various scholars (Belmartino, 1989, 1991; Laurell, 1992; Lerner, 1992; Lerner & Garcia Raggio, 1991; Pautassi, 2001; Tobar, 2000) concur that during those times, capitalist accumulation directed the changes implemented in Latin-American countries, but the crisis is blamed on state inefficiencies rather than on social policies. Therefore, a "program of adjustment and structural change" needs to be created. While neoliberalism was worldwide, the socio-economic situation (that is, the early Keynesian model) in the core industrial first world countries (United States, England, France, and Germany) was not comparable to that in the peripheral countries in the second, third, and fourth world. The core states executing policy (and the corresponding societies) had completely different levels of development than those on periphery. Lerner (1992) commented on social class interests in this way:

> As is well known (in the core or central countries), class commitment func-
> tioned as long as the economy preserved its ability to thrive. An investment
> blockage appeared in 1970, as the rates of growth and profitability for businesses
> decreased. Business people focused on the unlimited social burden of State
> programs and on the excessive power of trade unions that destabilized the
> system with inflated expectations. (p. 21)

Neoliberal globalization is ideologically linked to the values of individual freedom, autonomy, and inequality. These are considered motivators for personal initiative and the competition of individuals in the market. In a neoliberal economy, these driving forces are regarded as the only means of correcting economic and social ills.

Neoliberal globalization posits the idea that the ideal State must curtail its inter-vention in the economy (its planning, leading and participation as direct economic agent), but must also guarantee the proper conditions, through the appropriate legal framework, for the expansion of the market. At the same time, it must reduce its functions related to social welfare, intervening only so as to secure a minimum to alleviate poverty and to produce those services that private enterprise cannot, or may not want to, produce. For neoliberals, social welfare is a private matter taken up by private organizations on an "as needed" basis. The State need not intervene with additional services. For neoliberals:

> . . . a public good provides benefits that are indivisible, that is, benefits for which
> one can state in advance of individual participation. Examples are security and
> national defense . . . but not education and health care services, where the
> benefits can be easily calculated and thus become divisible leading to a "private
> profit." (Lerner & Garcia Raggio, 1991, p. 37)

Core countries (e.g., the United States, Canada, England, France, and Germany) were able to "overcome resistance to the withdrawal of the State from the economy, but have been unable to abandon their commitment to social rights" (Laurell, 1992, p. 5). This issue, a contested topic in electoral campaigns, forced core country governments to conclude that "withdrawal of the State from social institutions is not possible nor legitimate" (Laurell, 1992, p. 5). The impact of neoliberal policies in these core countries (limited to the economic aspect without totally dismantling the welfare system) has been the regressive distribution of income and the increase of relative and absolute poverty with the additional effect of social exclusion (Davis, 1989).

Lerner and Garcia Raggio (1991) list the basic tenets for neoliberal state reform that are uncritically applied to Latin America, based on the following so-called value-free technical and economic explanations:

1. An excess of democracy makes it necessary to discipline society by means of the market as a natural barrier to the growth of expectations and to the coercive strengthening of state authority.
2. The hypertrophy (or swelling) of the State caused by its social intervention.

According to neoliberalism tenets, welfare programs can be summarized as:

- Collective services, organized on universality and free access, promote an "unlimited demand" for those very services that necessarily leads to a process of over-expansion of the public sector.
- The over-expansion of collective services requires a costly infrastructure that increases social expenditures.
- State control of goods and services generates social public institutions that become bureaucratized and controlled by special interest groups. Ironically, this dynamic is not egalitarian and instead benefits those special interest groups who have more, not those who need it the most.

Unfortunately, Argentina has a history of authoritarian regimes during which unfair social policies caused the population to suffer great inequalities. For example, during the 1975-1986 military regime, expenditures for social programs decreased by 6.4% and were maintained at that constant level in the GDP. These regressive social policies resulted from the Argentinean internal revenue system that relied to a great extent on consumption and wage taxes, not on property or investment taxes.

The 1990s represented a particularly active period for the implementation of neoliberal restructuring and reform in Argentina. Scholars (Laurell, 1992) identify the following strategies used to decrease the Argentinean social welfare activity:

> . . . cut-backs in social expenditures, eliminating social programs and reducing benefits; the focusing of expenditures, that is, channeling *(resources)* towards destitute groups once (only after) their poverty has been demonstrated; the privatization of the production of services; and the decentralization of public services *(including health services)* at the local level. (Laurell, 1992, p. 29)

Implementational of such dramatic cuts in social policies required an initial public relations phase where the reforms were publicized as part of the so called *"process of modernization of the State,* and were advertised as being an unavoid-able requirement for economic consolidation and institutional change" (Pautassi, 2001, p. 18).

This public relations phase facilitated the next phase that included legislative changes to avoid any "obstacle(s) to the modernization of the State" (Pautassi, 2001). During this second phase, significant legislation was passed that had a serious impact on all aspects of social life including (a) the law deregulating *"Obras Sociales"* (b) the federal Education and Higher Education Law, and (c) the Labor Reform Law. Additional impact also came from the landmark Argentinean constitutional reform of 1994 that incorporated "an extensive list of rights encompassing wide aspects of citizenship" and also inserted into the text of the Argentinean Constitution a series of international Agreements and Treaties. This inclusion made the Constitution an influential document that did not derive from labor rights, but rather sought to "legitimize the (neoliberal) reform project, while the population was forced to accept reforms to welfare institutions that in no way represented egalitarian values" (Pautassi, 2001, p. 19).

Evolution of The Argentinean Health Care System

If the Argentinean health care system could be characterized in two words, they would be: "fragmentation and heterogeneity" (Belmartino, 1991, 1992, 1995, 2000; Findling, Tamargo, & Redondo, 2000; Pautassi, 2001; Tobar, 2000). The conditions that contribute to this fragmented and heterogeneous system are partly the result of the organization of services and of fiscal and budgetary issues. The Argentinean health care system has multiple jurisdictions (national, provincial and municipal) with little or no coordination among them. Additionally, different normative, financial and organizational capacities (programs and resources) exist, according to Katz (1993, as cited in Pautassi, 2001) that make it difficult to produce a "national" analysis with conclusions that are accurate for the entire country.

Historically, the Argentinean health care organization was viewed as three separate sub-sectors:

a) "the *public sector*—dependent on the national, provincial and municipal administrations (financial and management) and made up of a network of health care providers;

b) the *private sector*—including a complex network of private diagnostic centers, hospitals, and clinics. (The State has no financial relationship with the private sector); and

c) The *social health insurance system,* integrated by the *Obras Sociales* (O.S.)." (Pautassi, 2001, p. 23)

The financial function of the State is *"to regulate"* by managing a fund consisting of contributions from *Obras Sociales.* In order to compensate the lesser financial ability of the weaker *Obras Sociales,* the contributions are proportional to the members' incomes. The public sector delivers direct health care services and sets the direction and norms for the entire health care system. The private sector provides selective private services, and the *Obras Sociales,* the social health insurance branch, handles the finances and budget of the entire health care system.

However, because the configuration of the three sectors has undergone so many changes over the last decade, the categories of public, private and *Obras Sociales* are no longer as relevant (Pautassi, 2001). Also, the system encourages inequality in care received because people from different socio-economic strata use different sectors of the health service. Pautassi (2001) elaborates:

> . . . disadvantaged and poor groups seek the public system; low, middle and upper-middle class groups have social health insurance through one of the *Obras Sociales* (connected to one's occupation, employment or wage category and area of work), and finally members of the upper class are not insured by the *Obras Sociales* and use the private sector." (Pautassi, 2001, p. 24)

The cause for the fragmented health system is rooted in the Argentinean state's poor control over the health care sector and ultimately its inability to provide the population with equal access to health care services.

Health historian Susana Belmartino, sees the 1940s in Argentina as pivotal in how the health care system took its current shape because of "the pioneering character of the political restructuring of health care and its characteristics such as unity of command, rationality and planning" (1991, p. 14). However, to explain the resulting fragmentation and inequality, it was necessary "to consider the conditions by which the problem is framed in the midst of civil society" (Belmartino, 1991, p. 14).

Health care services before 1940 reflected liberal Argentina: individual professions; not-for-profit hospitals, charitable institutions, and mutualities (organized according to the criterion of belonging to the collective) with similar characteristics and few ties to government. Legislation regarding health care was minimal and restricted to work-related accidents (Belmartino, 1991, p. 15). Eventually, growth in the size and complexity of society and industry as well as insufficient private resources to finance health care services resulted in a popular call for government to take an active role in the organization of health care services. Many, but not all wanted more State intervention in health care. Some who did not were those who held power and prestige.

Nonetheless, Argentinean health care in the 1940s took on a new face. Strong labor organizations and support for the concept of social rights spurred a movement that placed the State in the role of "guardian" of social rights. Strong labor unions successfully pushed for a system of social health insurance through the *Obras Sociales*. The *Obras Sociales* and the Argentinean Medical Association (COMRA) together with the Confederation of Clinics and Hospitals representing the private sector defined the relationships of the health care sector. While initially these three disagreed with each other on policy issues, after 1955 they joined together in a common distrust for State proposed health policies (Belmartino, 1995, p. 8). Two things are worth noting regarding this event.

First, the union movement (which controlled the *Obras Sociales*) held enough political power to place the unions in a privileged negotiating position vis-à-vis the State; thus, they were often the recipients of "special favors." While publicly claiming to represent the rights of workers, the union movement internally generated unequal power relationships. The unions' hierarchical electoral system denied minorities representation and depended on the productive and financial capacities of the sector to which they belonged. Unions had access to funds for which they never were accountable, a source of additional power and corruption.

Second, the Argentinean Medical Association had a powerful corporate identity and role in the regulation of the job market. It "got involved in the design of policies and provided its expertise and support to consensual regulation attempts of health care practices in the private sector" (Belmartino, 1991, p. 19). These policies determined professional benefits, tax rates, free choice for professionals and others. Because the *Obras Sociales* in turn contracted the services of the private sector, it ensured that the private section and the union bureaucracy became the greatest beneficiaries. Obviously, as the role of the private sector and the *Obras Sociales* expanded, the role of the State in the regulation of health care diminished (Belmartino, 2000; Pautassi, 2001).

Over time, the Argentinean health care system grew increasingly unequal in its complexity and benefit coverage. Not only was the public sector reduced in importance and "recapitalized," but it also became "a catch-all for people without health coverage and for the chronically ill" (Pautassi, 2001, p. 25). The public system came to assume responsibility for "all preventive actions, the care of infectious diseases, psychiatric hospitalizations, and it also maintained a network of medical emergency services and hospital guards, especially in the provinces and in the most economically depressed regions" (Pautassi, 2001, p. 24). In essence, the public health sector grew to assume most of the services that were not profitable economically, and in fact, could fiscally drain a system.

The State attempted repeatedly to introduce rationality in the health care sector but their efforts failed. The most significant changes were put into place in the 1960s. Although the State tried to infuse efficiency and reason into the health care system, it passed a landmark law involving the *Obras Sociales* that actually broadened coverage "under a multiple professional system controlled by the unions" (Belmartino, 1991, p. 21).

With this legislation, the Argentinean health care system was consolidated and financed by the *Obras Sociales*. The law made coverage mandatory and employers were forced to contribute, establishing different levels of coverage. With significant power in the hands of the unions, the demand for *private enterprise* devoted to the health care services and medical technology also increased significantly. As mentioned before, the Argentinean Medical Association and the Confederation of Clinics and Hospitals negotiated these changes. As a result of these events, the private health care sector no longer had a responsibility to coordinate a rationale and effective health service. In fact, the full burden of responsibility for the regulation, control and supervision of the system was relegated to the public sector.

In 1966 the "Ministry of Social Welfare was created. It included the Health Care Secretariat which, supported by a group of public health professionals, attempted to reorganize the program . . . in accordance with technical and organizational directives prepared by the OPS/WHO" (Organization of Pan-American States/World Health Organization) (Belmartino, 1995, pp. 10-11). These ambitious proposals gave the public system the role of reorganizing the whole health care system, based on the OPS/WHO criteria for regionalization according to levels of complexity and the responsibility of creating nursing departments in ministries, health care secretariats and hospitals.

This decision was important for nursing since it gave it visibility by making nursing appear in the organizational charts of the institutions with corporate headquarters and clear command relationships. Even though in some cases nursing still reported formally to physicians (Director, Chief of Clinical Services, etc.) or was "an auxiliary" service, this inclusion in organizational charts was still a major milestone for nursing. This also pressured Universities to echo this demand and to prepare their students to hold managerial positions. Education in the area of administration was solid and still constitutes a central strength of the "licensed" (*Lincenciado*) nurse.

While a new national policy attempted to introduce more equity into Argentina's heterogeneous and fragmented health care system, most of the policy goals were not achieved. The weaker government could only move as allowed by the more powerful corporate sector. Indeed, some analysts use the term "corporate pact" to describe the corporate main actors, so the government was not able to oppose the position of powerful and dominant private corporations.

The government supported increased democratization, a broadening of basic benefits, and a reasoned use of technology. However, the system could function only as long as growth was maintained. Thus, the economic crisis, the liberalization of the economy, the shrinking of the industrial apparatus and the resulting reduction of the workforce, and a fall in real wages all negatively affected the functioning of the health care system. At the same time, private corporations attempted to maintain their advantage, thus increasing the fragmentation of health services and reducing the availability of health care services overall.

In 1973, just before the military junta, the Integrated National System of Health Services (*Sistema Nacional Integrado de Servicios de Salud*–SNISS) that had the same political affiliation as the union leadership, tried to strengthen the public health care system, but failed. By this time, the public sector was weak in all aspects of government, not only in health care. Additionally, it is interesting to examine the contradictions between words and actions as demonstrated by the military government during the (1976-1986) dictatorship. For instance, the Secretary of Public Health in the military government agreed with the positions of the Organization of American States (OAS) that were put forth during Alma Ata (in 1980). But, they failed to implement any of the policy recommendations such as: (a) regionalization of public health services, (b) expansion of public health coverage, and (c) coordination of the three sectors (public, private, and *Obras Sociales*) to avoid duplication of services. It is telling that during the military dictatorship, the national health care budget was reduced from 6% of GNP in 1975 to 2.5% of GNP in 1983.

In 1980, after 2 years of debate, the important *Obras Sociales* law passed. Heated debate over the role of government in health care provisions, especially whether or not health care provisions should cover life-threatening risks for working people, had blocked the passage of the law for over 2 years.

Further complicating matters, in the democratic period that began in 1983, the National Health Care Insurance Project was not handled as a global initiative and ended up a bargaining chip in the alliance with the unions. The negotiations ended with the issuance of revised *Obras Sociales* and National Health Care Insurance that had little relation to the original proposal.

Argentinean Health Care Reform of the 1990s

The government that assumed office in the 1990s did so with overwhelming support. The majority of the provincial governors, the parliament, and the unions supported it. In 10 years it achieved what authoritarianism had not been able to do in the previous decade. It re-instituted a neoliberal model, concurrently reducing the State's influence by means of discourse on efficiency and of a debate on "public vs. private." Still, this new version of neoliberal government contributed to the fragmentation of the labor movement.

In the "recipe" proposed by the World Bank (1993), one can recognize that the same two policies were applied to Argentina: (a) reduction in social expenditures and (b) focus on the expenditures, decentralization, deregulation, and privatization. In Argentina's health care field, the application of the recipe was manifested by *budget cutbacks* in health care (and also in other aspects related to social well-being that were directly related to the health of the population); by *focused programs* financed by international organizations (for instance, *Programa Materno Infantil–* Maternal and Infant Program PROMIN) soft credits; decentralization or the *transfer of national health care providers* to the *provinces and municipalities*; the *deregulation of the Obras Sociales*; and privatization that for the public hospitals meant the incorporation of *self-management* processes and for the private sector meant the *strengthening of private health insurance.* These policies exacerbated the existing fragmentation, thus "increasing the complexity, stratification, and inequality that were the most critical features" (Belmartino, 1992, p. 5).

Without a doubt, the deregulation of *Obras Sociales* was the most important change that took place in the health care sector. Deregulation allowed the beneficiary's free choice of *Obras Sociales* and opened the health care market to private capital (Tobar, 2000, p. 7). The World Bank awarded a credit of "375 million dollars between 1996 and 1997 for the purpose of restructuring the system of *Obras sociales*" (Findling et al., 2000, p. 130). This "restructuring" of the *Obras Sociales* attempted to guarantee a compulsory basic benefit (*Prestacion Médica Básica Obligatoria–*PMO), which consisted of medical benefits with universal characteristics guaranteed for all beneficiaries (Tobar, 2000). Different professional groups made up its composition increasing the cost of health care. At the same time, employee contributions were reduced. Those *Obras Sociales* that could not comply had to be merged or liquidated. Driving the above-mentioned strategies were the economic needs of the new capital accumulation pattern.

The *public sub-sector* was also affected, as Pautassi states, "the axis of the reform—discussed since 1991—this is based on a redefinition with respect to the role of the State in the health care system, on the future of the public hospital and its reconversion on the basis of criteria of efficiency and competitiveness" (Pautassi, 2001, p. 29). One strategy prior to the reform of the Public Hospital was strengthening the decentralization—started at the beginning of the 1980s— of the health care providers. Decentralization as social policy was argued for on the basis of its advantages to a highly bureaucratized State. But in actuality, "provinces confronting serious financial problems have transferred health care providers to the municipalities, dependent on the will and ability of local governments to consolidate their own health care services management hospitals" (Pautassi, 2001, p. 29). However, preventive actions, aid plans and programs, maternal child health programs, and, since 2002, the REMEDIAR (program for the supply of medications), continue to be the responsibility of the National Ministry of Health.

The Decree number 578 on Self-Managed Public Hospitals (*Hospitales Publicos de Autogestion*–HPA), issued in 1993, forces all agents that are part of the National System for Health Insurance (public and private service providers) to pay the benefits that their beneficiaries demand from public hospitals. Each Self Managed Hospital (HPA) has the power to: "I) carry out agreements with social security entities, ii) complement their services with those offered by other providers, iii) charge for the services to those that can pay for them or to third parties (*Obras Sociales*, prepays, etc.), and iv) provide medical care on an egalitarian basis and without distinction to all the population, and particularly is obliged to provide service to poor patients once their 'indigence' is verified" (Pautassi, 2001, p. 30). The decree states that the HPA will continue receiving the budget assigned to it by the corresponding jurisdiction and *according to the production, yield and type of population.*

The role of the World Bank's 375 million dollar credit for the reform of the *Obras Sociales* can also be perceived as ideological and financial support specifically targeting the reform of the Public Hospital as evidenced in the World Bank's 1995 report (quoted by Pautassi, 2001, p. 30). While there are no studies available about the impact of the health care system reform, presented at the time as an "alternative" to the existing situation, its implementation (824 hospitals in 1996) has led to demand segmentation, creating a division between those HPAs who have financial backing and those who do not. There are two groups of data that illustrate the effects that are becoming manifest:

1. Between 1980 and 1995, there was growth in the number of establishments devoted to providing aid, both public and private. The number offering ambulatory care doubled: in 1980 there were 6,038 health care providers without hospital admission while in 1995 the number rose to 12,775 (health care providers with internment went from 3013 to 3310). As Pautassi points out, the increase in the public sector is due to the primary care centers while in the private sector, the growth is clearly related to the addition of new technologies, including imaging, and diagnostics. These data exhibit a trend toward strengthening primary care (first level of attention) and the reduction in hospital admissions.

2. The composition of health care expenditures viewed as simple percentages is misleading, as pointed out by Pautassi (2001, p. 27). Health care was 4% of the GDP in 1987 and seemed to drop to 3.78% of the GDP in 1997. However, in absolute terms, these expenditures expanded at a constant rate: from 1980 until 1997 the total expenditures in the sector increased 40% while the expenditures per capita grew by 12%. This better analysis points to the importance of looking at all the data (for instance, while the consumption of medications decreased by 20% in 5 years, medication costs increased by 107% between 1991 and 1997).

The analysis of the portion of household finances going to health care expenditures shows the efforts that families make to cover the increasing gap between deteriorating coverage and benefits of the public care systems: in the case of Greater Buenos Aires, the National Poll on Home Expenditures 1996-1999 (carried out by the INDEC) revealed an increase in the total share of families' expenditures associated with "medical attention and health care costs" from 6.6% to 9.8%. The lower quintile of the poorest homes now apportions a significantly smaller share of their income to "health," 4.2% versus 9.1% that would indicate greater reliance on the public hospital service. The significance is that for the poorer families, public hospital services help reduce their health cost burden.

But as Belmartino (1995) points out, for the beneficiaries of the health care system, the changes do not constitute a favorable tradeoff. The stratification of access is now more transparent. While the financial situations of the public sector and of *Obras Sociales* may have improved and while the benefits provided by those suppliers with more concentrated services and with more technology may have broadened, the access and the quality of the care to the covered population have not improved.

PART 3: NURSING IN ARGENTINA

The 1990s application of neoliberal policies (and the abandonment of the Welfare State) produced adaptative changes that promoted: the auto-management within the health care public sub-sector; the members' free choice of which *Obras Sociales* to belong to (before, members were obligated to belong to the *Obras Sociales* according to their work category); and "pre-payments" as the way to improve financing of the private sector, through the contributions of the organized members, following the insurance model.

With the purpose of decentralizing and improving the internal efficiency of organizations, many sectors of the economy adopted strategies such as soft technologies in management and the privatization of those services conducive to being independent. Within the health team, nurses were seen as the most feasible professional to manage because of their educational background and the nature of nursing service (24 hours a day, 7 days a week).

On the other hand, in order to transfer labor costs to workers, neoliberalism promoted the increase of the so-called "professional" categories through a legal framework. For nursing, this trend meant the implementation of "Professional Practice Law," regulated in some provinces, as well as the creation of professional schools. These new laws promote more autonomy assuming self-regulation by the professionals to control and regulate themselves. These requirements have also been useful for stimulating and increasing the collaborative spirit among nurses and to inspire them to register as professionals. Additionally, these changes as well as the escalating demands of the health sector, increased the demand for higher education nursing programs.

Nursing "Auxiliary" to "Nurse" Completion Programs

Bridge programs were designed specifically for "nursing auxiliaries" (1-year non-university education programs) to complete the requirements for the title of "Nurse" (normally a 3-year non-university-based program). These 2-year completion programs are open to all nursing auxiliaries who have completed secondary education. University and non-university schools of nursing as well as the unions collaborated to create these programs because they understood the need for nursing auxiliaries (the largest percentage of nurses in Argentina) to advance in the field. The completion programs were first instituted through agreements with universities in the year 2000 and they have an ongoing positive impact on nursing in Argentina.

- *Enhanced Licenciados Workforce:* An increase in the number of university-prepared nurses with the qualification of "*Licenciados* in Nursing" through innovative techniques such as distance learning.
- *Nurses with Masters and Doctorates:* An increase the number of nurses with the qualification of *Licenciados* who also complete graduate degrees.
- *Creation of Graduate-Level Nursing Programs:* One masters level, one doctoral level, and one university-based nursing specialization program were opened in Argentina.

Nursing in the Context of Globalization in Argentina

Toward the end of the 1950s, concerns about the nursing workforce became widespread in Argentina. Development programs such as the National Development Program (*Program Nacional de Desarrollo*) and its philosophy of efficiency and rationalism had a great impact on health care. Provisions for nursing in the National Development Program called for the expansion of university-based nursing programs and the creation of departments of nursing in public hospitals. However, in the private sector, development initiatives for nursing were slow to take hold. One private sector strategy was to hire a small number of university-educated nurses to supervise and make decisions for large numbers of non-professional workers who provided the actual nursing services. The non-professional workers had little or no formal nursing education.

Departments for health "health care providers" were created. One of their responsibilities was to set the nursing wage structure and personnel policies (e.g., the departments determined nurses' job descriptions, benefits, and requirements for promotions within the system.) The disproportionate numbers within the nursing workforce, that is, the small numbers of university-educated nurses versus the large number of nursing paraprofessionals (nursing auxiliaries without a high school diploma and "nursing aids"—nurses trained in hospitals without any formal program) made it impossible for nursing departments in clinical settings to attain a rational division of nursing duties and responsibilities.

During the 1960s, the division of labor for nurses in Argentina became even more blurred. In response to recommendations made by international organizations, the Ministry of Health sponsored a large number of 1-year non-university-based educational programs to prepare *nursing auxiliaries* at both the national and provincial levels. As stated previously, students who completed middle school but who did not hold high school diplomas were allowed to enroll in nurse auxiliary programs.

The new programs for nurse auxiliaries had broad support from the PAHO/OPH. This effort has increased the complexity of the nursing workforce by adding new levels of non-professional nursing service providers. However, the initial purpose for creating educational programs for nursing "auxiliaries" had been to phase-out the role of the less prepared nurse aids. But instead, the lack of differentiated roles for nursing personnel and the rapid preparation of the new auxiliaries created large numbers of auxiliaries. They became a hegemonic presence in health care institutions. Their presence further blurred the role of the university-educated professional nurse, a situation that continues today despite the dramatic rise in the number of professional nurses. One explanation for the power of nursing auxiliaries is that because of the clear delineation of their subordinate role, they adapted much better than professional nurses to the needs and requirements of the hegemonic physician based medical power. Unlike professional nurses, auxiliary nurses follow medical orders without discussion or questioning. In brief, compared to professional nurses, nursing auxiliaries have very little autonomy, but because of their large numbers within the health care system, they wield power. The following Table 1 offers a breakdown of the numbers of nursing personnel while Table 2 offers workforce estimates for some health care professionals in Argentina.

Table 1 shows recent numbers of nursing personnel over a 25 year period. It shows a 52.67% increase in nurses. But, while professional nurses are increasing in number, nursing auxiliaries are, by far, the fastest growing category of workers in the nursing labor force. The gradual replacement of aids by nursing auxiliaries is another example of the "deskilling" in the nursing workforce.

Table 2 shows that growth in the overall number of health care workers has slowed over the last few years. The increase (61.1%) in professional nurses (licensed and university and non-university prepared nurses) is partly due to new education programs designed for nursing auxiliaries to gain certification as professional nurses. Between 1990 and 2000, the Ministry of Health, professional nursing associations and the Organization of American States (OAS) implemented these programs at

Table 1. Nursing Personnel in Argentina
(Absolute Values)

Educational level	1969[a]	1979[a]	1988[b]	1989[b]	1994[c]
Licenciatura	357	286	383	500	1,000
Professional nurse	14,114	16,090	17,118	19,800	25,000
Nursing auxiliary	8,862	24,746	21,820	26,000	49,000
Aids	16,894	2,529	24,988	25,000	10,000
Total	40,225	64,691	64,309	71,300	85,000

[a]CANARESA, 1980.
[b]Estimates from the Study of Nursing Schools and Services. Direction of Human Resources and OPS/OMS, 1988.
[c]Analysis of the situation and Plan for the Development of Nursing in the Argentinean provinces 1988-1994.

Table 2. Workforce Estimates for Health Care Professional
Categories 1992-1998

Category	1992	1998	Change (%)
Physicians	88,800	108,800	22.5
Dentists	21,900	28,900	32.0
Pharmacists	10,500	15,300	45.7
Biochemists	7,500	11,100	48.0
Psychologists	32,000	43,000	34.4
Kinegiologists (PT)	6,000	9,800	63.3
Dieticians/nutritionists	4,000	5,300	32.5
Professional nurses	18,000	29,000	61.1
Nursing aids	51,000	57,000	11.8
Public health engineers	1,000	1,000	0.0
Social workers	3,300	3,300	0.0
Veterinarians	11,500	13,000	13.0
Technicians (not including professionals)	90,000	11,100	−87.7
Administrators and general service workers	95,000	103,500	8.9
Total	442,492	440,100	−0.5

Source: Abramzón and Cadile (2001).

both the national and provincial levels. Today, those programs are still in place where the local demand for nurses continues. Abramzón and Cadile (2001) note the regional variation in the supply of nurses and urge analysts

> . . . to consider the context of the multiple transformations Argentinean nursing has undergone, the changes in the educational processes for professionalization, in the framework of the more complex practices than technology imposes on the professional model and the impact of reform on the health sector. These changes have affected different (geographical) jurisdictions to different extents. (p. 77)

While auxiliary nurses sought a higher level of quality academic preparation for the nursing workforce, the market valued the quantity rather than the quality of nursing personnel. This trend is related to several issues: I) nursing is viewed as an expenditure (not an investment), ii) there is little concern for the quality of nursing care, and iii) health providers demand nurses mainly for caring for the hospitalized patients.

In reality, there is a shortage of nursing personnel that is hidden by the failure of the health service to implement primary care (e.g., to develop health promotion and illness prevention programs and other health care providers of primary care— developed over the last decade). In Argentina "shortages" are measured merely by what physicians need, rather than by what patients or programs need. A true concern for the quality of patient care is not yet imbedded in the health care system.

In fact, no serious studies have been done in Argentina on the outcomes of quality patient care. Even in inpatient services, few studies measure patient care and nurse decision making as related to the levels of care. Therefore, there is no data to make comparisons among the types of care provided. Additionally, the differences between the care given and what care is actually necessary cannot be determined.

Table 2 also shows that nurses make up 9.54% of the health care workforce. The health care sector itself makes up 3% of the 15,500,000 strong national workforce as documented in the statistics provided by the National Institute for Statistics and Census (INDEC *Instituto Nacional de Estadistica y Censo*). Note, however, that because few statistics are available for the health care sector, data such as workforce availability can only be indirectly calculated using the number of university graduates in the professional categories as well as information provided by organizations.

Privatization and outsourcing health services to third parties have further diminished the quality of the aggregate information available. Thus, "important groups of people carrying out their activities in the sector and who are part of its workforce are not considered as such because their work is computed by the company or unit providing the service. . . . This has an impact on the calculation of the number of technical personnel" (Abramzón & Cadile, 2001, p. 75). This discrepancy could explain the decrease in "technicians" which includes third party contracted services such as transportation, housekeeping, food services, etc.

The problem of accurate statistics also appears when one classifies the various professional groups. Pautassi (2001, p. 46), followed the classification of Wainerman and Geldstein (1990), and identified the categories of: university professionals, technical workers and aids and helpers. The data is important because the title of nurse appears in all three groups. The following data represent the partial results from the 1998 Inventory of Health Care Resources and Services (*Catastro de Recursos y Servicios de Salud de 1998*) and are the most recent that have been published.

Tables 3 and 4 show a broad view of numbers of health professionals. Table 3 shows that for the most part, non-professional workers support professional nurses. Nurse aids with no formal education and nursing auxiliaries with 1 year formal education make up almost three-quarters (69.1%) of the positions, though there are significant regional variations. The shortage of professional nurses is disguised not only by the high ratio paraprofessionals to nurses but also by the oversupply of paraprofessionals (nursing auxiliaries and nurse helpers). Tables 4 and 5 show that physicians greatly outnumber nurses when nurses are considered in the aggregate as well as when they are divided into categories based on educational level.

However, nurse-physician ratios have actually improved slightly over the last decade. A 1993 study found one nurse for every 4.9 physicians while 5 years later in 1998 there was one nurse for every 3.5 physicians (Abramzón & Cadile, 2001, p. 78). This is still far from meeting the international standard of three nurses for every physician. There are many reasons for the lack of professional nurses and despite advances in nursing education, professional organizations and legislation, nursing in Argentina continues to be a discipline with "less social recognition than others and with low levels of pay" (Abramzón, 2003, p. 122).

PART 4: NURSING SALARIES AND WAGES

Argentinean health care workers have restrictive employment contracts with fixed wages based on a 36- to 40-hour work week. Neoliberal economic reforms implemented in the 1990s focused first and foremost on the deregulation of labor. Employment was an adjustment variable: "during the 1990s the search for labor flexibility became one of the driving forces in the management of personnel (. . .) Labor laws passed during that period adopted "flexibility" as essential criterion to reduce labor costs and foster a competitive environment" (Novik & Galin, 2003, p. 15).

Argentina successfully used neoliberalism's tenet of deregulation to create a more flexible and expendable workforce even though it makes workers' job security precarious. Argentinean health care workers are a unique group because they are made up primarily of professionals (more than 60% of them are professionals, while in other sectors of the Argentinean economy barely 10% of workers are professionals). Novik and Galin describe different factors of employment flexibility in the Argentinean health care sector:

1. In hiring conditions: (a) for an *indeterminate time*, typical of current hiring, (b) *temporary contracts*, which have combined with other types such as

Table 3. Nursing Positions

Nursing	Positions					Percentage				
	13 Provinces	Total 9 jurisdictions district capital	District Mendoza	Buenos Aires	TOTAL	13 Provinces	Jurisdictions district capital	Mendoza	Buenos Aires	TOTAL
Licenciatura nursing	345	688	30	660	1,723	1.6	4.2	1.2	3.6	2.9
University nursing	1,232	1,205	210	427	3,074	5.8	7.3	8.6	2.3	5.3
Professional nursing	2,093	3,687	229	7,242	13,251	9.8	22.5	9.4	39.5	22.7
Subtotal	3,670	3,580	469	8,329	18,048	17.2	34.0	19.3	45.4	30.9
Nursing auxiliaries	16,821	10,429	1,944	9,675	38,869	79.0	63.6	79.9	52.7	66.5
Nursing aids	795	400	21	350	1,566	3.7	2.4	0	1.9	2.7
Subtotal	17,616	10,829	1,965	10,025	40,435	82.8	66.0	80.7	54.6	69.1
TOTAL	21,286	16,409	2,434	18,354	58,483	100.0	100.0	100.0	100.0	100.0

Source: Abramzón (2003).

Table 4. Physician and Nursing Positions

	Human resources				
Positions	13 provinces	9 jurisdictions capital district	Mendoza	Buenos Aires	Total
Total nursing	21,286	16,409	2,434	18,354	58,483
Total physicians	21,824	26,836	2,874	26,530	78,064
Total human resources	85,949	83,813	9,788	83,806	263,356

Source: Abramzón (2003).

Table 5. Ratio Physician-Nurse According to Classification

Ratio	13 provinces	9 jurisdictions capital district	Mendoza	Buenos Aires	Total
Physicians/university nurses	17:7	22:3	13:7	62:1	25:4
Physicians/licenciatura in nursing	63:3	39:0	95:8	40:2	45:3
Physicians/professional nurses	10:4	7:3	12:6	3:7	5:9
Physicians/total professional nurses	5:9	4:8	6:1	3:2	4:3
Physicians/nursing auxiliaries	1:3	2:6	1:5	2:7	2:0
Physicians/nursing aids	27:5	67:1	136:9	75:8	49:8
Physicians/total non-professional nurses	1:2	2:5	1:5	2:6	1:9
Physicians/ total nurses	1:0	1:6	1:2	1:4	1:3

Source: Abramzón (2003).

subcontracting, internships and learning contracts; (c) *unregistered employment* ("under the table") and *free employment* or "volunteerism."
2. In pay: (a) based on time worked and (b) based on results. Both are used as mechanisms to reduce costs (for instance, by transforming a fixed wage into a wage for a specific task or benefit), or to increase motivation, stimulate productivity or increase the commitment to the institution.
3. In work shift: New forms of computing shifts to extend or flex the work shift appear based on "modular" criteria that are more responsive to demand fluctuations. This form of shift extension is "naturalized" in such a way that it does not involve the payment of overtime.
4. In the structure of work: this means the "tendency to subcontract and/or externalize some stages (such as cleaning, security, maintenance, etc.), the elimination of hierarchy (middle-level management); the reduction in systems of control and supervision; the introduction of new modes: work teams, work modules, etc.; cross-training; requiring greater understanding of processes and situations rather than concentration on their own work environment." All the above forms of employment structures are present in Argentina in the nursing labor market (2003, pp. 35-48).

Abramzón (2003), in analyzing the various *forms of contracting* for the professional category of "nurse" in Argentina, concluded that employment is the most frequent form for all categories and sub-sectors, 90% in the public sector. In contrast, the type of relationship based on a *"contract"* appears in the private sub-sector primarily for the category of "university nurses."

Still, in some provinces, many nurses are hired "by contract" since permanent positions have not been available since 1992. Also, private health care providers offer scholarships to auxiliary nursing students with low-paying internships promoted as a kind of "contract" to them. This scholarship-internship package gives private health providers a two-fold advantage: (a) it allows them to pay workers low (internship) wages while at the same time (b) it enhances the providers' prestige because intern contracts are obtained through agreements with universities.

The most notable change pertains to the loss of strong structures in nursing departments, so instead of a hospital nursing department chair whose sole responsibility was to manage the nursing staff, now there is the chair (even though still perhaps a nurse) whose responsibility is to manage the hospital's entire health cares service.

Also, some nursing professionals transform themselves into "managers" and contract themselves out to provide nursing services to a hospital or to a specific service. A positive outcome of this practice is that professional nurses with better education are increasingly sought out. This characteristic has given nursing a greater competitive edge over other health care professionals.

Nursing and Gender

Gender issues in Argentinean nursing are a rarely studied topic and the data that do exist are not always easy to interpret. Gender comparisons are often impossible because the data sets of nursing and health care workers are not always categorized by sex. A landmark study by Laura Pautassi entitled *Equidad de género y calidad en el empleo: las trabajadoras y los trabajadores en salud en Argentina* (Gender equity and quality of employment: female and male health workers in Argentina) is regarded as the most complete and timely study on the topic. It identifies important issues in the Argentinean health care workforce and recommends ongoing analysis of the problem. With the reform of the Argentinean health care system in the 1990s, the gender breakdown of health care workers became a pressing issue. Pautassi found that (a) personnel costs in the health care sector make up the largest percentage of its expenditures, (b) health care workers in service organizations occupy the role of "social agent," and (c) health care workers engage in symbolic exchanges and social relationships that mobilize the process of illness care. Still, the health care sector has not yet accounted for the gender composition of its workforce which can impact all three of these factors. Implications for nursing in Argentina are particularly acute since nursing is historically a "feminine" occupation made up of over 70% women (Pautassi, 2001).

Women in the Argentinean health care sector make up the largest proportion of workers in intermediate level positions, while males make up the largest proportion of workers (a ratio of 2:1) in upper level positions (Pautassi, 2001, p. 40). The majority of women (42%) work in the public sector, with 26% in the private sector. Educational levels of workers are higher in the public sector, which corresponds to the type of benefits and practices. For example, in the private sector, there are greater numbers of housekeeping, food, and aid services that do not require qualified personnel.

The median income of women employed as direct caregivers is 73% that of males (Pautassi 2001, p. 42). This percentage may be influenced by the fact that women generally work fewer hours than men. Another peculiarity of the health care sector is that "women in supervisory positions are 43.67% of all supervisors, a proportion that is significantly larger than that found in the economy as a whole (18.1%)" (Pautassi, 2001, p. 43). Still another feature of the sector is the larger number of males in technical levels positions and in semi-qualified levels, while the number of women in professional categories increases. This increase in female professionals is related to the feminization of university enrollments (Saber, 1997, p. 4).

Pautassi (2001) cites three factors influencing the increasing number of males entering the health professions:

1. an employment crisis that led males to seek employment in health care,
2. the supposed greater cost of employing women due to maternity leaves and higher incidences of absenteeism, and
3. the change in historical patterns of occupations such as nursing. (p. 41)

The presence of males in the Argentinean nursing profession is not negative. Rather, it produces a positive change in the historic social definition of nursing as a "feminine" field. However, interviews with female nurses reveal worrisome trends "that discriminatory ideas persist (e.g., the stereotype of male nurses as homosexual) and the idea that more males in nursing will simply reproduce the patterns of domination connected to the hegemonic medical model" (Pautassi, 2001, p. 51).

Unions, Professional Associations, and Nursing *"Colegios"*

In general, the success of a professional workforce such as nursing is directly related to organizational forms that enhance best practices. When key players collaborate well, more positive outcomes are possible both inside and outside the profession (e.g., in its ability to influence public policy). Autonomy distinguishes a profession from an occupation and is linked to the institution granting professional certification.

In Argentina, certification helps the professions maintain reliability and autonomy in practice. Nursing certification is awarded by the professional *"Colegios,"* organizations at the local level to control professional practice and are made up of professionals delegated by the state and the Provincial Ministries of Health. *Colegios* are the "first [local] level organizations charged with the administration of mandatory requirements for the exercise of the profession both in private practice and in staff employment relationships" (Pautassi, 2001, p. 48). Second level organizations are aggregates of the first level ones, for instance, the Federations that bring together *"Colegios."* Third level organizations, Confederations, such as the Medical Confederation of the Argentinean Republic (*Confederacion Medica de la Republica de Argentina*–COMRA), coordinate with the second level organizations and are responsible for creating a compatible national system to respond to questions related to the practice of the profession and to the functioning of the insurance system.

Struggles for status and autonomy characterize the history of professional nursing organizations in Argentina. The professional organizations seek to reinforce the social need for nursing. Yet, the Nursing Professional Practice law, issued in 1994, has been enforced in only a few provinces; only three provinces have nursing professional *"colegios."* In the remaining provinces, physicians still manage and control professional nursing.

History of Nursing Associations

Although formal professional nursing education began at the first Argentinean School of Nursing founded by Dr. Cecilia Grierson in Buenos Aires in 1886, the first nursing association was not created for almost another 50 years. It was created in 1935 by Monsignor Miguel de Andrea in response to a call by Pope Pius XI to formally bring Catholic nurses together in an association (Heredia, 2004). This group later joined with the Catholic Union of Nurses and the Association of Catholic Samaritans and Nurses to create the "Federated Association of Catholic Nurses." In 1946, during the presidency of General Juan D. Peron, the government offered the Federated Association of Catholic Nurses the chance to become the "Union of Nurses" as long as they were willing to stop using the word *Catholic* in their name and adopt the postulates of the official Argentinean government. The Federation rejected the proposal. In response, the government created the private sector public health workers guild (ATSA), the first guild representing health care workers, including, but not restricted to, nursing.

A few years later in 1953, the "Argentinean Association of Nursing Instructors" was created as a result of Argentinean professionals meeting at the 4th Regional Congress of Nursing held in Brazil. And 4 years after that, in 1957, the Argentinean Association of Nursing Instructors was transformed into the "Argentinean Association of Diploma Holding Nurses." This association has legal status and functions as a national nursing organization. Since Argentina is politically organized along federal lines, provincial level associations also exist in Santa Fe, Cordoba, Entre Rios, Tucuman, Buenos Aires, and Salta. These provincial nursing associations joined together in 1965 to form the "Argentinean Federation of Nursing" (FAE), referred to in some publications as the Argentine Nursing Federation (Perich, 2004), and based in the nation's capital. This Federation remains active today. Its objective, as stated in its bylaws, is to improve the quality of life of the Argentinean people by serving without discrimination as a nucleus of member organizations, associations, *colegios,* and other groups.

In 1967 another professional nursing organization, the "Association of University Schools of Nursing of the Argentinean Republic," or AEUERA, was created. AEUERA is a consortium of four universities including the Universities of Tucuman, Cordoba, del Litoral (now the National University at Rosario), and Buenos Aires. AEUERA collaborates with the Association of Medical Schools of the Argentinean Republic and with the PAHO's Office of Public Health connected to the WHO.

The Civic Association of Tertiary Schools of Nursing of the Argentinean Republic (ACETERA) is another professional nursing association made up of Tertiary Schools of Nursing. Tertiary Schools of Nursing are non-university affiliated schools that award nursing degrees after a program of study equivalent to that of the first cycle of the *licenciatura.*

In 1999, AEUERA and FAE developed a set of professional nursing standards for the first decade of the millennium. The group determined that professional nursing organizations should serve as the leadership vehicle to promote and consolidate a united profession, to strengthen nursing's identity and image, and to enhance nursing's position and recognition within society.

For over 10 years, professional nursing organizations and PAHO have supported Argentinean nurses in their campaign to transform nursing toward:

1. the essential and comprehensive development of human resources at all levels in nursing;
2. the development of nursing services;
3. the creation of nursing laws;
4. the increased participation by nurses in the political arena and in decision-making processes affecting health;
5. the development of professional associations; and
6. the incentives to produce and disseminate new nursing knowledge.

Argentinean law allows individual provinces to create professional "*Colegios*" which are responsible for professional certification. However, as noted previously, only a handful of provinces in Argentina have done so. In the remaining provinces, nursing certification is carried out by the respective Health Ministries under provisions made by the National Law for the Practice of Nursing (Law 24.004/91).

Argentinean professional nursing associations maintain relationships with a variety of international institutions. They have particularly strong links to the Canadian Nursing Association, the Regional Commission of MERCOSUR, the Pan-American Federation of Nursing Professionals (FEPEN), the Latin American Association of Nursing Schools (ALADEFE), and the Geneva-based International Council of Nursing (ICN). Without doubt, some of the greatest benefits of the ongoing partnerships have been the transnational collaboration and support as well as the mutual exchange of knowledge and the opportunity to develop projects together. Also, the international nursing community has supported the positions and advocated for the requests made by nurses on the Argentinean national scene.

Finally, it is important to point out how Argentinean nursing as a discipline has changed as a result of its participation in national and international professional organizations. For example, international organizations oppose the deskilling of nurses and support educational incentives that move nurses through the educational process in a rational manner. Technical nurses are given the opportunity to return to school to obtain professional qualifications. Reciprocity among programs and reciprocal licensure agreements cross-nationally allow nurses to study and work abroad more easily. Yet, despite significant efforts to create professional associations, nursing has not been able to create a union capable of representing and defending the rights of the professional nursing workforce. Interestingly, nursing is one of the few professions in Argentina unable to achieve this goal.

The development of the major nursing organizations is consistent throughout the country. For example, nearly all of the provinces have a local branch of the "Argentinean Nurses Association." However, relatively few provinces (three) have local branches of the *Colegios*. The FAE has long-term stability and as an organization, it has participated most actively in national decision making and in political action (e.g., it is a consulting member of the COFESA Federal Health Council, and it advises the National and Provincial Health Ministries on health policy making, although their inclusion is not permanent). Despite these gains and its voice in the wider political realm, FAE has been unable to implement changes vis-à-vis the job market. Rather, the job market is the domain of the unions and the FAE's counterpart, the Argentinean Medical Association, has had an important role in the health care job market for many decades.

Partly as a consequence of the above, the solidarity needed to establish a self-regulating workforce is not present. Additionally, the prevailing individualism in nursing weakens the struggle for nursing labor rights. And, poor leadership characterizes the labor organizations representing nurses. Also, since professional certification processes for nurses are controlled by non-nursing organizations, the profession is further fragmented and stripped of power in that area.

MERCOSUR

MERCOSUR is a regional trade alliance or block in South America. Its goals are to allow free circulation of goods, people, services, and skills and to establish common tariffs and trade policies. Also known as the "Common Market of the South," MERCOSUR created a free trade area including Argentina, Brazil, Paraguay and Uruguay. Bolivia and Chile are affiliated members. Since its inception in 1991, the MERCOSUR partnership has influenced advances in the health care sector. MERCOSUR's health care focus is to analyze common problems, to establish epidemiological programs, and to collect and analyze relevant information regarding (a) health problems, (b) resources and other factors affecting health problems, (c) health sector development and operation policies, and (d) population trends regarding growth, aging, urbanization, and predominant pathologies. The "MERCOSUR Regional Council of Nursing" and the FAE brings together nursing scholars from member countries. The group has worked for several years to create explicit statements concerning common nursing competencies expected of nurses with the "*licenciados*."

Legislation of Professional Practice in Nursing

Two important laws, one passed in 1967 and other in 1991, regulate professional nursing practice in Argentina. Law number 17,132, passed in January 1967, defined professional nursing practice as "the daily performance of activities related to the care and assistance of the sick." Nursing included "personal collaboration with the physician or with dentist." While Law 17,132 described nursing and medicine as collaborative professions, the two professions were not equal under the law. In fact, Law 17,132 mandated nurses to act "only under the direction and control of physicians, within the limits authorized by their certification and under the conditions of existing regulations."

But National Law number 24,004 brought important legal changes to professional nursing in Argentina. Passed on September 26, 1991, Law 24,004 superceded the earlier law and gave Argentinean nurses an impressive leap into the future. Under the new law "within the limits of competency derived from the respective professional certification, nurses were given the authority to (a) autonomously promote health and wellness, (b) carry out disease prevention and screening tests, (c) provide nursing interventions and treatments, and (d) engage in rehabilitation measures. Moreover, teaching, research, consulting in their area of expertise, and the management of services was also considered part of professional nursing practice as long as the services are carried out by individuals authorized by the above law to practice nursing." Law 24,004 clearly discriminates the functions of the professional nurse from that of the auxiliary nurse with the latter working under the direction and/or supervision of the professional nurse.

Nursing Higher Education in Argentina

Argentinean nursing education has evolved significantly since the late 19th century when Cecilia Grierson, the first Argentinean female physician, founded the first school of nursing in Buenos Aires. Since that time many historical and political factors helped shape the development of nursing and nursing education.

For example, before 1947, the State had no control over the academic education of nurses. Academic nursing education took place without standardized requirements regarding prior academic background or over professional certification. In fact, until 1947, a large number of people practiced nursing without having any academic preparation at all.

In 1947, the Argentinean Secretary of Health created the "Public Health Cultural Commission." The Commission designed a model school of nursing, which implemented an innovative curriculum based on the International Nursing Council (*Consejo Internacional de Enfermeria*–CIE) standards and essentials. The first to complete the new program was a group dedicated to nursing education, not just to nursing practice. As a result, a decision was made for the new schools to be administered by nurses who specialized in education. A diploma from junior high school or, alternatively, a diploma from elementary school and a passing score on a general aptitude exam qualified a person for admission into the school. Later, the curriculum was extended to 3 years and the practical contents were consolidated.

Although the preparation of nurses working in public health and in community health centers improved somewhat during that period, the focus was on preparing nurses to function in acute care, inpatient settings. The capacity of the public hospital sector in Argentina grew dramatically during this time and quickly absorbed the graduates from the new nursing schools.

As a result of political economic shifts in the world capitalist system, Argentinean policy makers began to target specifically cost cutting efforts and on economic efficiency and development in general. After 1955, significant revisions in Argentinean national policy sought to optimize resources in the health care system including the cost of educating health care professionals.

A review carried out by PAHO/WHO in 1956 found irregularities specifically in the field of nursing. The PAHO study reported that the majority of Argentina's 120 schools of nursing did not comply with existing national regulations. Among other suggestions, the PAHO evaluators recommended the creation of nursing schools within the universities and emphasized the need to prepare nurse administrators and educators capable of improving nursing education as well as nursing care.

Some nursing schools within universities existed prior to 1956. In 1942, for example, the *Universidad Nacional del Litoral* created the first "School for Nurses and Hygiene Visitors" in the city of Rosario. However, shortly after its foundation, it was closed down by the national government. The feverish activity of *Peronism* during this period spurred the Eva Perón Foundation to create a School of Nursing in 1950. Though not university-based, the school was "oriented to medical and social specialization" (Rapoport, 2006, p. 327). Later and beginning in 1952, schools of nursing appeared in the following national universities: Tucuman in 1952; Cordoba in 1956; Rosario in1958; and Buenos Aires in 1960.

Still, as a result of the 1956 PAHO study, there was a 5-year agreement between the Argentinean government and the PAHO, which had PAHO external consultants to help design the curriculum for the new Argentinean nursing schools. The consultants also advised local professionals and scholars on ways to modernize existing programs in nursing and public health as well as in the overall administration of health care services.

Without a doubt, incorporating nursing in the university produced a change in the profession's status, making it more attractive. The length of time it took to complete a nursing program was reasonable (compared to other academic programs) and the opportunity for employment at the completion of the degree was high.

During the 1970s, new university-based nursing programs were created and by 1989, a total of 21 nursing programs existed. Most of the new programs were part of the public university system, although some were at private universities. With these new programs, all the provinces had their own university-based nursing schools. There were also 36 non-university schools controlled by the Superintendence of Private Schools, a branch of the National Health Ministry.

However, despite the number of schools and the significant increase in the number of incoming students, a high dropout rate led to low (program completion) graduation rates, leaving persistent lack of qualified nurses.

In response to pressure by service provider administrators to increase the number of nurses in the labor pool and recommendations by international health organizations to follow the U.S.-based model for the use of "nursing auxiliaries," training programs for nursing auxiliaries were created in 1960. Education programs for nursing auxiliaries requires candidates to complete junior high school before entering the 9-month long program of study to become a nursing auxiliary.

In 1967 the university-based program of study toward the nursing degree was split into two phases. The degree of "technician" is awarded upon completion of Phase One. The degree of *Licenciado* in Nursing is awarded on completion of Phase Two and offered only at the university level.

The *Licenciado* prepares nurses for leadership positions in management, staff development, and research. However, the State created nursing leadership positions during the 1950s that were filled by nurses who did not have the educational qualifications to assume such positions. As noted, the health sector is fragmented; as one example, in the case of the public health sector in the Province of Rosario, all the administrative positions are in charge of *Licenciados*, who must apply for positions through a public competition. The need for university-educated professional nurses must be addressed by the Ministry of Health as well as the Ministry of Education.

To regulate and supervise the non-university schools of nursing and the nurse aid programs, a 1968 agreement was passed that unified and streamlined the criteria and competencies of the different nursing educational programs. The agreement was responsible for regulating academic education programs in nursing and assigning appropriate levels of preparation to university and non-university professional nursing courses.

In 1989, an important study carried out by the PAHO on nursing in Argentina showed that from a total of 57 university and non-university schools of nursing, only 500 students graduated each year. It also showed a high 60% dropout rate and a significant shortage of professional nurses. Even more troublesome was the PAHO finding that little connection existed between nursing education and nursing service and that great disparities existed within nursing programs and levels of education (OPS/OMS, 1995, p. 43).

As a result of this and other studies, the Plan for the Integral Development of Nursing was launched with the participation of various stakeholders: service providers; educational institutions; professional associations; and national, provincial, and municipal government organizations. The PAHO supported the effort through its local representatives. The Plan for Integral Development instituted a strategy of offering additional education to nurses so that they could upgrade their skills and become qualified at a higher level. For example, nursing auxiliaries were offered educational opportunities to study to become nurse technicians, while technicians were offered educational opportunities to study for the *licenciatura*, and so forth. The Plan for Integral Development also instituted other innovations: (a) distance learning programs for Licenciatura candidates, (b) nursing internships and residencies, (c) specialization courses in nursing, (d) nursing and interdisciplinary graduate programs leading to the master's degree, and (e) doctoral programs in nursing.

The inclusion of innovative educational techniques (distance education systems) initiated during the 1990s at the Universities of Cordoba and Rosario has had a great impact on enrollment and has been extended to the majority of university-based schools of nursing by means of inter-university and training agreements for the application of these technologies. There was great enthusiasm among the personnel in achieving increased levels of education. Significant growth in the professional nursing category occurred as a consequence of the changes detailed above. During 1999, the 17 nursing schools based at national universities produced 1,334 graduates. Fifty-three percent of the graduates were "nurses" (having completed Phase One of the university education) and 47% were *licenciados* in nursing (having completed Phases One and Two of the university program. This process received broad support through the "Nursing Policies for the Decade of 2000" issued by the Argentinean Federation of Nursing.

Regarding graduate studies, the majority of the master's degree granting programs developed in Argentina have an interdisciplinary design, although there is one program that focuses on nursing administration at the National University of Rosario and another that focuses on maternal child health nursing at the National University of Cordoba. The first doctoral program in nursing science and philosophy was created in 2001 at the National University of Tucuman. Today, the Universities of Rosario, Cordoba, and Buenos Aires offer interdisciplinary doctoral programs that include nursing content.

Clearly, this noticeable transformation of professional nursing education is the result of collaboration and joint action by academics, service providers, and representatives of professional nursing associations. One must also note the valuable contributions of the national and provincial health and education ministries as well as the contributions of international organizations such as the WHO/PAHO and the K. W. Kellogg Foundation. What happened to nursing education in Argentina is an indication of nursing's passion for growth and for enhanced abilities to contribute to community health issues. This passion exists despite the fact that health care providers fail to provide incentives for the continuing education of their personnel.

It is important to note that Argentina is slow to modernize its health care system, particularly in terms of innovative best practices. Currently, Argentina's health care system needs to strengthen its programs for disease prevention and community health care. The hegemonic role of the physician and the lack of a mechanism for nurses to participate in decision making, planning, labor organization, and political circles only postpones and makes it more difficult for the public to take advantage of the transforming potential of nursing. It also discourages new generations of professional nurses working productively and makes it more attractive for them to emigrate to other countries or into other professions as they search for advancement.

A LOOK TO THE FUTURE: CHALLENGES FOR THE THIRD MILLENNIUM

The prediction for the future involves increasing globalization and neoliberal reforms in Argentina specifically and in Latin America in general. In this context it not possible to anticipate the precise role nursing will assume. However, it is safe to say that the health care system will become more complex and difficult for patients to maneuver. Consequently, nursing will have to overcome its current isolationism from other professions and push for greater integration and coordination. Only then will Argentinean nursing really respond to the increasing health and social needs of its people.

To be more effective and future-oriented, Argentinean nursing can benefit from focusing not only on its internal development, but also on helping to shape relationships in other sectors and in community development at both the local and national levels. As a result, Argentinean nursing will be able to increase its visibility and become recognized as a powerful force among health care workers. By moving beyond their differences and using their common strengths, Argentinean nurses in different sectors (e.g., education, service, and labor organizations) can work together collaboratively to foster change. In this way, they can serve as advocates for nursing as a profession as well as for Argentinean society as a whole.

The production of a qualified nursing workforce through advanced education is an essential element for the advancement of the nursing profession. Therefore, and despite the progress achieved to date, it is necessary, in the authors' opinion, to pursue the actions required to address the following priorities:

Priority 1 considers the role of nursing, including its position in the health care system and addresses the historical and social nature of nursing care. Priority 1 was drafted because nursing practice in Argentina is essentially the traditional view with an acute care, bio-medical focus. It is not well oriented toward a changing health care environment. Also, despite nursing education's focus on public health issues, nursing practice does not reflect this trend.

Priority 2 considers that while nursing care services are regarded as the autonomous axis of the profession, no clear definition of nursing practice exists that focuses on the clinical aspect of care.

Priority 3 considers the need to produce new knowledge, theories, and practices in light of the fact that scientific nursing evidence and texts are minimal in Argentina.

Priority 4 focuses on the necessity to develop a single degree awarded in the university setting so that nursing can develop within the context of other disciplines. The proposal would be that two levels of nursing preparation exist (both granted by the university system): one for the *Licenciado* degree, a 5-year program and granted by universities, and the other a nursing technician degree, a 3-year program. The technician degree may also be granted by the Tertiary Schools of Nursing (non-university institutions). Although different institutions could develop such programs, the curriculum must comply with that stipulated in a national law framed by the Ministry of Education (similar to decree law 35/69).

While the *Licenciatura* was an important achievement because this type of academic preparation offered nurses the possibility to develop and form independent practice, no higher levels of professional self-sufficiency has been achieved to date by the degree. Moreover, its insertion into clinical practice did not produce significant changes in the quality of care and it has not been possible to define a differentiated role with respect to the rest of the nursing team.

The newly-designed nursing graduate courses and curricula desperately need to be expanded geographically so as to provide skills in the conceptualization and implementation of change strategies, to influence and increase the viability, and to take better advantage of the current structure of the profession.

Finally, the development of nursing research networks is vital. These network can provide the necessary information to conceptualize and implement transformative programs in nursing. The support given to the doctorate in nursing is fundamentally important to the future of nursing in Argentina.

REFERENCES

Abramzón, M. C. (2003). Los recursos humanos en salud en Argentina. Una mirada a los datos [Human resources in health in Argentina: Looking to the data]. *observatorio de recursos humanos en salud en Argentina*. Información estratégica para la toma de decisiones. OPS. Programa de desarrollo de Recursos Humanos en las reformas sectoriales de salud (OPS/OIT/CEPAL) Representación OPS/OMS en Argentina. No. 58, pp. 91-166.

Abramzón, M. C., & Cadile, M. del C. (2001). Recursos humanos en salud en Argentina: Análisis de su evolución 1992-1998 [Human resources in health in Argentina: Analysis of its evolution 1992-1998]. *Recursos Humanos de Salud En Argentina/2001* (pp. 61-82). Observatorio de Recursos Humanos en Salud. Representación OPS/OMS en Argentina.

Araújo de Mattos, R. (2002). Las agencias internacionales y las políticas de salud en los años 90: Un panorama general de la oferta de ideas [International organizations and health policies in the nineties: A general overview]. *Cuadernos Médico Sociales, 82*, 77-93.

Areces, N. (1999). *Historia II* [History II]. Mimeo. Cátedra Historia II. Facultad de Ciencias Políticas. Universidad Nacional de Rosario.

Arzani, E., & Micozzi, T. (2003). Niveles de enfermería en la República Argentina y políticas de desarrollo [Levels of nursing levels in Argentina and development policy]. Cátedra Enfermería Comunitaria y Hospitalaria. Escuela de Enfermería. Universidad Nacional de Rosario: Rosario. Argentina.

Asociación de Escuelas Universitarias de Enfermería de la República Argentina [AEUERA]. (1967). *Acta Fundacional AEUERA* [AEUERA Constitutive Acts].

Belmartino, S. (1989). La crisis de las políticas sociales: Discusión de una alternativa [The social policy crisis: The debate for an alternative]. *Cuadernos Médico Sociales, 55,* 49-50.

Belmartino, S. (1991). Políticas de salud en Argentina: Perspectiva histórica [Healthcare policy in Argentina: A historical perspective]. *Cuadernos Médico Sociales, 55,* 13-33.

Belmartino, S. (1992). El sistema de salud en Argentina: Perspectivas de reformulación [The healthcare system in Argentina: Perspectives on reform]. *Cuadernos Médico Sociales, 61,* 1-5.

Belmartino, S. (1995). Estado y obras sociales: Desregulación y reconversión del sistema [The state and the social security system: Deregulation and reconversion]. *Cuadernos Médico Sociales, 72,* 5-24.

Belmartino, S. (2000). Argentina: Nuevas modalidades y espacios de regulación en la Seguridad Social Médica. Estado y Sociedad. Las nuevas reglas de Juego [Argentina: New regulation in Social Medical Security in the state and society: New rules of the game]. Oscar Oszlak (compilador). Vol. 2. *Colección CEA (Centro de Estudios Avanzados).* Eudeba. Buenos Aires, pp. 185-215.

Collier, P., & Dollar, D. (2002). Aid allocation and poverty reduction. *European Economic Review, 46*(8), 1475-1500.

Davis, M. (1998). *Prisoners of the American dream: Politics and Economy in the history of the U.S. working class.* Verso, American London.

Ferrer, A. (1996). *Historia de la Globalización. Orígenes del orden económico mundial [The history of globalization: Origins of the world economic order].* Fondo de Cultura. Económica, Buenos Aires.

Findling, L., Tamargo, M. del C., & Redondo, A. (2000). Las obras sociales ante la desregulación estatal: Actores y estrategias [Social Security faces state deregulation: Actors and strategies]. Estado y Sociedad. Las nuevas reglas de Juego. Oscar Oszlak (compilador).Vol. 2. *Colección CEA (Centro de Estudios Avanzados).* Eudeba. Buenos Aires, pp. 121-133.

Heredia, A. M. (2004). Educación en enfermería en la Argentina. Su último medio siglo [Nursing education in Argentina: It's last half century]. *Asociación de Escuelas de Enfermería de la Capital Federal (AECAF).*
http://www/mercosulsalud.org.spanhol/links/LinksUruguai.htm

Kosacoff, B. (1995). *Hacia una estrategia exportadora: La experiencia Argentina, el marco regional y las reglas multilaterales* [Toward an export strategy: The Argentinean experience, regional framework and multilateral regulation] (423 pp.). Buenos Aires: Universidad Nacional de Quilmes.

Larousse Enciclopedia médica [Larousse medical dictionary] (5th ed.). (1997). Barcelona, España (Spain): Historia Universal.

Laurell, A. C. (1992). La política social en el proyecto neoliberal. Necesidades económicas y realidades sociopolíticas [Social politics under neoliberalism: Economic needs and socio-political realities]. *Cuadernos Médico Sociales, 60,* 3-17.

Lerner, L., & Garcia Raggio, A. (1991). El discurso neoliberal en las políticas sociales [Neoliberal rhetoric in social policy]. *Cuadernos Médicos Sociales, 58,* 33-45.

Lerner, L. (1992). *Análisis crítico de las Políticas Sociales* [Critical análisis of social policy]. Cátedra de Medicina Preventiva y Social. Curso de post grado. Facultad de Ciencias Médicas. Universidad Nacional de Rosario.

Luna, F. (1996). *Yo soy roca* ["I am a rock"]. Ed. Atlántida.

Novick, M., & Galin, P. (2003). *Flexibilidad del mercado de trabajo y precarización del empleo. El caso del sector salud* [Labor market flexibility and employment destabilization]. Observatorio de Recursos Humanos en Salud en Argentina. Información estratégica para la toma de decisiones. OPS. Programa de desarrollo de Recursos Humanos en las reformas sectoriales de salud (OPS /OIT/ CEPAL) Representación OPS/OMS en Argentina. No. 58. Octubre, 11-90.

Organización Panamericana de la Salud [OPS/OMS]. (1995). *Dessarrollo en enfermeria en Argentina 1985-1995: Análisis de situación y lineas de trabajo* [Nursing development in Argentina 1985-1995: Situational analysis and labor force] (44 pp.). Argentina.

Pautassi, L. (2001). Equidad de género y calidad en el empleo: Las trabajadoras y los trabajadores en salud en la Argentina [Gender equity and employment quality: Female and male healthcare workers in Argentina]. Unidad Mujer y Desarrollo. Proyecto CEPAL-GTZ Institucionalización del Enfoque de Género en la CEPAL y en Ministerios Sectorial. *Serie Mujer Desarrollo No. 30.* Naciones Unidas, CEPAL, ECLAC. Santiago de Chile, 84 páginas.

Perich, E. (2004). *Nuestras organizaciones* [Our organizations]. Asociación de Enfermería de Capital Federal. Edición Especial 50 aniversario AECAF Buenos Aires, Argentina.

Previch, R. (1949). *El desarrollo económico de América Latina y alguna de sus principales problemas* [The economic development of Latin America and its main issues]. Santiago de Chile: Secretaria Ejecutiva de la Comisión Económica para América Latina (CEPAL).

Rapoport, M. (2006). *Historia económica, política y social de la Argentina (1880-2003)* [Economic, political and social history of Argentina] (1st ed.). Buenos Aires: Editorial Ariel.

Romero, J. L. (2002). Breve Historia de la Argentina [A brief history of Argentina]. *Fondo de Cultura Económica.* Séptima edición, Buenos Aires.

Saber, G. (1997). *Enfermería, Profesión de Mujeres. Un estudio de caso* [Nursing, a woman's profession: A case study]. Universidad Nacional de Santiago del Estero. Presentación en el Encuentro de la Latin American Studies Association. Guadalajara, México, Abril, 18 páginas.

Tobar, F. (2000). *Economia de las reforamas de los seguros de salud en Argentina* [The economic reform of the social security health insurance system in Argentina]. Organización Panamericana de la Salud (OPS/OMS). Retrieved April 26, 2004, from http://www.PAHO.org/espanish/HDP/HDD/tobar.pdf

Tobar, F., Garraza, L. G., Monsalvo, M., & Falbo, R. (2002). Impacto de la politica nacional de medicamentos en al ano 2002 [The impact of national politics on prescription drug policy in the year 2002]. Retrieved April 26, 2004, from http://www.federicotobar.com.ar/pdf/publicaciones/17.pdf

Wainerman, C. H., & Geldstein, R. N. (1990). *Condiciones de Vida y de Trabajo de las Enfermeras en la Argentina* [Living and working conditions for nurses in Argentina]. CENEP. Centro de Estudios de Población, Buenos Aires.

World Bank. (1993). *World development report: Investing in health.* Oxford, England: Oxford University Press.

CHAPTER 5

Nursing in Brazil[1]

Maria da Gloria Miotto Wright,
Maria Cecília Puntel de Almeida,
Maria Itayra Coelho de Souza Padilha,
Helena M. S. Leal David,
Gelson Luiz de Albuquerque,
and Jaqueline Da Silva

Brazil is the largest nation in South America and the only Portuguese speaking country in the Americas. Nineteenth and early 20th century Brazil developed as a peripheral capitalist state, with globalization taking over in the late 20th century. For 21 years between 1964 and 1985, Brazil was run by a military dictatorship. Currently, global and local insecurities have influenced Brazilian nationalized health and education systems and affected the complexities of the health care workforce.

The chapter "Nursing in Brazil" conceptualizes nursing as a social practice and uses Wright's (2000) "Critical-Holistic Paradigm for an Interdependent World" as a guiding framework. The paradigm offers a multidimensional view of Brazilian nursing by considering the relationship among various international (macro) determinants and national (micro) conditions, and identifies the complex relationships in nursing as it attempts to transform itself in the 21st century. The Critical-Holistic Paradigm provides a framework for looking at (a) international and national market demands and their primary effects on the national health system; (b) social and professional demands and their primary effects on nursing practice; and finally (c) the science and technology demands with their primary effects on nursing higher

[1] The opinions expressed in this chapter are the sole and exclusive responsibility of the authors and do not represent the opinions of the organizations and the administration where they are employed.

education and research. Furthermore, the chapter presents an analysis of contemporary demands and trends in Brazilian nursing and concludes with an examination of proposals for transformative action.

Brazil was colonized primarily by Portugal and is the largest country in South America, with almost 200 million people, mainly of three races and ethnicities: European, Native Brazilian, and African (Singer, Campos, & Oliveira, 1978). It is a complex country with many disparities and social injustices, evident in all of its systems, regions, and social groups. Brazil's federal republic, democratic government consists of legislative, judiciary, and executive offices. At the local level, the country consists of 27 states (including one federal district) and more than 5,500 municipalities, which are all autonomous.

Brazil is rich in natural and mineral resources and is home to the largest section of the Amazon Rainforest. The country is bounded by Uruguay, Argentina, Paraguay, Bolivia, Peru, Colombia, Venezuela, Suriname, Guyana, and French Guiana on its southern, western, and northern borders. Brazil's long eastern seaboard faces the Atlantic Ocean and its territory includes a number of archipelagos. The large Brazilian population—one of the largest in the world—is more concentrated in large urban areas along the coastline with the internal area having a lower population density. Although Brazil is primarily a Roman Catholic country, Protestant religious groups have increased somewhat in popularity over the last several decades. Culturally, Brazilian practices and traditions stem from all of its multiracial population groups.

After a long period of colonization and imperial rule, Brazil declared independence from Portugal in 1822. Its independence was recognized in 1825 and it became the Federal Republic of Brazil in 1889 with autonomous regions and states. Political upheaval and military rule marked the early years of the 20th century interspersed with some periods of democratic rule.

By the 1950s, Brazil had become dominated by a nationalist ideology, which saw "development" as the sole solution to social problems (Rodrigues, 2003a). Unfortunately, social and health care policies did not, in fact, benefit. The nationalistic ideology excluded certain groups of people who were perceived by those in power as neither strategically nor economically important to the country. Such ideology also served as a challenge and prompted nursing to increase its critical involvement in politics during this decade.

The 1960s were years of economic prosperity, controlled and dominated by multi-national and national *bourgeoisie* who were aligned with foreign capital and military forces (Simões Paes, 2002). The control began in 1964 when military forces staged a successful *coup d'état* and installed an authoritarian military dictatorship with unlimited power that lasted 21 years (Simões Paes, 2002). During this period, outspoken intellectuals, artists, and politicians who were not politically tolerant of the U.S.-supported dictatorship were exiled (Simões Paes, 2002). During the military rule, colloquially known as the "years of lead" ("*anos de chumbo*"), a number of proactive nurses, along with other health professionals with educational interests different from the government's, were investigated. A few nurses were arrested, questioned, and released, while other nurses were imprisoned for some years.

The 1970s was a decade characterized by the military dictatorship, with selected areas of capitalist development and the integration of Brazil into the world capitalist system. The government and prominent multi-national companies (e.g., automobile, chemical, pharmaceutical, mining, and agriculture) celebrated the country's high rate of economic growth as the "Brazilian Economic Miracle." Unfortunately, the "Miracle" stood on three unstable and unsustainable pillars: (a) increased working class exploitation through unfair, stagnant wages, poor working conditions, and political repression; (b) state influenced capitalist expansion and large national and international mergers; and (c) massive influx of foreign capital as investments (Habert, 2003). During this decade, in addition to the campaign against the organized left, the government used para-military and police-like groups to spread fear and insecurity. Subsequently, nursing, peoples' health, workplace conditions, and social conditions worsened.

During the 1980s, the multinational capitalist growth and the military dictatorship began to lose its appeal within Brazil. International opinion and pressure also mounted against the dictatorship (Albuquerque, 2001). In the 80s—the "Lost Decade"—the country experienced considerable political and economic change when Brazil and other Latin American countries acquired extensive external debt. Brazilian nurses participated in a massive people's movement to reestablish direct elections (Rodrigues, 2003b). In 1985 the military rule ended in a peaceful conversion to a transitional government termed the "*Opening*" followed by democratic elections.

In the 1990s, Brazil adopted a new industrial paradigm derived from globalization processes, economic opportunities, privatization of public companies, and industries, and labor *de-regulation*.[2] The consequences—the concentration of wealth in a small percentage of the population—became quite visible (Chossudolski, 1999; Demo, 1996; Junior, 2000; Lacerda, 2004).

During the 1990s, globalization intensified via neoliberal economic policies changed Brazil's relation to international markets as the influx of foreign capital created significant changes in Brazil's social, judicial, and regulatory relations. The process of *de-nationalization*[3] also had political, social, cultural, and economic effects, which resulted in institutional fragility and external vulnerability (Arruda & Boff, 2000; Gonçalves, 1999). As one example, structural adjustment programs (SAPs) initiated to mediate on behalf of international capital demands had a significant impact on social policies, as reflected in Brazil's employment data. The Brazilian Institute of Geography and Statistics (BIGS)[4] (April 2004) showed that at the time only 50% of Brazil's employable citizens were working: the other 50%, or

---

[2] In terms of the health care system "de-regulation" means that health workers had, among others, precarious work contracts with low wages, excessive work hours per week, increased experience period, no social security or other benefits, and no dismissal wages.

[3] When national assets are privatized and sold to multinational, international companies and corporations.

[4] In Portuguese: Instituto Brasileiro de Geografia e Estatística – IBGE.

2.8 million employable citizens, were not. Though consistent with world trends, these data also indicated that the highest unemployment figures were in Latin American countries, according to the Applied Economics Research Institute (AERI)[5] (IPEA, 2004). The precarious employment situation—including that in the health sector—perpetuated job instability, which in turn increased absenteeism and turn-over. Ultimately, the health care workers' mobility created additional problems for the National Health System [NHS], most noticeably in the number of terminated projects and programs.

Globalization has created other problems for Brazil's diverse populations. Regional disparities in literacy, wealth concentration, child labor, and violence are the products of the state's neoliberal economic policies. For example, despite the continuity of state policies supporting interventions aimed at reducing mortality rates and expanding nutrition and education programs, these programs have not been uniformly available in all Brazilian regions.

GUIDING FRAMEWORK

The following examination of Brazilian nursing uses four different lenses: (a) the macro-political, emphasizing international and national scenes; (b) the micro-political, discussing international and national market demands as they influence national health care system; (c) the social and professional demands, highlighting professional practice, nursing organization, and social-cultural issues such as racism and gender; and finally through (d) the science and technology demands, high-lighting higher nursing education, graduate education, and research evolution and consolidation.

Brazilian nursing as a social practice is best considered outside the usual academic stratification with its emphasis on the immediate, direct application of technical and scientific knowledge. This chapter accomplishes this by using the Critical-Holistic Paradigm as an analytical tool (Wright, 2000). The framework considers the rela-tionships among both international (macro) determinants and national (micro) conditions and provides a way to treat (a) international and national market demands, and their primary effects on the national health system (b) social and professional demands, and their primary effects on nursing practice and finally (c) the science and technology demands, with their primary effects on nursing higher education and research (see Figure 1—*Critical-Holistic Paradigm Theoretical Model for Brazilian Nursing* developed by Wright in 2004).

In Figure 2, the *Operational Model of Brazilian Nursing Critical-Holistic Analysis* developed by Wright in 2004, applies the theoretical paradigm in Figure 1 specifically to Brazil. Figure 2 depicts the operational relationships which have contributed to Brazil's and Brazilian nursing's position in the Americas and the world. These complex relationships influence nursing's evolution and its attempts to consolidate and transform itself in the 21st century.

---

[5] In Portuguese: Instituto de Pesquisas Econômicas Aplicadas – IPEA.

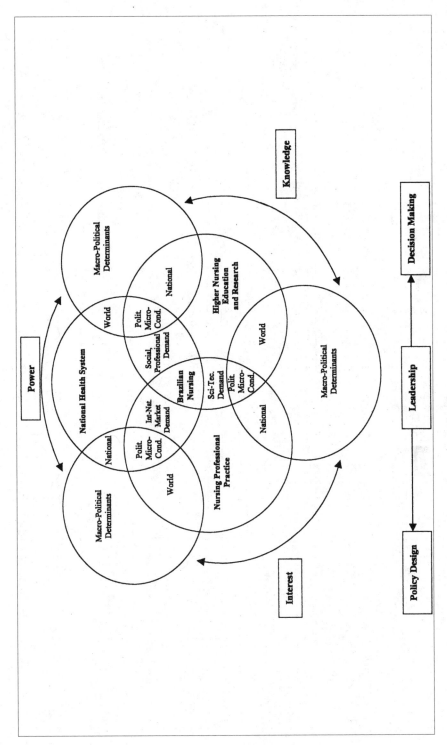

Figure 1. Critical-Holistic Paradigm Theoretical Model for Brazilian Nursing (used with permission © Wright, 2004).

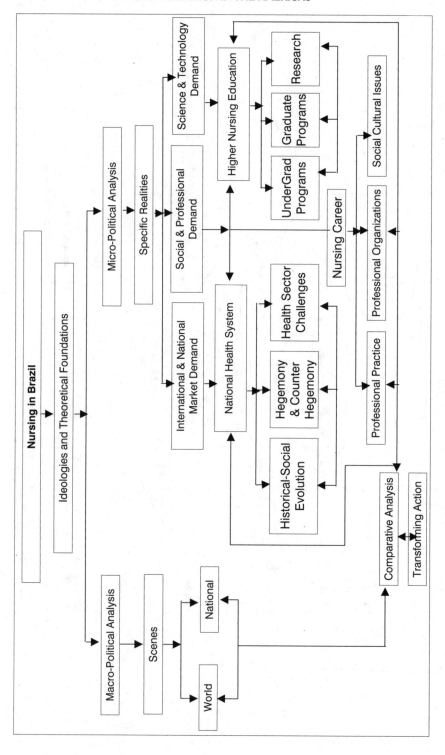

Figure 2. Operational Model of Brazilian Nursing Critical-Holistic Analysis (used with permission © Wright, 2004).

MACRO-POLITICAL ANALYSIS

The macro-level political analysis looks at relationships among determinant factors (both international and national) that affect Brazil and its place in the globalization process. Rourke (2003) identifies the eight most important macro-level determinants: the consequences of the two World Wars; the creation and expansion of large multi- and trans-national corporations; the changes in international relations, patterns and disputes; the [violent] conflicts for independence; the disparities between rich and poor countries; the United States' imperialist domination over Latin America and other developing countries; the creation of international organizations to alleviate tensions; and, finally, scientific and technological advances. It's especially important to note that certain events within globalization have impeded the choices and opportunities available to nursing as a social practice.

MICRO-POLITICAL ANALYSIS

Today's Brazilian nursing and universal health care system developed as a direct response to influences such as: (a) the country's political and administrative structures and ideologies; (b) the effects of people's movements; and (c) nursing's history as pro-active advocates for universal health care.

Although globalization has shaped Brazil's and nursing's development, it is the micro-political aspects of globalization that have had the most powerful impact on Brazilian nursing. Analyzing the micro-political level helps elucidate concrete reality (Wright, 2000). The following three aspects of this level of analysis are most pertinent (a) international and national market demands, highlighting the Brazilian health care system, (b) social and professional demands, highlighting nursing's position in the country's health care system, and (c) science and technology demands, highlighting an analysis of higher nursing education and research and its impact on the development of the profession. Each of these is discussed below.

International and National Market Demands

Wright's 2004 "Operational Model of Brazilian Nursing Critical-Holistic Analysis"© suggests that international and national market demands drive the NHS in three major areas (a) Historical and Social Development, (b) Hegemonic and Counter Hegemonic Movements, and (c) Financial Health Sector Challenges. Since the population's current health status is the result of several economic models and policies that have impacted the NHS, the analysis presented here focuses on just the challenges these pressures cause for the NHS and for nursing as a social practice.

Socio-Historic Development—16th to 21st Century

In Imperialist Brazil, local authorities were responsible for keeping cities clean and the population safe by monitoring garbage collection as well as many aspects of food commerce. Sick care was the province of religious hospital mercy orders and Jesuit fathers. From the 16th to the end of the 18th century, nursing was considered an "informal practice" performed by healers, midwives, religious, and lay people (Herson, 1996). A more formal medical policy that targeted overall population health and welfare began in 1808, when Portugal's Royal family migrated to Brazil after fleeing Napoleon. At that time, keeping the country's population healthy helped to maintain the social order and the high immigration levels from different parts of Europe (Araujo, 1982; Padilha, 1998).

From late 19th and early 20th century onward, the country's development into what is an essentially capitalist system obviously changed economic, political, social, and health policies. By the end of the 19th century, Brazil was a coffee-based economy—an industrialized coffee exporter. The State was interested in public health solely to maintain the sanitation of all components associated with the exportation of coffee (Braga, 1978). In early 20th century, with an expanding coffee-based economy, personal health emerged as a social issue as workers became better organized and sought their rights, such as social security, benefits, and services. In conjunction, administrators were interested in the economic impact of commerce-related health issues, such as endemic and epidemic diseases—on exploitation of the workforce (Braga, 1978).

Within this social-political context, and inspired by the U.S. sanitation model, there was an increase in the number of primary health units that provided individual and collective medical care. Paradoxically, however, the concentration of primary health care units in politically strategic areas precipitated an overall decrease in public health services, so regrettably, services did not meet the overall population's social needs (Campos, 1987). Additionally, despite the strong medical focus during these decades, health care and social needs still demanded a highly-qualified nursing practice. Thus, nursing education became both socially and medically necessary.

In late 20th and early 21st century, globalization provided new directions for policy design and decision-making, resulting in health care services with improved access, more efficient organization, and new funding and management opportunities. The autonomy of Brazilian states and municipalities led to the decentralization of much of the country's health care system.

Accordingly, a new national public health service was organized as the precursor of the National Department of Public Health.[6] In 1922, influenced by North American nurses, the *National Public Health Department School of Nursing*,[7] was also created, later becoming the *Anna Nery School of Nursing* (ANSN).[8] Most significant for nursing, the school introduced sanitation education and scientifically-based public health administration principles in its early years (Bertolli-Filho, 2001; Rodrigues, 1967).

From 1930 to 1970 the health care system improved by expanding from local to national services (Campos, 1987). The NHS clearly had two foci: (a) a public health focus on prevention and control of endemics and epidemics and (b) an individual

[6] In Portuguese: Departamento Nacional de Saúde Pública (DNSP).

[7] In Portuguese: Escola de Enfermeiras do Departamento Nacional de Saúde Pública (EE-DNSP).

[8] In Portuguese: Escola de Enfermagem Anna Nery (EEAN).

focus on clinical diagnosis and treatment. These foci expanded nursing employment opportunities—both for preventive and curative health services—as well as nursing leadership and political representation at local, municipal, state, national, and international levels. Although this division between preventive and curative services did increase health coverage, it did not provide equal access, since only the working class had full access to services (Donnangelo, 1975; Donnangelo & Pereira, 1979).

It is important to note that the nursing profession's involvement in politics increased during the 1950's and nurses have remained active in politics ever since. More specifically, over the last 50 years, nursing began to play a significant role in the implementation and maintenance of the National Health System (NHS) structure, policy design, and decision-making. This expanded role for nursing directly influenced nursing education, certification and leadership in Brazil, the Americas, and the world (Almeida & Rocha, 1997).

Currently, Brazil's health care is divided into three systems: (a) the public Unified Health System (UHS)[9], (b) the private Supplementary Medical Care System (SMCS),[10], and (c) the private Direct Disbursement System (DDS).[11] The private SMCS receives direct and indirect subsidies from the State under fiscal and contributive waivers and has four components: (a) group medicine, (b) self-management, (c) medical mutual company, and (d) health insurance. The SMCS provides services to an estimated greater than 25% of the population at the cost of approximately US$16 billion per year (Campos, 1992; Mendes, 2002a, 2002b; MPAS, 1982).

Hegemonic and Counter-Hegemonic Movements

During the 1970s and 1980s, hegemonic and counter-hegemonic movements emerged in response to various national and international crises and to the profound national fiscal crisis (Mendes, 2001a, 2001b). In the dominant health care model, which was based on curative procedures and technology, there was a move toward greater hegemony. This consolidation influenced both medical and nursing labor markets, professional education, and the private health sector. Further consolidation occurred in some regions, where most health services are offered by the private sector through a service delivery contract with public administration. In addition, highly complex, highly technological, and costly diagnostic and therapeutic procedures such as magnetic resonance or hemodialysis are usually provided by the private sector.

The counter hegemonic movements that took place during the 1970s were influenced by the Alma-Ata report. The Alma-Ata report prompted several primary care strategies the NHS implemented over the following two decades (OMS, 1978). Also in the late 1980s professionals, intellectuals, and activist groups, whose goal was to force the legislative and judiciary sectors to structure a new public health policy, initiated *the Sanitarian Movement*. Several nurses were leaders in this

---

[9] In Protuguese: Sistema Único de Saúde – SUS.

[10] In Portuguese: Sistema de Atenção Médica Suplementar – SAMS.

[11] In Portuguese: Sistema de Desembolso Direto – SDD.

movement as well as public advocates in favor of the policy. The Sanitarian Movement eventually became the Unified Health System (UHS). As a result, the National Constitution, in 1988, approved a health care system that established principles that were more inclusive (a) universal access, (b) equity, (c) people's participation, (d) integrality and hierarchy, and (e) regionalization. Thus, the health care system that had been formerly separated into preventive and curative health care was transformed into comprehensive health promotion, prevention and curative services.

Although the UHS regulatory policies define the private sector as a complementary provider of health care services, the private sector still plays an important role for complex diagnostic and therapeutic procedures, because the public services system cannot afford high cost procedures. Paradoxically, nurses employed to provide such high-cost services—who care for UHS clients through governmental/institutional agreements—still must work under private sector rules. Thus, these nurses generally work longer hours and have lower salaries compared to nurses in public services.

Unified Health System Financial Challenge

Funding the public UHS has been chronically difficult. Finally, in 2000, 12 years after the UHS was established, Brazil set baseline tax percentages for funding the UHS as follows—the national government would pay 5%; the states, 12%; and the municipalities, 15%. These percentages were based on research as to what was adequate in maintaining the country's public health services (Campos, 1992; Carvalho, 2002).

The UHS has been profoundly positive, both for the organization of services and for progress toward a more equitable and efficacious technical-assistance model. According to the National Institute of Consumers' Protection (NICP)[12] (IPEA, 2004), the UHS performed 84% of all complex procedures and more than 7,000 organ transplants. In addition, the system's 60,000 basic health care units and 6,500 hospitals handled over 350 million appointments per year, on average of 2.4 appointments per person per year. These numbers, along with a steady movement toward more equitable and efficacious technical-assistance model and best practices, suggests that the demand for nursing care has also been on the rise.

The most viable public health strategy is surveillance of health, which is based on an understanding of health as a complex product of social, biological, historical, political, and cultural issues. Relying on the healthy surveillance paradigm, the UHS seeks to identify and meet population health needs by reorganizing health services into partnerships with the community and using "light technologies" known as "acknowledgment" and "humanization" (recognizing the health care sector's responsibility for "defense of life") (Mehry, 1987; Mehry, Chakkour, Stéfano, Stéfano, Santos, Rodrigues, et al., 1997).

---

[12] In Portuguese: Instituto Nacional de Defesa do Consumidor – INDC.

This extensive transformation of public policy not only poses a number of challenges but also increases social and professional demands for nursing professionals. For example, one of the UHS principles is community participation, to be achieved through effective representative councils in local areas. Recently, participatory democracy and inclusive strategies—such as *"health fairs," "popular theater,"* and *"experiences' systematization"*—have been added to strengthen the community (Stotz, David, & Wong-Un, 2005).

The UHS has been a key part of major health changes in Brazil. Despite existing difficulties with funding, community participation, the follow-up of invested money in health care, overall, the UHS has met nurses' ideals and demands for a more equitable health system—and for the profession as a social practice.

Social and Professional Demands

In keeping with Wright's 2004 *Operational Model,* the analysis of nursing's social and professional demands reviews how they are closely related to the career issues of nursing's professional practice, their professional organizations as well as their social-cultural issues.

Professional Practice

Brazilian professional nursing has evolved via a dynamic and continuous process. Movements (both divergent and convergent with the profession's goals, as well as during periods of prosperity and decline) have punctuated nursing history (Padilha, Silva, & Borenstein, 2002).

During the 1920s, nursing was institutionalized as a career in response to both international macro- and national micro-level demands. At an international level, the endemic and epidemic diseases such as tuberculosis, yellow fever, and syphilis threatened Brazil's ability to export food, textiles, and other products. Importing countries demanded that Brazil intervene in these health issues. Such international demands (as well as national micro-conditioning factors) resulted in programs "to solve" people's health problems. The first such programs involved health care teams trained to work as sanitary visitors and to organize mass vaccination campaigns.

Initially, the nursing profession responded to these international market demands by using Rockefeller Foundation's model of public health. That model emphasized public health services administration and sanitary education as the basis of medical sanitation and nursing practices. In theory, the National Department of Public Health would employ a group of nurses to conduct home visits for the detection and control of infectious diseases, and the director of the National Department of Public Health would oversee the professional team that worked systematically with the population. The ideal was that the visiting-nurse would be the "health educator" for the communities. However, in the actual practice of the model, because there were not enough baccalaureate prepared nurses, the newly-graduated professionals were forced to accept leadership positions in health care institutions rather than provide direct patient nursing care in the communities. At the national level, a number of micro-conditions shaped nursing into its current multi-level educational and professional careers. This stratification has generated academic, professional practice and social status challenges based on the standardized criteria for the tasks and technical responsibilities of these professional categories as established in the 1986 Brazilian Nursing Professional Practice Law No. 7.498[13].

Nursing Education and Practice

Yet, the stratification of the nursing profession did not occur in a vacuum. From the 1940s to the 1960s, nursing underwent major educational and service changes. Prior to that time, "practice nurses" had no formal education. They were trained "on the job" or by courses organized by the Brazilian Red Cross. These "practice nurses" provided all nursing care services in all hospitals.

Early in the 1940s, to address the shortage of registered nurses with Bachelor of Science degrees and the pressure from hospitals for a professional nursing category that could be educated in a shorter period of time, the profession created nurse auxiliaries. These nurses had at least an elementary and/or high school degree, graduated from 2-year programs, and were trained to function as nurses' helpers. The majority of nurse auxiliary graduates were employed in the NHS hospitals' public and private units. Additionally, the National Nursing Association, the Nursing Council, and the government approved the new nursing category and nursing auxiliary programs. This new professional category divided nursing work into levels of complexity, making the nursing auxiliaries responsible for performing elementary nursing care such as patient feeding, hygiene, and transportation and making the baccalaureate-prepared RN responsible for nursing care management.

During the 1960s, as health care became more sophisticated and technology dependent, demands for yet another category of nursing care worker emerged—that of nurse technicians—a category qualified to function in both public and private hospital networks. Despite all of the new categories of workers, it was not until the end of this period, in 1962, that Brazilian nursing became a liberal profession and entered the university as a legitimate educational program. Not surprisingly, the heightened demand for baccalaureate-prepared RNs increased the number of baccalaureate programs and in 1986, approximately 20 years later, the Professional Nursing Practice Law passed Congress. Ten years after that, the New Minimum Nursing Curriculum was approved and came into effect in 1994, more than 30 years after nursing was reestablished as a liberal profession. These changes have had far-reaching effects.

One change concentrated on the distribution of nursing resources through the country. The Ministry of Health (Department of Management in Health Labor and Education),which was responsible for the definition and implementation of health human resources education, created Permanent Health Education Units[14] in various regions of the country. This policy defined the four essential segments: the

---

[13] In Portuguese: Brasil, Lei do Exercício Profissional de Enfermagem n° 7.498, de 25 de junho de 1986.

[14] In Portuguese: Pólos de Educação Permanente em Saúde.

education sector (universities and technical schools), the local health system administration, the health services, and social control through people's participation. The policy regulated all undergraduate health sciences programs, the formation of personnel at the technical level, and lifelong education of health care providers in the service networks. These interrelated educational components were integral to health care and teamwork (Ministério da Saúde, 2004). *Nursing care* became part of the UHS agenda and part of different professional specialties whose goals were to improve the quality of community and hospital nursing care. This was a dramatic change and health policy revolutionized nursing practice.

Prior to the 1980s, nurses functioned primarily within hospitals in specialty areas and had their professional practice subject to the demands of the national labor markets. In 1983, the Integrated Health Actions (IHA) proposed curricular changes and provided a technical base as well as strategic principles for the Health Reform. The IHA and the "Health for All by the Year 2000" compelled academic and service environments to create generalist RN curriculum that met the nation's social and public health concerns.

In the 1990s, as an initiative to deliver primary health care, a new category of health worker was established through the Community Health Agents Program (CHAP).[15] These workers, unlike hospital auxiliaries, received no education, but they were included as a new professional category in the basic health care network to function primarily in the Family Health Program (FHP). Then, in 2003, Community Health Agents were recognized as part of the public health care system, with a formal mid-level curriculum. Although the IHA is developing professional regulations, nurses are the main supervisors and educators of this category nationwide (David, 2001).

Clearly, these socio-political forces increased the numbers of care givers thus extending health care to more of the population, but these increases also presented new challenges to nursing as it aimed for higher standards of care and social status for the profession. Currently there are three levels in the nursing team: the RN-BS nurse; the nursing technician and the nursing auxiliary. A descriptive profile of each category including the nursing attendant follows:

RN-BS Nurses are educated in 4-year university-based programs. Graduates are generalists who are prepared to accept management, direct health care, or university positions at schools of nursing. Master's degrees are required for nurse educators/faculty positions in undergraduate programs. Doctoral degrees are required for faculty positions in Master's and Doctoral programs.

Nursing Technicians are high school graduates with an additional diploma from a 2-year training programs. Graduates are prepared to accept positions that assist RN-BS nurses by providing medium-level complexity care.

Nursing Auxiliaries are high school graduates with 1 year of training courses. Graduates are prepared to perform low complexity care. In the absence of nurse technicians, they also perform medium-level complexity care. The nursing profession

---

[15] In Portuguese: Community Health Agents Program – CHAP.

and the NHS are in the process of reclassifying nursing auxiliaries through further training courses—to become nursing technicians.

Nursing Attendants with elementary school education perform elementary tasks such as patient transportation, bed linen care, equipment cleaning, and sterilization. Currently, the nursing profession and the NHS are in the final process of reclassifying and eliminating this level.

In total numbers, Brazil's nursing workforce includes 875,545 nursing professionals, divided into five different categories and five geographical regions (see Table 1). Nursing auxiliaries (504,885) represent the majority of the workforce, followed by nursing technicians (228,030), RN-BS nurses (116,457), and nursing attendants (26,132). Midwives (41) have the smallest numbers in both nursing and the NHS.

Brazil has a total population of over 179 million people, of which 79% are urban. Including all five levels of nursing, the ratio is 1 nursing professional to 229 people, with only 1 RN-BS to approximately 1,700 people. These ratios indicate that the number of nursing professionals does not yet come close to meeting either the population's needs or public and private health sector's demands, when the ideal ratio is 1 RN- BS nurse to 30 hospital beds. Brazil's infant mortality rate is 33.1 for every 1000 births and its maternal mortality rate is 74.5 for every 100,000 deliveries. These statistics are glaring evidence of the need for more RN-BS nurses. However, these numbers do not characterize and/or foresee a severe shortage of nurses because numbers of entries of high school graduates in BS nursing schools and of BS graduate nurses in the labor market are on the rise.

Nursing Organizations

Nursing organizations and unions, as advocates and critical social change agents, also work to confront the issues of nursing education and supply that contribute to

Table 1. Brazilian Nursing Workforce According to Categories and Regions

Region	RN-BS	Nursing technician	Nursing auxiliary	Nursing attendant	Midwife	Total
North	6,484	22,433	21,471	126	15	50,529
Northeast	26,951	33,256	89,168	1,578	19	150,972
Center-West	8,327	27,706	28,074	92	0	64,199
Southeast	55,834	100,341	290,853	13,343	4	460,375
South	18,861	44,294	75,319	10,993	3	149,470
Total	116,457	228,030	504,885	26,132	41	875,545

Source: Conselho Federal de Enfermagem (COFEN) [Federal Council of Nursing] (2006).

the disproportionate number nurses compared to the general population. The professional and labor organizations emerged, representing the diversity among Brazil's health professionals and workers, in the context of global and national economic and political development.

Brazilian Nursing Association

The former Diploma Nurses Brazilian National Association established in 1926 was renamed the Brazilian Nursing Association (BNA)[16] in 1954. RNs, nurse technicians, auxiliaries, and students are eligible to become members. With a membership of 10,000, it is recognized as the primary political nursing organization within Brazilian society and it continues to represent Brazilian nursing today. Yet, its proportionately small membership evokes an interesting question. Why have only a small number of the 116,457 RNs become members? Some possible reasons are: (a) membership is voluntary; (b) there are other scientific and cultural affiliations; (c) the majority of members are academicians. Professional practitioners often cite low salaries as one of the reasons for their non-affiliation. Yet, despite its proportionately small membership, BNA is powerful. Nursing unions as well as the Professional Council originated from and are supported by the BNA, which encouraged and fostered the expansion of all Brazilian nursing organizations. In fact, BNA's bylaws stipulate its collaboration with other labor and non-labor entities and education, scientific, and health care institutions (Albuquerque, 2002).

As Brazil's most assertive professional nursing organization, the BNA has intervened in struggles to transform the nursing profession, arguing for it to address broader issues, such as freedom and democracy (Albuquerque, 2001). Thus, all nursing organizations are indebted to the BNA. Indeed, at each BNA sponsored Brazilian Nursing Conference (BNC), it is easy to discern the synergy among the conferences' official themes, nursing perspective, country's current status, health system, and education and political transformations. The conferences also reveal how Brazilian nurses are actively engaged in health and education policies and socio-cultural changes (Padilha et al., 2001).

The BNA's societal relevance is evident in the fundamental role it played in the campaign to end the military dictatorship. The BNA provided leadership in the movement known as *"Diretas Já!"* or *"Direct Elections Right Away!"* Of all nursing organizations, the BNA is the most political and contributes accordingly to the nation's health, education, and social policies. Scientific events organized by the BNA have contributed to political strategies that have furthered nursing's transformation. As just one example, BNA established minimum standards for nursing curricula as well as the delineation of basic competencies for nurses employed in the health care system. Equally important, BNA continues to play an important role in the development of partnerships among national and international organizations that define the socially-relevant nursing practice and research priorities.

---

[16] In Portuguese: Associação Brasileira de Enfermagem – ABEn.

Federal and Regional Nursing Councils

The regulation of professional nursing changed dramatically in 1973 with the authorization and creation of the Federal Nursing Council (FNC)[17] and the Regional Nursing Councils (RNCs)[18] within the Ministry of Labor (ML), which legitimatized Brazilian nursing. These councils regulate professional nursing practice and issue licenses to RNs, nursing technicians and auxiliaries. They manage professional practice, provide the ethical framework for nursing, and submit legislative proposals to Congress. Since the FNC is the federal regulatory body, practicing nurses are required to register with it. Thus, a total of 875,545 (100%) of nursing professionals are members.

Nursing Unions

The political development of nurses has been interwoven with their evolution as members of the labor force. The struggle to become unionized that began in 1933 in Rio de Janeiro, D.C., has been marked by contention among nurses with different goals for the profession. For example, during the 1940s, some groups fought for and won the designation of "liberal professional." But the existing union protested the change and the designation of "liberal professional" was revoked in 1943 (as noted previously, it would be another 20 years, not until 1962, before RNs would be designated as "liberal professionals"). In 1945, the first fledging union became the Hospital and Clinics Workers' Union (HCWU).[19] Its membership included all health care workers, even non-nurses. During its existence, the HCWU was effective in organizing and bringing together all health care workers—except physicians. Another major transition occurred during the 1970s when the first national Nurses' Pre-Union Professional Association, the Guanabara Nurses' Association, became the pro-active Nurses' Union of Rio de Janeiro.

These early attempts at unionization laid the foundation for the RNs-only Nurses' National Federation (NNF)[20] begun in 1986. The NNF's bylaws stipulated "promoting nationwide RN union conferences and meetings" to guide nursing labor endeavors. Currently, the RNs' union[21] has 13 branches in different states and pre-union associations in 10 other states. Gradually all licensed levels of nursing became unionized in one or another organization. The National Nursing Auxiliaries' Association, (NNAA)[22] created in 1950, became the National Nursing Auxiliaries Union (NNAU)[23] in 1959. And, during the 1970s, it opened its membership to nursing technicians and became the National Union of Nursing Auxiliaries and

---

[17] In Portuguese: Conselho Federal de Enfermagem – COFEn.

[18] In Portuguese: Conselhos Regionais de Enfermagem – COREns.

[19] In Portuguese: Sindicato dos Empregados de Hospitais e Casas de Saúde – SEEHCS.

[20] In Portuguese: Federação Nacional dos Enfermeiros.

[21] In Portuguese: Sindicato dos Enfermeiros.

[22] In Portuguese: Associação Nacional de Auxiliares de Enfermagem – ANAE.

[23] In Portuguese: União Nacional dos Auxiliares de Enfermagem – UNAE.

Technicians (NUNAT).[24] Presently, all unions representing nurses are funded by union taxes and yearly membership dues. All unions are associated with the NNF and the NCCE.[25]

Non-licensed health workers had a slightly different evolution. A 1978 decision of the Ministry of Labor designated nursing attendants—workers with no specific training in basic nursing services—as unlicensed personnel. That status changed with the passage of the Nursing Professional Practice Law, Number 7498/86, which provided nursing attendants' licensure but time-restricted and dependent on their registering in the next higher level of education—the nursing auxiliaries programs. Thus, in this sense, the Law provided a mandatory career ladder for those at the bottom of the nursing work force hierarchy.

In Brazil, 95% of nurses are affiliated with some union: one of the nursing unions, or health sector unions, or another specific sector's unions, or the workers' general union. Brazilian unions negotiate salaries and the choice of union membership is not dictated.

Social and Cultural Issues

Nursing faces issues that are inherent to Brazil's socio-cultural system. Among the many, two issues—racism and gender—are pertinent, though there have been few nursing studies conducted on them. The following succinctly presents a discussion of racism and gender as ongoing socio-cultural issues for Brazil and nursing.

Racism and Nursing

An understanding of racism in nursing requires some knowledge about race in Brazilian society. The objects of racism in Brazil are Blacks (African heritage) and native Brazilian (Indian heritage) populations. Racist behaviors and prejudicial attitudes inherent in the country's socio-cultural system are common occurrences in the everyday lives of these populations (Haddad, 2002). Data about the differences in opportunities among black, native, and non-white populations indicates the kinds and numbers of social injustices and inequities. According to the Institute of Applied Economic Research (IAER)[26] (as cited in Seyferth, Silva Bento, Silva, Borges Pereira, Siqueira, Silvério, et al. 2002, p. 11):

1. Blacks (African heritage) constitute less than 50% of the population. There are 33.7 million black and 15.1 million native Brazilians living in poverty;
2. Black male workers earn 53.99% less and black women workers earn 49.47% less than their white counterparts;

---

[24] In Portuguese: União Nacional dos Auxiliares e Técnicos de Enfermagem – UNATE.

[25] In Portuguese: Confederação Nacional dos Trabalhadores do Comércio – CNTC.

[26] In Portuguese: Instituto de Pesquisas Econômicas Aplicadas – IPEA.

3. Twenty-seven percent of the black population between 11 to 14 years of age is in 5th or 6th grades, while 44% of white 11 to 14 year olds are in 5th or 6th grade; and

4. Twenty-five-year-old black persons have attended school for approximately 6.1 years compared to 25-year-old white persons who have attended for 8.4 years.

The data also suggest that the social and economic outcomes of racism are predicated on Brazil's socially constructed color stratification system. Race in Brazil is not solely biological. Since slavery, Blacks have struggled to be recognized as integral to Brazilian society. Their struggles have been documented in movements (e.g., Brazilian Black Front) precipitated by political and social system changes (Pereira, 2002). Globalization has further stimulated Blacks to dispel negative stereotypes and to build political and ideological power in different spheres of Brazilian society. Concomitantly, the government has recognized the social injustices and inequities (Seyferth et al., 2002).

Most recently, media and academic discussions feature ethnic inclusion policies (i.e., affirmative action policies). One such policy reserves seats in public universities for minorities. Fierce debate waged about this policy because of the inability to define ethnicity. Many believe that the country has a long tradition of tolerance of ethnic mixture, and that the injustices and inequities are the result of class rather than race or ethnicity, but no such debates have occurred in nursing.

In nursing, the issue of racism has been approached quite superficially. Existing documents show that racism has existed in nursing since the early 20th century. At that time, racism was evident in the selection of nursing program applicants. For example, black applicants' admission records from the 1920s were marked "*The applicant did not meet all the requirements*," but since it was clear that the applicants had indeed met all admission requirements, the only logical reason for their rejection was their phenotypic characteristics (i.e., skin tone). Interestingly, racist behaviors became more evident in nursing during the 1960s when the restricted access and exclusion educational model of the United States was adopted. During this decade, one admission criterion was "*to have a good appearance,*" which seemed to translate to "not black." Black applicants also self-excluded—even when they met all admission criteria—to avoid the arbitrary exclusion by white admission committees (Lima, 1994).

Overt racist behaviors decreased during the late 1960s with the passage of new laws. After the 1968 University Reform, which declared that any person could enroll and take the admission examination, all university careers were open to black men and women. Despite the open door policy, few Blacks were admitted because the majority of the black population had few opportunities to receive the formal education that would permit them to compete successfully for university undergraduate programs.

Additionally, despite nursing being a primarily female profession, white females who were in power either denied all women or made inclusion as difficult as possible for women who did not look like them. Paradoxically, racism is similar to the gender power struggles that deny access to women and grant most leadership positions to men.

Society, Women's Roles, and Nursing

In Brazil the women's movement was lead by women who were futurists. Bertha Lutz assumed leadership of the feminist movement in 1918, 50 years prior to its worldwide explosion (Badinter, 1986; Miranda, 1996; Muraro, 1992), and founded the League for Women's Intellectual Emancipation (D'Ávila Neto, 1979).

Despite Lutz's "intellectual emancipation," prior to the 1960s, one's sex directed professional career choices. Women's careers fit "feminine" stereotypes such as those of elementary school teacher, secretary, nurse. These career choices were perceived as less rigorous and less competitive (Michel, 1989). Indeed, nurses were expected to have internalized the feminine role, which had supposedly prompted their choice of this professional career. Scholars commonly acknowledge that the feminine stereotype is the source of feelings of inferiority as well as self-deprecatory attitudes in interactions between males (e.g., physicians, male nurses, and other male professionals) and even female nurses (Padilha, 1990, 1998; Padilha, Bornstein, Santos, & Cartana, 1998). The subordinated role in the private-domestic sphere extended to the public-professional sphere in part because the majority of nursing functions replicated those of private life. The hypothesis that women's professional career choices are based upon both their families' and their own personal social histories and reflect their "feminine roles" remains relevant even in today's environment (Padilha, 1990; Wright & Carneiro, 1984).

The major challenge for Brazilian nursing as globalization increases is to expand the scope of ideas and modify the stereotypes in order to promote nursing as a career for both men and women. Only 12.7% of Brazil's professional nurses are men and of those, only 1.6% are male RNs. The gender issue in nursing continues to represent a challenge that the profession needs to address in order to achieve a better balance of males and females within the profession.

To confront this challenge, nurse researchers must investigate and expose gender relations to stimulate new research questions. Until that time, nurses are becoming more qualified professionally and participating in international movements related to transforming women's roles. Additionally, female nurses are accepting positions that once were occupied exclusively by males including leadership positions. For example, women are now 50% of the students in the medicine and law, historically male professions. These societal leaps forward match the increased numbers of women in the work force and as single heads of households (Padilha et al., 2001). In Brazil, these advances for women indicate a change in the balance of power between men and women.

Also, mixed-gender health care teams have demonstrated a slow yet positive trend toward improved relationships. Although a patriarchal rigidity still exists, some advances in female and male roles indicate emancipation for women.

Generally, labels and stereotypes within the human categories (e.g., class, ethnicity, gender, generation, sexual orientation, and religion) lead to perceptions about power, dominion, and subjugation. As women have changed their roles within society, there are ruptures in traditionally social roles, models, and paradigms.

SCIENCE AND TECHNOLOGY DEMANDS

As previously noted, the international and national macro-determinants and micro-conditioning factors and the country's socio-historic development interweave throughout the history of nursing's undergraduate and graduate educational programs. Science and technology demands also shape nursing higher education.

Higher Nursing Education

Brazil's undergraduate nursing programs are offered at federal, state, and municipal public and private universities. Public universities at the three governmental levels are free of charge. Even though smaller in number, nursing schools in public universities are the most traditional and institutionally accountable. Private universities have the largest number of nursing schools, but with less tradition and institutional accountability. Graduate programs—master's and doctoral—are predominantly offered in federal and state public universities. The private universities have been much slower to offer graduate education for all careers because of a lack of facilities, funding and research infrastructure. In fact, it was not until 2004 that the first private master's program was offered, at the University of Garulhos. [27]

Agencies regulate educational policies. The *Coordenação de Aperfeiçoamento de Pessoal de Nível Superior* (CAPES)[28] and, at the Ministry of Science and Technology, the *Conselho Nacional de Desenvolvimento Científico e Tecnológico* (CNPq)[29] are Brazil's major educational regulatory agencies. CAPES is the national entity responsible for Brazil's graduate policy as well as the follow-up and evaluation of undergraduate and graduate education. CAPES also provides scholarships and grants for highly qualified graduate personnel who are accepted into excellent programs within Brazil and overseas. The CNPq also provides a variety grants. It funds the research of senior and junior investigators and provides graduate scholarships based on the same criteria as does CAPES.

Undergraduate Education

As noted at the beginning of this chapter, Brazilian undergraduate nursing education emerged in late 19th century as a response to the country's struggle to control the epidemics threatening its economic model. Nursing education initially focused on the preparation of nurses to function in public health (e.g., epidemic control and vaccination) (see Socio-Historic Development 19th to 20th century). As mentioned previously, during the first decades of the 20th century, nursing education sought to support the health sanitary model and meet the demands of an

---

[27] In Portuguese: Universidade de Guarulhos.

[28] Translation: Coordination for Further Education of Graduate Personnel – CFEGP.

[29] Translation: National Council for Scientific and Technological Development – NCSTD.

industrialized economy and urban workforce. The social and economic changes resulted in the development of medical assistance programs and the expansion of hospitals. Nurses who graduated from programs with this educational model joined philanthropic hospitals such as the *Santas Casas de Misericórdia*[30] and psychiatric or charity hospitals—thus continuing the charity work and the submissive nursing ideology originally initiated by lay people and nuns.

Also of note, during these early decades, nursing schools were associated with hospitals and were not part of the country's formal education system. As previously discussed, the first school in the Nightingale system, *The Anna Nery School of Nursing* (ANSN), opened in 1923. It became known as the "Reference or Gold Standard School" until 1949, when the State government, through the Ministry of Health and Education, formulated standards. In 1975, the Ministry of Education and Culture, Department for University Affairs–MEC/DAU[31] identified a number of problems related to the development of health sector human resources, particularly in nursing (MEC/DAU, 1974). The MEC/DAU recommended and implemented specific measures for the national expansion of undergraduate nursing education.

National Curricula Guidelines and Expansion of Undergraduate Programs

The macro-international demands and the micro-national factors constituted the most important referents for the advancement of nursing education, culminating in its inclusion in the university system. Nursing became a university-level, higher education career at public and private institutions, through the Law of Higher Education[32] passed in 1962. However, the growth of nursing schools was slow. By 1974, there were still only a total of 41 nursing schools and programs in different regions of the country. However, after the implementation of the 1975 MEC/DAU recommendations for health sector human resources, the number of schools increased in the mid-1970s; 22 new nursing schools and programs opened across different regions of the country and culminated in 63 nursing schools and programs in public universities (MEC/DAU, 1977; MEC/SES/CEEE, 1987; Wright, Paim, & Rodrigues, 1982). And, by 1980, there were 79 undergraduate schools and programs. Of these, 49 were in public (i.e., 30 federal, 11 state, and 8 municipal), and 30 in private universities (MEC/CAPES, 1996; MEC/SES/CEEE, 1987). Twenty years later, in the early 2000s, the number of nursing schools and programs had more than quadrupled to 354, with 114 in public and 240 in private universities (Ceccim & Feuerwerker, 2003).

The large number of undergraduate schools and programs in public institutions, supported by State subsidies from the military regime, helped precipitate an expansion of nursing schools and programs in private universities as well. The increase was facilitated through international agencies such as the United States Agency for International Development (USAID) and the Rockefeller, the Ford,

---

[30] Cultural note: Charity/Mercy Hospital Institutions run by Roman Catholic nuns.

[31] In Protuguese: Ministério da Educação, Departamento de Assuntos Universitários – MEC/DAU.

[32] In Portuguese: Lei de Educação Superior.

and the Kellogg Foundations. In summary, economic and industrial sector demands, pressures from organizations, and demands for efficacy, as well as the 1964 military *coup d'état* all forced the reformulation of the higher education system (Batista & Barrera, 1997a, 1997b).

Consequently, nursing schools and programs became part of the Universities Health Sciences Centers or Biomedical Science Centers that ensured integration into the university system. The university admissions system moved to the "Unified and Classificatory Vestibular Exam." Thus, a national examination system allowed the filling of all available seats in the university, in nursing and any other science undergraduate programs (Almeida & Maranhão, 2003). In conjunction, the credit system was implemented, and the nursing curriculum was divided into basic and professional programs, after the United States model (Nakame, 1987).

The Federal Council of Education (FCE)[33] established the minimum requirements and both schools and programs were responsible for developing their total nursing curricula to meet them. Initially, undergraduate programs, as recommended by the BNA, were to be 4 years in length and consist of 4,000 hours. Recently, the "National Curricula Guidelines for Undergraduate Nursing Education"[34] changed the requirements for hours and curricular content. Now baccalaureate students had to demonstrate the application of principles, foundations, conditions, and procedures in their early course work. This curricular content is to be the national template for the organization, development, and evaluation projects of undergraduate schools/ programs in the educational system under the Ministry of Education (Almeida & Maranhão, 2003).

These recommendations propose incorporating specific concepts that provide training for generalist nurses who would then function as integrated team members in interdisciplinary situations and possess both general and specific competencies. Furthermore, programs are to foster the principles of autonomy, flexibility, and plurality, which permeate the interdependency among teaching, research, and application/extension. Therefore, undergraduate curricula must possess an interdisciplinary perspective, conceptualize curricula in view of culture, faculty and students' backgrounds, and assure baseline levels of competence in graduates (Ramos, 2003).

In addition, programs must be based on the principles of the UHS, and include the political, social, economic, and cultural aspects of Brazil. In public universities, UHS principles guided nursing's curricular development, resulting in the high quality rating of programs in the public universities. But the discrepancy between the superior quality of education in public universities in contrast to private universities has been detrimental to the overall educational excellence of nursing. Unfortunately, initially (up to 2003) there was no official mechanism, similar to UHS, to control the quality of the increasing number of programs offered by private universities. In addition to the UHS monitoring mechanisms, the quality of public and private

---

[33] In Portuguese: Conselho Federal de Educação.

[34] In Portuguese: Diretrizes Curriculares Nacionais do Ensino de Graduação de Enfermagem.

universities differ in terms of faculty qualifications and roles. Public university schools and programs follow very strict rules and norms for faculty qualifications that reinforce the importance of research. However, the vast majority of private university nursing schools and programs do not. In fact, the majority of private universities do not have as priorities the three-fold academic roles of teaching, research, and service. Private universities focus solely on the faculty's teaching role, and typically, very little or no research is conducted.

Currently, the UHS considers the quality discrepancies in the recent boom of undergraduate programs a challenge to be addressed by nursing associations, councils, and unions. Despite the struggle over responsibility, these disparities in the quality of undergraduate programs reinforce the need for the government to be the gatekeeper that grants new programs permission to open. Fortunately, in 2004 the Ministry of Education (ME) placed a moratorium on the creation of new undergraduate programs for 180 days. During this period, new mechanisms for issuing credentials and authorizations for institutions and new programs were generated. These mechanisms tightened up the "looseness," created during Fernando Henrique Cardoso's (1999-2002) presidential mandate. The Ministry of Health, Department of Management in Health Labor and Education–DMHLE[35]—through its Permanent Education Centers located all over the country established an education policy in the health sector—for the existing 16 health care careers in Brazil (Ceccim & Feuerwerker, 2004a, 2004b).

Undergraduate Education Contrasts

Some of the contrasts in higher education in general and in nursing education in particular are related primarily to the fact that Brazilian public universities are completely tuition free. Public universities receive state financial support for the operating costs to develop and promote high quality teaching, research, and service[36] activities in underserved communities. As a result, Brazil's public universities rank higher nationally and internationally in terms of teaching, research, and knowledge production than do its private universities. Thus, the majority of public universities are able to attract students from high and upper middle class backgrounds and who have attended the better preparatory schools. In contrast, private universities admit students from middle and lower class backgrounds because their families cannot afford expensive, prestigious elementary, middle, and high schools. Most students who attend nursing programs in private universities without state supported financial aid have to work during the day to afford evening school tuition. The following summarizes the situations of both faculty and students.

In the majority of public universities, faculty members are full-time employees and able to dedicate their time and effort to their academic roles of teaching,

---

[35] In Portuguese: Departamento de Gestão do Trabalho e da Educação na Saúde – DEGES.

[36] Cultural Note: University faculty, staff and student service activities are community programs and services developed, implemented/delivered, and evaluated with community participation.

research, and service. In contrast, faculty members in most private universities are hired as hourly (class-hours) employees and are not remunerated for the other aspects of the faculty role. Students in both types of universities face the same dilemmas as faculty. For example, the majority of undergraduate students in public universities do not have to work. They are able to dedicate more time to their studies and become involved in activities such as faculty-sponsored research. Students at private universities generally do not have the luxury of such opportunities.

However, despite an increase in the number of seats in public universities' nursing programs there have actually had a decrease in the number of applicants. The number of applicants reached its nadir during the 1980s, during the *"Lost Decade."* However, beginning in the 1990s, the number of applicants for nursing schools and programs began to move upward because of (a) rise of job diversification in the labor market; (b) increase in school years of the employed workforce; (c) increase in school years in the different categories (leading to higher qualifications); and (d) expansion of health care jobs (mainly in the ambulatory care sector net/referral system) and in basic health care services (Ferraz, Nakao, & Mishima, 2004).

Although Brazil still does not have a sufficient number of nurses to meet the population's needs, at no time during its evolution has there been a general or severe shortage in the nursing workforce that required Brazil to import nurses from other countries.

Regionalization of Undergraduate Programs

Despite the severe nurse shortage in many countries of the world, Brazil faces a different situation. Brazil's geo-economic distribution influences the numbers of nurses produced, and consequentially, the health services delivered. However, because of economic inequity among the country's regions, there is unequal access to undergraduate nursing programs. The North, Northeast, and Center-West regions have a smaller number of nursing schools and programs compared to the more populated Southeast and South regions (Ferraz et al., 2004). Currently, the regions with unequal access to nursing education and health services do not meet the recommended proportions of baccalaureate prepared RNs, nursing technicians, and auxiliaries.

Some of the disparities among regions are related to nursing's discriminatory processes in regional opportunities. However, recent changes have occurred—one is the opening of undergraduate education to all eligible students. Whether or not this change in eligibility will increase the number of applicants has yet to be determined. Unfortunately, the history of graduate programs at Master's and Doctoral levels consists of the same unequal opportunities to access.

Graduate Education

World War II created the world's demands for more sophisticated science and technology. International and national pressures compelled Brazil to expand its science and technology base. Even though nursing schools were fulfilling their traditional roles, these pressures pushed the schools, primarily in the most developed regions, to advance their science and technology components. Thus, the establishment of graduate education occurred in response to two main demands at the height of an economic-industrial boom: The first, the need for a specialized workforce for new positions required by the expected economic development. The second, the need for scientists, researchers, and technicians capable of conducting research critical to the country's economic-industrial change (Rocha et al., 1988; Zucco, 1996).

In response to these powerful determinants and conditioning forces, the scientific community (located in institutes, techno-bureaucratic government organizations, and larger universities), developed organizations that demanded more voice in political matters and to be included in the benefits of the economic industrialization and modernization that the world and Brazil was experiencing (Córdoba, Gusso, & Luna, 1986). For example, the *"Brazilian Society for the Progress of Science"*[37] (1948), the *"Brazilian Center of Physics Research"*[38] (1949), the CAPES and the CNPq (1951) were created as a result of scientists' struggles for more resources such as more educational and research funds, better equipped libraries, up-to-date computer laboratories, latest software, and new/renovated buildings and facilities within the universities (Córdoba et al., 1986).

During the 1950s and 1960s, the Ministry of Culture and Education (MCE)[39] and the Federal Council of Education (FCE),[40] issued a report about distinctions between graduate programs. The distinctions consisted of graduate *"lato sensu"* (specialization) programs and graduate *"stricto sensu"* (master's and doctoral) programs. The national financial institutions such as CNPq, CAPES, Technical and Scientific Development Fund (TSDF),[41] the São Paulo State Foundation of Research Support (SPSFRS)[42] and international foundations such as Rockefeller and Ford emphasized and funded Brazilian involvement in international programs. Universities financed and supported faculty and scientists willing to leave the country for additional education by continuing to pay their salaries (Rocha et al., 1988). During this time, several other factors emerged in the country's push toward graduate education: (a) university reform; (b) increased registration for higher education programs; (c) quantitative expansion of institutes and departments; (d) need for better-qualified faculty; and (e) a decisive increase in the demand for graduate programs.

These factors resulted in the organization of *"stricto sensu"* (master's and doctoral programs) and the Sucupira Decision,[43] approved by the FCE in 1966, and the 1968 University Reform. The latter instituted the undissolvable interdependency between teaching and research, created the unit/credit system, and formalized departments as the smallest units of the graduate system (Almeida & Barreira, 2000).

---

[37] In Portuguese: Sociedade Brasileira para o Progresso da Ciência – SBPC.

[38] In Portuguese: Centro Brasileiro de Pesquisas Físicas.

[39] In Portuguese: Ministério da Educação e Cultura – MEC.

[40] In Portuguese: Conselho Federal de Educação – CFE.

[41] In Portuguese: Fundo do Desenvolvimento Técnico e Científico – FUNTEC.

[42] In Portuguese: Fundação de Amparo à Pesquisa do Estado de São Paulo – FAPESP.

[43] In Portuguese: Parecer Sucupira.

Graduate nursing education in Brazil actually began in the 1950s with specialization programs and then advanced in the 1970s with master's programs. Doctoral programs were not available until the 1980s. In both cases, educational policies precipitated the establishment of these levels of nursing education. These advances demonstrated that organized nursing was capable of assessing and performing concrete actions geared to professional development and to addressing the country's needs. Nursing's abilities to foster professional growth are also evident in the current demographic data. Currently, the breakdown of nursing faculty in Brazilian universities is: 9% have earned doctoral degrees, 34% have earned master's degrees, 48% have earned specialization (or advanced practice) degrees, and 9% have earned bachelor of sciences degrees. These percentages indicate a significant demand for nurses with earned doctorates, which, in turn supports the need for more doctoral programs in Brazil. More specifically, for a masters or a doctoral program to open, there is the legal requirement of at least eight doctorally prepared nurses, with a relevant scientific production. Thus, nationwide, doctorally prepared nurses are in demand to teach in graduate nursing programs at specialization (or advanced practice), master's, and doctoral levels. Last but not least, any graduate program—new or old—is required to be allied with a policy-prioritized project and geared toward meeting the needs and demands of both the country and the region where it is located.

Specialization Programs

The specialization (or advanced practice) programs were created to meet the need for nurses with specific expertise. These programs were expected to stimulate the development of leaders for the nursing labor market as well as expose students to conducting and using research. Thus, the graduates from these programs were expected to assume management and advanced care positions in specialty areas. The goals for these programs were, and are, to create high-quality nursing services, reaping high levels of patient satisfaction.

The specialization programs, begun during the 1950s, have demonstrated distinct trends over the years. For instance, the specialization in nursing administration experienced significant increases during the 1970s, and during the 1990s, there was a boom in specialized technology programs in response to major technologic development. Currently, the areas of specialization reflect less economic and technological developments and are more matched with applicants' interests. Oddly, it's been the regional, rather than national, demands that have promoted specialization programs.

Overall, these programs targeted nurses in the biomedical sector who want specialized training. The programs consolidate the scientific knowledge of nurse professionals who provide direct health care. At the same time the programs prepare nurses for more competent, satisfying, and fulfilling performances in an expanding labor market. These programs reflect the diversity of job opportunities and nursing practice that result from: a) changes in the labor market as result of reforms in the health sector and b) incorporation of technologies that concretely address the population's health care needs (Sena & Villalobos, 2001). The Ministry of Education (ME) established a minimum of 360 hours for specialization programs and the majority of programs offered do not exceed 600 class hours in one academic year.

In general, most of the specialty programs are grounded in critical thinking and a humanistic, multidisciplinary, holistic, and integrative conception of health care in order to meet both students' and clients' needs. The majority of faculty in these programs have master's and doctoral degrees and are affiliated with public universities. As competent university faculty, they dedicate a number of their work hours to the specialization programs ensuring that students receive a quality education.

There have been different approaches to funding these specialty programs. For instance, the Ministry of Health (MH) has funded those programs that mirrored components of the national health policy. These specialties have included Nursing Obstetrics; Specialization and Residency in Family Health (interdisciplinary); Specialization in Alcohol and Drugs (interdisciplinary); and in Gerontology (interdisciplinary). Another targeted program, the Drug Phenomenon Research (health professionals and related areas), is supported by the Organization of American States (OAS/CICAD). In general, however, student-paid tuition funds the majority of specialization programs.

During the last decades of the 20th century, state investment in education has fluctuated due to restrictive neoliberal policies. Unfortunately, these policies have prioritized areas directly connected to industrial production and infrastructure rather than those related to health, human, and social sciences. These priorities have not boded well for the specialization programs. Overall, specialization programs have been responses to economic policies in the health sector internal market. The health service needs of institutions drive the internal market. For example, the need for nurse administrators prompts a specialty program in Nursing Administration. Similarly, the need for Intensive Care or Emergency personnel prompts the development of specialty programs designed to meet that need. Finally, universities have taken advantage of the latest teaching technologies and offered some programs as blended or distance learning to open access to nurses throughout the country.

Master's and Doctoral Programs

In the 1970s, public universities began requiring their faculty to have master's degrees and, in the 1990s, to have doctoral degrees. To adequately prepare potential teaching faculty for these requirements, the first master's program was established in 1972 at the Federal University of *Rio de Janeiro,* Anna Nery School of Nursing. Shortly thereafter, in 1981, the first doctoral program was established at the University of *São Paulo,* through the *São Paulo* and *Riberão Preto* Schools of Nursing. The objective of these new programs, legislated by the Orientations and Fundamentals Law (OFL),[44] was to produce faculty who were qualified to teach and conduct research. Consequently, beginning in the 1990s, faculty from public

---

[44] In Portuguese: Lei de Diretrizes e Bases – LDB.

universities in the less populated Northeast, Center-West, and North migrated to the Southeast and South regions of the country to attend the doctorate-granting university programs clustered there.

The growth of the graduate, *stricto sensu*, nursing programs was relatively uniform in the 1970s and 1980s, but during the 1990s, the numbers increased significantly. However, again these programs were concentrated in the São Paulo and Rio de Janeiro states (Gutiérrez, Vieira, Almeida, Elsen, & Stefanelli, 2001). Still, Brazil, with a total of 40 programs, has the most nursing *stricto sensu* (master's and doctoral) graduate programs in Latin America. Of the 40 graduate programs, 13 offer doctorates; 23 offer master's, and 4 offer professional master's programs. See Table 2 for the distribution of graduate programs per geographical region.

The data indicate that the majority of graduate programs are in public federal and state universities and are located in the Southeast and South regions. The intensification of nursing's scientific and technological development, the production of theses and dissertations, and the publication of papers in refereed journals and books during the 1990s was vital to recognition by the scientific community.

Currently, Brazil is recognized as a leader in graduate education. Indeed, prior to the 1990s, it was the only Latin American country with doctoral programs. Brazil's leadership position is related to multiple factors, which include: (a) a predominance of public universities at state or federal levels; (b) a more developed infrastructure that supports program funding and academic resources (i.e., software, libraries, research facilities); and (c) most importantly, professors with earned doctorates either in disciplines other than nursing (e.g., education) or in nursing programs overseas (e.g., the United States, Canada, and Europe). Thus, Brazilian faculty were poised to support developing programs and nurse scientists in other Latin American countries such as Colombia, Chile, Equador, Peru, Argentina, and Mexico. In addition, the Government of Brazil, through its CAPES agency, provided and continues to provide scholarships to students from the South American, Central American, and African countries with which it has maintained exchange treaties or agreements (Pagliuca, Gutiérrez, Erdmann, Leite, Almeida, & Kurcgant, 2001). Thus, Brazilian nursing takes into account not only Brazilian needs, but also those of Latin America and Africa.

Admitting faculty prepared at the doctoral level, mentoring nurses in graduate programs, and fostering research skills have contributed to proposals for alleviating Brazil's health care problems. Currently, the *stricto sensu* graduate programs serve both national and international nursing. The Brazilian graduate programs have enhanced the qualifications of nursing professionals and the country's scientific advancement. These in turn, culminated in Brazil's prestige within both Pan-American and European contexts.

The total number of nursing faculty in all areas reveals that Brazil has exponentially increased the ratio of nurses with earned master's degrees to the population as a whole. In 1991 there were 3:0 nurses with master's degrees for every 100,000 Brazilians. In 1998, that ratio increased to 4.7 nurses with master's degrees to every

Table 2. Distribution of Nursing Graduate Programs per
Geographical Region

Region university	City and state	Graduate
SOUTHEAST		
Universidade de São Paulo (São Paulo)	São Paulo/SP	4 (M (2); D (2)
Universidade de São Paulo (Ribeirão Preto)	Ribeirão Preto/SP (Total)	6 (M (3); D (3)
Universidade de São Paulo (São Paulo/Ribeirão Preto)	São Paulo/SP Ribeirão Preto/SP	1 (D)
Universidade Federal de São Paulo	São Paulo/SP	2 (M (1); D (1)
Universidade Federal de São Paulo	São Paulo/SP	1 (MP)
Universidade Estadual de Campinas	Campinas/SP	1 (M)
Universidade Estadual Paulista (Botucatu)	Botucatu/SP	1 (MP)
Universidade de Guarulhos	Guarulhos/SP (private)	1 (MP)
Sub-Total: São Paulo		**17**
Universidade Federal do Rio de Janeiro	Rio de Janeiro/RJ	2 (M (1); D (1)
UNIRIO	Rio de Janeiro/RJ	1 (M)
Universidade Estadual do Rio de Janeiro	Rio de Janeiro/RJ	1 (M)
Universidade Federal Fluminense	Niterói/RJ	1 (MP)
Sub-Total: Rio de Janeiro		**5**
Universidade Federal de Minas Gerais	Belo Horizonte/MG	2 (M (1); D (1)
Sub-Total: Minas Gerais		**2**
TOTAL:		**24 (60.0%)**
CENTER-WEST		
Universidade Federal de Goiânia	Goiânia/GO	1 (M)
Universidade Federal de Mato Grosso	Cuiabá/MT	1 (M)
TOTAL:		**2 (5.5%)**
NORTHEAST		
Universidade Federal da Paraiba	João Pessoa/PB	1 (M)
Universidade Federal da Bahia	Salvador/BA	2 (M (1); D (1)
Universidade Federal do Ceará	Fortaleza/CE	2 (M (1); D (1)
Fundação Universidade Estadual do Ceará	Fortaleza/CE	1 (M)
Universidade Federal do Rio Grande do Norte	Natal/RN	1 (M)
TOTAL:		**7 (17.5%)**
SOUTH		
Universidade Federal de Santa Catarina	Florianópolis/SC	2 (M (1); D (1)
Universidade Federal do Rio Grande do Sul	PortoAlegre/RS	2 (M (1); D (1)
Universidade de Rio Grande	Rio Grande/RS	1 (M)
Universidade Federal do Paraná	Curitiba PR	1 (M)
Universidade Estadual de Maringá	Maringá/PR	1 (M)
TOTAL:		**7 (17.5%)**
TOTAL:		**40 (100%)**

Note: M = Master's; D = Doctoral; and MP = Professional Master's
Source: MEC/CAPES (2007).

100,000. Other data supported the increase. In 2003, according to the CAPES Nursing Assessment Committee,[45] the number of nurses from Brazilian programs with master's (3,176) and with doctorates (834) was at an all time high. Like all other areas of knowledge (e.g., engineering, biology), the university internal commission conducts yearly (and the Ministry of Education–ME/CAPES conducts alternate yearly) assessments to evaluate nursing graduate programs in order to maintain their integrity. Thus, all programs are subjected to both rigorous governmental and scientific quality assurance and control.

Graduate Program Perspectives

For the future, there are strategies for the expansion and consolidation of nursing graduate programs (Padilha, Pires, Martins, & Wright, 2003). These include, but are not limited to: (a) the expansion of the "Regional Centers of Nursing Graduate Education" to other regions in the country that do not have graduate programs, for example, the "REPENSUL" (this project aimed to increase the numbers of nurses with master's and doctoral degrees in the region as well as the number of new graduate programs); (b) the increase of lines of research to conduct national, trans-national, and multi-center studies which would strengthen specific areas of knowledge and consequently Brazilian nursing science; (c) the consolidation of post-doctoral programs among the existing seven in the country and overseas which would enhance the quality of university graduate programs and faculty; (d) the increase in the number of "Sandwich Doctoral Programs"[46] that are nationally and internationally supported by funding agencies of science and technology development to improve doctoral education as well as to enhance international interchange and partnerships; and (e) the identification of unexplored areas of nursing research that will facilitate knowledge and would reduce the number of graduates who have to change programs, reducing program costs. These objectives indicate a heightened interest in the future of nursing scholars and scientists.

Graduate Education Impact in Latin America

The emerging investment in nurses earning graduate degrees is aimed at forming leaders, critical thinking, investment in scientific knowledge, and building capacity. Nurses with master's and doctoral degrees contribute to the development of a professional practice by seeking solutions to critical health problems, while simultaneously supporting the country's development through their representation and presence in major political decision and policy making. In addition, these professionals have developed a higher level of professional practice, structured by

---

[45] In Portuguese: Comissão de Avaliação de Enfermagem da CAPES.

[46] Cultural note: *Sandwich Doctoral Programs* (Programas de Doutorado Sanduíche) are programs currently funded by CAPES and CNPq agencies. In this modality of scholarship the sponsored graduate student takes half of her/his doctoral program in Brazil and the other half overseas at a graduate program/institution that has excellence in her/his research question/area.

the critical thinking processes learned while developing their master's theses and doctoral dissertations.

However, these efforts have been insufficient to fully change the quality of professional practice or the nation's social inequities. What is missing are national strategic plans grounded in an ideology about the value of science and technology. Such strategic plans would permit the organization of a robust cadre of nurse researchers. Indeed, past national strategies for higher education expansion in Brazil could serve as a reference for such a strategy. And, financial and techno-logical support from national and international funding agencies would result in quality improvement of undergraduate and graduate education and science and technology production.

Even until the advent of national strategies, progress will still continue with the development of partnerships among teaching, service, and research. The partner-ships foster new opportunities to incorporate innovative scientific and technological knowledge into solutions for real-life situations. These solutions occur in both undergraduate programs and specialty graduate programs where practicing nurses share their experiences and faculty provides their expertise. Thought-provoking interactions occur in seminars where practicing nurses, faculty and undergraduate students discuss problems and reach consensus. The challenges of the 21st century require more such interactions structured by an intense critical thinking process, aimed at alternative solutions based on scientific evidence. In time, graduates of nursing programs will spearhead this necessary revolution.

Slowly but steadily, nursing graduate education has improved the quality nursing care, as indicated by the increased number of clinicians with master's and doctoral degrees, who introduce, enhance or foster critical thinking in non-academic practice settings. The Brazilian graduate faculty's support to Latin American and African countries (especially those countries whose first language is Portuguese) has been multifaceted. They have trained the first doctorally prepared groups in some of these regions in order that those students can then initiate doctoral programs in their own countries. Also, Brazilian nursing has also established agreements with other Latin American and African universities to create nursing graduate programs to meet these countries' specific needs and requests.

Research Evolution and Consolidation

Nursing research in Brazil evolved with the creation of the master's (1970s) and doctoral degree programs (1980s). Little by little, nurse researchers developed and refined both qualitative and quantitative scientific methods as well as con-tributed to technological and scientific advancement for applied research in day-to-day nursing practice. Thus, over the past 30 years, there has been an increase in nursing knowledge production. However, because of the complex relationships among knowledge production, dissemination of research findings and improvement in practice, determining the actual quality of the research findings—in the light of its limited societal impact—requires additional investigation. Another serious and equally important aspect of research has been the lack of exclusive criteria for evaluation of scientific production.

Despite these limitations, the incorporation of research results into professional practice is an important achievement. In Brazil, evidence-based practice is still a "work in progress" (SEPLAN/CNPq, 1982). Although evidence-based practical applications have been common and systematically incorporated in non-nursing disciplines (medical and social sciences), it is only within the last 30 years that evidence—both international and national—begun to systematically inform nursing practice. Since the 1970s, nursing leaders—with the support of the Brazilian government—have set national priorities and research guidelines for the production of nursing knowledge in conjunction with science and technology policies. During the 1980s, with the incentives of SEPLAN[47]/CNPq (1982), Brazilian nurses defined (a) strategies for the scientific and technological development of nursing, and (b) the three priorities for government research funding. Doing so opened up opportunities for more political space, funding (grants) and representation in SEPLAN/CNPq, and a research planning office for the profession.

During the late 1990s, after national discussions among science and technology graduate program coordinators, the 1970s document which set research priorities was revised based on the scientific products of master's and doctoral programs. A second document was produced that grouped into broad themes scientific evidence produced by various researchers and research groups. Because of its obvious contribution, as a result, nursing gained representation in the MEC/CAPES agency as a consequence of its new position in the country's scientific and technologic community (Gutierrez et al., 2001).

The 1980s and 1990s were decades of multiple advances for nursing, both in the spheres of science and technology policy and in graduate nursing education. Generally, the production of scientific knowledge has come from: (a) dissertations[48] and data-based research reports from graduate theses or faculty selection exams;[49] (b) faculty research at nursing schools either with graduate programs or those associated with nursing and multi-professional research groups; and (c) research requested by the Brazilian Nursing Association or other professional organizations and conducted by research nurses and developed by faculty and non-faculty researchers (SEPLAN/CNPq, 1982, p. 16).

Specific theoretical and methodological trends (Neves & Vargens, 2003; Santiago, 2000) that influenced research include: (a) the combination of qualitative and quantitative (mainly historic materialism or phenomenology) methods seeking

---

[47] In Portuguese: Secretaria de Planejamento – SEPLAN. Translation: Planning Office.

[48] Cultural note: In Brazil the word "*dissertação*" stands for Master's (Honor) Thesis and the word "*tese*" stands for Doctoral Dissertation.

[49] Cultural note: Available faculty positions at public universities are advertised. Interested applicants join the selection process, submit their CV, and go through exams. Most selection processes have a curriculum analysis, a clinical practice exam and a lecture delivered on a topic drawn 24-48 hours in advance. The applicant who scores highest in total takes the position.

answers to questions emerging from professional practice and population needs; (b) the use of research findings to produce a professional practice based on scientific evidence; and (c) the insufficient financial and technological support from the existing funding agencies—for both consolidated and emerging nursing research groups. These trends also consolidated the means of disseminating nursing knowledge: (a) peer reviewed national and international nursing and non-nursing journals; (b) monographs and books; and (c) bulletins, brochures, and university papers, such as catalogued master's theses, doctoral dissertations, conference proceedings, and oral presentations at national and international conferences.

Most nursing research is operational, applied, or intervention studies. Such studies have an impact on health and nursing care in: (a) care management developed with active participation of nursing team; (b) better communication processes with increased interaction between staff and patients; (c) nursing care focused on patient and families using qualified listening, responsible autonomy, and integral care; (d) application of educational methods to improve the life style of adults with chronic conditions such as diabetes, hypertension, obesity; (e) humanization of nursing care; and (f) interactive educational technologies to improve treatment adherence and follow-up for patients with tuberculosis, AIDS, and other chronic diseases (Almeida, Mishima, & Peduzzi, 1999). During the 1990s, the number of Brazilian nursing journals increased from 6 to 20. Unsurprisingly, this trend paralleled the trend of new graduate nursing programs. By the year 2004, Brazil had 18 indexed nursing journals, classified by the CAPES Nursing Area Evaluation Committee based on normalization criteria and on their national and international circulation (Pagliuca et al., 2001).

Despite these advances in the conduct of research, there is still not much international visibility. The most significant barriers to the international publication of Brazilian research reports and scholarly papers include: (a) English as a second language and Brazilian researchers' limited English language proficiency; (b) diverse criteria of international journals; and (c) the power relations among nurse scientists in different countries.

Brazilian nurse scientists must also eliminate national barriers. Scientific knowledge is produced primarily in research networks or centers concentrated in Brazil's Southeast region. Other regions must be involved to stimulate exchange among researchers and the scientific community must determine their priorities. Focus on eliminating these barriers would promote a national financial and technology policy to: (a) promote the advancement of existing research networks and centers, and (b) establish research centers for career development in priority areas that do not currently have them.

Both graduate programs and nursing research in Brazil have achieved their major objectives to become consolidated in different regions of the country. Currently, the goal is to accelerate incorporating research findings into professional practice, to hasten the development and consolidation of scientific and technological evidence-based nursing that improves health care for all Brazilians, with positive repercussion in the Americas.

COMPARATIVE ANALYSIS: BRINGING IT ALL TOGETHER

The World, the Americas, and Nursing Trends in the 21st Century

Several macro-determinants and micro-conditioning events have entirely changed the direction of international and national relations during the early 21st century. These factors include: economic relations and policies, security measures, communications and dissemination systems, health systems organization and management, social security, education, sports, and specific components such as the socialization of knowledge. Nursing's evolution in the world and in Brazil will particularly be affected by the following six levels of world trends (International Council of Nursing, 1999; Rourke, 2003; Wright, 2003).

Political Trends

Globalization and a new geopolitical era characterized by strong religious fundamentalism and by terrorism have influenced a number of politically unstable countries. The more stable countries have reorganized and created political partnerships as approaches to balancing hierarchical power relations. The consequences of these political partnerships at the same time as democratic and "welfare" states have weakened, is yet to be determined. Hopefully, the political instability and the emergence of daring but peaceful globalization processes may integrate heretofore excluded countries and non-hegemonic markets. Pinning its future on the possibility of more inclusive processes, nursing has helped construct political and health policies aimed at reducing health-care disparities. These policies aim to: (a) integrate underserved and excluded groups and individuals into society; (b) expand participative democratic arenas; (c) voice clients' concerns; and (d) ensure equal, integral, and universal access to health care services.

Economic Trends

These political trends meld with a new global economic paradigm that assumes the privatization of public properties, increased interdependence among countries, and dependence of developing countries on developed countries, a fresh and elaborate form of "21st Century Colonization." This current paradigm has serious and deleterious effects because the greater discrepancies and inequalities between the world's rich and poor nations have left major populations seriously behind. For Brazil, the most pressing challenge of this "fresh" colonization has been the health and economic disparities directly affecting the health care system.

Most countries confronted the globalization of medical/health systems with their own medical health care delivery system reforms. The medical/health model that emphasized privatization and managerial and organizational efficiency also changed the relations between the health care team and patient. The changes empowered patients as consumers to demand their rights and have also affected nursing evolution in unanticipated ways. Brazilian nurses had to become better prepared philosophically and academically to provide equal and universal health care, in a country with a high incidence of poverty, disparities, and absolute inequalities.

Health and Environmental Trends

Although recent scientific, health, and environmental developments have contributed to increased life expectancy and well-being among many populations, these developments have not always been positive. The technology monopoly is concentrated in core capitalist nations and the polluting industries are concentrated in developing ones. But risk is not limited to just the populations in developing nations. As Godue (1997) points out, in a world more and more interconnected, the concept of invulnerability is not valid. Instability at the periphery increases vulnerability in the center. That is, problems affecting "others" may become threats to the "self." An example of Godue's point is Avian Flu. It initially affected a developing country, but has spread to developed countries, despite all efforts to contain it. Thus, no developed nor developing nation is immune. There are increased probabilities for new diseases, the recurrence of diseases thought to be eliminated; higher incidences of acts of violence; increased licit and illicit substance abuse; changes in patterns of migration and immigration; as well as natural or human-induced disasters. These risks necessitate nursing to investigate and alleviate medical/health problems caused by "environmental racism"—health problems created from placing populations in developing countries at risk from environmental and non-environmental causes. There is a moral imperative as well. Nursing's involvement in the prevention of "environmental racism" is grounded in its mission to provide services to all people.

To meet this mission, nurses' roles must be multifaceted. Nurses must also promote health as well as prevent disease. Also, as educators, nurses must participate in raising patients'/consumers' consciousness about environmental health risks and threats. Brazilian nurses need to use "clean" technologies and nursing interventions as effective strategies which at the same time also help promote the population's health consciousness. One example of a wellness intervention is "environmental alphabetization," being carried out in several cities in Brazil, where knowledge about ways to conserve and protect natural resources is exchanged. Another example is nursing's investment in health promotion policies such as—Healthy Cities[50] and Agenda 21—which are aimed at the development of new ways of working with and caring for people and conserving planetary resources through collaborative partnerships.

Scientific and Technological Trends

The majority of the world's nations are interconnected in this information-technology age. Nursing has incorporated innovative technology and computer

---

[50] In Portuguese: Cidades Saudáveis.

science in its educational programs. Schools of nursing have developed under-graduate and graduate nursing curricula using virtual/distance learning classrooms, which provide educational accessibility to candidates and professional nurses from different parts of the country. Simultaneously, Brazilian citizens, weary of the biomedical model, have begun to demand better access to both traditional and homeopathic therapies. Nursing has initiated new course offerings (at all degree and certificate levels) about alternative therapeutic practices and has created joint spaces for the practice of more pluralistic and holistic services. Such trends have compelled nursing to recognize that multiple, comprehensive, and innovative thera-peutic modalities are necessary and must be incorporated into educational programs alongside the advances in science and technology.

Nursing Education and Professional Trends

In Brazil, nursing schools have developed curricular models based on nursing and other theories. Pedagogical approaches are grounded in participative forums and critical thinking methodologies[51] as well as in the use of distance learning, blended and virtual technologies. These and other approaches are now integral compo-nents of graduate school curricula for Brazilian nurse educators. Curricular content includes international and environmental health; licit and illicit drugs; family health; human and population aging; social inequalities; and approaches to natural and "man-made" disasters. Studying these content areas prepares politically-aware nurse scholars and advocates. Thus, nurses are more visible in both the political and scientific communities. Nurses have achieved their visibility by accepting leader-ship positions in community health care as well as in national and international organizations' health promotion and preventive services.

Despite these professional advances, efforts directed toward better health con-ditions and the formulation of an equitable, universal, free of charge health system have been an ongoing, and largely unsuccessful struggle. Yet, Brazilian nursing professionals continue to be visibly involved in political actions aimed at reducing inequalities and social exclusion among the many population groups. As dynamic international macro-determinants and national micro-conditioning factors shift, which challenges will Brazilian nursing confront as it struggles to ensure its pro-fessional leadership? The following section addresses this question from two per-spectives: (a) the economic, social, professional, science, and technology market demands and (b) the globalized market economy's contradictions and inequities.

Market and Other Demands

Economic Demands

The neoliberal economic policies imposed on Brazil and other Latin American countries by funding agencies such as the International Monetary Fund (IMF), the World Bank (WB), and the Inter-American Development Bank (IDB) can be

---

[51] In Portuguese: metodologias problematizadoras da realidade.

viewed as promoting the well-being of all Brazilian people, or as promoting positive benefits for only selected population groups. In fact, a combination of these two views is the true perspective.

Social, Professional, Science, and Technology Demands

UHS demands highly-qualified professionals, with in-depth scientific and technical knowledge to develop and to implement health programs and projects in accordance with the diverse populations' needs. This continual demand ensures nursing's value to the NHS. A case in point is nursing's representation on negotiation teams with international funding banks. The UHS's demand has assisted nursing in garnering representation at: the Ministries of Health and Education, state health offices and health centers as well as international financial organizations, such as the IDB (office representation in Brazil), the Pan-American Health Organization (PAHO office representation in Brazil), and non-health agencies such as the Organization of American States (OAS) which includes the Commission for Inter-American Drug Abuse Control Commission (CICAD) in Washington DC, U.S.A. (Wright, 2002). These leadership positions enhance nursing's visibility and continued demand for leadership positions.

To insure that future nursing professionals are qualified for such work, at both national and international levels, programs involving more than one scientific knowledge domain have been added to the curricula. Examples of interdisciplinary programs include combinations such as nursing and business management; nursing, nutrition, and food engineering; and nursing, international relations, and public health. In tangent, faculty has increasingly adopted different pedagogies such as Wright's Critical-Holistic Paradigm Theoretical Model for Brazilian Nursing, and other theoretical models.

During the 1970s, the country's administration realized that the number of nurses was not increasing as rapidly the numbers of other health care professionals. In response to the neoliberal international economic policy and the UHS demands, the Ministry of Education initiated a national policy for qualification of nurses. The Ministry of Health, through the *Human Resources Observatory,* funded in the mid-1980s, has been following the expansion of public and private nursing schools based on the specific needs of the country's geographical regions (Ferraz et al., 2004). The expansion of nursing education at universities also created nursing graduate programs that met the requirements to qualify nurses for leadership positions.

A major hurdle that hindered the advancement of higher education, specifically during Fernando Henrique Cardoso's administration, was the reduction of faculty positions in public universities. Additionally, many faculty positions were lost after faculty retired.[52] The decrease in numbers of faculty meant heavier workloads and additional stress for the remaining faculty as they strove to maintain high standards

---

[52] This problem did affect almost all public universities programs.

and quality programs. Regardless, these hurdles have not prevented Brazilian faculty from assisting "sister schools" in Latin America and Africa.

At more than 30 years, Brazilian nursing has the longest history in Latin America of university and graduate education and research, and has attempted to meet Latin American and African countries' needs for nurses with graduate degrees as well. Currently, several Brazilian graduate nursing schools (the Schools of Nursing of the University of *São Paulo,* the Federal University of *Rio de Janeiro,* and the Federal University of Santa Catarina[53]) have "faculty qualification" agreements and treaties with schools of nursing in other Latin American countries. In turn, these schools have been pivotal in the opening of doctoral programs in Latin America, graduating their first cadre of nurses with earned doctorates and in advising about the processes of implementing new doctoral programs in nursing. Finally, universities and technical nursing schools have taken responsibility to reclassify nursing auxiliaries as nursing technicians. The technical nursing programs are offered through distance learning. So far, the evaluations based on cost-benefit, efficacy, and efficiency indicators have been positive.

Contradictions in the Global Market Economy

In the lifelong education and professional practice model, Brazilian nursing has much to master in order to provide health services for all Brazilians. There are obvious and continuing disparities in health services, accessibility to these services and nurses' work conditions among the different regions in the country as a result of the country's neoliberal policies adopted in the last decades of the 20th century. Brazilian nursing and its organizations have participated actively in nationwide and local movements aimed at new health policies to improve living conditions of the population and the work conditions of health care professionals and workers in general.

Immigration and migration has increased worldwide and nurses have not been exempt from this phenomenon. Nursing "brain-drain" has been observed in many countries though not in Brazil. Interestingly, the *MERCOSUL* establishment has resulted in the immigration of nurses from other Latin American countries into Brazil. Consequently, the Federal Nursing Council and the Brazilian Nursing Association have reviewed and updated their bylaws and regulations as they contemplate new demands from the nursing labor market. The influx of non-Brazilian nurses will provide future challenges for Brazil's nursing workforce.

Future Challenges to Transform Nursing

Considering the intricately interwoven challenges imposed by the dynamic forces of the 20th and 21st centuries, nursing proposals centered on new approaches to nursing leadership are essential. Additionally, nursing leaders who are confident and

---

[53] In Portuguese: Universidade de São Paulo, Universidade Federal do Rio de Janeiro, and Universidade Federal de Santa Catarina.

skilled in mobilizing all nurses as members of a team are needed to develop educational programs, research projects and interventions that will influence the health of the nation.

In general, the economic and social challenges faced by developing countries in the world are that certain populations will be excluded from the development process. To avoid this future, an alternative would be to implement radical changes in economic policies of developed countries for a future with a more ethical and humane social reality. It is imperative that nursing attend to the factors and determinants that drive social systems. From the authors' perspectives, nursing education and professional practice must be grounded in a socially responsive view of the world while at the same time being constructed within the domains of science and technology. Nursing leadership in Brazil and beyond can benefit from collaborating with governments and international organizations to challenge and respond to economic, social, professional, scientific, and technological market demands.

Higher Education Demands

Curricula that are flexible yet adhere to evolving science and technology need to be implemented with innovative pedagogies that incorporate new educational paradigms. Discipline-specific and theory-based historic-social, cultural, ethical, political, and humanistic issues must be required in professional practice teaching-learning processes at all levels of the nursing curriculum. Programs for researchers, faculty and professionals at all post graduate levels require financial assistance (e.g., grants and scholarships) to increase Latin American countries' competitiveness in national and international labor markets. To foster cultural, scientific, and technological enrichment, more programs (such as "Solidary University"; "Rondon Project"; "See UHS"; and "Learn UHS"[54]) for exchange, networking, mentoring and service need to be implemented.

In summary, Brazilian higher education must also: (a) intensify the use of current undergraduate and graduate technologies such as teleconferences, distance learning, and blended programs; (b) introduce the application of science and technology; (c) develop and manage technological-scientific cooperation treaties; and (d) create science and technology laboratories for undergraduate and graduate nursing education.

Professional Practice Demands

Workforce labor issues can be addressed through the establishment of policies for priority issues in the public and private sectors such as precarious nursing work (e.g., temporary or part-time contracts, low wages, excessive weekly work hours); technological and evidence-based nursing practice; policies that regulate the expansion and implementation of permanent education centers specifically to update technological nursing services; and professional leadership. Additionally, issues created by the culture of nursing practice—(a) task classified social divisions within

---

[54] In Portuguese: Universidade Solidária; Projeto Rondon; Ver SUS; and Aprender SUS.

the profession; (b) decreased value of teamwork; and (c) problematic professional social dynamics and inter-relations—need to be solved.

Research Demands

Research for Brazilian nursing has evolved slowly, but continually. Still needed, however, are collaborative networks, joint publications among faculty at national and international universities, and additional investigations into the country's priority areas. Researchers' social and professional needs encompass: (a) conducting macro-structural investigations that involve political, economic and social aspects of nursing and health; (b) breaking down the dichotomy between disease prevention and health promotion; (c) developing multi-center research studies; and (d) contributing to the knowledge base about ethnicity and gender. Additionally, studies about the intersection of research, science, and technology and new technologies for nursing education and practice require funding.

FINAL CONSIDERATIONS

Nursing in Brazil has evolved over time within the context of the country's social, economic, political, scientific, and technologic development. As of 2005, the numbers of nurses and nursing technicians have continually increased. At the same time, the numbers of nursing attendants have decreased, but many have become nursing technicians through the *PROFAE* program. Historically, the number of registered nurses in Brazil always has been less than other nursing professionals. This trend will undoubtedly continue for some time. Currently, Brazil does not have the same shortages of nursing professionals that Canada and the United States do. The primary challenge faced by Brazilian nursing is where the majority of nurses are located, with a concentration in the southeast region. Salary disparities among the different regions contribute to nurses migrating for better pay. Nursing itself is being characterized as a "migratory" profession. In general, nurse professionals have assumed leadership positions at the macro level (i.e., international organizations and international development banks); and micro level (i.e., within the NHS, management of national programs and projects, state and local level management, and as directors of multi-professional teams).

Obviously, leadership positions provide higher salaries and in general, head nurses' salaries are comparable to those of physicians who are employed by the public health system. However, most physicians also work autonomously in the private sector, accounting for the monthly income difference. Nurses' working conditions need to improve for them to maintain only one job, rather than two, or sometimes, three jobs as they currently do. The current need to hold down two or three jobs speaks loudly about distinctions between nurses and physicians and their perceived societal value. The fact that a majority of the nursing workforce belongs to unions (95%) has not translated to an increase in salaries or improvement in work place conditions. Unfortunately, nursing unions are losing their bargaining power in today's political arena. One last major contention which Brazilian nurses have not openly discussed is gender and ethnicity issues.

The number of nursing schools has expanded numerically and geographically, contributing to an increase in the programs for general practice. Scientific production and research projects by nurses, as principal investigators, have also increased exponentially. Brazilian researchers have fostered international research partnerships in order to overcome barriers to international publishing. Despite being the home of the most graduate nursing programs in Latin America, Brazilian nursing practice and scientific production still face difficulties with international and national visibility and funding, as well as internal labor struggles and health care challenges common to a number of Latin American countries, although a few are common to North America as well. Throughout this chapter, the "Critical-Holistic Paradigm" (Wright, 2000) facilitated the identification of ideologies that have affected the profession of nursing and how current nursing education, research, and social practices were developed based on a strong political participatory tradition.

In conclusion, Brazil is a country in transition, from a capitalist economy and deeply unequal society to a steady and self-sustained democratic country. In this sense, Brazil's nursing evolution reflects the socio-political and historical evolution of the country. Nursing research, education, and practice in Brazil should continue effective participation in those social and political movements that favor inclusion in and accessibility to a health care tailored to the needs of all Brazilians.

ACKNOWLEDGMENTS

The authors would like to express a special thank you to Dr. Cornelia P. Porter, who assisted with multiple editions of the chapter, specifically the English edition; as well as to Dr. Jaqueline Da Silva, who translated the Portuguese version of the chapter into English, for her effort, dedication, and suggestions to improve the editing of the chapter.

The authors also thank Cristiane Gramari Say, grantee of CNPq Technical Support in Dr. Maria Cecilia Puntel de Almeida's project "Work Technological Organizations in Health Care" for her valuable logistic and technological collaboration in the making of this chapter. We express special thanks to the InterAmerican Drug Abuse Control Commission–CICAD of the Organization of American States–OAS for fostering nursing integration and advance in the Americas, with special emphasis in Latin America and the Caribbean Regions.

With great sadness we inform the readers that Dr. Maria Cecilia Puntel de Almeida passed away on February 15, 2009. No words in Portuguese or in English can translate how much she and her work will be missed—she truly was an admirable nurse scientist and a person who enriched the minds and lives of those she met. We were privileged to have had the opportunity to work with her in this endeavor and to share with you some of this experience.

REFERENCES

Almeida, M., & Maranhão, E. (2003). *Diretrizes curriculares nacionais para os cursos universitários da área da saúde* [National curriculum standards for undergraduate courses in health] (p. 8). Londrina, PR: Secretaria Executiva da Rede Unida.

Almeida, M. C. P., & Barreira, I. A. (2000). Estudos de pós-graduação em enfermagem na América Latina: Sua inserção na comunidade cientifica [Nursing graduate education in Latin America: Inclusion in the scientific community]. In R. Rosângela de Sena (Ed.), *Educación de Enfermería en América Latina* [Nursing education in Latin America] (pp. 139-145). Bogotá, Colômbia: Universidad Nacional.

Almeida, M. C. P., Mishima, S. M., & Peduzzi, M. (1999). A pesquisa em enfermagem fundamentada no processo de trabalho: em busca da compreensão e qualificação da prática de enfermagem [Nursing research based on the work process: Seeking to understand and recognize nursing practice]. In *51º Congresso Brasileiro de Enfermagem e 10º Congresso Pan-americano de Enfermería* (pp. 259-277). Florianópolis Anais, Florianópolis: Associação Brasileira de Enfermagem.

Almeida, M. C. P., & Rocha, S. M. M. (1997). *O trabalho de enfermagem* [Nursing work]. São Paulo: Cortez.

Almeida, M., & Maranhão, E. (2003). *Diretrizes curriculares nacionais para os cursos universitários da área da saúde* [National curriculum standards for undergraduate courses in health] (p. 8). Londrina, PR: Secretaria Executiva da Rede Unida.

Albuquerque, G. L. (2001). *O movimento participação na Associação Brasileira de Enfermagem—Seção Santa Catarina, na visão de suas principais lideranças* [The Brazilian Nurses Association Participation Movement: Leaders from the Santa Catarina Chapter]. Florianópolis. Tese (Doutorado)—Departamento de Enfermagem, Universidade Federal de Santa Catarina.

Albuquerque, G. L. (2002). *A luta pela identidade profissional: participação e enfermagem* [The fight for professional identity: Participation and nursing]. Florianópolis: UFSC/PEN.

Araújo, A. R. (1982). *A assistência médica hospitalar no Rio de Janeiro no século XIX* [Nineteenth century hospital medical care in Rio de Janeiro]. Rio de Janeiro: Conselho Federal de Cultura.

Arruda, M., & Boff, L. (2000). *Globalização: desafios socioeconômicos, éticos e educativos* [Globalization: Socio-economical, ethical and educational challenges]. Petrópolis: Vozes.

Badinter, E. (1986). *Umé o outro* [One is the other]. 4ª ed. Rio de Janeiro: Nova Fronteira.

Batista, S. S., & Barreira, I. A. (1997a). *A luta da enfermagem por um espaço na universidade* [Nursing's struggle for space in the university] (pp. 51-52). Rio de Janeiro: Universidade Federal do Rio de Janeiro.

Batista, S. S., & Barreira, I. A. (1997b). As escolas de enfermagem na sociedade brasileira. In: *A luta da enfermagem por um espaço na universidade* [Nursing schools in Brazilian society] (pp. 43-48): Rio de Janeiro: UERJ.

Bertolli-Filho, C. (2001). *História da saúde pública no Brasil* [The history of the public health in Brazil] (4th ed). São Paulo: Ática.

Braga, J. C. S. (1978). *A questão da saúde no Brasil: Um estudo das políticas sociais em saúde pública e medicina previdenciária no desenvolvimento capitalista* [The Brazilian health care question: A study of social public health policy and social medicine during capitalist development]. Tese de Mestrado, Campinas: UNICAMP.

Campos, G. W. S. (1987). Subordinação da saúde pública à dinâmica da acumulação capitalista: Ou, breve história do "ocaso" da saúde pública [Healthcare subordination to capitalist accumulation: Or, the brief history of public health "decadence"]. In E. E. Merhy (Ed.), *O capitalismo e a saúde pública* [Capitalism and public health] (pp. 111-134). Campinas: Papirus.

Campos, G. W. S. (1992). *Reforma da reforma: Repensando a saúde* [Reform of the reform: Rethinking health]. São Paulo: Hucitec.

Carvalho, G. C. M. (2002). *O financiamento público federal do Sistema Único de Saúden– 1988-2001* [Public funding of the integrated National Healthcare System: 1988-2001]. Tese de Doutorado, Faculdade de Saúde Pública, Universidade de São Paulo.

Ceccim, R. B., & Feuerwerker, L. M. (2003). *Abertura de cursos da área da saúde* [Course development in the area of health]. Brasília, DF: Ministério da Saúde.

Ceccim, R. B., & Feurwerker, L. M. (2004a). *O quadrilátero da formação para área da saúde: Ensino, gestão, atenção e controle social* [The health area education square: Education, management, care and social control]. Brasília, DF: Ministério da Saúde.

Ceccim, R. B., & Feurwerker, L. M. (2004b). *Mudança na graduação das profissões de saúde sob o eixo da Integralidade* [Changes in health profession graduation rates under the integration partnership]. Brasília, DF: Ministério da Saúde.

Chossudolski, M. (1999). *A globalização da pobreza* [The globalization of the poverty]. São Paulo: Moderna.

COFEN/Brasil. (2006). *Conselho Federal de Enfermagem* [Federal Council of Nursing]. Retrieved March 23, 2006 from http://www.portalcofen.br

Córdoba, R. A., Gusso, D., & Luna, S. V. (1986). *A pós-graduação na América Latina: O caso brasileiro* [Post-graduation studies in Latin America: The Case of Brazil] (p. 80). UNESCO/CRESALC/MEC/SeSu/CAPES, Brasília, DF: Ministério da Saúde.

D'avila Neto, M. I. (1979). *O autoritarismo e a mulher. O jogo da dominação macho-fêmea no Brasil* [Authoritarianism and women: The male-female domination game in Brazil]. Rio de Janeiro: Achiamé.

David, H. M. S. L. (2001). *Religiosidade e cotidiano das agentes comunitárias de saúde: Repensando a educação em saúde junto às classes populares* [Religiosity and the everyday life of community health providers: Rethinking health education for the working class]. Rio de Janeiro: Tese de doutorado em saúde pública–ENSP/FIOCRUZ.

Demo, P. (1996). *Combate à pobreza: Desenvolvimento como oportunidade* [The war on poverty: Development as opportunity]. Campinas: Autores Associados.

Donnangelo, M. C. F. (1975). *Medicina e sociedade* [Medicine and society]. São Paulo: Pioneira.

Donnangelo, M. C. F., & Pereira, L. (1979). *Saúde e sociedade* [Health and society]. São Paulo: Duas Cidades.

Ferraz, C. A., Nakao, J. R. S., & Mishima, S. M. (2004). *Tendências do Mercado Educativo de Enfermagem* [Market trends in nursing education]. (Mimeógrafo—documento interno Ministério da Saúde—Observatório de Recursos Humanos).

Godue, C. (1997). *La salud em los procesos de globalización y de internacionalización* [The globalization and internationalization of healthcare]. In Relaciones Internacionales, Politica Social y Salud: Desafios en la Era de la Globalización [International relations, social and healthcare policies: Challenges in the era of globalization] (pp. 25-45). Grupo de Salud Internacional. Pontificia Universidad Javeriana. Bogota, Colombia.

Gonçalves, R. (1999). *Globalização e desnacionalização* [Globalization and denationalization]. São Paulo: Paz e Terra.

Gutiérrez, M. G. R., Vieira, T. T., Almeida, M. C. P., Elsen, I., & Stefanelli, M. C. (2001). *Acompanhamento e avaliação da pós-graduação no Brasil: Retrospectiva histórica da representação da enfermagem* [Monitoring and evaluating graduate studies in Brazil: A nursing historical retrospective]. *Escola Anna Nery Revista de Enfermagem, 5*(2), 161-172.

Habert, N. (2003). *A década de 70: apogeu e crise da ditadura militar brasileira* [The 1970's: Apex and crisis of the Brazilian military dictatorship] (4th ed., pp. 7-83). São Paulo: Ática.

Haddad, S. (2002). *Apresentação do livro "Racismo no Brasil."* [Introduction to the book: "Racism in Brazil"] (p. 9). São Paulo. Editores (Seyferth, G., Silva Bento, M., Da Silva, M. P., Borges Pereira, J. B., Siqueira, M. L., Silvério, V. R., da Silva, M., Gomes, J. B.). São Paulo: Petrópolis: Editora Fundação Petrópolis.

Herson, B. (1996). *Cristãos novos e seus descendentes na medicina brasileira de 1500-1850* [New Christians and their descendents in Brazilian medicine 1500-1850] (p. 227). São Paulo. Ed. USP/SP.

Instituto de Pesquisas Econômicas Aplicadas [IPEA]. (2004). Ipeadata on-line. *Consulta a séries históricas, consistentes e atualizadas das principais fontes das estatísticas econômicas brasileiras* [Updated, historical sources of Brazilian economic statistics]. Retrieved June 11, 2004 from http://www.ipeadata.gov.br

International Council of Nursing [ICN]. (1999). *Guidebook for nurse futurists: Future oriented planning for individuals, groups and associations*. Genebra: Suíça. http://www.esg.br/publicacoes/artigos/a008.html

Lacerda, A. C. (2004). *Globalização e investimentos estrangeiros no Brasil* [Globalization and foreign investments in Brazil] (2nd ed). São Paulo: Saraiva.

Lima, M. J. (1994). *O que é Enfermagem* [What is nursing?] (pp. 50-60). São Paulo: Brasiliense.

MEC/CAPES. (1996). *Infocapes: Edição comemorativa dos 45 anos* [Infocapes: 45th Anniversary Edition]. Boletim Informativo da CAPES.

MEC/CAPES. (2007). *Relação de Cursos Recomendados e Reconhecidos*. Retrieved March 20, 2007 from http://conteudoweb.capes.gov.br/conteudoweb/ProjetoRelacaoCursos

Mendes, E. V. (2001a). *Os grandes dilemas do SUS* (Tomo I) [SUS great dilemmas, Vol. 1]. Salvador: Casa da Qualidade Editora.

Mendes, E. V. (2001b). *Os grandes dilemas do SUS* (Tomo II). [SUS great dilemmas, Vol. 2]. Salvador: Casa da Qualidade Editora.

Mendes, E. V. (2002a). A evolução histórica da atenção primária á saúde no Brasil [The historical evolution of the primary healthcare in Brazil]. In E. V. Mendes (Ed.), *A atenção primária à saúde no SUS* [Primary healthcare at SUS] (pp. 23-29). Fortaleza: Escola de Saúde Pública do Ceará.

Mendes, E. V. (2002b). *A atenção primária à saúde no SUS* [Primary health care at SUS]. Fortaleza: Escola de Saúde Pública do Ceará.

Merhy, E. E. (1987). *O capitalismo e a saúde pública* [Capitalism and public health]. Campinas: Papirus.

Merhy, E. E., Chakkour, M., Stéfano, E. Stéfano, M. E., Santos, C. M., Rodrigues, R. A., & Oliveira, P. C. P. (1997). Em busca de ferramentas analisadoras das tecnologias em saúde: A informação e o dia a dia de um serviço, interrogando e gerindo trabalho em saúde [Searching for healthcare analytical tools: The information and the daily routine of a public service, questioning and managing a healthcare service]. In E. E. Merhy & R. Onocko (Eds.), *Práxis en Salud—Desafio para lo público* [Health praxis: The challenge for government] (pp. 113-150). São Paulo: Hucitec.

Michel, A. (1989). *Não aos estereótipos. Vencer o sexismo nos livros para crianças e nos manuais escolares* [Say "no" to stereotypes: Overcoming sexism in children books and school manuals]. São Paulo: UNESCO.

Ministério da Previdência e Assistência Social [MPAS]. (1982). *Reorientação da assistência à saúde no âmbito da previdência social* [Restructuring health care in social medicine]. Brasília, DF: MPAS, Brasil.

Ministério da Saúde. Secretaria de Gestão do Trabalho e da Educação na Saúde. Departamento de Gestão da Educação na Saúde (2004). *Política de educação e desenvolvimento para o SUS: Caminhos para a educação permanente em saúde: Pólos de educação permanente em saúde* [SUS education and development policy: Ways to permanent health education: Permanent health education clusters]. Brasília, DF: Ministério da Saúde.

Ministério da Educação e Cultura, Departamento de Assuntos Universitários [MEC/DAU] (1974). *Estudo sobre a formação e utilização dos recursos humanos na área de saúde* [Research on the development and use of human resources in health] (pp. 15-22). Brasília, DF: MEC/DAU, Brasil.

Ministério de Educação e Cultura, Departamento de Assuntos Universitários [MEC/DAU]. (1977). *Desenvolvimento do ensino superior de enfermagem no Brasil* [Nursing higher education development in Brazil] (pp. 19-22). Brasília, DF: MEC/DAU, Brasil.

Ministério de Educação, Secretaria da Educação Superior, Comissão de Especialistas de Ensino de Enfermagem [MEC/SES/CEEE]. (1987). *Ensino superior de enfermagem—Relatório Final do Seminário Nacional* [Nursing higher education—National seminar final report] (pp. 107-111). Rio de Janeiro: MEC/SES/CEEE, Brasil.

Miranda, C. M. L. (1996). *O risco e o bordado—Um estudo sobre formação de identidade profissional* [Risk and stitches: A study of professional identity formation]. Tese de Doutorado apresentada ao Centro Biomédico da UERJ–RJ, Rio de Janeiro.

Muraro, R. M. (1992). *A mulher no terceiro milênio: Uma história da mulher através dos tempos e suas perspectivas para o futuro* [Women in the third millennium: A women's history over time and their perspective on the future]. Rio de Janeiro: Rosa dos Ventos.

Nakamae, D. D. (1987). *Novos caminhos da enfermagem* [Nursing new pathways] (pp. 100-101). São Paulo: Cortez.

Neves, E. P., & Vargens, O. M. C. (2003). La contribución de los programas de doctorados de enfermería ante los avances científicos y tecnológicos: el estudio de caso de Brasil—un análisis preliminary. [The contribution of nursing doctoral programs to scientific and technological advances: A case study of Brazil—A preliminary analysis] (pp. 9-24). In CICAD, *Los nuevos programas de doctorados en enfermería y su contribución en la reducción de la demanda de las drogas en America Latina: Retos y perspectivas* [New nursing doctoral programs and their contribution to drug demand reduction in Latin America: Challenges and perspectives]. Washington, DC: Inter-American Drug Abuse Control Commission CICAD/Organization of American States–OAS.

Organizacion Mundial de la Salud [OMS]. (1978). *Atención Primaria de Salud—Informe de la Conferencia Internacional sobre Atención Primaria de Salud Alma-Ata* [Primary health care: International Primary Health Care Conference Report]. Genebra: Organización Mundial de la Salud.

Padilha, M. I. C. S. (1990). *O resgate das raízes—A influência da formação familiar e social na escolha e exercício da enfermagem* [Rescuing the roots: How family and social background influences choice in nursing work]. Tese de Livre docência apresentada a UNIRIO/RJ.

Padilha, M. I. C. S. (1998). *A mística do silêncio: A prática de enfermagem na Santa Casa de Misericórdia do Rio de Janeiro no século XIX* [Mystique of silence: Nineteenth century nursing practice at Santa Casa de Misericórdia Hospital in Rio de Janeiro]. Pelotas: Palotti.

Padilha, M. I. C. S., Borenstein, M. S., Santos, M. L. S. C., & Cartana, M. H. (1998). Acordando a bela adormecida—Gênero ou sexismo no discurso da enfermagem [Waking up "Sleeping Beauty": Gender or sexism in nursing discourse]. Florianópolis: Revista Ciências da Saúde, 17(1), 43-66.

Padilha, M. I. C. S., Silva, A. L., & Borenstein, M. S. (2001). Os congressos brasileiros— Pontes para a liberdade e transformação da enfermagem [Brazilian congresses: Bridges to nursing freedom and transformation]. Ribeirão Preto: Revista Latino-americana de Enfermagem, 9(3), 7-13.

Padilha, M. I. C. S., Silva, A. L., & Borenstein, M. S. (2002). Um contraponto entre os personagens dos congressos brasileiros de enfermagem e da Revista Brasileira de Enfermagem no período de 1977 a 1987 [Comparison of participants in the Brazilian Nursing Congresses and the Brazilian Nursing Journal from 1977 to 1987]. Brasília: Revista Brasileira de Enfermagem, 55(3), 323-330.

Padilha, M. I. C. S., Pires, D. E. P., Martins, C. R., & Wright, M. G. M. (2003). As perspectivas dos programas de pós-graduação em enfermagem e o uso de ciência e tecnologia na América Latina frente aos desafios do século XXI. [Perspectives on nursing graduate programs and the use of science and technology in Latin America: Facing the challenges of the 21st century]. In CICAD, La situación de los programas de postgrado de enfermería en nueve países de América Latina frente a los desafíos de la reducción de la demanda de drogas [How graduate nursing programs in nine Latin American countries deal with the challenges of drug demand reduction] (pp. 111-117). Washington, DC: Inter-American Drug Abuse Control Commission CICAD/Organization of American States–OAS.

Pagliuca, L. M. F., Gutiérrez, M. G. R., Erdmann, A. L., Leite, J. L., Almeida, M. C. P., & Kurcgant, P. (2001). Critérios para classificar periódicos científicos de enfermagem. [Criteria for the classification of scientific periodicals in nursing] São Paulo: Acta Paulista de Enfermagem, 14(3), 9-17.

Pereira, J. B. B. (2002). O Negro e a identidade racial brasileira [Black men and Brazilian racial identity]. In Racismo no Brasil (pp. 65-71). São Paulo: ABONG/ANPED.

Ramos, F. R. S. (2003). Acerca de diretrizes curriculares e projetos pedagógicos: um início de reflexão [Curricular standards and educational projects: A reflection beginning. Revista Brasileira de Enfermagem, 56(4), 340-342.

Rocha, S. M. M. et al. (1988). O ensino da pós-graduação em enfermagem no Brasil [Post-graduate nursing educational programs in Brazil]. Brasília, DF: Cortez.

Rodrigues, B. A. (1967). Fundamentos de administração sanitaria [Fundamentals of health care administration]. Rio de Janeiro: Freitas Bastos.

Rodrigues, M. (2003a). A década de 50: Populismo e metas desenvolvimentistas no Brasil [The 1950's: Populism and development goals in Brazil] (4th ed., pp. 9-91). São Paulo: Ática.

Rodrigues, M. (2003b). A década de 80: Brasil: Quando a multidão voltou as praças [The 1980's: When people returned to the streets] (4th ed., pp. 7-66). São Paulo: Ática.

Rourke, J. T. (2003). International politics on the world stage. Connecticut: Dushkin.

Santiago, M. M. A. (2000). O saber acadêmico de enfermagem: Constituição e represen- tações em três programas de pós-graduação [Nursing academic knowledge: Constitution and representation in three graduate programs]—Tese de doutorado— Rio de Janeiro: Universidade Federal do Rio de Janeiro, Escola de Enfermagem Anna Nery.

Secretaria de Planejamento [SEPLAN]; Conselho Nacional de Desenvolvimento Científico e Tecnológico [CNPq] (1982). Avaliação e perspectivas [Evaluation and perspectives]. Brasília, DF. Vol. 6/Ciências da Saúde, # 38-Enfermagem.

Sena, R., & Villalobos, M. M. D. (2001). A especialização: mecanismo para excelência. In *Recursos de enfermagem: Contribuições ao processo de desenvolvimento* [Nursing resources: Contributions to the development process]. Colômbia: Editorial UNIBIBLOS.

Seyferth, G., Silva Bento, M. A., Silva, M. P., Borges Pereira, J. B., Siqueira, M. L., Silvério, V. R., Silva, M., & Gomes, J. B. (2002). *Racismo no Brasil* [Racism in Brazil]. São Paulo: Editora Fundação Peirópolis.

Simões Paes, M. H. (2002). *A década de 60: Rebeldia, contestação e repressão política* [The 1960's: Disobedience, protest and political repression] (4th ed., pp. 7-91). São Paulo: Ática.

Singer, P., Campos, O., & Oliveira, E. M. (1978). A evolução da situação de saúde no Brasil [The evolution of health care in Brazil]. In *Prevenir e curar—O controle social através dos serviços de saúde* [Prevention or cure: Social control through health care services] (pp. 88-137). Rio de Janeiro: Forense-Universitária.

Stotz, E. N., David, H. M. S. L., & Wong-Un, J. A. (2005). Educação Popular e Saúde: Trajetória, expressões e desafios de um movimento social [Popular education and health: Documenting protests and challenges of a social movement]. *Revista de Atenção Primária à Saúde, 8*(1), 49-60.

Wright, M. G. M. (2000). A critical-holistic paradigm for an interdependent world. *American Behavioral Scientist, 43*(5), 808-823.

Wright, M. G. M. (2002). La contribución de la enfermería frente al fenómeno de las drogas y la violencia en América Latina: Un proceso en construcción [Nursing's contribution to the drug phenomenon and violence in Latin America: A developmental process]. *Ciencia y Enfermería-Revista Iberoamericana de Investigación, 8*(2), 9-19.

Wright, M. G. M. (2003). La profesión de enfermería y el fenómeno de las drogas. In CICAD, *Los nuevos programas de doctorado en enfermería y su contribución en la reducción de la demanda de drogas en América Latina: Retos y perspectivas* [New nursing doctorale programs and their contribution to drug demand reduction in Lain America: Challenges and perspectives] (pp. 43-51). Washington, DC: Inter-American Drug Abuse Control Commission CICAD/Organization of American States–OAS.

Wright, M. G. M., & Carneiro, A. M. (1984). Espaço da mulher brasileira e o espaço da enfermeira brasileira [The sphere of Brazilian women and the sphere of Brazilian nursing]. *Revista Gaúcha de Enfermagem, 5*(2), 341-356.

Wright, M. G. M., Paim, L., & Rodrigues, K. H. (1982). Desenvolvimento do ensino superior de enfermagem na região centro-oeste: Indicadores de qualidade para cursos de graduação [Nursing higher education development in the Central-West Region: Quality indicators for undergraduate programs]. *Revista Brasileira de Enfermagem, 35*(6), 60-73.

Zucco, C. (1996). Relação entre pós-graduação e graduação. A pós-graduação no contexto histórico educacional. In *Discussão da pós-graduação brasileira* [Analysis of Brazilian graduate programs] (pp. 79-96). B. 1, Brasília: CAPES.

CHAPTER 6

Nursing in Mexico

Lucila Cardenas Becerril,
Maricela Sanchez Gandara,
Beatriz Carmona Mejía, and
Beatriz Arana Gómez

What can be considered modern nursing first appeared in Mexico at the beginning of the 20th century. Most believe its development was motivated by the creation of Mexico's General Hospital in 1905 because 2 years later the first nursing school was built. During the next 100 years, nursing education and professional practice evolved based on three models:

1. schools of nursing connected to hospitals;
2. schools of nursing connected to schools of medicine;
3. university-based nursing programs offering undergraduate and graduate degrees.

We draw in part from the following works: Cárdenas (1997, 2000, 2005), Barbosa and De Souza (1999), Casasa (2001), CNE/INEGI (2001, 2002), De Monterrosa and Lange (1991), Donahue (1985), Frank and Elizondo (1987), Martinez and Latapi (1993), Nava (2000), Cleaves (1985), SEP/DGP (2001a, 2001b, 2003).

At the beginning, the professors who taught theory, all of whom were doctors, focused on what they themselves considered important and emphasized their own area of specialization. Nurses who worked for them in clinical settings, learned by apprenticeship through observation and imitation without reflection on or analysis of the purpose of the demonstrated technique or procedure. Such apprenticeships gave rise to an empirical model based on the practical and experiential where learning takes place by doing. Subsequently, some nursing courses were structured in a loosely systematic manner, giving rise to the "practical-empirical" model, which dedicated the majority of the students' instructional time to practice in clinical areas. However, much more recently, that ratio has been reversed. The "practical theoretical" model, which dedicates 60% of the curriculum to the acquisition of knowledge with 40% in clinical and community practice, has proved to be a favorable advancement for nursing in Mexico.

In considering Mexican nursing, we see an inconsistency between academic preparation and the type of job individual nurses actually perform. This inconsistency affects the recognition nurses receive as measured by their salaries and their status. In other words, nurses in Mexico face a reality that does not honor them. This has been a concern to nurses in Mexico over the last half century and particularly over the last 15 years, due mainly to (a) the increasing number of nurses earning graduate degrees, (b) the influence of North-American nurses, and most importantly, (c) the increased recognition of the professional and social contexts of the nursing profession.

In this chapter, we examine historic and contemporary factors influencing the social recognition of nurses in Mexico. We explore socialization as a phenomenon, including the role of nursing labor within the socioeconomic structure as well as the nurse's social mobility. We also evaluate the prestige of nursing and other dimensions of social stratification. Finally, we close this chapter by considering political economic factors relevant to the Mexican context.

It is important to point out that now, at the onset of the 21st century, healthcare in Latin America, specifically in Mexico, demands more than at any other time. Today, health system challenges need to be solved not by individual care providers but rather by "teams" of professionals (e.g., nurses, physicians, social workers) who, depending on their knowledge base, can analyze and offer innovative strategies to address public health issues. Currently, there is a high incidence of preventable infectious diseases as well as the so-called "diseases of industrial development" such as cardiovascular illnesses, chronic degenerative diseases, and respiratory infections.

During the 20th century, the health care system in Mexico was affected by foreign influences that advocated a new focus on health and not on disease. This focus led to new practices, to promote and maintain health, as well as to prevent disease and to achieve major coverage of services, low costs, non-invasive care, and risk reduction, among other considerations. This philosophy was embodied in the World Health Organization "Health for all by the Year 2000" program.

Even though the theoretical move to make "health" a high priority and the political will to channel actions toward primary health care existed, the established structures still support a disease-oriented model to cure and treat disease rather than to prevent it. The disease-oriented model dates back to the 1940s when the biological, individual and historical events encouraged the creation of large hospitals and other health care institutions, thus creating a vertical, hierarchical system where the physicians assume leadership.

However, within the last 10 years, the health care discourse has focused on primary care (promotion, prevention, and maintenance of health), but there are still incongruencies, with respect to who provides this level of care, the education of the primary care professionals, and the economic interests of transnational corporations producing health care equipment and pharmaceuticals. Also controversial are the costs, in general, of the products and services used to treat illness and diseases and to provide rehabilitation services.

In sum, over the last century, the profession of nursing in Mexico has been altered or influenced by two significant factors:

1. the development of primary care in the nursing profession, that is, the epistemological work in recognizing that *care* is for the individual, his family and the community;
2. the external factors (the social, political, economic and cultural dimensions) where the politics of health and education play out.

THE CONTEXT OF NURSING IN MEXICO

Nursing in Mexico did not evolve in isolation. Rather, various social, cultural, political, and economic factors influenced its origin and development. Indeed, the social and cultural traditions in Mexican nursing were shaped by three main factors: religion, gender, and the military.

Religion and Nursing

A close relationship between religion and nursing is not peculiar to Mexico as it is a worldwide phenomenon. During the early Christian period, the church undertook care of the sick. Such care was carried out by deacons and deaconesses organized to devote their time and money to the goal of aiding the ill—as well as all those in need—and inspired by their religion and by the intrinsic virtue of charity. Mexican society's Christian faith in human kindness and illness became characterized as a means of gaining God's grace, a Christian duty.

Because society considered the practice of "helping the sick" a religious duty, institutions were created to accomplish just that task. Health care services were established and offered to all regardless of their background or origin. Greeks, barbarians, free men, slaves, the rich, and the poor were offered health care without discrimination. And, of course, counseling, free health care, and therapeutic and moral care were included. This egalitarian practice stood in stark contrast to that of the non-Christian world (Weber, 1998).

Nursing in Mexico was in religious hands for over 3 centuries; thus, nursing values were marked by religious values, particularly "Christian" values. From this perspective, nursing itself is regarded as a "service to fellow human beings," a "personal calling," a "mystical experience." Consequently, nursing health care is seen more as "Christian charity" (the patient is regarded as a person in the image of God) than as a citizen's right (Frank-Elizondo, 1987).

Religious sisters did "everything that charity inspired them to do." The spiritual side required them to provide care with a charitable spirit and without showing discomfort, always trying to focus on the well-being of their patients' souls rather than only on their bodies. Indeed, the care of the body was performed because it supported the care of the spirit. Given the spirituality of the times, even pain, suffering, and death were seen as positive values toward the salvation of the soul.

Weber notes that all modern Mexican disciplines have a religious origin that views a profession is "something that man must accept because it is granted by Providence, something he has to adjust to, as professional work is considered a mission imposed by God" (Weber, 1998, pp. 104-105). During the 19th century, care of the sick was charity and self-sacrifice that the nursing agents, typically people linked to the church, were providing as they worked toward both the salvation of their own and the ill person's souls. Indicative of the view at the time is the statement that "the nurse owes herself to the sick" (Cárdenas, 2005, p. 307).

Obviously, then, the fee for services rendered has always been low in comparison to other professions since nursing was regarded as a job performed for the sake of "salvation." Consequently, nursing care was not viewed as a salaried job, nor were there limits to its duration, the number of patients assigned, the kind of activities performed or the occupational risks associated with the job. Since the job was done "for the love of God, then the reward for it was not in this world" (Frank-Elizondo, 1987, p. 38). Also, because of its perceived spiritual value, the job could not be compared to any other job and the Sisters never benefited from labor laws. The job's reward was satisfaction, the "praxis" of the love of God through the service to fellow human beings. This tension in determining the economic value of nursing care—varying between that of a salaried job and a donation—constituted a significant obstacle toward the social and economic recognition of nursing care in later times (Gaitan, 1999, p. 138).

Eventually, nursing as a lay profession grew in the West as a political response to Great Britain's industrial revolution and subsequent economic transformation, resulting in new value on the concept of work. Even so, the nursing reform which took place in Victorian England (resulting in modern nursing or "Nightingale nursing"), integrated the Catholic mystique of charitable care for the poor and the disabled with the Protestant ethic and the notion of work as a virtue and source of personal satisfaction (Barreira, 2000, p. 2). Even though with the advent of modern nursing, a scientific paradigm replaced the religious paradigm, nursing continued to be regarded as a charitable, pious, and unselfish activity that demanded resignation, docility, and conformity.

The religious paradigm in nursing also influenced nurses' attire. The expression "since the cloth makes the priest" has as its corollary: "a nurse without her uniform is not a nurse." Nurse's uniforms were very similar to the attire worn by nuns (Velandia, 1995, p. 38). Religious values also manifested themselves in the concepts of discipline, schedules, and wages. Not surprisingly, nursing only emerged as a profession when certified lay nurses began to occupy the positions left vacant when the size of religious congregations decreased over time.

Gender and Nursing

Nursing is included among the so-called "feminine professions," that is, those occupations that prepare women not only for a job, but also express the richness of their gender (regarded as of primary importance) as mothers, wives, daughters, and sisters. The "feminine question" is strongly connected to religion: the prototype of the feminine image as either the "Virgin Mary," innocent and obedient, for unmarried women or the "Suffering Mother," suffering and sensible, for married ones. As a result, feminine characteristics are similar to the expected behaviors of nuns, namely submissiveness, kindness, gentleness, and courtesy, among others (Velandia, 1995, p. 39).

The direct relationship that exists between woman and nurse implies that the latter must be assigned values traditionally associated with femininity: submissiveness, obedience, and self-denial. In addition, until the early decades of the 20th century, women's education took place mainly within the family. It prepared women for domestic chores, for her "housewife" activities.

In Latin America, the first nursing schools opened their doors toward the end of the 19th century. At that time only an elementary school education was required of applicants. The heads of these schools were either nuns or foreign nurses. Prospective students were not recruited from among members of the upper class since social prejudices did not allow such women to "work" outside the home. Their primary occupation was to remain at home, waiting to be married. This phenomenon was more cultural than social. Although upper class women could study nursing, they had many more options because they could choose other topics. They could become teachers or they could study art, culture, or home economics, useful fields once they reached the age of marriage because they would have learned skills necessary for being considered "good housewives." Within Mexican culture and family traditions, appropriate roles for women ranged within the realm of "domestic service" to "natural healer."

Today, women's roles have changed significantly because of feminist movements. As a result, society now considers gender-based skills as socio-cultural fact and not simply as biological predestination. For nursing (in Mexico 95.8% are women— SEP/DGP, 1999, p. 8), it means overcoming the image of nurse as the *lady in white* and nurses recognizing their own social responsibility in promoting the growth of their field.

The Military and Nursing

The military shaped nursing in Mexico by promoting a strong hierarchical organization of the work force. Thus, the nurse's uniform became a symbol and not, as one might assume, an accessory to prevent the transmission of disease or for self-protection. Without the uniform, the nurse seems to lose her identity. This identification was promulgated by Florence Nightingale and the care she and her nurses provided the wounded during the Crimea War. Nightengale brought the same rigid norms to the Saint Thomas School of Nursing which she later founded in England. These traditions spread to nursing in Latin America. Symbols that are still preserved in Latin American nursing are the use of the nurses' *cofia* (cap) and *toca* (cape), where the different lace alludes to the hierarchical level the nurses possess, a symbolism that compares to military rank (Cárdenas, 2005; Velandia, 1995).

The military paradigm also reinforced the values inherited from the religious model, especially the concept of discipline—orders must be followed without discussion, enforced through supervision in order to govern, control, and direct the person so as to obtain high productivity.

Contemporary Mexican Nursing

The economic and political aspects characteristic of the 20th century had a decisive impact on nursing education as well as practice. Government health and education policies directed educational practices as well as methods to incorporate nursing into the job market. During the first 80 years of the 20th century, these policies emphasized individualistic, ahistorical, and biology-based training in Mexico. However, health does not depend solely on biological factors. Rather, it is also the product of the relationships that exist between humans and nature.

During the last 2 decades of the 20th century, however, nurse educators in Mexico emphasized a more integrated, holistic approach and tried to develop nurses who could care for individuals, families, and society as a whole. As a result, contradictions now exist between the professional abilities of recent graduates and the demands of the workplace. For instance, nursing education focuses on "preventative" care at the "primary (pre-disease) level" while most nursing jobs continue to be in "secondary (disease) level" acute care facilities or "tertiary (post-disease) level" chronic care or rehabilitation facilities.

This fundamental disparity between the education of nurses and the nursing workplace derives from the politics of health and education embedded in the Mexican health care system. While educational institutions focus nursing education curricula and the academic load mostly on primary care (disease prevention, health promotion and screening), the health care workplace is focused largely on curing existing illness. The percentage of the Mexican Gross Domestic Product (GDP) allocated for health services is less than 5% of the national GDP, and most of it is used to care for those in secondary and tertiary health care facilities. Consequently, acute care hospitals have many more economic resources than those units dedicated to prevention and primary health care. Most new nursing graduates find employment in secondary care disease-oriented hospitals and medical centers that focus their efforts on curing acute disorders and rehabilitating recovering patients.

As we moved into the 21st century, the National Health Plan for 2001-2006 (whose motto is "democratization of health care in Mexico: toward a universal system of health care") faced many challenges (PNS, 2001). The plan has four main goals:

1. to eliminate health inequalities;
2. to improve the general health of Mexican citizens;
3. to provide appropriate treatment; and
4. to ensure fairness in the financing of health care.

Currently, Mexico allocates 5.6% of its wealth to health care. Most people feel that the allocation must be increased since many basic needs still go unfulfilled and because health care costs rise continuously (PNS, 2001).

The Mexican state believes that investment in health care services that are fair, efficient, and of good quality has a positive impact on economic activity since such investment increases human capital, increases the efficiency of investments in education, improves income distribution, and raises the productivity and competitiveness of the work force. This view also believes that a vigorous economy creates the necessary resources to better serve the health needs of the population, leading to a true equality of opportunities. In this way, a vigorous economy creates a virtual circle between economic development and good health (PNS, 2001, pp. 17-18). The National Educational Program, in turn, is linked to health policies by promoting continuing education, internationalization, and curricular flexibility. This view thus implies that new generations of nurses need to be trained for self-learning, a commitment to service, solidarity, and national equality (PNE, 2001).

The Beginning of Modern Nursing in Mexico

It is widely regarded worldwide that modern nursing[1] began during the 19th century with the work of Florence Nightingale. Nightingale contributed to the technical and administrative aspects of the profession and created a theoretical model of patient care. Nursing in Mexico began within this same framework and is the result of the need for a care-giver for the sick and disabled once the illness had been diagnosed and treated by a physician. In fact, physicians themselves were the ones who recognized the need for nurses and thus proposed and promoted the creation of the first Nursing school in 1907. From that time, the nurse's scope of action was defined, since physicians never regarded *patient care* as part of their own responsibilities. However, because of the professional interdependency created, physicians were responsible for establishing the foundations of nursing during the first 20 years of the 20th century.

The consequences of these beginnings have become more concrete over the last century. First, the activities of nurses were based on a model of the empirical-practical type. That is, nursing actions were based on an apprenticeship model that focused on "how" an activity was performed, but not "why." Notably, the apprenticeship model was not unique to nursing since from the 19th century industrial revolution on, the majority of jobs used those same methods of teaching and learning. Furthermore, nurses only learned the dominant view of medicine based entirely on biology and which gave primary importance to the body over the psychological or spiritual dimensions.

---

[1] One must note that Nursing started as an empirical practice as a result of observation and experience. In Mexico, from prehispanic times, the Tlamatquiticitl and the Ticitl prescribed drinks, provided intestinal enemas, gave treatments, placed ferules, and watched the temascales, among many other activities. Throughout time, women have been the ones that have provided care and comfort for the sick. Because of that, they have been considered healers "by nature."

This approach to the care of the body, focused on the biological and the individual patient, originated toward the end of the 18th century when hospitals[2] became centers for medical attention: "the medical perception must not be directed toward groups but rather must be structured as if one were looking though a magnifying glass in such a way that, when applied to the various different parts of an object, brings into focus other parts formerly not perceived and with this the never-ending work of acquiring knowledge about the individual" (Foucault, 1997, p. 33).

The apprenticeship model also reinforced nurses' dependency on the physician. That dependency influenced the development of nursing in Mexico and was based mainly on the history of the medical profession and of the physicians who gained importance toward the end of the 18th century when the organization of the hospital constituted itself as an "examination" apparatus. The ritual of "the visit" became the noticeable feature.

Stepping back for a moment to understand the ritual of the visit, during the 17th century, the physician, always coming from outside, combined his patient examination with various other forms of control—religious and political. He seldom participated in the day-to-day management of the hospital. Little by little, the "visit" became more regular, more rigorous, broader and covered an increasingly more important part of the functioning of the hospital.[3] In this manner, the examination that was formerly erratic and brief became regular physician rounds that placed the ill person in almost perpetual observation.[4] This evolution changed the internal hierarchy of the hospital, since the physician, until then an external element, began to acquire preeminence over the religious personnel running the hospitals. Physicians became entrusted with a definite role that was always revolved around the examination technique. It is then that the category of "sick" appears for the first time. Thus the hospital became a place for learning about disease as well as the formation and application of knowledge. It also became a place where the power relationships were inverted (Foucault, 1997, pp. 190-191).

Mexican Nursing Enters Academe

From about 1900 to 1950, Mexican nursing advanced its knowledge and practice, a trend that greatly enhanced it as a profession. First and foremost, nursing schools

---

[2] In the middle ages, the concept of *Hospital* was broader. Not only the sick were taken care, but the term "patient" was used to describe the person in the hospital (Foucault, 2000, pp. 46, 123).

[3] In 1661, the physician of the *Hotel-Dieu* in Paris was responsible for one daily visit. In 1687 an "expecting" physician should examine in the afternoon those more severely ill people. The rules of the 18th century specify the schedule and duration of visitations (2 hours minimum). They also stress that in order to ensure the effectiveness of rotating service it must take place every day "inclusive of Easter Sunday." At last, in 1771, the resident physician was instituted with the mission of "lending the services of the profession, day and night, during the span of time between external physicians visits" (Foucault, 2000, p. 191).

[4] The examination, with all its documentary techniques, transforms each individual into a "case" that in turn becomes and object of knowledge and a prey for power. "The examination is at the center of procedures constituting the individual as object and effect of power, as object and effect of knowledge" (Foucault, 2000, pp. 196-197).

became independent from hospitals; second, nursing curricula and study became formalized; third, nursing school applicants were required to have completed junior high school for admission to nursing programs (an improvement over the earlier elementary school requirement); and fourth, a theoretical-practical model was emphasized.

While physicians still served as heads of nursing schools, the discipline of nursing officially entered academe. Among a number of educational changes, nursing was institutionalized as a part of the university system. In regard to professional practice, nursing labor was regulated and limits were placed on work schedules. Mexican nurses with formal preparation in nursing administration took over as supervisors and department heads, and nurse health officers were developed. Also, during this period the first professional association, the Mexican Association of Nurses (AME), was formed. It sought professional education and continuing education for nurses as well as the betterment of their social standing.

During the next 30 years (1950-1980), nurses became more important to the health system and demonstrated their skill in public health services as well as in various hospital specialties. This period was marked by great advances in the theoretical education of Mexican nurses. The programs and plans of study were standardized, and they also included new programs in a number of nursing specialty areas. Although specialization in nursing paralleled that of physicians (in that it followed the medical model), the nursing specialty area programs were affiliated with non-university technical nursing schools, which meant that candidates could enter the nursing specialty programs without a high school diploma. Ultimately, nurses with specialty preparation in a special area remained academically inferior to physicians with training in the same area. In broad terms, this time period was characterized by the following innovations in nursing within the structure of the National Health Service: (a) a restructuring of the academic nursing programs and initiating bachelor's degree preparation in nursing, (b) a nursing focus on disease prevention, (c) a nursing emphasis on theory over practice, and (d) teaching the nursing process called the *Proceso de Enfermería* and abbreviated as *(PAE)* in Latin America.

As nurses became part of the university system, it was necessary for them to adjust to existing policies regarding curricula and the currency of academic faculty. In 1980, the first nurses completed graduate studies. Nursing, as part of a university system, provided opportunities for nursing students to study other academic disciplines such as management, education, sociology, and the humanities. But professionals in these other disciplines began to question how nurses were undertaking master's level studies and carrying out research. The prevailing view was that nurses were only assistants to physicians and not professional in their own right. Hence, they concluded that the rationale for graduate studies in nursing was not warranted.

Despite this prevailing attitude, one of the advantages of nurses participating in the broad academic environment was the opportunity for them to study and understand the profession within its social, cultural, and political economic contexts. This resulted in some nurses in Mexico borrowing sociological theories for the first time and adapting them to nursing science, thus leading to the initial nursing studies in Mexico using a sociological perspective.

During the same 30-year period, from approximately 1950 to 1980, Mexican nurses focused predominantly on hospital-based care and on responding to the expectations of the prevailing biomedical model of care. During this period, nursing failed to account that certain social aspects (such as the value attributed to the various professions, status and prestige) can translate into an income. The social conditions that determined the evolution of the profession also influenced its status and prestige, and nursing was still seen as merely an occupation that somehow managed to evolve into a profession.

It was not until the 1980s that Mexican nurses started to question their social and professional role and, thus, they initiated a series of important changes. Nursing education, academic activities, and curriculum plans were revised, thus posing questions about the new generation of nurses.[5] Graduate study in nursing was initiated with specialization programs, master's degree programs and, most recently, doctoral programs. Now interested in health promotion and preventative care during this time, nursing adopted innovative methodologies of investigation such as constructivism and competencies.

It was also during the 1980s that nursing began to develop a theoretical and scientific foundation for the discipline, fueled somewhat by a general interest in conceptual models, frameworks, and theoretical foundations, including "care" and "caring" as central tenets of nursing. Additionally, national professional nursing organizations in Mexico tightened their accreditation and certification processes so as to encourage professional self-regulation.

THE FIRST NURSING SCHOOLS

The first nursing schools in Latin America appeared during the last decades of the 19th century generally under the leadership of medical professionals, English or North American nurses, or of Catholic or Protestant institutions. Often, the schools appeared next to hospitals or under the sponsorship of organizations such as the Rockefeller Foundation or the Pan-American Health Organization (OPS).[6] In more than 90% of cases, physicians initiated nursing schools in response to the need to satisfy the care demands of the sick. As noted previously, the foundation of some of the nursing schools coincides with the reforms of Florence Nightingale that were brought to America at the start of the 20th century.

---

[5] Precisely, another way in which nurses achieve greater academic levels was to work in direct parallel fashion with physicians. This is the result of the fact that the directives and policies in the health care field and particularly in the hospital, have been dictated by physicians and have been modulated by the economic political system of the Mexican State.

[6] In 1890 the first Latin American school of nursing was founded in Argentina. Between 1900 and 1912 schools appear in Cuba, Chile, Mexico, and Uruguay. In the decade of the 1920s, schools linked to public health service appear in Chile and Brazil. The appearance of those first professional nursing schools marks the start of secularism in nursing in Latin America.

The development of nursing in Mexico paralleled that of many Latin American countries, such as Argentina, Chile and Brazil, among others. Since the early Mexican nursing schools appeared at the beginning of the 20th century, nursing education in Mexico has gone through three educational phases or periods which are detailed here. Based on characteristics such as institutional dependency, academic aspects, and human resources, the three phases are: (a) nursing schools integrated in hospitals settings; (b) nursing schools connected to medical schools; and (c) nursing schools offering graduate degree programs.[7] This classification recognizes the characteristics present in each of the stages, particularly because the school belonged to an institution of health or education, until it reached physical, structural and systematic independence (Cárdenas, 2005; Velandia, 1995).

Phase One: Hospital-Based Nursing Programs

In the early 20th century, changes were made in the organization of the Mexican health system, including the provision of health services and the education of health care professionals. Phase One in nursing education lasted for about 30 years (1900-1930). In 1900, physician Eduardo Liceaga, director of the Center for Maternal and Infant Care, asked Mexican President Profirio Diaz permission to create a school of nursing in Mexico City. Two years later Liceaga, then president of the Health Council and head of the School of Medicine, planned training courses for nurses sponsored by the "Public Charity," a position supported by the Mexican state and by non-governmental organizations (NGOs) that lobby for the poor and disenfranchised.

Inspired by European hospitals and schools of nursing, Liceaga established Mexican nursing schools based on the European nursing curriculum model, which in turn was inspired by the French nursing health care model. The initial goal was to serve the needs of the Mexican General Hospital, about to be built. To recruit nurses, Liceaga ran newspaper ads inviting Mexican women to receive instruction at the Hospital for Maternal and Infant Care. Requirements for admission included elementary school completion, good health, good behavior, and being 20 years old or thereabouts.[8] On February 9, 1907 the Mexican General Hospital School of Nursing was inaugurated[9] with 20 students in the first class. By 1911 the majority of nurses had completed their diplomas, awarded by the Director of Public Charity (Perez Loredo, 1986, pp. 9-11).

---

[7] These phases of nursing education were taken from Velandia (1995, p. 219).

[8] Jamieson states that from 1902 to 1905 only 4th grade of elementary education was required. As part of their "education" they learn to take vital signs (Jamieson, 1968, p. 219).

[9] Although some authors such as Jamieson (1968), Bravo Pena (1980), and others point out that the first Mexican nursing school was at the General Hospital of Mexico, other schools started before that, specifically in *San Luis Potosi, Oaxaca,* and in the State of Mexico that started on March 25th, 1896 when the local House of Representatives authorized the creation of the Theoretic-Practical School of Obstetrics at the Maternity and Children's Hospital House *Concepcion Cardoso de Villada,* a branch of which also operated in *Toluca.* Today, it is known as the Department of Nursing and Obstetrics of the Autonomous University of the State of Mexico.

The rules of the school were in place the following year. Hospital-based nursing education programs continued to grow for two reasons: (a) hospitals needed nurses from the schools to provide care to the sick, and (b) the schools did not have their own physical space, nor the necessary academic and administrative framework to mount independent institutions. These factors determined the make-up of Mexican nursing schools during Phase One.

In terms of academic and practical preparation, from the first day of nursing school, students worked on the hospital wards, taking cues from "nurse helpers" and "religious sisters," and observing how their mentors took care of patients. The nurse helpers themselves learned their skills "on the job," while religious sisters continued helping the sick even after the reform movement expelled some religious groups from the country. Despite their charge to provide "cues" to the students, Roman Catholic sisters (nuns) had little experience in developing nursing education programs. Their primary concern was to provide benevolence and to help the sick and needy. Later, some Roman Catholic nuns subsequently completed formal academic preparation and were awarded degrees.

In addition to observing procedures, nursing students took informal academic classes on anatomy, physiology, hygiene, and treatments. Physicians served as both their program directors and professors. They taught material based on their own interests and areas of clinical expertise. The educational focus was biomedical, individual, and ahistorical. The concept of health focused on disease treatment, that is, physical or bodily pains, without any concern for the environment, family, or social history of the person treated. Under this vision, health care became medicalized and the nurse's role was reduced to providing support for the physician.

According to physicians, the goal of nursing education was to produce qualified personnel capable of carrying out prescribed treatments to hospitalized patients. Its approach was based on "learning by doing." To accomplish this goal, nurses were incorporated into hospital activities very early, echoing some physician's remark that: "nursing students must be in contact with the hospital from the very beginning of their education, at the very least, to smell it." As could be expected, the job market for graduates of nursing programs was in the same hospital environment and this, in turn, exacerbated the dependency on and service to physicians.

The National University of Mexico reopened in 1910 when Mexican independence reached its 100th anniversary. At that time, all professional schools became part of the university and nursing programs were placed under the auspices of medical schools. On December 30th, 1911 nursing programs were actually integrated into the medical schools. The new nursing "degree" was awarded after 2 years of schooling; the degree of "midwife" also required 2 years. As a result of this process, nursing programs of study were updated with emphasis on practical and objective teaching. Disciplinary measures for faculty, students, and other employees were established and a junior high school diploma became the requirement for admission into nursing programs.

Although there have been subsequent changes in the nursing curriculum, program administration and the dependent relationship of nurses on physicians, there are still a few hospital-based schools of nursing in existence. A few examples of hospital-based nursing programs that exist today are the Mexican Institute for Social Security (IMSS), the Institute for Social Security of State Workers (ISSSTE), Escandon, Nutrition, and Cardiology.

Phase Two: Medical School-Based Nursing Programs

This period of Phase Two spanned 30 years from 1930 to 1960 and is characterized first and foremost by the dependency of nursing programs on undergraduate and graduate medical schools. Another feature of Phase Two was the introduction of nurses as teachers, even though physicians continued to teach most of the courses and to direct the nursing schools.

In 1935 the School of Nursing was physically separated from the School of Medicine and based at the National Autonomous University of Mexico. All professional schools then became part of it. After that, to pursue the degree of *Midwife* one must have first completed the degree in nursing. Beginning in 1949 nurses with the appropriate academic background taught specific courses dealing with nursing skills. The School of Nursing as well as the Department of Medicine belonged to the Autonomous National University of Mexico, the latter continues to prepare physicians.

It should be noted that the objectives and the methodologies in teaching nursing barely changed, but the relevant feature was the introduction of professional nurses as teachers in academic activity using a "theoretic-practical" perspective. Thus, nurses were the ones who formed the new generations of nurses, not only in the classroom, but also through community and clinical practice, generating a vision of "nurses for nurses" and not of "physicians for nurses" as it had been previously. Plans and programs of study and clinical practice sessions were formalized and required for successful completion of the program. This had the effect of prioritizing education with a "theoretic-practical" view within the hospital environment. The great specialty-based institutes in nutrition, cardiology, and pediatrics, (among others) were created during this period (1940s) and had a strong positive influence on the education and practice of nursing. In essence, during this phase, nursing was institutionalized and, as previously mentioned, it adhered to an ahistorical, biomedical model focusing on the individual (Cárdenas, 1997, p. 196). Also, in this period, nurses had no problem finding employment. In fact, demand for nurses was so high that nursing auxiliaries were hired. Nursing auxiliaries completed a training program lasting 2 to 6 months. This situation encouraged the development of heterogeneity of nursing personnel,[10] and a large number of nursing schools were founded.

Each year a significant number of graduates were produced; however, the majority were interested in attending to births rather than in providing assistance to the sick. This created an important deficit in public health nurses and nurses with hospital

---

[10] In reality, these labor characteristics are not unique to nurses as all professionals go through the same process, which is congruent with the economic model of the nation, called *Modelo Desarrollista*. The strategy is based on import substitution. The model encouraged industrial expansion and development of the service sector.

skills to care for acutely ill patients. Again, demand drove the creation of large numbers of nursing schools all over the country to meet this need. Physicians almost always directed the schools, especially those connected to hospitals and designed to satisfy the demand for nurses in those institutions.

Phase Three: University-Based Nursing Programs

Throughout Latin America nursing underwent great transformations during the 20th century. As nursing was incorporated in the university system, there was an increase in the number of schools of nursing as well as in the number of nurses. Graduate programs in nursing were created, starting first with master's level studies and continuing to the recent initiation of doctoral programs in nursing. Mexico was a big part of the Latin American transformation of the profession of nursing.

The primary features of Phase Three for the Mexican nursing educational system are: (a) that it gained independence from medical schools, and (b) that it was incorporated into the university system. In Phase Three, deep changes in academic life were demanded, as nursing programs became part of the university. Theoretical knowledge was differentiated from practical know-how and various viewpoints on nursing philosophy were developed. Criteria and conditions required for the degree—aimed at providing advanced professional education, high quality professors, the production of research in basic and applied science, and the development of the service and productive sectors—were set. Under the new academic culture, programs of nursing formalized their plans and programs of study, and at the successful end of 3 years of study, the degree of "Technical Nurse" or "General Nurse" and the license for professional practice are granted.

The "Licenciatura" Degree

A significant event in Mexican nursing took place in 1970, when nurses took over as heads of university-based nursing programs. In 1975 the *University Council* authorized the implementation of a special course leading to the degree of *Licenciatura* in nursing and obstetrics. This was done with the aim of allowing nurses (who had completed high school and who had at least 5 years of professional experience) the opportunity for further advancement by means of a course specializing in nursing. The first course started in February 1976. Toward the end of the 1980s, the curriculum leading to the *Licenciatura* in Nursing in the School of Nursing of the National Polytechnic Institute was approved. The school offering the *Licenciatura* degree was called the Advanced School of Nursing and Obstetrics (ESEO/IPN).

Unfortunately, at this time, in an attempt to reduce health expenditures, health care administrators began hiring health care workers who were less qualified. This led to both unemployment and underemployment of the more qualified and higher wage professionals. Although the effect on professional nursing was minor, since there was at this time already a shortage of nurses, an inconsistency developed between the professional profile of nursing graduates and the specific needs of the institutions employing them. While universities sought to increase professional quality in order to respond to the health needs of society, health care institutions were looking for ways to lower costs. Moreover, a discrepancy existed: the educational curriculum focused on preventive health care, while the workplace hired health care personnel primarily to provide help for the sick.

The *Licenciatura* in nursing began in Mexico under these precarious political and economic conditions. While some pushed to increase the academic level of nurses, others supported the State's position for technical level health care workers prepared in the National Schools of Professional Studies (ENEP) and the National College of Technical Professionals (CONALEP).

This situation placed the nursing *Licenciatura* in a critical position. During the 1980s the degree did not fulfill the promise of better positions upon graduation. In fact, *Licenciatura* degree prepared nurses were under-employed, accepting jobs requiring a lower level of academic preparation and at similar wages as nursing technicians. And, nurses had to struggle with a lack of definition of the functions of professional practice.

SYNOPSIS OF NURSING EDUCATION IN MEXICO

Nursing education in Mexico used an "empiricist-theoretical" process, meaning that nursing was a social activity that became increasingly professionalized. This occurred initially in the health area and subsequently expanded upon recognizing that "health" required the bio-psycho-social cultural equilibrium of the individual, the family, and society as a whole.

When the first general hospital was created, Dr. Liceaga realized it was necessary to prepare the personnel for providing hospital services, and thus, the first hospital nurses were trained for that purpose alone. The curriculum for nurses was formulated in 1906. All students lived on the premises and the plan of studies and practices lasted from 7:00 in the morning until 2:00 in the afternoon, alternating with night shifts, from 8:00 in the evening until 7:00 in the morning (Pérez Loredo, 1986).

At the end of the second decade (1920), when the Health Council was reorganized, a section devoted to child hygiene was created which required the training of personnel capable of providing hygiene tasks. This focus allowed for the development of public health nursing where nurses played an outstanding role, especially in the eradication of infectious-contagious illnesses such as smallpox. The "Office of Sanitary Nursing" was created to allow nurses to plan, implement, and evaluate nursing actions autonomously and with decision-making power.

In 1927, the first preparatory course was established where prospective nurses studied biology, mathematics, Spanish, physics, and chemistry. All these courses were aimed not only at preparing nurses to become physician's aids, but also to help them better understand the foundations of the profession. Three years were required for completion. Despite all this, academic education in nursing was not very advanced as it focused only on the curative aspect of care.

In 1933, the first Congress of Nursing was organized and it was here that the idea of requiring junior high school completion for admission into nursing school was proposed. At the same time, the Department of Public Health regarded nurses as integral to their health team because nurses carried out organizing activities and provided health services to the population. Once it had 658 nurses established and distributed all over the country, the Department of Public Health initiated training designed to implement programs which created federal district health centers as well as those in the provinces.

Soon after, the first nurse instructors appeared as a result of Public Health programs. These instructors visited the most remote towns and had training in rural hygiene, the laboratory, and maternal and childcare.

As nursing was incorporated into the university system between 1950 and 1965, besides implementing the idea of the admission requirement of junior high school completion, nursing updated the plan of study to 3 years to include other courses such as social work, ethics, physiotherapy, as well as laboratory work. The program changed continuously, a course in public health was introduced and the performance of fieldwork in health centers was also required.

Still, prior to 1968, the curriculum lacked educational objectives and content. Physicians developed plans of study and there was no relation between theory and practice. Also, more emphasis was given to health problems than to preventive care (Cárdenas, 1997, p. 196). So in the late 1960s, plans of study in schools of nursing were restructured to attempt to equalize the time devoted to theory and to practice, and nurses began to design plans of study.

Throughout the 1970s and specifically in 1972, the main goal of the 10-year health plan for the Americas was "to increase life expectancy" by increasing health care coverage. In 1977, Mexican primary health care was regarded as the main strategy to achieving this goal. Nursing curricula were reoriented toward community public health nursing goals. Recommended were (a) preparation of nurses for the provision of primary care, and (b) changes for advancing the levels of nursing education (Sanchez Hickman, 1991, pp. 91-92).

In the majority of Mexican undergraduate and graduate nursing programs, a plan of study at a technician's level prevailed for about 20 years (1970-1990). Students came in after completing junior high school; they studied for 3 years; carried out social service, and upon a professional evaluation, received their diploma and their professional license. Also during this period, nursing educational institutions restructured their plans of study and relied on a theoretical focus called *educational technology*.

Nowadays, despite all the efforts at collaboration by nursing schools, there is still no national plan for the academic curriculum that results from unified criteria concerning the appropriate education of the nursing professional at the various degree levels matched to the real-life requirements of the job. In other words, there is no consensus on nursing's professional profile or even on how to push for appropriate legislation of professional practice through professional organizations.[11] As a result of this situation, one encounters great discrepancies in the academic preparation of

---

[11] The FEMAFEE has worked since 1996 to establish the foundations of a nursing curriculum. It is also working on the analysis and reformulation of criteria allowing "curricular homologation." This means the definition of mechanisms fostering student mobility, professional identity, and group cohesion by creating consensus about the knowledge nurses must possess at the national level, regardless of geographic location, health conditions or the specific morbidity indices.

nurses, from (a) the *licenciatura* (university program) through (b) the nurse at the technician's level (3 years of education following junior high school), (c) the nurse specialist (general nurse with a post basic course of 10 months duration on average), (d) to the nurse's aid (with training from between 6 months to a year following junior high school). The situation is further complicated because the institutions which employ nurses use various levels of nurses to provide the same service, without taking into consideration that various degrees of responsibility are associated with the various levels of preparation (Verde Flota, 1991, p. 47).

MEXICAN NURSING EDUCATION TODAY

Today, nurse educators in Mexico strive to transform nurses by instituting best practice protocols, through their teaching of the nursing process, nursing theory, and conceptual models. Additionally, nursing education seeks to establish a body of nursing knowledge. The transformation process faces great obstacles, the most significant being the lack of knowledge, commitment, and responsibility of nursing faculty for whom "innovative" curricula specifies that they must teach these methodologies as a foundation. Mexican nurse educators are not always prepared to teach such material and thus they continue to transmit material that has little relevance to students for their clinical or community practice.

The characteristics of Mexican nursing education, knowledge, and practice led to two distinctive worlds: the "academic world" and the clinical world or the "world of the hospital." In academe, the emphasis is on achieving (a) higher academic ranks, (b) the deployment of knowledge, and (c) the application of innovative educational models to train new generations of nurses and for nursing care and research. All this is the result of the "strategic objectives" which were issued as an outcome of policies in higher education in Mexico. On the other hand, in the hospital, health care policies focus on productivity and quality. Emphasis is on the ability to do more with less and with a high degree of efficiency. This emphasis implies that a reduction in personnel costs, in raw materials and in process costs have an impact on the structure and organization of health services.

Nurses in Practice versus Nurses in Academe

A dichotomy in the vision and mission of academic and clinical settings negatively influence the quality of nurses' relationships. This academic-clinical divide in nursing is played out in multiple settings (e.g., in the workplace, in labor organizations, and in the social and economic environment.) In the end, the split negatively affects the status of nurses.

Because a healthy connection between education and practice is so important to nursing and its development, bridging the divide is necessary. How to create synergy and promote reconciliation between the practice and educational setting is not yet clear. Certainly, the different labor and trade union systems and different conditions of work that exist in the two realms create the illusion and perhaps the reality of separate occupational categories.

In Mexico, nurses in academe and nurses in practice are split by both ideological and theoretical differences. They identify differently with nursing, have different interests, methods of work, and areas of concentration. Because different labor systems exist, nurses in the two realms have little in common and may identify primarily, for example, either with unions or with the employer. It follows that the education and know-how of the nursing profession must come to terms with the features of work in the nursing workplace.

A lack of agreement about nurse unionization also exists among practicing nurses and nurses in academia. Healthcare professionals, particularly nurses, align themselves more with their employer and their workplace than they do with unions. Thus nursing identity and professional development is secondary and often ignored. In Mexico, this phenomenon is not directly connected to the nurse's social class as both practicing nurses and nurses in academia belong to the same socioeconomic class.

The second situation to be addressed concerns the relationship between the education and the prestige or status of Mexican nurses. Ever since the beginning, nurses struggled for social and professional recognition from other health care professionals as well as from society as a whole. Because Mexican nurses believe there is a direct relationship between education and status, they believe academic accomplishments, titles, and credentials allow them to achieve a better standard of living and status among professionals.

But the authors believe that education is only one part. We must consider the genesis and historic aspects of the profession, the characteristics of incorporation into the workforce, the structural and working policies of the health care system, the institutions providing health care, the participation of the State, and the value society places on each profession.

Therefore, the situation cannot be considered in the linear terms that made up the predominant view since the 1970s when nurses became concerned with advancing their knowledge. Even today, when nurses are asked about self-regulation, autonomy, status, and union issues, a significant percentage of them still state that one must have more knowledge, preparation, and education (Cárdenas, 2005).

Even though they spend a large portion of their lives preparing themselves educationally, they still do not consider this sufficient. Very few nurses, primarily those in clinical practice, recognize the importance of being involved in social, political, or cultural activities which allow them to identify the dynamics of professional development as well as to actively partake in those avenues to seek to transform and promote Mexican nursing. On the other hand, nurse educators in academic settings are less likely to view education as the panacea for recognition and prestige of the profession. They not only have significant information on the topic, but also they already are more involved in social participation.

The Construction of Nursing Knowledge and Practice

The urge to develop a theoretical perspective in nursing appeared in the United States during the second half of the 20th century. The need to base nursing practice on its own unique knowledge foundation followed the development of master's level nursing education programs. Clarifying that nursing was not only technical but also theoretical was important. Thus, attempts to establish the essence of nursing as something philosophically sound and conceptually based were pivotal to creating a unique and distinct profession.

The scientific literature in nursing expanded as nursing programs linked to institutions of higher education were developed. Interest in developing a theoretical basis grew, initially in the United States, through other theoretical frameworks using holistic theory based on rigorous scientific arguments.

Thirty years later, the same concern for nursing theory development appeared in Mexico. In the 1980s, Mexican nurses developed a series of activities to increase the scientific rigor of the discipline. They began to measure empirical knowledge on a systematic basis and to broaden the concept of the "nursing process" toward the "nursing diagnosis." Nurses in Mexico addressed the health-illness continuum differently than did medicine, developing their own professional thinking and broadening their understanding of the nursing role. The actions and scope of nursing were viewed as a profession, not an occupation. It was at this point that Mexican nursing aspired to attain the full merits and obligations of a profession (Fuerbringer et al., 1995, p. 45).

As part of theory development, Mexican nursing reached the pre-paradigmatic phase in both the academic and clinical settings. Nursing strove to develop practice-based as well as research-based philosophies, methods, and conceptual frameworks. Nursing aimed to construct an autonomous, scientific-based theoretical body of knowledge. The aim was to strengthen the foundation of the discipline and to enhance everyday practice through the description, explanation, prediction, and control of the health care phenomena.

The advantages are obvious: a sound theoretical base allows Mexican nursing to offer students an autonomous educational preparation and to develop human resources capable of performing well in the different health care arenas as expected by society. Theory development can be used to strengthen the profession of nursing throughout Mexico (*Secretaria de Educación Pública/Dirección General de Profesiones* [SEP/DGP], 2001, p. 24). Models and theories are regarded as a part of nursing's conceptual basis. Because these models focus on wellness as well as on disease, they allow nursing to expand its clinical field beyond just the care of the sick, offering alternatives for its practice.

Exactly at this time (during the 1980s) two perspectives of nursing study began to appear: the epistemological and the sociological. Under the epistemological perspective, a scientific discipline is constructed from history, its professional practice, the philosophy of science and the comparative history of the sciences. From this perspective, the practice of nursing is seen as a combination of the sciences and the art of health care: a humanistic mix of scientific knowledge, philosophy, clinical practice, the social sciences, and the basic sciences.

The nature of a professional discipline is characterized, above all, by a conceptual nucleus. The body of knowledge constituting this nucleus can arise in various ways. In some disciplines, the nature and organization of the body of knowledge itself establishes the epistemological statute of the basic sciences. In contrast, in other disciplines, as is commonly the case with applied, technical, or practical disciplines, the process of scientific configuration takes place as determined by social and historical factors. This is the case of nursing which because of its asystematic origin based on practice, has been organized through the centuries as an activity with a very high level of structure, with a broad range of specific knowledge relevant to its practice, with a precise and well-defined methodology, and with a material and formal object which is perfectly identifiable (Velandia, 2000).

The conceptual structures of nursing connect development with conceptualization into a precise discipline through the introduction of theory. Each one of these structures constitutes a different school of thought. In an epistemological sense, there is relative agreement about the four central concepts supporting the development of nursing as a discipline and as a profession: (a) *person* (patient or user and nurse), (b) *context* (setting: of the patient and nurse), (c) *health* (life), and (d) nursing *health care* (action, therapeutic intervention).

Nurses need specialized knowledge in order to be the decision-makers in professional interventions for their patients. Such knowledge must have a unique structure and organization to be recognized as "known." It is not enough that only nurses know it, but it is essential that other professionals as well as the public can recognize, appreciate and value it. "Knowledge is important for nursing because it [nursing] is a scientific discipline and its process is based on logic and the scientific method. Since nursing has actively participated in the development of its own theory during the last 20 years, it is clear that it is committed to its own beliefs regarding its own professional existence. The integration of a philosophy within the nursing process and the assumption that the philosophy of a person determines his or her actions support the need felt by nursing professionals to develop and reflect about their own philosophy and practice" (Martinez, 1998, p. 127).

Beginning in the 1990s, the development of knowledge and practice in Mexican nursing aimed toward establishing two forms that systematize and support nursing: (a) the nursing process and (b) nursing theories and models. Doing so has focused on the importance of clearly defining the object of study and the work of the profession. With this focus, nursing reached consensus that its essence is *health care* and that the activities of nurses are directed toward the patients, the family, and the community. This focus on health care replaces the widespread belief that the work of nurses was centered on the physician and physician activities. The other outcome is the organization and systematization of the actions derived from a nursing diagnostic, which is based on an analysis of the needs of patients. A systematic process provides a basis for independent and interdependent nurse interventions as well as for the evaluation of nursing actions and the reassessment of their effectiveness.

Graduate Studies in Nursing

In 1980, a university-based specialization program in nursing opened at the graduate level. In 1982, this program of specialization became a master's degree in nursing. Today in Mexico, 10 master's level programs in nursing exist. According to Espino:

The pressure of medical specialties and the requirements that must be fulfilled to qualify as university faculty appear to be what explain, for the most part, the appearance of specialties and master's programs for nursing . . . in actuality the phenomenon of the globalization of the economy, of technology, and of communications and the rapid pace with which knowledge becomes obsolete, professionals, academics, and scientists are required to promote the vital development of the nation, not only of their own disciplinary fields. (Espino, 1997, p. 7)

It is appropriate to point out that the design and operation of these academic programs occurred erratically and often in isolation, without taking into consideration a foundation and basic structure that could allow academic exchanges both at the national and international levels. The wide disparity of master's and specialization programs at the national level suggests a weakness in the teaching and research personnel and in the infrastructure required for the development of these programs (Espino, 1999, pp. 5, 15).

Professional Practice

Nursing first became part of the labor market in Mexico in the early 20th century, coinciding with the creation of the General Hospital of Mexico in 1905. Jamieson et al. (1968) points out that the first Mexican nurses "were devoted mainly to providing treatment inside hospitals and jails, they were women of middle age, single, or widowers and earned about $50.00 per year. Their occupation was regarded as being so humble that no license or exam was required for the practice of the activity in contrast with the situation of physicians and surgeons" (Cárdenas, 2005, pp. 62-65).

When the new hospital opened its doors on the fifth of February, 1905, 54 nurses covered all of the services and direct care. All of the nurses lived inside the hospital. There were two work shifts, one from 7:00 in the morning until 8:00 in the evening, and the other one from 8:00 in the evening until 7:00 in the morning. These shifts, however, were not fixed and were adjusted according to service needs. Relief from the work schedule was based on a rotation system (Perez Loredo, 1986, p. 10). This practice of two 12-hour work shifts left a deep mark on the evolution of Mexican nursing during the entire 20th century.

Further, because of patient needs and the dynamic of the hospital itself, 12 hours was often just the minimum. To get all of their work done, nurses would often need to work 24 hours. Patients were too sick and the census was too high for the number of nurses on staff. Additionally, the infrastructure, such as medical equipment, pharmaceuticals, and overall budget was insufficient to meet patient care needs.

Also, beginning Mexican nurses often assume many additional duties. While some of these added responsibilities are relevant to nursing, others—such as answering telephones, taking messages, transporting patients, and processing forms—do not need to be done by a nurse. Even though Mexican nurses perform these duties, their salaries do not compensate for them. This situation has persisted because the agencies are accustomed to nurses completing these extra tasks without compensation and nurses have "gotten used to" the excessive work. Finally, while nursing working conditions and salaries have improved of late, they are still low when compared with other health professions.

During the 20th century one can distinguish three job models: the midwife, the public health nurse, and the hospital nurse (Nájera et al., 1992, p. 9). Although the profession of midwifery, the *Aztec Ticitl*, existed in pre-Hispanic times offering health care to mothers and their children according to Nájera et al. (1992), it exploded during the 20th century, particularly from 1933 to 1943. The most important feature of midwifery was its accessibility—within the familiar and domestic context—at an acceptable cost, provided to women by other women. But the practice lost ground as specialized physicians appeared and the care of birth became institutionalized toward the end of the 1950s.

The predecessors of public health nurses, visiting nurses, first appear at the start of the 20th century. The visiting nurses performed activities aimed at preventing illness and promoting health in the community. Public Health nursing itself appeared in 1921, relatively late compared to midwifery and hospital nursing. At this time, the public health services had 10 practical nurses for the purpose of carrying out its activities, mainly vaccination for the population (Perez Loredo, 1986, p. 16). In 1945, the General Office of Public Health Nursing was created. It was composed of nurses that had studied public health in the United States and Canada under Rockefeller Foundation Fellowships.

During the 1950s and the first few years of the 1960s there were numerous groups of public health nurses, many of them with excellent preparation and broad experience. Their duties included carrying out community studies, recruitment and training of personnel, and the organization, and the start-up and supervision of health centers. Public health nurses contributed to the development of priority health care programs such as the control of communicable diseases, the health care of mothers and children, public health campaigns, and more generally, the systematization of community health work.

In 1951, the Ministry of Health chose to increase the number of nurses because nurses are the one group of health care providers who maintain direct, individual, and ongoing contact with both the healthy and the sick. From this perspective, nurses were the decisive agents in the public health services and the nursing schools were charged with promoting enrollments all over the nation (Perez Loredo, 1986, p. 51). This decision started the growth of the institutions responsible for developing human resources in nursing. Unfortunately, this growth was not well planned, leading to wide disparity in academic training and background, making difficult the clear definition of the duties of the various levels of nursing. This disparity in training and lack of defined roles remains one of the main obstacles to defining a standard educational policy, enabling the cohesiveness of the nursing profession.

The numbers of hospital nurses boomed at the start of the 1960s as hospital health care focused on the middle class working population. The boom contributed, according to Nájera (Nájera et al., 1992, p. 35), for almost 2 decades (1972-1985) to a crisis in nursing manifested primarily by the suppression of the organizational structures of the profession within health care institutions. While overall nursing schools proliferated due to the lack of a normative system regulating nursing education, many nursing programs with dubious academic quality appeared. The problem was more acute with the education of nurses' aids, as these programs were and are located outside of the formal national educational system. Most nurses began their nursing education after junior high school, despite the fact that other technical courses (like elementary school teachers, nutritionists, and social workers) require the additional years of senior high school completion as a basic requirement for admission.

During the 30-year period from 1950 to 1980, professional nursing in Mexico experienced other major developments, especially in community public health nursing. One was the establishment of the *Direccion Nacional de Enfermeria* (National Secretariat in Nursing), which standardized nursing responsibilities on a national level, not only for nursing practice, but also for nursing education. For example, community public health nurses organized and directed community health promotion programs, conducted home visits that allowed them to examine and observe the health of families, implemented preventive maternal child health practices, examined and treated infectious-contagious diseases, and mounted immunization and vaccination programs for children.

According to Margarita Navarro, the first National Nursing Director (Secretary), the *power* that the Mexican nurses acquired was so great that physicians decided to close down the *Dirección Nacional de Enfermería,* which in addition to interior conflicts within the profession, generated the crisis described previously (Navarro & Cárdinas, 2002).

Before it closed, in 1979, the Office of Nursing required that the heads of nursing departments in hospitals and clinics to have completed a university degree and a specialization program. The Office's objective was to improve nursing care and to implement a handbook of nursing levels and positions (Perez Loredo, 1986, p. 147).

During the last 20 years the integration of nurses into the workplace has not changed significantly. Those who hire nurses, that is, hospitals, industries, schools, communities, and physicians, determine the distribution of nurses. Most nurses work under a contract and their performance is dependent on a contractual situation. Therefore, although nurses are educated to be professionals, they lack autonomy because they work under the control of others outside the profession.

Free Trade Agreements and Nursing

The North American Free Trade Agreement (NAFTA) involving Mexico, the United States, and Canada motivated new models for health care services. For nursing, it also highlights the existing nursing weaknesses in regard to accreditation, certification, professionalization, and the link between teaching and service. Still, the process of globalization, as framed by "neoliberal health care policies"[12] has allowed

[12] "Neoliberal Health Policies" are the set of policies adopted since 1973 in industrialized nations resulting from the application of economic formulae designed to restrict public expenditures and freeze wages so as to solve the so-called "fiscal crisis of the state."

nurses to realize that the nursing profession is embedded in the social, cultural, political, and economic contexts existing not only in the nation, but also in the world.

Today, nurses' work is not necessarily defined by their academic preparation. Professional nursing resources are underutilized in health care institutions. Also, work methods are organized so that care is provided through routine activities which do not encourage the development of professional nursing interventions aimed at personalized primary care. Thus, nursing practice is restricted to sub-ordinate activities preventing the creative and reflexive performance that should be the outcome of the knowledge base of the nursing discipline and a humanitarian approach to health care.

Another feature of the actual conditions of nursing practice is the lack of an organizational structure that encourages professionalism. The existing [health care] structures, going back to the 1960s, still assign nursing personnel, significant loads of administrative activities that should be performed by other workers. This implies a decrease in the time nurses have available for the actual health care required by patients. On the other hand, the activities assigned to supervisors and heads of nursing departments does not allow effective development of the administration and assessment of the quality of health care as they are confined to taking care of a large number of administrative activities aimed at the control of the resources (Jiménez, 2001).

In other words, in the distribution of activities that are carried out by the health team in hospitals, it is the nursing personnel that perform a broad set of tasks that do not correspond, at least in a direct manner, to their objective of study and work: health care. In fact, 60% to 70% of nurses' time is spent on administrative chores and only 30% to 40% on providing actual nursing care.

Working Conditions for Mexican Nurses

Unfortunately, information about numbers and qualifications of nursing per-sonnel in Mexico is incomplete. The National College of Nurses A.C. together with the Ministries of Public Health and Health Care published a report "Nursing and Obstetric/Gynecological Resources in Mexico" with the results from a study conducted in 1970 (CNE-INEGI, 1979). At that time, there were 38,955 Mexican nurses. Twenty-eight percent of the nurses were in the "professional category."[13] The distribution of the personnel throughout the country ranged from 1.9 and 7.6 nurses per 10,000 inhabitants. These numbers are consistent with a significant nursing shortage.

More research on nursing as an occupational category was carried out in 1985 (Nájera, 1992a, 1992b; CNE-INEGI, 1993, 2001; Health Care Ministry, 1999, 2000;

---

[13] This differentiation is based on academic background. Professional nurses are those who study nursing for 3 to 5 years subsequent to completion of high school. They earn the degree of General or Technical Nurse or "*Licenciatura*" in Nursing. Non-professional or technical personnel may or may not have completed elementary school and have taken short courses in nursing with duration between 3 months and a year.

Inter-institutional Nursing Commission, 2000). The studies explored how nurses throughout Mexico make decisions, plan and manage resources, and track and evaluate the profession. Findings from the 1999 study conducted by the "System for the Management of Human Resources in Nursing" (Health Care Ministry, 1999) reported a total of 152,157 nurses[14] with 22.46% of them based in the Federal District; 6.46% in the State of Mexico; 5.73% in Veracruz; 5.61% in Nuevo Leon; and 4.97% in Jalisco. The studies report that 95% of all Mexican nurses are female. A mere 7% of the nurses hold the qualification of *licenciatura* with 60% of them prepared at the technical level and 30% of them at the level of the nurse's aids.

As previously noted, in Mexico health care services, in general, are classified as primary (prevention), secondary (treatment/cure), and tertiary (rehabilitation) levels, whether provided in community health, in acute care hospitals, in industries, in school settings, or in the emerging private professional practice. The assignment of nurses in terms of these levels of health care is as follows: first level, 21.81%; second level, 55.19%; third level 18.44%; and teaching 0.56%. The main settings of employment for nurses are hospitals, the community, and industry (CNE/INEGI, 1993; SEP/DGP, 1998).

Nursing Status

The status of Mexican nurses is low. There are two perspectives on the reasons for this low status:

1. The sociological perspective derives from the job market, the relationships within and among professions, and the context of nursing practice. Sociologically, nurses' low status derives from the perception that there is no special knowledge or skill required to provide their services. One aspect supporting this idea is the religious and feminine legacies of nursing. These legacies created an image of the nurse as charitable, selfless, and wholly devoted to their fellow persons. Such an image "justifies" low remuneration and compensation for nursing work. These legacies have also created the impression that nurses have it "in their nature to provide health care" so that they are only transporting domestic activities from the home to the hospital.
2. The epistemological perspective includes the development of the nursing discipline and the human and professional relationships within labor organizations, the identity and cohesion of the group, as well as the professional self-perception.

After almost a century of existence of modern nursing in Mexico, the professional discipline has not been able to create a firm epistemological foundation for the body of nursing knowledge. Nonetheless, nurses have made valuable efforts to evolve from an empirical health care model to a theoretic-practical model. Simultaneously, they seek not only to better define their focus, study, and work, but also to refocus their practice toward holistic interventions incorporating the various supporting disciplines.

---

[14] Nájera et al. (1992b).

It is common that social valuations of a profession are made without considering the possession and dominion of knowledge. Often society places value based on the honor and prestige acquired early in the profession's history or through movements demanding professional, labor, and social rights. Given this context, Mexican nurses hold an inferior position among the professions. Thus consumers are willing to pay less for the professional services of a nurse than for the services of other professionals.

The job market assigns characteristics to nursing that reinforce the image of it as a weak profession. In principle, nursing functions are associated with obedience, submission, and respect for authority. Labor relations are ruled by contract and thus there are few opportunities within the profession for independent practice. Generally, nurses carry out their labor in an institutionalized setting, typically in hospitals at the secondary and tertiary level of health care where the wages are, by nature, low. The nursing profession is caught in a vicious circle leading from low status and little prestige to low wages.

The internal perspective is complicated since nursing is under the aegis of physicians whose vision of health care is mainly bio-medical in nature and taking place mainly inside a hospital. Still, after about 20 years of labor struggle, Mexican nurses have been able to define their unique professional participation as part of the health team. Nowadays, it is generally acknowledged that the body of nursing knowledge is developing, and there is a set of actions that are performed uniquely and exclusively by the professional nurses.

This is a still big challenge since physicians have historically had the necessary political strength to prevail over other professionals in the health field, as they have been the interface between the state and national health care projects. Professional relationships within the profession, educational disparities, the various labor categories, and the lack of definition of functions have hindered the formation of effective labor organizations. There is no close, direct relationship between the academic level and the degree of status and social and professional prestige of the profession. Nurses must review their opportunities for development, starting from the internal and external conditions existing within their professional, labor, and social interactions. Then, they can establish viable strategies to achieve consistency in the perception of a nurse's status, prestige, and income.

In summary, the profession of nursing in Mexico, from the time of its beginning and development, is populated by people with unequal academic preparation— ranging from nursing assistants (auxiliaries), who study for 12 years beginning with kindergarten, to *licenciadas,* or those with masters or doctorates in nursing, who have studied between 23 to 27 years, respectively. This disparity should generate a different prestige for *licenciadas,* not only because of the vastly different academic preparation in nursing, but also because of the cultural capital, the social and labor environment.

Nursing's Social Image

Mexican society's image of nursing does not match the image Mexican nurses have of themselves. For instance, society does not differentiate between a university-educated nurse and a nurse aid with much less education. The practice of undervaluing manual labor carried out by women also leaves a scar on the nursing profession that permeates all social relationships.

Furthermore, the longstanding association of nursing with charitable service to the poor reinforces its unfavorable position in the prevailing hierarchy in the health care field. The lack of nursing's social prestige turns the profession into a provider of cheap, efficient, and disciplined labor. Although nurses have always taken care of all human beings who get sick, both the rich and the poor, from the beginning nursing care has been primarily associated with the needy.

Professional Self-Perception

Professional self-perception is shaped by the broad social context, including family and educational institutions as well as exposure to professional practice. Nurses' professional self-perception is incongruent with its actual social status and prestige in Mexico. This situation motivated Mexican nurses to mount a long-standing struggle for recognition in the workplace. Specifically, Mexican nursing sought to enhance their status by increasing nursing knowledge, competence, and by focusing on the humanistic dimensions of health care. However, they mounted their strategies for increased recognition and status within the profession only and not with other constituents.

The diverse composition of nursing in Mexico makes it difficult for all nurses to have uniform interpretations of the nature of their profession. Widely different academic background and experience create a diverse membership pool. Administrators in health care settings (primarily inside hospitals) fail to differentiate between auxiliary and professional nurses. Thus, all nurses are treated the same, regardless of their educational background. This situation has resulted in battles within nursing and within the hierarchical authority systems, ultimately exacerbating the fragmentation and serving as an obstacle to solidarity among nurses. The net result is weak cohesion among working nurses.

Professional Self-Regulation and Autonomy

In Mexico, the autonomy of the nursing profession depends on the work setting, the position nurses hold in organizations, the structure of the health care system, the educational level of the nurse, as well as other factors. Tension exists between the *ideal* autonomy and the *real* situation for nurses. Although nursing began as dependent on medicine and physicians, now in the 21st century, professional autonomy of any discipline in the health field is in question. From our perspective, in a strict sense, a profession that does not depend on others does not exist. Fundamentally, nursing seeks and creates interprofessional relationships within the national health care system.

Today, nurses continue to struggle to justify and legitimize their position in society and in the workplace. They have done so from several vantage points. One such vantage point is professional autonomy strongly linked to the work setting. To enable nurses to achieve an unambiguous autonomy, one must analyze the nursing job market, the organization and structure of the employing institutions, and interdisciplinary professional relationships.

From this perspective, nursing education should focus on socialization that prioritizes the assumption of norms, values, and attitudes grounded in professional knowledge. Nursing education must also be based on professional freedom and autonomy in decision-making instead of on the nurse solely as someone who helps, provides comfort, and assists in emergency situations.

It is also worthwhile to consider professional autonomy from the perspective of interdisciplinary professional relationships existing among members of the health team. That is, if the patient or consumer of health care services is regarded as the key linking all the health care professions, the question is to determine which professions are able to reestablish the health of the patient. Strictly speaking, the "concept of *autonomy* should be replaced by that of *interdependency,* the integration of the knowledge and actions of the health team as a whole aimed at fostering, preserving, or reestablishing the health of the sick individual, his or her family, and society as a whole" (Cárdenas, 2005, pp. 207-208).

In addition, health care policies and educational policies have been transformed with the implementation of the Free Trade Agreement (NAFTA) among the United States, Canada, and Mexico. *Quality* is the factor that links education to the job market and underlies the accreditation processes of institutions and educational programs. The ultimate goal is to incorporate health care and educational institutions to international competitiveness.

Two of the primary commitments that Mexican nurses established in these trilateral meetings, a little before the vigorous entry of the Free Trade Agreement in 1994, was to begin the process of accreditation of academic programs and the certification of the nursing professional, creating academic, labor, and union platforms to accomplish this purpose.

Despite the fact that Mexican nursing is still characterized by its focus on acute care and hospital institutions, nursing can use this opportunity to create a critical consciousness among nurses by modifying the existing vertical relationships in the nursing labor force and by empowering nurses.

Although the initial "free transit" of nursing professionals through the countries that signed the Free Trade Agreement (Canada, the United States, and Mexico) is not yet finalized, Mexican nurses have entered into a dynamic of professional development that favors (a) the quality of care consumers of health care services receive, and (b) the social transformation of the nursing practice. To do so requires carrying out the process of planning, organizing, intervention, and evaluation, having as a standard that guarantees quality as well as relying on the international indicators or standards.

At the same time, nursing in Mexico is not completely self-regulated. While it is true that there are norms regulating the profession, these norms are not universally applied to all of nursing. Instead, each educational or service institution creates, applies, and interprets its own norms and controls. This inconsistency can be due to the lack of a national nursing profile with sufficient status and power to regulate and guide itself within the health care system. Because of this, the norms for nursing are often dictated by non-nursing professionals such as physicians or hospital administrators. Moreover, the standards for the regulation of professional nursing practice are not yet well developed. Although the regulation of nursing is a process that has been underway since 1988, the results are not yet tangible.

It is not easy to achieve the goal of having nurses regulate their own profession. Numerous obstacles exist and each day battles are fought both inside and outside the profession. The external battles relate to the sociopolitical position physicians have achieved in the health care system as they head and direct the majority of offices where decisions are made and where the policies guiding the actions of the various job markets are issued. Struggles inside the profession are generated mainly between nursing personnel who have different distinct educational levels and work categories, but also between male and female nurses.

Despite all of the above, hope exists that Mexican nursing leaders are able to combine their efforts and their collective will to crystallize professional regulation. By doing so, these leaders can encourage the participation of nurses to implement normative schemes that favor public recognition of the discipline.

LABOR ORGANIZATIONS

From their creation in 1947 until now, professional nursing organizations in Mexico have sought to improve nursing's labor and social conditions. However, they suffer from lack of visibility and their actions often go unnoticed. Several conditions that contribute to the invisibility of the nursing organizations include the lack of personnel and financial resources required to publicize Mexican nurses in their work settings (schools, hospitals, industries, homes, etc.) in an appropriate fashion. Another reason nursing fails to promote itself is the lack of collaboration within the nursing organizations. More collaboration would allow nursing to develop an evidence-based practice which is fostered through writing, carrying out research, offering conferences, working in networks, without compromising the completion of nursing's other professional roles. In any case, there is no certainty that the most geographically distant nurse is being reached.

It is difficult to foster the growth of labor union membership and participation among nurses since nurses are scattered throughout Mexico, in primary, secondary, and tertiary health care settings and in many different work environments. In Mexico, union membership is not required as it is in some other Latin American countries. Instead, membership is completely voluntary.

Certainly, nursing attributes many of its problems and weaknesses to its inability to promote itself and its inherent lack of positive publicity. Mexican nurses overwhelming concur that mass media distorts the image of nursing through its portrayal of them as women with little knowledge, subordinate to physicians, and interested in sexual liaisons. Even the best portrayals show nurses as women who only give injections, administer intravenous solutions, and check vital signs.

Nurses have had little effective participation in professional labor associations and unions. Their participation has been sporadic and has had little impact on the conditions of nurses' work and on the public perception of nursing. The reasons for this are easy to understand. The diverse roles they play, such as daughter, sister, mother, wife, friend, among others, have not been of great help to professional and labor organization causes. Their apathy, their lack of critical thinking, and their indifference to the situation have caused great harm and have also created great obstacles to the development of labor organizations, resulting in a negative impact on labor demands such as the recognition (in terms or wages) of *licenciadas* or the inclusion of nurses in the tax code at the level of a "trade." Their labor union affiliation also prevented nursing from achieving the desired social prestige as recognized by professional social services and the integration of civilian groups focused on social welfare. In the end, it seems that Mexican nurses have yet to acknowledge the importance of their individual and collective participation in the workings of society. In effect, nurses need to develop a social consciousness.

The contributions of professional organizations of nurses in Mexico during the last 5 years can be summarized as: (a) updating legislation regarding the profession; (b) updating the official norms on health care in Mexico; (c) the establishment of nursing standards; (d) creating the Mexican Council for the Accreditation and Certification of Nursing (COMACE); (e) implementation of the System of Administrative Information about Human Resources in Nursing (SIARHE); (f) revision of plans and programs for the education and continuing education of nurses; (g) participation, productivity and self-improvement of nursing personnel; (h) determining guidelines for a Nursing Code of Ethics; (I) fulfillment of the professional social service and the education of professional experts; and (j) proposing national policies designed to direct the education and professional practice of nursing within the rules of the health care sector.

CONCLUSIONS

In summary, the characteristics of Mexican nursing are strongly linked to the historical, social, and political conditions associated with its origin and development. Nursing is now part of a complex occupational social structure and is viewed as a subordinated occupation whose members perform according to the demands of institutional practices. Nurses themselves, regardless of their education, are considered salaried employees under contract. Moreover, nursing faces circumstances that exclude their advancement primarily because there is no direct relationship among nurses' educational background, their employment responsibilities, and their professional and social recognition.

To further exacerbate the issue, most nurses have a poor understanding of the relationship between education and status. They expect that increased education will automatically translate to increased social recognition. Why the status of nursing does not increase with more education is not well studied, but it is clear that Mexican nurses regard education as the single most important vehicle needed to attain professionalism, social status, and prestige.

Their view stems from two main factors. The first one relates to characteristics associated with the origin of nursing. Historically, nursing was primarily empirical and experiential in nature with low income and status. Consequently, nurses may have assumed—consciously or unconsciously—that if their scientific knowledge and academic level were higher, both their income and their prestige would increase. The second reason relates to the proximity of nurses to physicians who continually update their knowledge. Nurses may have assumed that medicine's high status comes from medicine's high level of knowledge. However, nursing paid little attention to the differentiation between medicine and nursing that society, the social dynamic and struggles for legitimization have made on their respective status and prestige.

There is a tension between the professional structure and the job market because, in Mexico as well as in most underdeveloped countries, it is widely believed that as a profession enhances its "scientific" base, it also gains social prestige and income. This belief is supported by neoclassical economic theory that inspired educational strategies that fostered marked inequalities between those professionals who possess commonly held knowledge (and thus are unable to claim high salaries) and those who justify their salaries based on the high value placed on their knowledge (Duviel, 1982, p. 2).

In this sense, Duviel argues that an "*unequal exchange*" exists among the professions based on the value society places on the services each offers. Obviously, this phenomenon erodes the economic potential as well as the prestige attainable within those professions where knowledge is commonly held. As a result, some professions either do not get paid or get paid little, as in the case of nursing. Thus, nurses are highly motivated to search for professional and social legitimacy.

Nursing argues that although the functions and activities they perform gravitate around *health care,* nursing also possesses an autonomous scientific bases. However, society regards the contributions of nursing to society to be of little significance because it is believed the knowledge applied to care for the sick is "common knowledge" and not owned exclusively by nurses. Mexican society maintains that it is a part of a woman's biological and historical nature to be caregivers and healers. It is precisely this assumption that "nursing knowledge is common knowledge" held by society and the idea that anyone is capable of providing nursing care to the sick that creates the unequal valuation of the profession.

This view of nursing also allowed the indiscriminate opening of private schools of nursing in Mexico by persons or organizations that regard nursing education as a "for-profit" business. The new private schools are not focused on the quality programming nor student outcomes. This explains in part the disparities of nursing education in Mexico (Barrón, 2003).

In their everyday practice, Mexican nurses continue to increase their academic preparation. They hope that higher education will enhance the recognition they receive in the workplace from colleagues and employers, *as if* their will and commitment were enough to make nursing stand out.

While Mexican hospitals are still the primary work setting for nurses, an initiative is underway to foster community health, occupational health, and private nursing consultation. Unfortunately, acute care settings are dominated by a system of health care that prioritizes the care of the sick. The dynamic within the Mexican health care system places the physician at the head as the decision maker and autocratic leader.

Despite all of the above, during the last 15 years nurses have successfully established for themselves professional independence. They subscribe to the view that all health care professionals (e.g., pharmacists, laboratory technicians, social workers, nutritionists, and nurses), use their knowledge and effort *for the patient* and that each of them, from their own vantage points, contribute to and support patient recovery. Professional autonomy becomes a relative concept since no single professional is capable of acting independently to carry out this mission.

This perspective allows a new view of the health professions in general and of nursing in specific. In reality, there is a thin line dividing the functions of diagnosis and care, causing nurses to think in terms of performing two kinds of activities: the *independent* ones dealing directly with care and which do not require the direction of other professionals, and the *interdependent* ones which are those actions carried out in coordination with the health team.

Professional self-regulation is another important factor. National nursing organizations regulate both professional nursing education and practice. However, the circulation of written policies and regulations to only nurses is inadequate to affect change. Further hobbling efforts at self-regulation, the health care administrators and nurses in the workplace do not know the regulations well enough to follow them. This has two major ramifications:

1. first, the national regulations are not always implemented which leads to weak labor organizations;
2. second, by not knowing the regulations or by not agreeing with them, each institution then establishes its own regulations adding to the fragmentation and confusion over nurses' roles.

From the standpoint of valuation, nursing recognition is an ongoing process that includes job performance, image, prestige, and wages. These factors are not always synchronized with the nurses' educational background. The perception nurses have of themselves as professionals does not correspond with that of society as measured by the indicators. From this point of view, it is not that society is not aware of nurses' work, it is that the various social sectors do not value it as much as the nurse does.

While Mexican nurses believe they do not hold the status and prestige of other professions, they are continually seeking strategies that enable them to attain it. They continually strive for self-improvement, for the accreditation of their institutions, and for the certification of their members. Nurses strive (a) to enhance their code of ethics, (b) to enhance professional development, (c) to control the practice of the profession in the workplace, and (d) to struggle for freedom and autonomy so that nursing can generate political power as well as professional and social legitimacy that ultimately may lead to their improved status and prestige.

However, the strategies Mexican nurses use cannot resolve the fundamental issues inherent to the profession. For example, because most nurse educators naively assert that the fundamental problem of Mexican nurses is their lack of education, nursing curricula are content-laded and overly saturated with information. Additionally, while students attend nursing programs full time, they are given little that enables them to be successful in the job market. At the same time, nurses employed in the health care area demand a say in what is taught in nursing schools.

Based on the above, nursing originated as an occupation and only later became a profession. While meeting the basic requirements, nursing is still regarded merely as the lowest level of a profession. Factors leading to the lack of social recognition of nursing as a profession include the existing tensions between academic training and the job market; between the social and labor conditions and the high spirit of volunteerism and struggle exhibited by Mexican nurses; and between autonomy and interdependency. Finally, the actions of the labor organizations aimed at producing evidence can impact both the job market as well as society as a whole.

Nursing evolved historically with a body of knowledge grounded mainly in biology and in the social and behavioral sciences. Today, there is some consensus on the definition of nursing as well as on the professional object of study: the holistic care of the person. Although the difference between "health care" and "health treatment" is a topic of ongoing debate, doctors diagnose and treat an illness, while nurses care for patients in a more holistic manner. How to integrate knowledge generated by other disciplines into research, education, and practice is also an ongoing issue for Mexican nursing. Knowing how to adapt and authenticate health care and nursing models developed outside of Mexico as valid for the Mexican context is another such ongoing dilemma. In order to address these, nursing must also form partnerships between the "academic world" and the "practice world" and to create mechanisms for diminishing and resolving professional differences in order to enhance the benefits that already exist and so achieve labor organization cohesion and identification.

However, as a professional group nurses have achieved a great deal even though a significant number of nurses, particularly those working in hospitals, in clinics, and in the community have lacked access to continuing education. As a result, they continue to use the biomedical model of care in their practice and to focus on the physician directing their practice. In the end, it is essential to establish an epistemological foundation for the profession. To do so requires that nursing discuss, analyze, and establish the process that it uses to adapt knowledge generated in other areas to become part of its own knowledge foundation.

Knowledge is not the only characteristic for gaining status and prestige. It is necessary, among other things, to work successfully on labor issues and on the structure and organization of health care systems. Nurses can benefit by analyzing how everyday language, symbols, and customs permeate the knowledge and culture. They also can discover ways in which socio-cultural networks in the profession are constructed. Doing so surfaces those traditions that create obstacles to nursing's ability to shape its own activities and evolution.

CHALLENGES FOR MEXICAN NURSES IN THE 21st CENTURY

The challenge for Mexican nursing in the 21st century is to transform itself. Because status and prestige have a direct impact on social position and income, it is important for nursing to clarify and define its roles within the profession as well as within health care labor settings (Cárdenas, 2005).

To make such widespread change is not easy. It involves structural, system-wide adjustments and includes political economic and labor dimensions. However, Mexican nurses possess strengths untapped by the "medically-driven" health care system and now have a great opportunity for social and labor reform since they constitute more than 60% of the health care labor force. Moreover, nurses are the only members of the professional health care team who are in direct contact with patients around the clock.

An informational campaign designed to disseminate how nursing knowledge is more than common knowledge is needed. While some nursing knowledge is borrowed from other disciplines, nursing has re-conceptualized this knowledge and adapted it to a nursing framework. The "nursing process" and "nursing models of care" are the objects of study and an essential part of the work of the profession.

It is urgent and necessary to use nursing academic preparation as the definition for levels of nursing practice and to establish labor profiles that meet the needs of the population. Nursing must promote interdisciplinary collaboration in which roles are complementary and harmonious where ever professional responsibilities are shared. To do so, it is essential that an organizational structure of nursing be developed that promotes new health care approaches and models to support education, research, professional identity, and cohesion.

Mexican nursing labor organizations cannot be restricted to merely the education and updating of nursing skills. Instead, these organizations can help nurses develop a consciousness of collegiality to improve the quality of relationships within the profession and set the groundwork for nursing's enhanced status and prestige.

While the nursing profession can benefit from more definition, identification, and dissemination of its object of study, it can also benefit from reaching a consensus on its body of professional knowledge. Doing so paves the way to develop new nursing models and create stronger links between education and practice. Joining theory and practice will enhance nursing cohesion and ownership and serve to combat the existing hierarchical structure of health care workplace organizations.

Nursing can shape, publicize, and support standards and methods of nursing care and be better able to clarify and explain the fundamental differences between diagnosing, treating, and *caring*. This should allow the determination of levels of educational preparation and clinical categories that have corresponding salaries commensurate with the nurses' professional background. Nursing needs to create more graduate programs in nursing and to continue gaining recognition of the Licenciatura in Nursing.

Finally, nursing can continue to disseminate evidence marking the contribution of nurses toward the reestablishment of the health of individuals and aggregates in communities. Finally, they can benefit from more involvement in other social, political, and cultural settings that may allow them to reorient the social image of the profession of nursing. These are some of the greatest challenges nursing in Mexico confronts.

REFERENCES

Barbosa, G. M. L., De Souza, B. S., et al. (1999). *A luta pela politizacao das enfermeiras. Sindicalismo no Rio de Janeiro: 1978-1984* [Fighting for the political awareness of nurses: Union work in Rio de Janeiro: 1978-1984]. Río de Janeiro, Brasil: Editora Anna Nery. UFRJ.

Barreira, I. E., & De Souza B. S. (2000). *A pesquisa e a documentacao en história de enfermagem no Brasil* [Nursing research and history in Brazil]. Ponencia presentada en el I Coloquio Latinoamericano de Historia de la Enfermería. Río de Janeiro, Brasil. 28-31 de agosto.

Barrón, T. C. (2003). *Universidades privadas. Formación en educación* [Private universities. Educational preparation]. México: CESU/UNAM/Plaza y Valdés Editores.

Bravo, P. F. (1980). *Nociones de la historia de enfermería* [Impressions on the history of nursing] (2nd ed.). México: Porrúa. notion

Cárdenas, B. L. (1997). *Historia de las organizaciones de enfermería en México* [The history of Mexican nursing organizations]. México: Tesis Maestría de Estudios Latinoamericanos, UAEM.

Cárdenas, B. L. (2005). *La Profesionalización de Enfermería en México. Un Análisis desde la Sociología de las Profesiones* [The professionalization of Mexican nursing: An analysis from the sociology of the professions]. México: Pomares/UAEM/ FEMAFEE/UAT.

Casasa, G. P. (2001). Aspectos ideológicos y socioeconómicos que inciden en la formación del profesional de enfermería [Ideological and socioeconomic aspects affecting professional nurses]. *Enfermeras, México, XXXVIII*(3), 35-44.

Cleaves, P. S. (1985). *Las profesiones y el Estado: El caso de México* [The professions and the State: The case of Mexico]. México: El Colegio de México.

Colegio Nacional de Enfermeras/Secretaría de Salubridad y Asistencia [CNE/INEGI]. (1979). *Estudio de recursos de enfermería y obstetricia en México* [Nursing and midwifery resources in Mexico]. México: SSA.

CNE/INEGI. (1993). *Censo nacional de recursos de enfermería* [Survey of national nursing resources]. México.

CNE/INEGI. (2001). *Enfermeras [Nurses], México, XXXVIII*(3), 4-9.

CNE/INEGI. (2002). *Reglamentación para el ejercicio y la formación de la profesión de enfermería en México* [Regulation of professional nursing practice and education in Mexico]. México.

De Monterrosa, E., Lange, I., et al. (1991). *Enfermería del siglo XXI en América Latina* [Latin American nursing in the 21st century]. México: Fundación W. K. Kellogg.

Donahue, P. M. (1985). *Historia de la enfermería* [History of nursing]. España: Doyma.

Duviel, I. (1982). *El capital humano después de la teoría neoclásica: Los profesionistas en los países subdesarrollados* [Human capital under Neoclassical Theory: Professionals in underdeveloped countries]. Pensamiento universitario. México: CESU/UNAM.

Espino, V. M. E. (1997). Avances en el curriculum de enfermería [Advances in nursing curriculum]. In *Memorias jornada científica cultural de aniversario VII reunión anual de estudiantes*. México: Escuela de Enfermería, Centro Médico Nacional Siglo XXI, Instituto Mexicano del Seguro Social.

Espino, V. M. E. (1999). *Elementos teórico-conceptuales en enfermería* [Theoretic-conceptual elements in nursing]. México: trabajo presentado en la XII Reunión Técnico Científica de la FENAFEE.

Flores, S. M. E. (1994). *Ausencia de órganos normativos para enfermería, ¿Qué factores lo han determinado?* [The lack of normative bodies in nursing. What are the determinant factors?]. México: Tesis, ENEO/UNAM.

Foucault, M. (1997). *El nacimiento de la clínica. Una arqueología de la mirada médica* [Birth of the clinic. An archeology of medical perception] (17th ed.). México: Siglo XXI.

Foucault, M. (2000). *Vigilar y castigar. Nacimiento de la prisión* [Discipline and punish. The birth of the prison] (30th ed.). México: Siglo XXI Editores.

Frank, CH. M., & Elizondo, T. (1987). *Desarrollo histórico de la enfermería* [Nursing's historical development] (4th ed.). México: La Prensa Médica Mexicana.

Fuerbringer, B. M., Villarreal, G. M. I., et al. (1995). *Enfermería disciplina científica (una aproximación epistemológica)* [The scientific discipline of nursing (An epistemological approach)]. México: Universidad Autónoma de San Luis Potosí.

Gaitán Cruz, M. C. (1999). *La enfermería en Colombia—Origines de audacia y compromiso* [Nursing in Colombia: The origins of challenges and commitments]. Universidad Pedagógica y Tecnológica de Colombia. Tunja, Boyacá.

Health Care Ministry. (1999). *Informe de la situacion de enfermería en Mexico* [Report of the case of nursing in Mexico]. SIARHE (Sistema de Información de Recursos Humanos en Enfermería, Mexico.

Interinstitutional Commission in Nursing. (2000). Plan Rector, Mexico.

Jamieson, E. M., Sewall, M. F., et al. (1968). *Historia de la enfermería* [Nursing history] (6th ed.). México: Interamericana.

Jiménez, S. J. (2001, May/August). Plan rector de la Comisión Interinstitucional de Enfermería SSA [Operations plan of the Inter-institutional Nursing Commission]. Revista de Enfermería del Instituto Mexicano del Seguro Social, 9(2), 105-111. México.

Martínez, B. M. M., Latapí, P., et al. (1993). *Sociología de una profesión. El caso de enfermería* [Sociology of a profession: The case of nursing] (2nd ed.). México: Centro de Estudios Educativos.

Martínez, P. C. (1998). *Marco teórico conceptual para la elaboración de los posgrados de enfermería* [Theoretical-conceptual framework to enhance graduate study in nursing]. México: Documento fotocopiado, Facultad de Enfermería y Obstetricia de la Universidad de Guanajuato.

Nájera, N. R. M. (1992a). *Tendencias de la investigación sobre la práctica en enfermería en México* [Trends in evidence-based Mexican nursing practice]. México: UAM-Xochimilco.

Nájera, N. R. M., et al. (1992b). *Estudio diacrónico, sincrónico y prospectivo de la enfermería en México* [Diachronic, synchronic and prospective research in Mexican nursing]. México: UAM-Xoxhimilco.

Nava, R. J. (2000). Enfermería y Filosofía [Nursing and philosophy]. *Enfermeras, México, XXXVI*(2), 64-67.

Navarro, S. M., Cárdenas, B. L., et al. (2002). *Colegio Nacional de Enfermeras. 55 años de vida* [National College of Nurses: A 55 year history] (2nd ed.). México: Prado.

Pérez Loredo, D. L. (1986). *Efemérides de enfermería 1900-1985* [Nursing events: 1900-1985]. México: Miguel Angel Porrúa.

Plan Nacional de Salud 2001-2006 [PNS]. [National Health Plan 2001-2006]. (2001). México: Secretaría de Salud.

Programa Nacional de Educación 2001-2006 [PNE]. [National Education Plan 2001-2006]. (2001). México: Secretaría de Educación Pública.

Secretaría de Educación Pública/Dirección General de Profesiones [SEP/DGP]. (2001). *Enfermería* [Nursing]. México: Comisión Técnica Consultiva de Enfermería. Fascículo 9.

SEP/DGP. Comisión Interinstitucional para la Formación de Recursos Humanos para la Salud. (1998). *Perfil del egresado de las carreras de licenciado y técnico de enfermería* [Profiles in bachelor and technical careers in nursing]. México.

SEP/DGP. Comisión Interinstitucional para la Formación de Recursos Humanos para la Salud. (1998). *Normas básicas de educación para la formación de licenciados y técnicos en enfermería* [Basic educational norms for bachelor and technical education in nursing]. México: Comité de Planeación/Grupo de Trabajo de Enfermería.

SEP/DGP. (1999). *Informe de la situación de enfermería en México* [Report of Mexican nursing conditions]. México: SIARHE.

SEP/DGP. (2000). *Lineamientos de educación continua para enfermería* [Guidelines for nursing continuing education]. México: Comité de Planeación/Subcomité de Enfermería.

SEP/DGP. Comité Intersectorial de Enfermería. (2001a). *Código de ética para enfermeras mexicanas* [Code of ethics for Mexican nurses]. México.

SEP/DGP. Subsecretaría de Innovación y Calidad. (2001b). *Plan rector de la Comisión Interinstitucional de Enfermería 2001-2006* [Inter-institutional Nursing Commission Governing Plan 2001-2006]. México.

SEP/DGP. Subsecretaría de Innovación y Calidad. (2003). *Proyecto vinculación docencia-asistencia* [The teaching Learning Connection Project]. México: Comisión Interinstitucional de Enfermería.

Universidad Autónoma Metropolitana Xochimilco. (1991). Las profesiones en México. *Enfermería.* [Professional nursing in Mexico]. México: UAM-X.

Velandia, M. A. L. (1995). *Historia de la enfermería en Colombia* [The history of Colombian nursing]. Colombia: Universidad Nacional de Colombia.

Velandia, M. A. L. (2000). *El cuidado de enfermería como objeto de estudio* [Nursing care as the object of study]. Puebla, México: Conferencia Oficial en el Primer Congreso sobre Investigación en Enfermería. 18 y 19 de Septiembre.

Verde Fiota, E. (1991). Niveles académicos de enfermería en México. Un problema a resolver [Academic levels of nursing in Mexico: A problem to solve]. *Revista del Colegia Nacional de Enfermeras, 28*(3), 45-48.

Weber, M. (1998). *La ética protestante y el espíritu del capitalismo* [The protestant ethic and the spirit of capitalism] (3rd ed.). México: Colofón.

SECTION TWO

CHAPTER 7

Nursing in Canada

Susan E. French and Jessica D. Emed

The development of nursing in Canada is inextricably linked with state interventions in the social sector, especially with regards to health and higher education, and with the rise and decline of medical dominance. The publicly-funded health care and educational systems reflect the underlying value of collectivism that permeates much of Canadian society. The health care system, known as medicare, is a source of pride to Canadians: "Medicare has been a success in making doctor and hospital care available under standard conditions to Canadians; indeed, medicare has almost come to define what it means to be Canadian" (Armstrong, Armstrong, & Coburn, 2001, p. 2). This chapter examines the evolution of the health care system and the development of the nursing profession along the three phases of capitalism—competitive, monopoly, and global capitalism—described by Ross and Trachte (1990; as cited in Coburn & Rappolt, 1999). As background, a brief geographical, economic, political, and cultural introduction to Canada is presented.

Following this brief background, the chapter first looks at the evolution of the health care system within the context of changing relationships among labor, capital, and the state, also considering Canada's historical ties with the United Kingdom and France and its current position vis-à-vis the United States. This section concludes with an examination of the political and cultural hegemony within Canadian health care as well as an examination of ensuing challenges, with a focus on those challenges associated with globalization and neo-liberalism within global capitalism. Globalization and neo-liberalism pose a great threat to both medicare and higher education, subjecting them to competition from a global market that is increasingly deregulated.

Next, this chapter presents a history of the evolution of professional nursing within the health care system and an examination of workforce issues related to globalization. The third section concentrates on the development of higher education in nursing, the current context and trends in nursing education, and the impact of education on professional and social development. Finally, the chapter concludes with a discussion of the challenges facing nursing in the 21st century and future directions for nursing and nursing education.

THE CANADIAN LANDSCAPE

Canada is bordered by the United States the south, by the Pacific Ocean to the west, by the Atlantic Ocean to the east, and by the Arctic Ocean to the north, and has an area of 9,984,670 sq. km, making it the second largest country in the world. Canada boasts an Inuit history dating back to 4500 BC, though Canada, as we now know it, grew from French and British colonization, with Great Britain being awarded sovereignty in 1763. Canada, independent of Great Britain since 1867, is governed by federal and provincial/territorial and municipal governments, each having defined areas of responsibility. Primary responsibility for the provision of health services, health sciences education, and the regulation of the health professions rests with the provinces/territories.

Canada counts 10 provinces and three territories. The territory of Nunavut, inaugurated in 1999, represents the most recent change to the geo-political organization of Canada, although the province of Québec has threatened to separate from Canada for decades, advocating its distinctly French-Canadian heritage and culture. The sovereignty movement in Québec resurges periodically after having lost its momentum in 1995 when Québecers voted in a province-wide referendum to remain in Canada with a 50.5% majority.

Canada is a member of many international organizations, including the United Nations (UN), the World Trade Organization (WTO), the North Atlantic Treaty Organization (NATO), the British Commonwealth of Nations, the Organization of America States (OAS), the G8, and the Organisation for Economic Cooperation and Development (OECD) (Turner, 2004). In addition, the provinces of Québec and New Brunswick, as well as Canada as a whole, are members of the international organization of French-speaking societies known as the International Organization of *La Francophonie*. While the influence of the United States is keenly felt through its participation in economic treaties with and geographical proximity to Canada, the Commonwealth represents another major influence on Canadian health and economic policy.

The Canadian Mosaic

According to the most recent census (2006), the population of Canada is over 31 million people, with 25 million (or just over 80%) concentrated in urban areas (Statistics Canada, 2007a). In the last 5 years, Canada had the fastest growing population among the G8 countries, which is attributed largely to an increase in international immigration (Statistics Canada, 2007a). The birth rate for 2004 and 2002 was 10.5 per 1,000 people, the lowest it has been since Canada began recording vital statistics in 1921 (Statistics Canada, 2004, 2006). As well, the Canadian population has been aging: in 2006, the portion of the population aged 65 years and over reached a record 13.7% at over 4 million, and the number of people nearing retirement (age 55-64) reached a record-breaking 3.7 million (Statistics Canada, 2007b). The leading causes of hospitalization are circulatory diseases (15.4% of hospitalizations), pregnancy and childbirth (14.0%), digestive diseases (10.9%), respiratory diseases (8.8%), injuries and poisonings (8.4%), and cancer (7.6%) (CIHI, 2002), while the main causes of death in 2002 were circulatory system diseases, cancer, and respiratory system diseases (PHAC, 2004).

Canada embraces a diverse and multi-cultural population, with the main ethnic groups being English, French, Scottish, Irish, German, Italian, Chinese, Ukrainian, and North American Indian (Turner, 2004). According to the 2006 census, Canada's foreign-born population reached nearly 20%, the highest proportion in 75 years (Statistics Canada, 2007c). Canada's immigration policies are well known to be liberal, with provisions for claims on gender persecution grounds as well, making it an attractive destination to many. Canada has one of the highest acceptance rates of refugees in the world and one of the lowest deportation rates for rejected claimants (CBC Canada, 2001). Canada was the first country to legally support multiculturalism through provisions in the Canadian Charter of Rights and Freedoms, the Multiculturalism Act, and the Canadian Citizenship Act (Fleras & Elliott, 2003). In a longitudinal study of newcomers to Canada, almost all stated that they did not have another country in mind when applying to Canada (Statistics Canada, 2003a).

In most of Canada, the official languages are English and French, though in Québec, a stronghold of French-Canadian patriotism, the only official language is French. Aboriginal people, defined as the descendants of the original inhabitants of North America, are divided into three main groups in Canada: the Métis (who are of mixed Aboriginal and European descent), the First Nations, and the Inuit. The Aboriginal population totals just over 1 million (Statistics Canada, 2008a). There are approximately 50 Aboriginal languages, though many are at risk of becoming extinct (Statistics Canada, 1998).

The Aboriginal population differs significantly from the general Canadian population, for example, along demographic measures (e.g., a higher fertility rate and younger median age), but the more staggering differences are in relation to health. The Aboriginal mortality rate is one-and-a-half times higher than the national rate, though trends show some improvement (Frideres, 2002). The leading cause of death among Aboriginal peoples is injury and poisoning (Waldram, Herring, & Young, 1995), though deaths related to "new" diseases within the population have been rising sharply, namely, diabetes and HIV/AIDS (Frideres, 2002).

THE HEALTH CARE SYSTEM IN CANADA

The main role of the federal government with regards to health is in setting national standards for the health care system. Those standards are based on the application of the Canada Health Act (1984), which establishes fundamental values for its health insurance program (medicare): portability of services across provinces, public administration, comprehensiveness, accessibility, and universality. The primary objective of Canadian health care policy is to protect, promote, and restore the physical and mental well-being of Canadians and to facilitate reasonable access to health services without barriers, financial or other. The federal government also shares responsibility for financing health care services through monetary transfers to the provinces and territories, and has responsibility for administering programs aimed at special populations (such as Aboriginal populations and military personnel), as well as ensuring the protection of the public through monitoring risks related to certain diseases, foods, drugs, and environmental conditions (West, 2004). It is up to the provincial and territorial governments, within national guidelines, to administer and manage health care programs according to their needs and resources, making the term *health care system* somewhat of a misnomer, given the variability in implementation of programs across provinces/territories (Deber, 2003; Storch, 2003).

The health care system is values-based, with collective welfare being a core concern. It is organized around publicly-funded services delivered by private (i.e., neither owned nor operated by governments or their agents) institutions, agencies, and practitioners (Chodos & MacLeod, 2004). The health care system comprises hospitals providing acute, chronic, or speciality services (such as rehabilitation, pediatrics, or mental health institutions), and long-term care facilities that are public or private (for-profit and non-profit); public health services; home care services; and services provided by health professionals. In the present system, there is universal public coverage for medically necessary/required services (i.e., hospital, public health, and medical services); mixed coverage for home and long-term care, as well as for out-of-hospital prescription drugs; and private coverage for other health goods and services. The services of most health professionals in private practice, exclusive of those provided by physicians, are funded through private insurance programs. Physicians are in a fee-for-service arrangement with the fee schedule negotiated at the provincial/territorial level by the medical association and the government.

Canada's expenditure-based GDP is $1,537,472 million (Statistics Canada, 2008b) and in 2007, the country spent an estimated 10.6% of the GDP on health care according to the Canadian Institute for Health Information (2007a). The total health expenditure per capita in Canada was expected to be $4,867 in 2007, placing Canada 8th among OECD countries for per capita spending, with the United States ranking highest (CIHI, 2007b). The public/private mix of health care expenditures varies among the provinces/territories, with public funds coming from federal, provincial/territorial, and municipal levels, Workers' Compensation Boards, and other social security schemes; and private sector funding coming mainly from households and private insurers. Currently, it is estimated that 70% of health care funds are from public sources while 30% come from the private sector, ranging from a high of 95% public funds in Nunavut (the sparsely populated northern territory) to a low of 67% in Ontario (the most populous and industrialized province). Hospitals (29%), prescribed and non-prescribed drugs (the fastest growing area of health expenditure, at approximately 17%), and physician services (14%) account for the bulk of the total health spending (CIHI, 2007b).

Socio-political and economic forces, as well as Canada's proximity to the United States and its historical relationships with France and the United Kingdom, strongly influenced the evolution of the Canadian health system. Two defining features marked its development: the establishment of medical professional dominance in the 19th and early 20th centuries and the emergence of demands for nationwide health insurance from the 1920s through 1970s (Torrance, 1998). Although capitalism is dominant in Canada, interventions by the government in economic matters to benefit industry (e.g., state intervention in the development of natural resources, construction of a national railway system) have been accepted, even demanded, since the country was settled. However, the evolution of the social security system, defined as health and social services, was more controversial.

From Traditional Healing Practices to Competitive Capitalism

Though Aboriginal peoples developed remedies and treatments involving massages, sweat lodges, and over 500 plants (Clarke, 2000), health services in Canada today evolved along two separate paths: public health and illness/hospital services. From the time that the first European settlers came to what is now Canada, communicable diseases such as smallpox and typhus drove the development of health services. Early efforts were directed toward control rather than prevention, as Boards of Health were established by governments to deal with epidemics and then disbanded. This marked the first involvement of the state in medical practices (Clarke, 2000).

Jeanne Mance, a wealthy woman from France and co-founder of the city of Montreal, established in that city the first Canadian hospital. That hospital provided services to Aboriginal people and settlers alike, and a system of apprenticeship training ensured a skilled nursing staff. By the time of transition to British rule in 1759, the traditions of a health care system under the religious orders and of caring for all regardless of race, nationality, or creed were firmly established (Ross-Kerr, 2003a, 2003b). Indeed, the pre-Confederation period (1604-1866) was characterized by limited government involvement in health services other than providing a modicum of services for the sick and the mentally ill (Meilicke & Storch, 1980).

From the 17th to late 19th centuries, hospitals (established under religious or lay auspices and serving the poorer groups in society) were seen as places of last resort. The mortality rate was high as was the probability of infection, and surgery was hazardous (Ross-Kerr, 2003b). Available treatments included whiskey, brandy, opium, purging and inducing vomiting, bleeding, and homeopathy (Clarke, 2000). Other than in Québec, where care of the mentally ill was delegated to families or religious orders, persons with mental illness were confined to poorhouses and jails and later to publicly funded asylums in which care was custodial in nature and generally harsh. Advances in scientific knowledge concerning health, disease, and treatment modalities resulted in much of health care moving into hospitals. Osler introduced clinical education in medicine, and hospitals associated with universities became teaching centres (Hanaway & Cruess, 1996). Although physicians were not salaried employees but private practitioners with hospital privileges, providing their services for a fee, they held dominant positions on most hospital boards.

The act creating the Confederation of Canada in 1867, in defining the areas of jurisdiction between the federal and provincial governments, allocated responsibility for social welfare (later called social security) and education to the provinces. Unfortunately, this move would become a source of unrelenting squabbling between the two levels of government even today as each blames the other for insufficient health care funding.

Barely 10 years later in England, with increasing awareness of the relationship between disease and environment and living conditions, the English Public Health Act was passed in 1875 impacting on public health in Canada as well. Starting in 1884, each province passed a Public Health Act that required every municipality to appoint a local board of health, a medical officer of health, and a sanitary inspector (Hastings & Mosley, 1980).

During these years, the economy moved from one of subsistence to one of competitive capitalism based on markets that were controlled by an ascendant corporate class that more or less controlled the state. The working class was unorganized and had little power (Ross & Trachte, 1990, cited in Coburn & Rappolt, 1999, p. 150). Medicine became part of the powerful business elite and seemed to have formed its own government within the government.

Monopoly Capitalism and the Rising Demand for a National Health Insurance Scheme

By the beginning of the 20th century, Canada had entered the phase of monopoly capitalism. Labor unions emerged as well as working class parties and movements (e.g., the Canadian Cooperative Federation, precursor to the New Democratic Party, in Saskatchewan). The country had experienced three economic depressions, the trade union movement and factory legislation were developing concurrently, industries were growing under protective tariffs, and better forms of communication and transportation were being developed. Settlement of the western regions accelerated; there was growing awareness of social insurance programs being developed elsewhere (e.g., Germany, England, and New Zealand), and a large number of immigrants from Great Britain arrived, bringing with them knowledge of the benefits of health insurance schemes. All those factors influenced the shift from individual rights and liberties to an emphasis on the well-being of the group and the wider interests of the community as a whole (Wallace, 1980). Socialism with respect to social security became established in Canada.

These social and economic developments were also changing public opinion, and there was increasing demand for government action, initially in the area of education. Public health services moved beyond environmental aspects of community health control to include school health services as well as maternal and child health services. In addition to the religious orders of women, community-minded women with high social standing became interested in addressing the health needs of immigrants and the poor, especially that of women and children. Despite opposition from medicine, in 1904, a private, not-for-profit, community nursing organization, the Victorian Order of Nurses (VON), was formed at the urging of the newly-created Canadian National Council of Women (CNCW). Medicine viewed these nurses as potentially eroding medical services and successfully lobbied against midwifery being considered part of community nursing practice. The secular VON became a major force in the development of community-based nursing services (Pringle & Rowe, 1992). As soon as such education became available, the VON required its nurses to have advanced educational preparation in public health.

World War I (1914-1918) raised awareness of the appalling profile of the health of Canadians, since many potentially military eligible young men were refused entry for reasons of ill health (Mansell, 2004). Education about measures for personal health and hygiene, immunization, screening programs for early detection of diseases, and initiatives for coping with new environmental hazards such as air pollution became valued. The publicly-funded departments of health introduced the role of the public health nurse, including visiting nursing services (Hastings & Mosley, 1980).

Also early in the 20th century, there was a move toward publicly supported hospital and medical care. A key step took place in 1916, when the province of Saskatchewan, a strong bastion of socialism, gave legislative authority to rural municipal councils to levy taxes based on assessment of property, thus enabling them to pay physicians retainer fees to provide services to residents. The economic depression of the 1930s was influential in increasing interest in publicly funded programs and concern with health insurance continued throughout World War II (1939-1945), but in 1945, the provinces rejected a comprehensive health insurance plan. In 1946, under the leadership of Premier Tommy Douglas, the province of Saskatchewan introduced a pioneer universal compulsory plan providing hospital care to all residents of the province regardless of financial means. Labor, in the form of the working and middle classes, increased in power and exerted pressure for access to health care and the implementation of health insurance. The dominant fraction of the business community, that is, the large corporations, was amenable to pressures for welfare state benefits as this would result in the state, rather than individual firms, picking up the cost. This fit with the interests of the state, as welfare state benefits would allow for a regulated and controlled health care system (Coburn & Rappolt, 1999).

Public pressure for a nationwide program of health insurance resulted in federal legislation in 1957, and by 1961, through federal-provincial agreements, hospital insurance was provided to 99% of Canadians. Under the Hospital Insurance and Diagnostic Services Act (1957) and the Medical Care Act (1966), the federal government contributed monies to the provinces to pay the costs of insurance programs as long as those programs met the criteria of public administration, universality, comprehensiveness, and portability from one province to another, thus laying the foundations for medicare. By 1972, medical insurance legislation was implemented in all provinces, insuring all Canadians for costs incurred with hospitalization, including medical and nursing services, drugs, and diagnostic procedures, but allowed for private practice of medicine and fees for medical services to remain

(Gelber, 1980; Hastings, 1980; Lindenfield, 1980; Torrance, 1998). The health care system moved from a phase in which there was relatively little or no state intervention, to a welfare state phase in which there was major state intervention in the form of hospital and medical insurance (Medicare). This phase was characterized by the dominance of the medical profession, including control over emerging occupations, such as nursing, and over health policy. Near the end of this phase, awareness of the broad determinants of health emerged and started to contribute to an erosion of medical dominance; that erosion escalated with the impact of global capitalism.

Global Capitalism and Pressures on the Health Care System

What does globalization mean to Canada in relation to health? It means greater participation in international collaborations and initiatives as well as increased access to health information and research. For example, the Global Public Health Network, an Internet-based alert system, was created in partnership with the World Health Organization (WHO) and Health Canada to monitor threats to public health such as disease outbreaks (Hagmann, 2001). Another example is the developing area of "eHealth," where, with advances in informatics technology and the development of networks of health professionals, medical consultations are possible without the need for travel (Cortinois, Downey, Closson, & Jadad, 2003). In general terms, globalization also poses a threat to Canadian health care through factors such as the globalization of the food supply (e.g., the emergence of avian flu, the spread of bovine spongiform encephalopathy, or "mad cow disease") and the increased pace of international travel, where incubation periods frequently exceed flight times (e.g., the spread of severe acute respiratory syndrome—SARS).

In particular, *economic* globalization poses a threat to the publicly funded Canadian health care system because of its underlying driving force: profit. With the ultimate aim being to increase international trade, that is, "corporate-centred trade" (Bezruchka, 2000), there is no doubt as to the core values behind the phenomenon. The pace of globalization has been growing dramatically (Cortinois et al., 2003; McMichael, 2000; Woodward, Drager, Beaglehole, & Lipson, 2001) and in parallel with this acceleration in trade, competition has become fierce. Neo-liberalism, a set of economic policies emerging in the past 25 years or so, is characterized by competition between private businesses in a deregulated market that is governed only by market forces (Martinez & García, 2000). However, "markets left on their own do not lead to equity" (Fleras, 2005, p. 241). As a result of globalization and neo-liberalism, pressures from foreign governments, multinational corporations, and international organizations have intensified, as has the power of these organizations relative to national governments (Coburn, 2001). This shift in power is particularly relevant to health care (Armstrong et al., 2001), as economic globalization impacts Canadian health care in numerous areas such as human resources (e.g., education and mobility of the workforce); clientele and their determinants of health; material resources such as drugs and medical technologies; as well as health care organization and policy.

International Trade Treaties versus the Canadian Health Care System

A key step in the development of the present Canadian economy was the North American Free Trade Agreement (NAFTA) with the United States and Mexico (implemented in 1994). While strengthening the Canadian economy and its competitiveness on a global scale, NAFTA has brought to the forefront the struggle between economic interests of corporations and those of Canadian social programs (Coburn & Rappolt, 1999). Describing the nature of Canada's relationship with its prevailing trade partner, the United States, Coburn and Rappolt refer to "continentalism" as analogous to globalization, as Canada struggles to preserve autonomy and authority over its economy despite enormous pressure from the United States.

In the case of Canadian health care policy, the most important international trade treaties are the General Agreement on Trade in Services (GATS) and the Agreement on Trade-Related Intellectual Property Rights (TRIPS) put forth by the WTO, as well as the NAFTA. Each of these agreements has far-reaching implications for health care delivery, from the availability of prescription drugs to the provision of services such as home care, but the driving force behind them is economic exploitation rather than patient need. This issue is described in the Summary Report on Globalization and Health of the Commission on the Future of Health Care in Canada:

> The principles underlying these international trade treaties are at odds with the principles upon which Canada's health care system is based. The treaties promote the freer flow of goods, services and investments—thereby facilitating international business by constraining and re-directing the regulatory ability of governments. These commercial priorities conflict with the fundamental public purpose of Canadian Medicare: the provision of health care to all, on the basis of need rather than the ability to pay. (Campbell et al., 2002, p. vii)

Though it remains unclear how certain provisions in these agreements will affect health care delivery, there is consensus that medicare is at risk: "Once private (and most likely American) health care corporations have their foot in the door, the North American Free Trade Agreement contains provisions that would hinder any attempt thereafter to 'discriminate' against them or to favor public delivery. NAFTA and the World Trade Organization (WTO) are biased against the public provision of goods and services" (Armstrong et al., 2001, p. 2).

Many of the provisions of these agreements are subject to a certain degree of flexibility in interpretation rendering their application, as well as their impact, ambiguous. Campbell and colleagues (2002) have highlighted several examples of potentially problematic provisions. For instance, non-discrimination provisions of the NAFTA require that foreign goods, services, and investors be given similar

treatment to that of their Canadian counterparts, ensuring that the competitive opportunities of foreign providers are not compromised in favor of those of local providers. Of relevance to Canadian health care, this provision directly threatens the
Canada Health Act tenets of universality and public administration, as it could
be used to challenge policies that favor not-for-profit providers, if these policies
negatively impact the business opportunities of foreign providers.

Another example involves restrictions on domestic regulation (Campbell et al.,
2002). In development under GATS, these restrictions allow foreign providers to
call on WTO panels to challenge domestic regulations (e.g., related to licensing,
certification, and other aspects of domestic regulation of services) if they are perceived as overly onerous. Similarly, the NAFTA provision for minimum standard of
treatment opens the door to challenges from foreign investors, if they suspect unfair
treatment with reference to international law. This type of challenge could be subject
to international commercial arbitration. Both of these scenarios could significantly
compromise the authority of the Canadian government in its defense of medicare.

A final example, involving international property rights, under NAFTA as well as
TRIPS, demonstrates the direct impact of these agreements on health care (Campbell
et al., 2002). Both NAFTA and TRIPS require a minimum of 20 years of monopoly
patent protection for pharmaceuticals, which limits the availability of less expensive generic equivalents. Compulsory licensing, allowing production of generic
drugs in exchange for royalties, was adopted in response to high drug costs in
the 1960s (Lexchin, 2002) and was vehemently contested by the pharmaceutical
industry. Despite intense lobbying from the pharmaceutical industry, compulsory
licensing remained until the Canadian government eliminated it in negotiations
of free trade agreements with the United States (the NAFTA and GATT agreements
in particular).

The Power of Corporations:
The Case of Pharmaceuticals

As illustrated in the example of compulsory licensing, the influence of the pharmaceutical industry in the political arena is considerable. While Canada advocates
access to generic drugs, the United States opposes the development of generic
drugs because of its powerful pharmaceutical industry. With the TRIPS agreement,
however, WTO members are required to adhere to patent laws that are similar to
those in the United States (Ostry, 2001). Though this provision allows for compulsory licensing, restrictions apply. Complicating the situation, a recent trend shows
increasing numbers of Americans purchasing prescription drugs through Canadian
Internet-based pharmacies (with annual sales exceeding US$1 billion), despite the
fact that it is illegal to import drugs into the United States (Picard, 2004b).

The pharmaceutical industry is considered the most important in terms of international trade in Canadian health care (Romanow, 2002). Canada is a net importer
of prescription drugs, and as it becomes increasingly reliant on drugs that were
developed and produced abroad, the ability of Canadian governments to negotiate
with pharmaceutical companies regarding the mounting costs of prescription drugs is

decreasing (Romanow, 2002). Meanwhile, the cost of drugs in Canada has been increasing, a tendency which threatens to cripple the health care system. Data from the Canadian Institute for Health Information (2007c) indicate that drug expenditure has grown at an average annual rate of 9.6%. Since drug prices have remained more or less stable over the past decade, increases in Canadian drug expenditure are thought to be related to a number of inter-connected factors, such as the introduction of newer drugs, which are usually marketed at higher prices, as well as the volume of drugs used, which is influenced, for example, by the health status of the population, changes in drug plan policies, and other factors such as direct-to-consumer advertising which reaches Canadians through international media (CIHI, 2007c).

The Regulation of Prescription Drugs in Canada

Though health care is insured by the federal government, only prescription drugs provided in institutional settings (e.g., hospitals) are included in the coverage. Some provinces have their own drug insurance plans (e.g., Québec) to cover out of hospital drug costs, and all provinces provide some form of prescription drug coverage to seniors and social assistance recipients. The development of a national Pharmacare program has been proposed by provincial and territorial leaders in order to increase their purchasing power as a group (among other benefits), though this issue is still under debate.

The federal government's Health Protection Branch (HPB), the Canadian counterpart to the U.S.'s Food and Drug Administration, holds almost all the responsibility for regulation of drug safety, quality, and efficacy. However, the HPB lacks sufficient funding and resources necessary to conduct clinical trials necessary to fulfill their mandate. In fact, funding for the HPB has been almost halved, from $237 million in 1993-94 to $136 million in 1996-97. As a result, pharmaceutical companies now fund parts of the HPB, compromising the independence (and transparency) of the organization and handing over greater regulatory power to private industry (Lexchin, 2002).

The domination of pharmaceutical companies is demonstrated also through their research and development agenda, which is determined based on profit potential (Lexchin, 2002). This influence is expanded by marketing and promotion campaigns. It is well known that pharmaceutical companies spend more on advertising than they do on research and development (Angell, 2004). Prescribers are targeted through a wide variety of means, such as sponsorship of continuing medical education conferences, advertising in medical journals, as well as direct visits to doctors' offices up to every 2 weeks (Lexchin, 2002), where the information provided on a drug is often biased toward a favorable representation of the product (Lexchin, 1997).

Changes to the Health Care System

Starting in the 1970s and accelerating in the 1990s, a paradigm shift from "Fordism" (mass production of a standardized product) was reflected in health services in Canada (Grispun, 2000). The years 1995 and 1997 were marked by nation-wide restructuring of health services (Armstrong, 1997) and deep federal and provincial cuts to health and social services. This also included a reduction in the number of seats in medical and nursing schools. The shift entailed a less hierarchical and more decentralized structure of management with each unit focusing on a specialized market. The labor force was segmented into white-collar, professional, technical, managerial workers and low-paid, easily dispensable, and mostly unskilled workers. Within health services, hospitals moved from a traditional cure-care paradigm to one that was business-oriented. Product-line and program management models and later, re-engineering, were introduced (Grispun, 2000).

New Challenges in the Health Care System

The Canadian health care system is under constant scrutiny and criticism. New challenges to emerge (or re-ignite) in recent years have been the private-public debate (heightened by the pressures of globalization and neo-liberalism) raising the question of the sustainability of medicare; accessibility of health care; the re-emergence of infectious diseases; patient safety; and the health of Aboriginal peoples as well as of immigrant and refugee groups. The challenges created by the increasing shortage of health human resources are discussed in the section dealing with globalization and nursing.

Public versus Private: A Fierce Debate

Two 2002 major federal reports on health services, the final report of the Standing Senate Committee on Social Affairs, Science and Technology (commonly referred to as the Kirby Report) and the Commission on the Future of Health Care in Canada (R. J. Romanow, Commissioner), reaffirmed the commitment of the Canadian population and governments to the single-payer, publicly-funded model of hospital and medical services. However, the reports differ on recommendations regarding the private vs. public debate, with the Kirby Report supporting expansion of the private sector. Amidst alarmist claims of escalating health care costs, authors argue that the Canadian health care system is financially sustainable. Sepehri and Chernomas (2004) write that previous analyses of the sustainability of medicare were based on inadequate models and they maintain that there is no evidence that Canada's public health expenditure is unsustainable.

Deber (2003) points out that the main area of Canadian health care that adopts a U.S.-style combination of public and private funding, that is, out-of-hospital prescription drugs, is the very area experiencing the fastest rising costs. Further, a comparison of certain elements of the Canadian and U.S. health care systems reveals several problems to the south. A review of the literature by Kenny (2002) shows that a number of for-profit U.S. hospitals fare worse than their not-for-profit counterparts on measures of cost containment and mortality. The Organisation for Economic Co-Operation and Development (OECD) health data (2004) indicate that Canada outperforms the United States in life expectancy and infant mortality, two standard criteria in measuring population health. It is postulated that part of the Canadian advantage stems from the efficiency of having a single provider of health insurance, thereby considerably reducing bureaucratic and administrative costs (Deber, 2003; Kenny, 2002). A 1991 report by the U.S. General Accounting Officer (cited in Deber, 2003) even suggested "if the United States could get its administrative costs to the Canadian level, it could afford to cover the entire uninsured population" (p. 22).

Neuschler (1998) argues that Canadians fare better with regards to health insurance coverage and health care cost by percentage of GDP, but that they may encounter difficulties regarding access to high-tech treatments. In fact, with NAFTA and the resulting increase in flow of people and services between Canada and the United States, it is argued that increasing numbers of Canadians who can afford to do so will turn to the United States for specialized medical care that is either not available in Canada or only available at the end of a long waiting list, with a resulting two-tiered system: medicare and a second, American tier (Pooler, 2000).

Accessibility: Reality or Idealism?

As elaborated in the Canada Health Act (1984), no Canadian will lack access to health care for financial reasons. However, with regards to drug insurance, Clarke (2002) comments, "In a system that relies so heavily on drugs and yet does not insure the out-of-hospital cost of drugs, it is impossible to claim universality" (p. 250), or accessibility, for that matter. Despite the promise of financial accessibility, waiting lists for consultations, tests, and procedures remain a reality for many, causing delays that may significantly compromise patients' health.

In response, the slippery beginnings of a two-tiered health care system have appeared, with private Canadian institutions offering specific services for a fee. This phenomenon is described as a "hemorrhaging of programs and services outside public coverage" (Williams, Deber, Baranek, & Gildiner, 2001). Examples are laboratories (e.g., for blood specimen analysis) and imaging centers (e.g., for ultrasounds and magnetic resonance imaging). Clarke (2000) gives the example of 13 Ottawa walk-in family practice clinics owned by Your Family Medical Centres, a company that has recently been added to the Alberta stock exchange.

Waiting lists for surgery, which can be considerable, are a manifestation of inadequate access to care. Over 50% of patients on waiting lists would be willing to have their surgery the next day, were there an operating room available (Ramsay & Walker, 1998) and among Canadians who reported difficulties getting their non-urgent surgery, long wait times was the most frequently reported barrier (CIHI, 2006a). In fact, waiting lists are playing a critical role in the debate over the development of private health care facilities. While courts had previously ruled that collective rights to a publicly-funded health care system over-rode individual rights to private health care, a historic case involving a year-long wait for hip replacement surgery prompted the Canadian Supreme Court decision that it was unconstitutional under the Québec Charter of Rights to ban private insurance for services covered under medicare, considering that the public system was failing to provide timely access to those services (CBC, 2005). Although long wait times for surgical procedures is one of Canada's most prominent health policy issues, wait times for diagnostic procedures, as well as appointments with specialists, are also significant (CIHI, 2006a).

Advocates for privatization argue that private services will relieve pressure on the public health care system, but evidence suggests that this is not true, due to a phenomenon similarly occurring in the pharmaceutical industry, where only goods and services that are considered profitable are developed and/or provided (Gray, 1999, cited in Kenny, 2002). In contrast with this definition of accessibility and its focus on payment modalities, the Canadian Nurses' Association (1989) has conceptualized accessibility as care that is accessible not only geographically, but culturally. Geographical and cultural barriers have had a devastating impact on the health of Aboriginal peoples (see section on Aboriginal health). Kenny (2002) argues that a "two-tier regime is already at work because of flaws inherent in the present system due to differences in access and quality related to . . . geographical circumstances" (p. 134). According to Pooler (2000), the main weakness of the health care system is the lack of equality in available services depending on where one lives, termed "geographical discrimination" (p. 198), where those living in larger communities are at a distinct advantage. For example, the territory of Nunavut, the largest territory with a population of 24,720, has one hospital and 26 health centers. For health needs exceeding these services, patients are flown to other provinces or territories (Turner, 2004).

Infectious Diseases Making a Comeback

The re-emergence of infectious diseases in Canada is a threat that has been receiving increasing media attention. SARS is an obvious example, where 30 Canadians died in the 2003 outbreak (Statistics Canada, 2003b). Another recent example involves the bacterium *Clostridium difficile,* which preys on patients who have received antibiotic treatment, and becomes lethal much more gradually. In fact, the same year as Canada faced the outbreak of SARS, 511 Canadians died in an outbreak of *Clostridium difficile* (Statistics Canada, 2003b). West Nile Virus, an illness contracted from the bite of an infected mosquito, is a newly emerging infectious disease in Canada (Health Canada, 2005). In most cases, the virus causes minor symptoms or none at all, but it can become fatal in severe cases. Since the first reported case of infection in 2002, there have been 201 cases including 10 deaths from the illness (Public Health Agency of Canada [PHAC], 2005a).

Tuberculosis is making a comeback in Canada, and rates among Aboriginal peoples are rising alarmingly, comparable to rates in Africa (Frideres, 2002). Despite significant public health efforts to reduce rates of HIV infection, the number of new infections has remained steady in the past few years (PHAC, 2005b). In addition to these current threats in Canada, it is predicted that infectious diseases are on the rise worldwide due to climate changes that have been associated with globalization, such as floods and global warming (McMichael, Martens, Kovats, & Lele, 2000).

Patient Safety and Human Error

A key event in the relatively young patient safety movement was the inquiry into 12 infant deaths in Winnipeg in 1994 (Sinclair, 2001). In order to begin addressing some of the safety issues within the health care system, there has been a trend toward full disclosure of medical errors to patients. This trend is part of a larger movement that espouses a blame-free approach in the hopes of increasing the reporting of medical errors and promoting learning on how they could be prevented (Baker & Norton, 2001). A report by the Canadian Institute for Health Information (2004) indicates that in 2000-2001, adverse events occurred in 7.5% of medical-surgical admissions, the majority of which were associated with surgical procedures and drug- or fluid-related events. This phenomenon is not limited to hospitalized patients: the report suggests that 11% of Canadian respondents in an international survey had experienced a medication error from a doctor, hospital, or pharmacy in the past 2 years. Because it is speculated that the majority of medical errors are still not reported, these figures represent a gross underestimation.

The Challenge of Aboriginal Health: An Issue with Deep Roots

The management of Aboriginal health requires special attention, as it involves a complex interplay of federal, provincial, and local agencies and organizations. Many health programs and policies have been implemented, with few succeeding in a context of poverty, isolation, crises of cultural identity, and power struggles.

The challenge of improving the health status of the Aboriginal population is long standing, but has recently become a major priority. Canadian history is well-versed on the horrors of colonization, residential schools, widespread racism, and assimilation, all forces that have contributed to the marginalization of Aboriginal peoples within Canadian society and to their poor health in comparison with the rest of the Canadian population. Aboriginal people "experience the kinds of health problems most closely associated with poverty, yet they also suffer from problems linked to their historical position within the Canadian social system" (Waldram et al., 1995, p. 3). The relationship of the Canadian government with Aboriginal groups has traditionally been hierarchical, with policies that reinforce and perpetuate Aboriginal dependence (Frideres, 2002). According to Wasekeesikaw (2003), the impact of colonization on Aboriginal peoples has been "cultural genocide" (p. 449), as early programs were aimed at relocation to remote locations (and requiring written permission to leave), education and conversion to Christianity. The traditional, sustainable lifestyle of Aboriginal peoples, characterized by hunting, fishing, and trapping has changed dramatically as a result. Changes in land ownership, economic development (e.g., hydroelectric dams), and environmental pollution through the exploitation of natural resources have compounded the situation. In addition, aspects of traditional Aboriginal culture and health care have historically been discouraged and, in some cases, were declared illegal and resulted in imprisonment (Frideres, 2002). In the search for jobs and a better lifestyle, Aboriginal people have been moving to urban centers and for many, this has meant assimilation and a loss of

Aboriginal culture (Frideres, 2002). Many Aboriginal communities have taken steps toward promoting their culture and their health, representing a sort of renaissance of Aboriginal culture, but the situation is far from resolved, with the media regularly reporting on conflicts regarding land claims as well as hunting and fishing rights, in addition to lawsuits regarding abuse suffered at the hands of the state (e.g., in schools and prisons) and innumerable accounts of environmental pollution leaking into the food supply.

Currently, health care is provided to isolated Aboriginal communities through nursing stations and hospitals and according to Gilbert (2003), since the mid 20th century, nurses have been the backbone of health care delivery to northern communities. Physicians are available in hospitals or may be reached by telephone from a nursing station. However, the responsibility for the administration of health care services is gradually being transferred to Aboriginal communities, with the goals of providing equity in access to health and healing services, a holistic approach to health issues, Aboriginal authority over health systems, and diversity in the provision of services in order to tailor to the unique needs of each community (Royal Commission on Aboriginal Peoples, 1996). Yet, according to O'Neil, Lemchuk-Favel, Allard, and Postl (1999), many barriers to successful health care delivery to Aboriginal people remain, such as the scarcity of resources, the ubiquity of the biomedical model, the lack of integration of health services among federal, provincial, and local efforts, and the historical reliance on the Canadian government for the provision of health services.

Health of Immigrants and Refugees

A new challenge, closely related to that of Aboriginal health, is the provision of health services to the immigrant/refugee populations. Despite the promotion of multiculturalism in Canada, inequities exist in relation to the immigrant and refugee population. A recent publication by Health Canada identifies the support for the "healthy immigrant effect," where newly-arrived immigrants enjoy superior health relative to the Canadian-born population (Hyman, 2001). Though this effect, however, decreases with time, there are some major discrepancies between the Canadian and foreign-born population with regards to the development of chronic diseases. Unlike the immigrant population, the refugee population is not screened for health conditions prior to entry and frequently arrives with major health problems (Gagnon, 2002).

Recognition of the Broad Determinants of Health

Medicine and the biomedical model dominated the development of health care, but in the 1960s, there emerged a general movement toward a broader approach to health and increased concern with wholeness, healing, and the determinants of health. In 1974, a working document entitled "A New Perspective on the Health of Canadians" (Department of National Health and Welfare [DNHW], 1974) was released. That document—often simply called the Lalonde Report after the Minister of Health at the time—as well as the report of the Castonguay-Nepveu Commission in Québec (Gouvernement du Québec, 1970), recognized that the health services were for the most part actually sickness or treatment services. Improvements in the health of the population would be dependent upon better knowledge of the human body, on the quality of the environment, and on individual lifestyles. The document proposed five strategies: health promotion, regulation, research, health care efficiency (balancing cost, accessibility, and quality), and goal setting (DNHW, 1974). The DNHW Report is considered to be one of the major achievements of the modern public health system because it brought into the mainstream the idea of socio-economic determinants of health (Picard, 2004a). The concepts espoused in the Report (1974) were reinforced with the release of the World Health Organization (WHO) report on primary health care (1978).

In 1978, with the creation of the Health Promotion Directorate, Canada became the first country in the world to establish an official health promotion government agency. The 1986 Ottawa Charter, the government's blueprint for achieving health for all, reinforced the importance of health promotion (WHO, 1986). The budgetary cuts in the 1990s, associated with global capitalism, placed an emphasis on controlling costs of illness care services, but also led to a renewed commitment to health promotion and disease/illness prevention as a means of sustaining the publicly funded health care system, a move that is strongly supported by health economists and epidemiologists (e.g., Evans & Stoddard, 1998). The Castonguay-Nepveu and Lalonde reports generated increasing interest in understanding the broad determinants of health and instituting changes in the provision of health services (Evans, Marmor, & Barer, 1994). However, as indicated by Torrance (1998), the health insurance program institutionalized a hospital- and illness-orientation of services, thereby increasing the difficulty of structural changes needed to make health care more responsive to societal needs.

The Pervasiveness of Medical Dominance

As in the United States and in the United Kingdom, the medical profession, part of the educated elite in Canada, dominated from the early 1900s. During the stage of monopoly capitalism, medicine ruled its own occupation, but also took action to exclude, limit, or subordinate competitor occupations such as nursing (Coburn, 1998). Organized medicine exerted a strong influence on how and where nurses were educated, what they did, where they worked, and on their conditions of work. Graduates of nursing schools working as private duty nurses and charging families for their services were dependent upon physicians for referrals. Despite this, in public health, nurses worked under the overall direction of the medical officer of health but had considerably more autonomy and independence, and there was less dissonance between obligation to the patient and obligation to the employer and medical officer of health (Storch, 2003).

By the 1920s, the Canadian Medical Association (CMA) had become a strong voice with close connections to the government and bureaucratic elites in the country. Physicians became dominant in local, provincial, and federal departments of health (Torrance, 1998). Medicine controlled health care policy "to such an extent that it formed almost a private government in which its committees . . . largely wrote health care policy" (Coburn, 1999, p. 153). Medicine's emphasis on disease and its treatment ignored the social-economic context of health, thus posing no treat to the business community and its powerful elite. Thus, medicine's historical alliance with the business elite established in the late 19th century continued. The alliance between the state and the medical profession has been described by Tuohy (1999) as an economic monopoly that relied strongly on "collegial" mechanisms in which patients and other health professionals were excluded from the decision-making process. The dominance of medicine reached its zenith in the immediate post-WWII period and started to decline with increasing state intervention in the management of health policy (Coburn & Rappolt, 1999).

Medical dominance was evident in the contentious evolution of medical insurance programs. The medical profession was supportive of hospital insurance, but opposed to any government plan that threatened its autonomy in fee-setting and control of work, as illustrated by the province-wide doctors' strike in Saskatchewan in 1962. It has also been argued, however, that the implementation of medicare favored the hegemony of medicine in health care by placing the emphasis on insurance coverage for curative, medical services at the exclusion of coverage for other types of services such as those focused on prevention or health promotion (Williams et al., 2001). As the cost of providing health care increased, there was a strong movement to introduce a combination of privately- and publicly-funded health services, such as additional fees levied by physicians for specific services. Legislation in 1984, the Canada Health Act, was a response to growing concerns about the imposition of user charges and premiums by the provinces, as these fees were considered an erosion of medicare. The legislation reaffirmed and clarified the basic principles of the health insurance program and gave the federal government power to levy financial penalties against provinces and territories failing to comply with those principles. The most controversial penalty was the loss of federal funds to any province passing on costs to consumers through hospital user charges or billing by physicians (i.e., the collection of fees in excess of those allowed by the medical fee schedule negotiated and approved by the provincial/territorial government and the medical association).

On the other hand, the CMA and many of the provincial medical associations are supportive of the introduction of a combined private-public health care system that will allow physicians to provide services to persons willing to pay. And, in fact, the recent ruling by the Supreme Court in Québec (CBC, 2005) in favor of a physician who challenged the government's ban on delivery of services through private health insurance may result in a resurgence of medical dominance.

DEVELOPMENT OF THE NURSING PROFESSION

As Canada moved through various stages of capitalism, nursing changed from an apprentice-system trade to a formally educated and regulated workforce, and eventually gained recognition as an independent health profession whose members meet increasingly higher formal educational standards. Nursing, concentrated primarily in hospitals and predominantly female, has been shaped by both internal and external forces, especially those impacting on women, paid work, and health care.

Competitive Capitalism and the Rise of Professional Nursing

Jeanne Mance, through her work in establishing a health care system including the first nursing apprenticeship training in North America, is considered the founder of nursing in Canada (Shaw, 2004). Under the auspices of religious orders, young women of good character and from reputable families were recruited into nursing (Ross-Kerr, 2003a). The Sisters of Charity of Montreal, a nursing order of nuns commonly known as the Gray Nuns, founded by Marguerite d'Youville in 1736, were the first visiting nurses in Canada. They played a decisive role in the opening up of the western areas of Canada through the establishment of hospitals, schools of nursing, and visiting nursing services in response to the needs of the Aboriginal and immigrant populations (Ross-Kerr, 2003b). In addition to leaving a legacy of providing health services to all, regardless of race, nationality, or creed (Ross-Kerr, 2003b), the religious orders left a lasting legacy of nursing as a female vocation characterized by altruism and obedience to superiors in hierarchical organizations (Shaw, 2004).

Formal nursing education made its appearance in Canada in 1874 with the establishment of a secular hospital-based school of nursing in the province of Ontario. That school followed the Nightingale model, as adapted in the United States, and was established at the instigation of a member of the hospital's medical staff, setting the stage for medicine's influence over much of nursing education that lasted until the 1960s. Commitment and loyalty to the hospital and its medical staff became an overriding value, even when it entailed silence regarding errors by physicians that resulted in harm to the patient, as reflected in the motto of the first Canadian school of nursing: *I see and I am silent* (Coburn, 1987).

Physicians and hospitals, including the secular hospitals in English-speaking settlements and those established by the religious orders in both the English- and French-speaking sectors, quickly realized the benefits associated with having a trained nursing staff, and hospital-based schools of nursing proliferated (Ross-Kerr, 2003b). The schools provided 3 years of training leading to a diploma, housing, and meals in a protective but highly controlled environment. In return, students provided labor. Depending on the institution, the quality of training varied and in many instances, the training was brief and haphazard; the students were exploited and the working conditions were dismal. As a result, the image of nursing and the quality of applicants deteriorated. However, educational standards improved in settings with strong nursing leaders who were from socio-economic backgrounds that were comparable to their colleagues in medicine and who, perhaps because of their common background, upheld prevailing societal beliefs regarding male dominance (Mansell, 2004).

The movement toward regulation in nursing began in 1893 with the foundation of the American Society of Superintendents of Training Schools for Nursing of the United States and Canada, the goal of which was to distinguish trained nurses from lay nurses (Rodger, 2003). This move, which would increase the status of trained nurses, was strongly opposed by hospital administrators and physicians, as it increased nurses' shared power over working conditions and salaries (Coburn, 1988).

Monopoly Capitalism and Changes Within Nursing: Professionalization and Unionization

In 1908, nursing in Canada formed its own professional organization, the Canadian National Association of Trained Nurses (CNATN) that, in 1924, became the Canadian Nurses Association (CNA) (Rodger, 2003). It focused on educational standards and control over those entering the profession. The societal trend toward increasing recognition of women's rights and of the value of nurses and their services during WWI were forces supporting the development of legislation for the registration of nurses (Kerr, 1996), a process that was accomplished in a relatively brief 12-year period across all provinces (Brunke, 2003), despite opposition from medicine in certain provinces.

The introduction of hospital and medical insurance, the rapidly changing technology along with ever-increasing scientific advances, the introduction of specialty services, and a rapid growth in the population as a result of immigration from Europe and the United Kingdom after WWII all drove an expansion of health services and an increased demand for registered nurses. Societal changes also caused more and more women, including nurses, to enter and remain in the workforce, additional employment opportunities within and outside of the hospital sector, and an increase in the proportion of nurses working part-time. The vast majority of nursing personnel worked in the hospital sector. Still, although the benefits of staffing complete units with graduate nurses was demonstrated in an experimental model in 1936 (Holt, 1936, cited in Ross-Kerr, 2003d, p. 336), hospitals continued to rely heavily on student labor until the late 1960s.

The economy was growing, and starting in 1948, federal government grants to provinces for hospital capital costs and expansion of educational facilities resulted in a rapid expansion of the hospital sector and of training facilities for registered nurses and nursing assistants. The introduction of nursing assistants (later registered nursing assistants (RNAs) or licensed practical nurses (LPNs)), was driven by a number of forces, including the nursing shortage associated with the closure of many hospital schools of nursing during the economic depression of the 1930s, the entry of nurses in the military during WWII, and the expansion of health services in a booming war-time economy. Unlike applicants to the diploma programs leading to RN status, applicants to assistant programs did not need to complete studies at the high school level. Unfortunately, the education of RNAs was and continues to be variable, occurring in diverse settings ranging from vocational tracks in high schools to programs in hospitals or technical institutions. The introduction of the RNA also created a class division within nursing. Finally, from the perspective of the general public, the distinction between the two cadres within nursing was blurred.

Models of Workforce Organization

In the early 20th century, the concepts of "Fordism" were introduced into health services management, that is, mass production of a standardized product, large-scale plants, inflexible production processes, rigid management structures, and the use of semi-skilled labor doing routine and repetitive tasks (Grispun, 2000). This management paradigm, along with that of "Taylorism," reinforced medicine's control over the work and workplace of nurses, as nurses in the hospitals were seen as functioning within hierarchical structures to implement the curative treatments ordered by physicians. The paradox was that despite trained nurses being seen as essential to health care, their work was undervalued and remuneration was low. However, the emergence of nursing unions contributed to improved working conditions and retention of nurses.

The Development of Nursing Unions:
The Canadian Federation of Nurses

The working conditions of nurses, a strengthening labor union movement in general, and the unionization of other workers in the health care system influenced the development of labor unions in nursing. Initially, the organization of labor unions for nurses was problematic, as many hospitals were staffed with student nurses rather than with nurses who were actually employed (Jensen, 1992). Nevertheless, in 1934, in Québec, the first Canadian collective agreement in a public hospital was signed, a movement later formally approved by the professional nursing association, the Canadian Nurses Association (CNA), in 1944 (Coburn, 1988). At that time, the CNA required that the bargaining agent be the provincial professional nursing organization (Jensen, 1992).

Following in the footsteps of Québec, the British Columbia Nursing Association approved collective bargaining in 1946 (Coburn, 1988), but it was not until the period between 1964 and 1970 that the nurses in the remaining provinces unionized. Factors leading to nursing unionization in these provinces included the growth of unionization in other sectors (thus creating pressure on nurses to join), increasing concern that nurses' poor working conditions would fail to attract strong recruits (Jensen, 1992), as well as the Royal Commission on the Status of Women in Canada (1967-70), which raised awareness of wage inequities based on gender (Ross-Kerr, 2003a). The division between professional organizations and unions took place in 1973, when the Supreme Court of Canada ruled that the Saskatchewan Registered Nurses' Association was inherently biased in its representation of nurses due to the involvement of nursing managers in the organization (Ross-Kerr, 2003a).

Unionization of the nursing workforce proceeded quickly. Currently, approximately 81% of nurses are unionized (Akyeampong, 2003), a relatively high proportion particularly when compared with nurses in the United States. The Canadian Federation of Nurses Unions is a federation that includes representatives from each provincial nursing union except Québec's. Unlike medicine, whose professional associations at the provincial level negotiate the fee structure directly with the government, in most provinces the nursing unions negotiate the contracts with the governments indirectly through provincial associations of employers, such as hospital associations (Coburn, 1988).

Globalization and Nursing

With globalization came new attention to efficiency in order to remain competitive. Re-engineering and restructuring designed to emulate the industrial models of productivity improvement by focusing on personnel allocation, production methods, and organizational structures did not address the concerns of the practicing nurses (Aiken et al., 2001). Instead, the new organizational structures strengthened the span of control of physicians and administrators, while diminishing that of nursing and other health care disciplines. In many hospitals, professional departments, such as nursing, were dismantled, while medicine's structure remained intact. Program management, in which physicians were placed as chairs or co-chairs of programs, exacerbated the power imbalances and increased the power of physicians and non-health professional managers. These planned changes unintentionally increased nurse dissatisfaction, increased voluntary turnover, and led to the loss of immeasurable expertise and skills in a time of unprecedented nursing shortages (Barry-Walker, 2000; Blythe, Baumann, & Giovannetti, 2001; Way, Baker, Chubbs, Davis, Barrett, & Parfay, 2001).

For nursing, restructuring or re-engineering of health services was a time of massive lay-offs and relegation to part-time and casual service, and in the province of Québec there was a government initiated incentive program of early retirement for health care workers, including nurses. Multi-skilling or cross-training, a key concept of re-engineering, described by Whetsell as "every employee would have the knowledge and skills to do every job" (as cited in Grispun, 2000, p. 37) was instituted. Unfortunately, as implemented, this concept encouraged the trend to replace RNs with RNAs and to introduce unregulated health care providers, despite concerns expressed by nursing. Subsequent research in Canada and the United States has shown consistently the negative impact on patient outcomes of decreasing the percentage of RNs in the staffing mix (e.g., Aiken, Clarke, Cheung, Sloane, & Silber, 2003; Ellis, Priest, MacPhee, & Sanchez-McCutcheon, 2006; McGillis-Hall, Doran, & Pink, 2004; McGillis-Hall et al., 2003).

Most seriously, organizational and systemic changes contributed to the nursing shortage, increased costs, and the creation of work environments characterized by overload, overtime, a flight of talent, and high levels of absenteeism associated with sickness and injuries (CIHI, 2006b; O'Brien-Pallas, Shamian, et al., 2004). Productivity gains by hospitals, achieved through staff reductions and fewer hours of care provided per patient day, have been questioned, given the longer-term crisis in health human resources, the increase in costly, non-productive hours, and the impact on patient morbidity and mortality (Shannon & French, 2005).

Employment Trends:
Full-Time, Part-Time, and In-Between

These changes introduced in the management of health services in the 1970s, but escalating in the 1990s, required specialization of the labor force with a skill-flexible core of employees working on a permanent full-time basis and a time-flexible larger proportion working on a part-time or casual basis. By 1997, the number of RNs employed full-time had dropped to 52.5% of the workforce from 73% in 1971. Between 1976 and 1999, part-time or casual employment in the general population grew from 12.7% to 18.5% whereas in nursing, between 1976 and 1998, and it increased from 33.6% to 50.8%. Notably, studies show that approximately 35% of those employed part-time or as casuals state that they actually prefer such employment (Grispun, 2003), and it has been suggested that part-time nurses actually achieve the equivalency of full-time by working for multiple employers (Grispun, 2003). Nurses may be using on and off full-time employment as a means of dealing with unsatisfactory working conditions. Recent research is showing that the degree of congruence between employment status and personal preference is a major factor in job satisfaction and retention (Mallette, 2005).

Younger nurses tend to be affected by the decrease in full-time positions more than senior nurses, who are more likely to be protected by seniority clauses in union contracts. One survey showed that 56% of the 35 years and younger contingent were working part-time compared with only 38% of nurses age 50 and over. As well, 23% of the younger contingent reported multiple employers compared to only 10% of nurses 50 years and over (CIHI, 2003).

To address these departures, a recent trend of creating more full-time positions is associated with concerted lobbying by the profession, supported by findings based on rigorous research. The percentage of RNs working full-time has increased each year since 1999 and, as of 2006, represents 56.3% of the nursing workforce. More importantly, in 2006 only 10.1% of new graduates were employed on a casual basis, compared to 39.3% in 2000. As well, the percentage of RNs working for more than one employer decreased, as did the percentage of nurses working on a casual basis (CIHI, 2007d).

Work Environment of Nurses

Technological innovations, such as same day procedures designed to decrease the number of hospital beds and the number of nurses required, actually increase the level of work intensity of the nursing staff, as more, not fewer, nurses are needed to deal with the increased patient acuity (O'Brien-Pallas, Thomson, et al., 2004). Nurses have consistently reported that their workload exceeds their capacity (Baumann et al., 2001; Priest, 2006). The concomitant need to continuously "rush to catch up" and the frustration of leaving important work undone have taken their toll on nurses' health and patient outcomes (CIHI, 2006b). Nurses report that the quality of health care is being seriously compromised as a result of cutbacks (Greenglass & Burke, 2001; Nursing Sector Study Corporation, 2005). What has shrunk in this changing environment is the amount of time nurses have to assess, monitor, and provide appropriate nursing care as well as be teachers, comforters, and communicators (Ontario Nursing Task Force Report, 2000, quoted in Canadian Nursing Advisory Committee Report, 2002).

Organizations, desperately short of nurses, use overtime as a regular staffing strategy (O'Brien-Pallas et al., 2001) and the vicious cycle of nurse dissatisfaction, burnout, and morale distress continues. The percentage (26%) of RNs working overtime every week is higher than the average of 22.5% among other workers. Recent research suggests an almost perfect correlation between overtime and sick time. Furthermore, overtime is highly predictive of increased lost-day injury claim rates among nurses (O'Brien-Pallas, Thomson, Alksnis, & Bruce, 2001; Shamian, O'Brien-Pallas, Kerr, Koehoorn, Thomson, & Alksnis, 2001). Oddly, understaffing, by design or circumstance, can lead to higher costs for employers through increased use of overtime, increased non-productive hours for staff, and poor quality care that leads to complications and increased lengths of stay for patients.

The rate of absenteeism for registered nurses because of injury, illness, burnout, or disability is 80% higher than the Canadian average at 8.1% for nurses, compared with a 4.5% average among 47 other occupational groups (Canadian Labour and Business Centre [CLBC], 2002). The CLBC estimates that the cost of overtime, absentee wages, and replacement for absent registered nurses is between $962 million and $1.5 billion annually.

Toward a Critical Shortage of Nurses

Since the early 1970s, Canada has had three regulated groups of nursing personnel. Registered nurses (RNs), comprise slightly more than three-quarters of the nursing workforce, and are educated at the diploma, baccalaureate, master's, or doctoral level. Registered psychiatric nurses (RPNs) are licensed in the four western provinces only, comprise less than 2% of the national nursing workforce, and have educational preparation similar in length to that of the diploma RNs but with a focus on mental health and psychiatric illnesses. Registered nursing assistants (RNAs) or licensed practical nurses (LPNs) comprise approximately 20% of the workforce, have a shorter length of educational preparation and a narrower scope of practice (CIHI, 2007d).

In the early 1990s, in response to the erroneous perception of a surplus of RNs, governments in a number of provinces decreased the number of seats in diploma programs. There was also a significant decrease in the number of applicants to nursing educational programs (RNAO & RNPAO, 2000). The flexible employment policies of the 1990s contributed to the shortage, and the migration of nurses within Canada as well as the loss of nurses, especially new graduates, to the United States was associated with the desire for full-time employment (Baumann, Blythe, Kotofylo, & Underwood, 2004b). There was soon a growing shortage of nurses in Canada.

Models for projecting the supply of nurses show that the overall supply of full-time equivalent RNs will not even keep up with general population growth over the next 20 years if other factors, such as the flow of new entrants as well as patterns of migration and retirement, remain at current levels. The demand for nursing services is expected to grow faster than the demand for physicians (Basu & Halliwell, 2004) and by 2011, it is forecasted that Canada will face a shortage of 59,000 to 113,000 registered nurses (Ryten, 2002). Additionally, the nursing workforce is aging and a high proportion will retire over the next 20 years. In Ontario, for example, 48.9% of head nurses and supervisors and 37% of staff nurses are expected to retire by 2010 (O'Brien-Pallas, Alksnis, & Wang, 2003). In 2006, the average age of an RN employed in nursing was 45.0 years and a third of nurses working in nursing were 50 years old or older. For every registered nurse under the age of 35, there are 9 aged 50 or greater (CIHI, 2007d).

The educational system will be unable to produce sufficient numbers of graduates to replace the numbers retiring let alone meet the need associated with the aging population: the average age of nurse educators is 49 years, and hence a wave of retirement is inevitable. Moreover, the numbers of admissions to nursing educational programs decreased by 26% between 1990 and 2000, and the number of nursing graduates decreased by 46%. Nursing school admissions must have an average annual growth of 13% to meet the requirements of population growth and an aging population, a rate that is not yet achieved (Canadian Nurses Association (CNA), 2002). Although the number of admissions has increased since 2000, the initial decrease was so severe that it will take some time and major increases to overcome the shortage (O'Brien-Pallas et al., 2002). And despite efforts to increase nursing school admissions, a recent progress report released in collaboration with the Office of Nursing Policy (Pringle, 2005) states that attrition from schools of nursing continues to be a reality, with "disillusionment with nursing as a career" being one of the major reasons nursing students cite for leaving.

International Recruitment and Mobility of the Workforce

The international nursing labor market affects the situation in Canada (Baumann, Blythe, Kotofylo, & Underwood, 2004a) and language is no barrier to external recruiters: Switzerland recruits about 500 nurses per year from Québec, primarily from the Francophone sector (Toupin, 2002). A strong influence is the United States, where a shortage of nurses and the development of trade agreements, such as NAFTA, have allowed for enhanced job mobility of health professionals, including RNs. Many border communities in the United States, such as Detroit, have come to depend upon a large contingent of Canadian RNs. However, changes in the work-visa requirements imposed by the U.S. Department of Homeland Security that are now applicable to nurses may impact negatively on the mobility of RNs across the Canadian-U.S. border.

Internationally-educated RNs constitute a relatively small proportion of the Canadian nursing workforce, 7.9% compared to 92.1% Canadian graduates (CIHI, 2007d). Recruitment of RNs is more global now than in the 1960 and 1970s, at which time the focus was on the United Kingdom, Australia, and New Zealand. Nurses currently come to Canada primarily from the Philippines (30.8%), the United

Kingdom (17.9%), the United States (6.4%), Hong Kong (4.73%), India (5.6%), and Poland (3.4%) (CIHI, 2007d). That pattern matches the country of origin of the overall immigrant population (Baumann et al., 2004a). Recruitment by many employers in Québec has been focused on France and other French-speaking countries.

Canada, along with several other countries, has signed a code of ethics stating that it is not appropriate to actively recruit significant numbers of trained health care providers from countries that are experiencing a nursing shortage. At the same time, actions are being taken to ensure that unnecessary barriers are not preventing foreign trained professionals already in Canada from working in the health field (Halliwell, Shamian, & Shearer, 2004).

Globalization has led to trends of decentralization and deregulation, phenomena that have an impact on the professional regulation of the nursing profession and by the same token, on nurses' mobility (Brunke, 2003). For example, at the national level, Canada's Agreement on Internal Trade requires that workers who are qualified in one province or territory have their qualifications recognized in other provinces or territories. Canadian nursing regulatory bodies have adopted the Mutual Recognition Agreement to this end. However, contrary to reciprocity across provinces, in 2004, *l'Ordre des infirmières et infirmiers du Québec* (OIIQ) ceased to recognize nursing licenses from other provinces. This follows their implementation in 2000 of a licensing exam that is considered significantly different from the one used across the other provinces. The OIIQ move is also due to the differential progress across provinces to require a baccalaureate degree for entrance to the profession (Ghislaine Desrosiers, personal communication, November 8, 2004). Another barrier to reciprocity with Québec is the OIIQ requirement for proficiency in French, which is mandatory for registration in that province.

Canadian Nurses in the Political Arena

The nursing profession responded to the changes occurring in the 1990s by becoming more assertive and politically active. As a result, stakeholders, especially politicians, government officials, and the general public, showed increased understanding of the problems existing in the quality of nurses' work life, and the impact on health services created by the growing shortage of RNs. The increased public understanding resulted in concern with the decrease in numbers entering the profession. For example, the Standing Senate Committee on Social Affairs, Science and Technology in Canada observed that "10 years of downsizing the Canadian health care system have only exacerbated the situation for nurses by producing unhappy patients, horrific workloads for nurses across the system, destruction of organizational loyalty, and decaying morale among all health care workers" (2002, p. 116).

In 1999, federal, provincial, and territorial Ministers of Health directed their ministries to prepare options to strengthen the development of health human resources. In 2000, after consultation with key stakeholders throughout the country, including Canadian nurses, "The Nursing Strategy for Canada" was released. The goal of that strategy is to achieve and maintain an adequate supply of nursing personnel who are appropriately educated, distributed throughout Canada, and deployed in order to meet the needs of the Canadian population. The strategy addresses four key issues: unified action; improved data, research, and human resource planning; appropriate education; and improved deployment and retention (Advisory Committee Health Delivery and Human Resources (ACHDHR), 2003).

The multi-stakeholder Canadian Nursing Advisory Committee (CNAC) was created to focus on improving the quality of work life for nurses and to provide advice to support the implementation of other strategies contained in the Nursing Strategy for Canada. In 2002, the landmark report, "Our Health, Our Future: Creating Quality Workplaces for Canadian Nurses" was released (CNAC, 2002). Progress is being made on the 51 recommendations contained in that report, such as the increase of 25% in registered nurses' education seats by 2004, with a further increase of 20% in each of four subsequent years. As a result, a 43% increase in RN education seats has been achieved (ACHDHR, 2003), though this remains insufficient due to the relative surplus of qualified applicants in many jurisdictions, including in provinces with a baccalaureate degree as minimum educational requirement for entry into the profession.

The CNA, with a membership of 120, 000 registered nurses and representing all nurses from eight provinces and five territories (given the partial membership of Ontario nurses and the lack of membership from Québec nurses) wields considerable political power. For example, it was involved in legislative changes to the Canada Health Act of 1984, and participated in the National Health Forum in 1997 and in the Romanow Commission in 2001 (Rodger, 2003).

The Role of the Canadian Nurses Association

Nursing is structured along two broad types of organizations: national/provincial professional and regulatory associations as well as national/provincial labor unions. Provincial and territorial governments have delegated the right to regulation of the nursing profession, giving provincial and territorial nursing self-regulatory bodies authority over the use of the title ("nurse"), scope of practice, standards of education and qualification, standards of practice and professional ethics, approval of educational programs for entry to practice, and continuing education requirements (Brunke, 2003). Thus, the functions of nursing organizations in each province/ territory vary, and while the mandates of public protection and representation of the nursing profession are fulfilled overall, the format is not uniform across provinces and territories.

The CNA, a federation of provincial and territorial nursing associations, is recognized as the voice of the nursing profession on a national and provincial/territorial level (Rodger, 2003) and is affiliated with the International Council of Nurses. The mission of the CNA is "to advance the quality of nursing in the interest of the public" (CNA, 2004). While each nurse must be a member of a provincial/territorial regulatory association, membership in a professional association (if separate) is optional. For example, in Ontario, two distinct organizations exist (regulatory and professional) because of the potentially conflicting interests of the dual mandate of protecting the public and protecting nurses. Québec nurses are another exception with regards to CNA membership. All Québec nurses are members of *l'Ordre des infirmières et infirmiers du Québec* (OIIQ), which speaks for regulatory and professional issues alike, but Québec nurses are not represented by the CNA. The OIIQ disaffiliated from the CNA in 1985 in the context of the Québec sovereignty movement.

HIGHER EDUCATION IN NURSING

Until the late 1960s, nursing retained its image as a trade despite many factors, such as expanding urbanization with its associated increasing numbers of women entering the workforce, a general shift toward a more secular society, expanded educational opportunities for women, and even other occupations (such as social work) being recognized as secular professions. Although nursing leaders had lobbied since 1905 and various studies recommended moving nursing into the educational sector (e.g., Mussallem, 1960; Weir, 1932), hospital-based training programs were deeply entrenched and any action to place nursing education within the post-secondary educational institutions (similar to those preparing teachers) was strongly opposed by physicians, administrators, and even many nurses. This model remained dominant until the 1960s with more than 95% of nurses receiving their education in hospital-based programs.

Philanthropic Organizations and University-Level Preparation in Nursing

The role of nurses in WWI and the 1918 influenza epidemic enhanced the public image of nursing. As well, the status of women was undergoing change with the suffragette movement. Governments were supportive, in principle, of university-level preparation for diploma-educated nurses for roles in the emerging public health services. However, it was financial assistance from the Canadian Red Cross (CRC) in 1919 that led to the first university-based nursing courses being established in five Canadian universities. Three of the five universities expanded the nursing courses into post-diploma undergraduate degree programs in nursing. The CRC's actions were influenced by its membership in the International Red Cross, whose goals were to increase standards of physical and mental health through health promotion and disease prevention (Gibbon & Mathewson, 1947, cited in Bajnok, 1992). From the 1920s onward, post-diploma nursing programs became the primary route to higher education. A second route was the basic university program introduced in 1919. The first programs were influenced strongly by the developments in nursing education in the United States.

The University of British Columbia (UBC), founded in 1915, had a utilitarian philosophic orientation common to the new western universities (Ross-Kerr, 2003c). Through the efforts of the medical superintendent of the teaching hospital and under the leadership of Ethel Johns, a 5-year non-integrated or "sandwich" program was established in 1919. Students enrolled in the university studied 1 year, then participated in the 3-year hospital school of nursing program, and returned to the university for the final year. The university had control of education only in the first and final years. That type of model was prevalent in the United States and became the norm for basic undergraduate programs in nursing in Canada.

The Rockefeller Foundation, a philanthropic organization in the United States, in combination with a strong nursing leader and support from academic medicine, was the instigator of a seminal change in university nursing education. That change was associated with the demand for intellectual expertise that emerged from the social and economic turmoil of the 1930s. The intellectual elite based in the universities formed alliances with politicians to use their expertise in dealing with the needs of society through programs combining humanitarianism with efficiency (Mansell, 2004). The University of Toronto School of Nursing, under the leadership of Kathleen Russell, received grants from the Rockefeller Foundation over a 30-year period beginning in 1923. Initially, the funding was to establish and implement an improved diploma program, and that program was created in 1933. It was financially independent of the hospitals and complete responsibility for the students rested with the School of Nursing. This change provided the opportunity for the nursing courses to be required to meet university standards. The School of Nursing became an autonomous unit within the administrative framework of the university, thus allowing it to participate fully in university governance. In 1942, the first integrated basic undergraduate program in nursing in Canada was introduced. The students were placed in clinical settings as learners, with faculty facilitating the integration of theory and practice, and fostering critical thinking and a questioning attitude. The entire program was controlled by the university and clinical education was integrated with nursing and non-nursing courses. The students received a liberal as well as a professional education (Ross-Kerr, 2003c).

Financial assistance from the Rockefeller Foundation was conditional on the provincial government's and the university's commitment to provide financial support to the School (Wood, 2003). This established a powerful precedent: In subsequent years, integrated basic nursing programs were developed and implemented by other universities with financial support from the provincial governments, and indirectly, from the federal government (Ross-Kerr, 2003c).

Diploma Programs Move into Post-Secondary Educational Institutions

Desire for quality education in the diploma programs and concern for the working conditions of students led to the Weir Report (1932), which was commissioned jointly by the CNA and the CMA. That report recommended that authority and responsibility for the schools of nursing be vested within the general provincial system of education and be financed in a manner similar to colleges providing teacher preparation. Unfortunately, the Weir Report was released in an environment of major economic depression. Universities were experiencing reduced revenues, staff layoffs and difficult working conditions, and varied amounts of financial support given by the governments and private resources. Despite the report's recommendations, governments were not interested in creating new or expanding existing educational institutions that would further drain on scarce resources. Furthermore, members of the medical profession were strongly opposed to the recommendations of the report, fearing both the loss of a pliable and cheap labor force in the hospitals and the competition in providing health services to the general public (Ross-Kerr, 2003c).

The beginning of WWII resulted in an improvement of the national economy. During the 1940s, the country again faced a shortage of nurses. Federal funds were directed to the universities in the form of training grants that were distributed through the CNA to schools of nursing. Following the end of WWII, the university-based nursing programs expanded. Many nurses who served in the armed forces used the funding provided to veterans for further education to enroll in the post-diploma baccalaureate programs. Many later became influential leaders in nursing.

Successive studies commissioned by the nursing associations or governments recommended that responsibility for basic nursing education be transferred from hospitals to educational institutions. In fact, the CNA sponsored a survey of schools of nursing and found that there had been little progress in improving basic nursing education since the Weir Report had been released in 1932 (Mussallem, 1960). University-based programs in nursing, although expanding in number and size, accounted for a relatively small proportion of the RN workforce. Still, graduate programs in nursing at the master's level had been established, and there was an ever-increasing demand for more university prepared nurses.

The 1950s and 1960s were a time of economic prosperity, a burgeoning population, a renewed demand for education at the post-secondary level, and a firmly-established belief in state intervention in social welfare, particularly in the fields of education, health, and social services. Prior to the 1960s, post-secondary education in Canada consisted largely of a limited number of private universities and educational institutions with very specific mandates (e.g., agricultural colleges and teacher colleges). In the 1960s, the applicant pool increased substantially as a result of the "baby boom" generation and the post-WWII wave of immigration. Federal and provincial governments took on a major role in post-secondary education, and the federal government replaced direct grants to the universities with generous transfer payments to the provinces. Universities remained independent, but became public institutions with the major portion of funding now provided by the provincial governments and, indirectly, by the federal government and students' tuition fees.

Additionally, a network of non-degree granting community colleges and technical and vocational training institutions was created (Larsen & Baumgart, 1992). These community colleges even today continue to play a key role in the post-secondary education sector: community colleges are more numerous and more accessible than universities as they are located in small as well as large urban centers and they require lower tuition, if any (there are no tuition fees for the community colleges in Québec).

The Royal Commission on Health Services (Government of Canada, 1964), acting on requests from the CNA, recommended that nursing education be organized and funded similar to other forms of professional education; that 10 more university nursing programs be established under administratively autonomous schools of nursing; that the non-integrated or "sandwich" programs be eliminated; and that baccalaureate programs be expanded in number to enable them to prepare approximately 25% of total recruits to the nursing workforce (Government of Canada, 1964).

As a consequence, the vast majority of hospital schools of nursing closed, and 3-year diploma programs were established in the community college sector. In many of the colleges, nursing was one of the largest programs and had a significant impact on the viability of the colleges. With the deletion of the service component, the programs became 2 years in length (Ross-Kerr, 2003d). During the period of transition, immigration also provided Canada with a pool of nurses trained elsewhere, thus transferring the cost of their training from Canada to the countries of the immigrants' origin (Wotherspoon, 1994).

A Baccalaureate Degree in Nursing for Entry into the Profession

In 1982, the CNA and its provincial associations (except the OIIQ) took the position that by the year 2000, a baccalaureate degree in nursing would be required for entry into the profession as an RN. Key strategies taken to achieve that goal included having universities improve access to nursing undergraduate programs, the promotion of collaborative programs between the universities and community colleges leading to an undergraduate degree in nursing, and the expansion of graduate education in nursing.

The goal could not become a reality until consensus was achieved among the various segments within nursing, that is, among faculty at the community colleges and universities, employers, professional associations, unions, regulatory bodies, and the members themselves. The ministries of education and health in the provinces/territories were key stakeholders as well, as they have responsibility for allocating resources for post-secondary education and for health personnel (Wood, 2003). Strategically, cohesiveness within nursing as well as the recognition of the value of higher education for nurses was necessary in order to achieve political and financial support from the provincial governments. To achieve the goal, compromises had to be made. For example, one provincial government would not support baccalaureate entry to practice, but did support collaborative programs between universities and community colleges with the proviso that a diploma-completion exit be offered. Through concerted and cohesive action by nursing, by 2005, all but three of the 10 provinces (Alberta, Manitoba, and Québec) had achieved the goal and those three are making significant progress to this end. Alberta has approved the requirement to be implemented by the year 2010, and in Québec, all diploma programs are now associated with universities (collaborative programs between colleges and universities lead to a degree, but students have the option of obtaining a diploma after 3 years and taking the licensing examinations).

In the provinces with strong community college sectors (e.g., Ontario, Québec, Alberta, and British Columbia), two routes to baccalaureate level education have emerged: first, direct entry to universities from secondary education into basic nursing programs of 4 years duration (3 in Québec); or second, entry through collaborative arrangements between community colleges and universities. The collaborative arrangements range from fully integrated programs given on different campuses to a 4-year curriculum of which the first 2 years (3 years in Québec) are provided by the colleges followed by 2 years at the universities. In the other provinces, there are no collaborative programs, and all basic nursing education is offered by the universities.

Graduate Nursing Programs

The increasing complexity of care, ever-expanding technology, changes in health and nursing services, standards for faculty appointments in universities and community colleges, and a recognized need for nurses to participate in the generation and utilization of knowledge were driving forces leading to the establishment of graduate programs in nursing. The first master's program in nursing was established at the University of Western Ontario in 1959. Other programs followed and focused on preparation in functional areas such as teaching or administration. Nurses wanting graduate preparation in clinical specialties in nursing went to go to the United States. In the 1960s, Canadian master's programs began including programs in clinical specialties. Also, in 1966, the Faculty of Nursing at the University of Montreal established the first French-language master's program in nursing in the world (Wood & Ross-Kerr, 2003b).

In the 1960s, research in nursing was embryonic, even though research and the presentation of a thesis were recognized as crucial components of graduate programs (Wood, Giovannetti, & Ross-Kerr, 2004). Thus, preparation for research became an integral component of all graduate programs in nursing at both the master's and doctoral levels. The focus in research is critical in a Canadian model for doctoral education that differs from that in the United States and the United Kingdom. Additionally, the combined clinical specialization and research is predominant at the master's level.

Implementing the new emphasis on research was underwritten by an American foundation. Although the CNA and individual universities played a major role in the development and support of graduate education, it was financial assistance from the U.S.-based W. K. Kellogg Foundation that was decisive. Over a 40-year period (1940-1981), that foundation provided grants to nine universities, including the University of Western Ontario, as well as monies for fellowships. That support financed a critical mass of nurses through graduate education in the United States as well as provided monies for faculty positions in Canada. The Kellogg Foundation also provided a grant directly to the CNA in 1962 to establish the Canadian Nurses Foundation (CNF) in order to provide nurses with fellowships for study at the master's and doctoral levels and for research assistance. The fellowship program has been the major thrust of the CNF, which has played a pivotal role in the development of a cadre of nurses at the master's and doctoral levels who have research expertise. A total of 494 fellowships for master's level study and 261 for doctoral studies were awarded between 1962 and 2002, representing a substantial return on the investment of start-up funds by the Kellogg Foundation (Wood & Ross-Kerr, 2003b). One last key development for master's level programs is preparation for nurse practitioner roles. There is general agreement that nurse practitioners require a master's degree in nursing and at least one province, Québec, has already made that level of preparation mandatory. This requirement added to the pool of nurses with master's degrees.

Doctoral Nursing Education

From the 1950s onward, as the number of master's prepared nurses grew, increasing (albeit small) numbers continued on to pursue doctoral level nursing education in the United States or the United Kingdom. Others continued their post-master's work within Canada but in disciplines related to nursing, since there were no Canadian nursing doctoral programs. The number of nurses engaged in research and obtaining external funding also increased (Wood & Ross-Kerr, 2003b). Still, by 1989, 257 nurses held doctoral degrees, representing only 0.14% of Canadian nurses (Wood et al., 2004).

The first Canadian doctoral program leading to a Ph.D. degree in nursing was established in 1991 and more were established over the following 16 years. A Canadian model emerged as these programs developed. That model "stood on middle ground between the traditional Ph.D. program from the United Kingdom and the American model" (Wood et al., 2004, p. 11). The model is characterized by a small number of required core courses, a firm grounding in research, a strong focus on the supervisor/ student relationship, and a requirement by many that a student identify a research area prior to admission. A 2004 workshop on doctoral education reiterated support for the "Canadian" model (Canadian Association of Schools of Nursing (CASN), 2004).

As it did with the undergraduate programs, the CNA played a key role in the development of graduate programs. In 1958, it publicly supported master's education and in 1978, it passed a motion to mobilize the necessary human and financial support to develop doctoral programs in nursing in Canada, although as noted above, it wasn't until 1991—some 13 years later—that the first Ph.D. program was established. The combined efforts of the CNA, the CNF, and the Canadian Association of University Schools of Nursing (CAUSN) in a plan, "Operation Bootstrap," initiated dialogue and debate, including a Kellogg Foundation-funded national seminar on doctoral education in nursing (Wood et al., 2004). The plan stimulated the development of research centers in nursing at several universities and influenced the major research funding agencies to make monies accessible to nurses on a competitive basis. Those efforts led to more nursing faculty members with funded research background now available as supervisors and mentors, a first step by universities for creation and/or expansion of doctoral programs.

Nursing Higher Education: Current Situation

The current applicant pool at the undergraduate level is changing. Many universities report an increase in the number of applicants who are in the mature student category and of those who have previous university studies. No national statistics are available, but individual universities are reporting a surplus of applicants to nursing higher education and waiting lists as long as 3 years (CNA, 2002). As a means of ensuring standards of excellence in nursing education, the Canadian Association of Schools of Nursing (CASN) developed and implemented a national system of accreditation at the undergraduate level and is embarking on a similar process for graduate programs. The move to an undergraduate degree in nursing for entry into the profession as an RN is placing tremendous demands on graduate programs to produce an adequate number of future faculty as well as clinicians to serve as mentors and preceptors.

In 2007, there were 30 programs at the master's level and 15 doctoral programs. These programs are spread out across the country and enrollment is steadily increasing. Currently, only 67 38 (2.7%) of RNs employed in nursing have master's or doctoral degrees (CIHI, 2007d). That is a very small pool in light of the expansion of the educational capacity and the demands from the health care system.

The average age of a student at completion of a Ph.D. program is around 40 years for nursing, compared with around 30 for the biomedical sciences and 32 in the social/behavioral sciences. Contributing factors to this older age are the insistence of some programs for considerable professional experience prior to commencing research training and the need to combine part-time studies with work (Wood et al., 2004). The older age upon completion of doctoral studies places nurses at a disadvantage when competing against peers in other disciplines for post-doctoral and career awards and research operating grants. Additionally, too many of the doctoral-prepared faculty carry heavy teaching loads, and thus have little time to develop as nurse scientists.

Also, the move to an undergraduate degree in nursing for entry into the profession as an RN has impacted on the educational preparation of the RPNs and/or LPNs. In most provinces, the education of that cadre has moved into the community colleges and the length of the programs has increased to 2 years. Strategies whereby members of that cadre can gain access to undergraduate programs in nursing are now a priority in many jurisdictions.

Impact of Higher Education on Professional and Social Development

As the number of nurses with baccalaureate, master's, or Ph.D. degrees in nursing increased, there were major changes in two areas: one—nursing research, including the transfer of knowledge into practice; and two—professional cohesiveness.

Nursing Research

Nursing has progressed from conducting very limited research to now being a competitive force for major operating grants and personal awards placing Canadian nursing research at the transitional stage of development (Alcock & Arthur, 2003). Canadian nursing is now engaged in research that influences not only how nurses and other health professionals practice, but also research that influences policy and addresses broad societal issues. For example, nurse researchers work with the automobile industry to make motor vehicles safer, especially for infants/children and the elderly (Snowdon, Miller-Polgar, Potvin, & Follo, 2004). Nurses are also on the adjudicating committees of the major research granting agencies. In general, the need to base the interventions of health care workers on the best scientific information available is recognized and valued within the health care system as a whole. The production through research and use of nursing knowledge through knowledge transfer has become a priority of professional nursing (White, Pringle, Doran, & McGillis-Hall, 2005).

Professional Cohesiveness

Nursing lobbied successfully to have Canadian governments address the crisis in nursing, including the nursing shortage and decreasing enrollment in numerous schools. Because of those successes and the raised awareness, nursing human resource development is now a priority of the federal government and many of the provincial governments. In recognition of the key role for nursing at the policy level, the Office of Nursing Policy (ONP) was established in 1999 by the federal government, with the mandate to influence federal health policy (CNA, 2004). A number of provincial governments now also have nursing policy officers or advisors.

The federal government's ONP, as well as CNA, CASN, the Academy of Chief Nursing Executives (ACEN), the Canadian Association for Nursing Research (CANR), and the CNF have joined to develop a strategic direction for nursing research, including preparation of future nursing researchers. That plan calls for a substantial increase in enrollment in doctoral programs and funding to allow for full-time studies (Griffin, 2004).

While continuing to advance its own interests, nursing is involved in promoting the welfare of society as a whole. Through its interests in the broad determinants of health, the nursing profession has become involved in socio-economic and environmental issues. For example, the nursing profession advocates for non-smoking environments, provides leading investigators in research on smoking, and implements and evaluates smoking cessation programs. Addressing the health of immigrants and refugees is another priority for nurse researchers, whose expertise is recognized and valued (e.g., Gagnon, 2002). Also, the plight of vulnerable populations such as the mentally ill, the homeless, and the aged, especially those in nursing homes, is the focus of nurse-led groups and organizations. For example, the first safe injection center in all of North America for intravenous drug users was established in 2003 in British Columbia, at the instigation of nurses working with this vulnerable population (Gold, 2003; Vancouver Coastal Health, 2004).

NURSING CHALLENGES IN THE 21ST CENTURY

Canada entered the 21st century with a shortage of nurses, less than desirable work environments, a gender imbalance, and limited educational capacity. Those challenges are exacerbated by a loss of expertise, knowledge, and productivity through an unprecedented wave of retirement. Further, the expansion of higher education in nursing and the generation of nursing knowledge are impeded by the paucity of doctoral-prepared faculty, the under-funding of universities in general, the limited funding available to prospective students for graduate education, and the limited funding available for nursing and others for health sciences research. The aging of the university faculty in nursing is a major concern as is the imbalance between the graduation rate from the graduate programs and the ever increasing demand for nurses with graduate education in nursing. This concern remains despite the efforts being directed to address those deficiencies (Griffin, 2004).

Addressing the Global Shortage of Nurses

The shortage of nurses is a global phenomenon with only Taiwan, Finland, and Spain reporting a surplus (Baumann et al., 2004a). Foreign-trained nurses comprised 7.9% of the Canadian RN workforce in 2006, with a predominance of nurses from the Philippines and the United Kingdom (CIHI, 2007d). Without recruiting more nurses from outside, Canada will be hard-pressed to meet the demands of its health care system. Such recruitment may be in violation of Canada's ethical position against stripping other countries of vital nursing resources (Halliwell et al., 2004). As recommended by Baumann et al. (2004a), the shortage of nurses is best addressed through the development of international standardized databases as well as through national and international collaboration in nursing workforce planning and research. Such planning has to be short-term, medium-term, and long-term. Although planning on a national level for the nursing workforce started in 2002 with the formation of the CNAC and subsequent nursing strategies, national plans are needed to enhance nursing capacity through recruitment and retention. The Canadian Institute for Health Information has created a national database on nursing and issues annual reports, and the Canadian Nurses Association and the Canadian Association of Schools of Nursing compile data and issue annual reports on nursing education.

Gender Inequities

In Canadian society, masculine work and attributes are traditionally being more highly valued than their feminine counterparts. Issues of gender and power are so important in nursing because of the ratio of men and women in the profession. Composition of the nursing workforce and its position in health services, as well as remuneration for services, were all shaped by society's view of women and women in the labor force. From its beginning, nursing was viewed as an extension of women's work, and paid work was seen as a secondary and usually a temporary facet of a woman's life. Nursing, along with teaching, was an acceptable occupation for women, but one that ceased at the time of marriage. Post-secondary educational opportunities for women were limited until the second half of the 20th century, as universities were considered primarily for men. Because of the view of nursing as "women's work," in the 1960s only 25 of Canada's 170 schools of nursing accepted male applicants (Hanvey, 2003). Furthermore, until 1969, the OIIQ denied entry to men, mostly because of the influence of female religious orders providing nursing care in Québec.

As societal trends are moving toward a greater acceptance of the nurturing role of men, both professionally and in the home, the numbers of Canadian men in nursing are increasing (Ross-Kerr, 2003b), albeit slowly. Yet, a man who is a nurse continues to be referred to as a "male nurse" whereas female nurses are simply "nurses." Currently, in Canada, men represent 6.6% of the RNs, 7.0% of the LPNs/RNAs, and 22.5% of registered psychiatric nurses (CIHI, 2007d). Almost half of all men employed in nursing as RNs work in Québec and slightly more than a quarter of men working in nursing as RNAs work in that province. Registered psychiatric nurses are employed in the four provinces of western Canada only. It is not clear why Québec differentiates itself to such a degree with respect to its numbers of men in nursing, though it has been speculated that the image of nursing in that province is more favorable to men. A major challenge will be to decrease or remove the many informal barriers to recruitment and retention of men interested in nursing, such as the value of nursing as seen by society, and even patient preferences.

Retention and Improving the Quality of the Workplace

A major challenge for health services in general, and nursing in particular, is the creation of quality workplaces in a time of fiscal constraints and ever-increasing competition for scarce health human resources. In addition to increasing the percentage of full-time job opportunities, innovative measures are required to reduce the use of overtime, absenteeism, and sick leave, and to maximize appropriate utilization of nursing personnel. The profession has learned the value of unity and of the responsiveness of governments when positions are supported by hard evidence (ACHDHR, 2003; CNAC, 2002). Innovative measures are being taken and studied (e.g., Ellis et al., 2006; Maslove & Fooks, 2004; McGillis-Hall, 2005; Priest, 2006).

Inter-Professional Collaboration and a Re-Orientation of the Health Care System

The competition between medicine and other health professions, especially nursing, for scarce resources will continue, but there will be more inter-professional collaboration in the delivery of health services. Through special funding, the federal government is promoting inter-professional education for collaborative patient-centered practice (Health Canada, 2004; Oandasan et al., 2006). Although its position has changed, medicine in Canada has been described as "still the most powerful health occupation, but [one that] is now surrounded by many other providers, all with increasing degrees of legitimation or state recognition and all eager to escape from under medicine's thumb" (Coburn, D'Arcy, & Torrance, 1998). There is strong support for recognizing that the nurse practitioner role in all levels of care is complementary, not assistive, to the physician (CNA, 2003). Finding and implementing the most effective RN: RNA/LPN ratio in terms of patient and nursing outcomes is a major challenge, and research to provide evidence is underway (e.g., White et al., 2005). Finally, although organized medicine in some jurisdictions continues to oppose the practice of midwifery, midwifery is recognized as a distinct, self-regulating profession in some jurisdictions and as a specialty within nursing in others.

One of the greatest challenges to the health care system is the promotion of health and the prevention of illness and disease. A health system in which disease prevention and health promotion are significant components is justified by the economical benefits of a healthy population requiring less attention from the already scarce health human resources. In addition to these political-economic forces, other forces are driving the increased presence of disease prevention and health promotion within the Canadian health care system. Those forces are a rapidly increasing understanding of genetics and the etiology of specific diseases; increasingly innovative treatments combined with an increasingly knowledgeable population; concern with patient safety; and the compulsory disclosure of information to patients and families. Indeed, now as always, nursing has a long history of being at the forefront of actions to improve the health of the population (Ogilvie & Reutter, 2003).

Multiculturalism

Nursing challenges in the providing health care to Aboriginal communities include providing culturally relevant care, improving access to health care, and recruiting health care professionals from Aboriginal backgrounds (Wasekeesikaw, 2003). Since Aboriginal peoples have experienced racism, prejudice, and insensitivity within the health care system, they commonly avoid seeking health services (see Browne & Fiske, 2001).

The Aboriginal Nurses Association of Canada (ANAC) has been pivotal in the development of health care in Aboriginal communities. Founded in 1974, this group of "Aboriginal caregivers to Aboriginal People" (ANAC, 2004) has pioneered research studies, publications, consultations, and recruitment, in addition to raising awareness of Aboriginal health issues. Now an affiliate of the CNA, the ANAC collaborates with many provincial/territorial and national organizations, such as CASN, the Canadian Hospital Association, and the Canadian Pediatric Society. One of the main nursing challenges is the provision of culturally relevant care, thereby allowing for flexibility in learning styles, beliefs, values, and health practices. In the case of immigrant or refugee populations, this same challenge applies (Davidhizar & Newman, 1998).

Recognizing the Value of Higher Education in Nursing

Major accomplishments with respect to nursing education are occurring at a time of massive budget cuts by governments in response to globalization. Within nursing, both the change in educational requirements and the need for graduate education are being cited by some critics as "creeping credentialism" or as self-serving interests of the health professions (exclusive of medicine). Critics argue that credential creep will result in underutilization of skills and higher costs for those seeking to enter the profession (CIHI, 2004). That accusation appears to be related to economic factors, though it is not leveled against occupations outside of health care or at its margins, such as teachers, social workers, or child care workers. At the federal level, the Advisory Committee on Health Delivery and Human Resources (ACHDHR) has established a process to manage proposals to change an entry-to-practice credential for medical and health professionals. That process is viewed as contributing to a sufficient supply of medical and health professionals and helping governments to determine if a change in credential serves the interests of patients and the health care system (ACHDHR, 2004).

A LOOK TO THE FUTURE

The health care system in Canada evolved considerably over the past 35 years, adapting to significant changes in the external environment and to changing needs and possibilities of the services themselves. The national health insurance program or "medicare," designed to ensure that all residents have reasonable access to medically necessary hospital and physician services on a prepaid basis, reflects the underlying values of equity and solidarity. Prior to and since its introduction, nursing has been a strong and articulate supporter. Medicare is congruent with the values evident throughout the history of Canadian nursing, that is, establishing hospitals and community-based services and providing care to populations in need regardless of ability to pay. Changes in the health and education sectors associated with the rise of neo-liberalism ideology in the 1960s-1990s negatively impacted on nursing. One of the cornerstones of that ideology of unregulated capitalism, that is, cutbacks to social programs, is reflective of values diametrically opposed to those underlying medicare. Pressures from internal and external sources on the governments from advocates of that ideology resulted in major cutbacks to the health and education sectors. Re-structuring and other changes all directed toward cost containment and cost reduction were destructive for nursing and the profession is still in the recovery phase. The forces of neo-liberalism are still present, but the governments are tempering their responses and reversing the cutbacks, for example, through the expansion of nursing positions and educational capacity. Canadian nursing through its collaborative networks, intensive lobbying, research and evidence-based position papers on the need for reforms in the health sector has been one of the leading pressure groups. Professional nursing has successfully positioned the future of nursing within the broader framework of the future health of Canadians (e.g., Villeneuve & MacDonald, 2006). Issues in nursing around education and training, scope of practice, workplace, and nursing human resource planning are being addressed by governments and other stakeholders as well as by nursing.

As Canada moved through competitive and monopoly capitalism into the current phase of global capitalism, nursing evolved from an apprenticeship trained workforce to a highly educated and politically active profession. With the pressures of globalization, such as corporate forces advocating for privatization of health care and the ensuing power struggle between business values and humanistic values upon which medicare was founded, the nursing profession will change again.

The present system of initial licensure or registration through examinations followed by fee-based annual renewal will be replaced by re-licensure or registration on a regular basis. Additionally, emphasis on continuing education will focus on lifelong learning and/or means by which this learning will be tested. The proportion of nurses with graduate preparation in nursing will increase substantially, the majority of RNs will have baccalaureate degrees in nursing and the role of RNAs/LPNs will change concomitantly with increased educational preparation. The body of nursing knowledge will expand as more research focuses on the evaluation of nursing interventions vis-à-vis patient outcomes, and there will be significant advances in evidence-based practice as well as administrative decisions and modalities for the transfer of knowledge to the work site (and to patients and members of the general public). A number of employers will have achieved reforms in the work environment designed to attract and retain nursing staff and nursing will strengthen its alliances with other health professionals as inter-professional education and practice become a reality and medical dominance decreases in favor of collaboration between health professions. The integration of education, research, and practice (e.g., the McGill nursing network) now seen only in limited extent across the country will gradually become the norm. Also, there will be increased collaboration across sites to maximize the use of scarce resources. Inequities in nursing education will be offset through more programs being offered through distance education and through international collaborative activities.

Though facing many challenges in the 21st century, nursing will become a stronger and more influential health profession. Nursing as a whole is engaged in intensive lobbying of the governments to accelerate the pace of reform focusing on health promotion, illness and injury prevention, and more effective management of disease, including addressing the underlying determinants of health; to decide on the range of health and illness services to be reasonably accommodated within the publicly funded system; to ensure the most appropriate and full utilization of all health professionals; and to establish structures supporting collaborative inter-professional health services providing patient centered care.

REFERENCES

Aboriginal Nurses Association of Canada. (2004). *Aboriginal caregivers to Aboriginal people: Background*. Retrieved September 23, 2004, from
    http://www.anac.on.ca/web/background.html

Advisory Committee Health Delivery and Human Resources [ACHDHR]. (2003). *A report on the nursing strategy for Canada*. Ottawa, Ontario, Canada: Health Canada.

Advisory Committee on Health Delivery and Human Resources [ACHDHR]. (2004). *New process for managing proposals to change an entry-to-practice credential for medical and health professions*. Ottawa, Ontario, Canada: Health Canads. Retrieved March 15, 2009, from
    http://www.hc-sc.gc.ca/hcs-sss/hhr-rhs/strateg/plan/credentials-criteres-eng.php

Aiken, L. H., Clarke, S. P., Cheung, R. B., Sloane, D. M., & Silber, J. H. (2003). Education levels of hospital nurses and patient mortality. *Journal of American Medical Association, 290*(12), 1-8.

Aiken, L. H., Clarke, S. P., Sloane, D. M., Sochalski, J. A., Busse, R., Clarke, H., et al. (2001, May-June). Nurses' reports on hospital care in five countries. *Health Affairs, 20*(1), 43-53.

Akyeampong, E. B. (2003). *Perspectives on labour and income.* Statistics Canada, Catalogue 75-001-XPE) 15(3). Retrieved November 30, 2004, from http://www.statcan.ca/english/studies/75-001/00802/fs-fi_200208_02.a.pdf

Alcock, D., & Arthur, H. M. (2003). *Federally and provincially funded nurses' research activity and capacity building in Canada in 2002.* Ottawa, Ontario. Canada: Office of Nursing Policy, Health Canada.

Angell, M. (2004). *The truth about drug companies.* New York: Random House.

Armstrong, P. (1997). Privatising care. In J. P. White (Ed.), *Medical alert: New work organizations in health care* (Rev. ed.). Toronto, Ontario, Canada: Garamond Press.

Armstrong, P., Armstrong, H., & Coburn, D. (2001). *Unhealthy times: Political economy perspectives on health and care in Canada.* Don Mills, Ontario, Canada: Oxford University Press.

Bajnok, I. (1992). Entry-level educational preparation for nursing. In A. J. Baumgart & J. Larsen (Eds.), *Nursing in Canada* (2nd ed., pp. 401-419). Toronto, Ontario, Canada: Mosby Year Book, Inc.

Baker, G. R., & Norton, P. (2001). Making patients safer! Reducing error in Canadian health care. *Health Care Papers, 2*(1), 10-31.

Barry-Walker, J. (2000). The impact of systems redesign on staff, patient and financial outcomes. *Journal of Nursing Administration, 30*(7), 77-89.

Basu, K., & Halliwell, C. (2004). Projecting the HHR impacts of demographic change. *Health Policy Research Bulletin, 8,* 17-21.

Baumann, A., Blythe, J., Kotofylo, C., & Underwood, J. (2004a). *The international nursing labour market.* Ottawa, Ontario, Canada: The Nursing Sector Study Cooperation. Retrieved from: http://www.buildingthefuture.ca

Baumann, A., Blythe, J., Kotofylo, C., & Underwood, J. (2004b). *Mobility of nurses in Canada.* Ottawa, Ontario, Canada: The Nursing Sector Study Cooperation. Retrieved from http://www.buildingthefuture.ca

Baumann, A., Giovennetti, P., O'Brien-Pallas, L., Mallette, C., Deber, R., Blythe, J., et al. (2001). Healthcare restructuring: The impact of job change. *Canadian Journal of Nursing Leadership, 14*(1), 14-20.

Bezruchka, S. (2000). Culture and medicine: Is globalization dangerous to our health? *Western Journal of Medicine, 172,* 332-334.

Blythe, J., Baumann, A., & Giovannetti, P. (2001). Health policy and systems: Nurses' experiences of restructuring in three Ontario hospitals. *Journal of Nursing Scholarship, 33*(1), 61-68.

Browne, A. J., & Fiske, J. (2001). First Nations women's encounters with mainstream health care services. *Western Journal of Nursing Research, 23*(2), 126-147.

Brunke, L. (2003). Canadian provincial and territorial professional associations and colleges. In M. McIntyre & E. Thomlinson (Eds.), *Realities of Canadian nursing: Professional, practice, and power issues* (pp. 143-160). New York: Lippincott Williams & Wilkins.

Campbell, B., Blouin, C., Foster, J., Labonte, R., Lexchin, J., Sanger, M., et al. (2002). Putting health first: Canadian health care reform, trade treaties and foreign policy (report prepared for the Commission on the Future of Health Care in Canada). *Globalization and health* (Ch. 11). Ottawa, Ontario, Canada: Health Canada. Retrieved October 30, 2004, from www.hc-sc.gc.ca/English/care/romanow/hcc0391.html

Canada Health Act. (1984). Ottawa, Ontario, Canada: Health Canada.

Canadian Association of Schools of Nursing. (2004). *Position statement on doctoral education*. Ottawa, Ontario, Canada: Author. Retrieved November 21, 2004, from www.casn.ca/education/graduate_programs.html

Canadian Broadcasting Corporation. (2005). Top court strikes down Quebec private health-care ban. Retrieved January 30, 2006, from http://www.cbc.ca/story/canada/national/2005/06/09/newscoc-health050609.html

Canadian Broadcasting Corporation, Canada. (2001). Retrieved March, 2004, from http://www.tv.cbc.ca/withness/refugee/refsmug.htm

Canadian Institute for Health Information [CIHI]. (2002). Hospitalizations by Leading Diagnoses and Gender, Canada, 2001/02. Retrieved February 15, 2006. from http://secure.chi.ca/cihiweb/dispPage.jsp?cw_page=statistics results topic hospital_e& cw_topic=Health%20Services&cw_subtopic=Hospital%20Discharges

Canadian Institute for Health Information. (2003). *Canada's Nursing workforce in 2003*. Ottawa, Ontario, Canada: CIHI.

Canadian Institute for Health Information. (2004). *Health care in Canada*. Ottawa, Ontario, Canada: CIHI.

Canadian Institute for Health Information. (2006a). *Waiting for health care in Canada: What we know and what we don't know*. Ottawa, Ontario, Canada: CIHI.

Canadian Institute for Health Information. (2006b). *Findings from the 2005 National Survey of Work and Health of Nurses*. Ottawa, Ontario, Canada: CIHI.

Canadian Institute for Health Information. (2007a). *Health care in Canada*. Ottawa, Ontario, Canada: CIHI.

Canadian Institute for Health Information. (2007b). *National Health Expenditure Trends, 1975-2007,* Ottawa, Ontario, Canada: CIHI.

Canadian Institute for Health Information. (2007c). *Drug expenditure in Canada, 1985-2006.* Ottawa, Ontario, Canada.

Canadian Institute for Health Information. (2007d). *Health human resources-nurses: Workforce trends of registered nurses in Canada, 2006; Workforce trends of licensed practical nurses in Canada, 2006 and Workforce trends of licensed psychiatric nurses in Canada, 2006.* Ottawa, Ontario, Canada: CIHI.

Canada Labour and Business Centre [CLBC]. (2002). Wortsman, A., & Lockhead, C. (PIs) *Full time equivalents and financial events costs associated with absenteeism, overtime, and involuntary part-time employment in nursing* (report commissioned for the Canadian Nursing Advisory Committee). Ottawa, Ontario, Canada: Health Canada, Advisory Committee on Health Human Resources.

Canadian Nurses Association [CNA]. (1989). Entry to practice. *Newsletter, 5*(3), 1-3. Ottawa, Ontario, Canada: Author.

Canadian Nurses Association [CNA]. (2002). *Nursing education data sets*. Ottawa, Ontario, Canada: Author.

Canadian Nurses Association [CNA]. (2003). *Position statement: The nurse practitioner*. Ottawa, Ontario, Canada: Health Canada.

Canadian Nurses Association [CNA]. (2004). *About CNA*. Ottawa, Ontario, Canada: Author.

Canadian Nursing Advisory Committee. (2002). *Our health, our future: Creating quality work places for Canadian nurses*. Ottawa, Ontario, Canada: Health Canada Advisory Committee on Health Human Resources.

Chodos, H., & McLeod, J. J. (2004). Romanow and Kirby on the public/private. Divide in healthcare: Demystifying the debate. *Healthcare Papers, 4*(4), 10-27.

Clarke, J. N. (2000). *Health, illness, and medicine in Canada* (3rd ed.). Don Mills, Ontario, Canada: Oxford University Press.

Coburn, J. (1987). I see and I am silent: A short history of nursing in Ontario. In D. Coburn, C. D'Arcy, G. M. Torrance, & P. K. New (Eds.), *Health and Canadian society: Canadian perspectives* (pp. 441-462). Markham, Ontario, Canada: Fitzhenry & Whiteside.

Coburn, D. (1988). The development of Canadian nursing: Professionalization and proletarianization. *International Journal of Health Services, 18*(3), 437-456.

Coburn, D. (1998). State authority, medical dominance and trends in the regulation of the health professions: The Ontario care. In D. Coburn, C. D'Arcy, & G. M. Torrance (Eds.), *Health and Canadian society: Sociological perspectives* (3rd ed., pp. 332-346). Toronto, Ontario, Canada: University of Toronto Press.

Coburn, D. (1999). Phases of capitalism, welfare states, medical dominance, and health care in Ontario. *International Journal of Health Sciences, 29*(4), 833-851.

Coburn, D. (2001). Health, health care, and neo-liberalism. In P. Armstrong, H. Armstrong, & D. Coburn (Eds.), *Unhealthy times: Political economy perspectives on health and care in Canada* (pp. 45-65). Don Mills, Ontario, Canada: Oxford University Press.

Coburn, D., D'Arcy, C., & Torrance, G. M. (Ed.). (1998). *Health and Canadian society: Sociological perspectives* (3rd ed.). Toronto, Ontario, Canada: University of Toronto Press.

Coburn, D., & Rappolt, S. (1999). The "logic of medicare," variants of capitalism and medical dominance: contextualizing profession-state relationships. In D. Coburn, S. Rappolt, I. Bourgeault, & J. Angus (Eds.), *Medicine, nursing and the state,* (pp. 139-167). Aurora, Ontario, Canada: Garamond Press Ltd.

Cortinois, A. A., Downey, S., Closson, R., & Jadad, A. R. (2003). Hospitals in a globalized world: A view from Canada. *Healthcare Papers, 4*(2), 14-32.

Davidhizar, R. E., & Newman, J. (1998). *Canadian transcultural nursing: Assessment and intervention.* St. Louis, MO: Mosby.

Deber, R. B. (2003). Health care reform: lessons from Canada. *American Journal of Public Health, 93*(1), 20-24.

Department of National Health and Welfare [DNHW]. (1974). *A new perspective on the health of Canadians: A working document* (Lalonde Report). Ottawa, Ontario, Canada: Author.

Ellis, J., Priest, A., MacPhee, M., Sanchez-McCutcheon, et al. (2006). *Staffing for safety: A synthesis of the evidence on nurse staffing and patient safety.* Ottawa, Canada: Canadian Health Services Research Foundation.

Evans, R. G., Marmor, T. R., & Barer, M. L. (1994). The determinants of a population health: What can be done to improve a democratic nation's health status. In R. G. Evans, M. L. Barer, & T. R. Marmor (Eds.), *Why are some people healthy and others not? The determinants of health of populations* (pp. 217-230). New York: Aldine de Gruyter.

Evans, R. G., & Stoddard, G. L. (1998). Producing health, consuming health care. In D. Coburn, C. D'Arcy, & G. M. Torrance (Eds.), *Health and Canadian society: Sociological perspectives* (3rd ed., pp. 549-579). Toronto, Ontario, Canada: University of Toronto Press.

Fleras, A. (2005). *Social problems in Canada: Conditions, construction, and challenges* (4th ed.) Toronto, Ontario, Canada: Prentice-Hall.

Fleras, A., & Elliott, J. L. (2003). *Unequal relations: An introduction to race and ethnic dynamics in Canada* (4th ed.). Toronto, Ontario, Canada: Prentice-Hall.

Frideres, J. S. (2002). Overcoming hurdles: Health care in Aboriginal people. In B. S. Bolaria & H. D. Dickinson (Eds.), *Health, illness, and health care in Canada* (3rd ed., pp. 144-166). Scarborough, Ontario, Canada: Nelson Thomson Learning.

Gagnon. A. J. (2002). *The responsiveness of the Canadian health care system towards newcomers.* Royal Commission on the Future of Health Care in Canada (Romanow Commission).

Gelber. S. M. (1980). The path to health insurance. In C. A. Meilicke & J. L. Storch (Eds.), *Perspectives on Canadian health and social services policy: History and emerging trends* (pp. 156-165). Ann Arbor, MI: Health Administration Press.

Gilbert, H. (2003). Great adventures in nursing: Colonial discourse and health care delivery in Canada's north. *Jouvert, Special Issue: Colonial Posts, 7*(2), 1-21. Raleigh, NC: College of Humanities and Social Sciences, North Carolina State University.

Gold, F. (2003). Supervised injection facilities. *Canadian Nurse, 99*(2), 14-18.

Gouvernement du Québec. (1970). *Rapport de la Commission d'Enquête sur la santé et le Bien-Etre social* (Vol. IV, Tome 2). Québec, Québec, Canada: L'Editeur officiel du Québec.

Government of Canada. (1964). *Royal Commission on Health Services* (Vol. 1) (Emmett Hall, Chairman). Ottawa, Ontario, Canada: Queen's Printer.

Greenglas, E. R., & Burke, R. J. (2001). Stress in nurses and hospital restructuring. *Canadian Journal of Nursing Research, 33*(2), 14-20.

Griffin, P. (2004). *Nursing research capacity in Canada: Challenges and future directions.* Ottawa, Ontario, Canada: Office of Nursing Policy, Health Canada.

Grispun, D. (2000). Taking care of the bottom line: Shifting paradigms in hospital management. In D. L. Gustafson (Ed.), *Care and consequences: The impact of health care reform* (pp. 25-48). Halifax, Canada: Fernwood Publishing.

Grispun, D. (2003). Part-time and casual nursing work: The perils of health care restructuring. *International Journal of Sociology and Social Policy, 23*(8/9), 54-70.

Hagmann, M. (2001). Globalization—How healthy? *Bulletin of the World Health Organization, 79*(9), 902-903.

Halliwell, C., Shamian, J., & Shearer, R. (2004). Health human resources: A key policy challenge. *Health Policy Research Bulletin, 8*(May), 3-7. Ottawa, Ontario, Canada: Health Canada.

Hanaway, S., & Cruess, R. (1996). McGill medicine. *The first half century, 1829-1885* (Vol. 1). Montreal and Kingston: McGill-Queen's University Press.

Hanvey, L. (2003). *Men in nursing.* Ottawa: Canadian Nurses Association.

Hastings, J. E. F. (1980). Federal-provincial insurance for hospital and physicians care in Canada. In C. A. Meilicke & J. L. Storch (Eds.), *Perspectives on Canadian health and social services policy: History and emerging trends* (pp. 198-219). Ann Arbor, MI: Health Administration Press.

Hastings, J. E. F., & Mosley, W. (1980). Introduction: The evolution of organized community health services in Canada. In C. A. Meilicke & J. L. Storch (Eds.), *Perspectives on Canadian health and social services policy: History and emerging trends* (pp. 145-155). Ann Arbor, MI: Health Administration Press.

Health Canada. (2004). *Interprofessional education for collaborative patient-centered practice (IEPCPCP).* Ottawa, Canada: National Expert Committee on Interdisciplinary Education for Collaborative Patient-Centered Care and Office of Nursing Policy of Health Canada.

Health Canada. (2005). *It's your health: West Nile virus.* Retrieved October 9, 2005 from http://www.hc-sc.gc.ca/iyh-vsv/diseases-maladies/wnv-vno_e.html

Hyman, I. (2001). *Health policy working paper series: Immigration and health.* Ottawa, Ontario, Canada: Health Canada.

Jensen, P. M. (1992). The changing role of nurses' unions. In A. J. Baumgart & J. Larsen (Eds.), *Canadian nursing faces the future* (2nd ed., pp. 557-572). St. Louis, MO: Mosby.

Kenny, N. P. (2002). *What good is health care? Reflections on the Canadian experience.* Ottawa, Ontario, Canada: CHA Press.

Kerr, J. R. (1996). Credentialing in nursing. In J. R. Kerr & J. MacPhail (Eds.), *Canadian nursing: Issues and perspectives* (3rd ed., pp. 363-372). New York: Mosby.

Larsen, J., & Baumgart, A. J. (1992). Overview: issues in nursing education. In A. J. Baumgart & J. Larsen (Eds.), *Nursing in Canada* (2nd ed., pp. 383-399). Toronto, Ontario, Canada: Mosby Year Book, Inc.

Lexchin, J. (1997). What information do physicians receive from pharmaceutical representatives? *Canadian Family Physician, 43*, 941-945.

Lexchin, J. (2002). Profits first: The pharmaceutical industry in Canada. In B. S. Bolaria & H. D. Dickinson (Eds.), *Health, illness and health care in Canada* (3rd ed., pp. 389-408). Scarborough, Ontario, Canada: Nelson Thomson Learning.

Lindenfield, R. (1980). Hospital insurance in Canada: An example in federal-provincial relations. In C. A. Meilicke & J. L. Storch (Eds.), *Perspectives on Canadian health and social services policy: History and emerging trends* (pp. 166-182). Ann Arbor, MI: Health Administration Press.

Mallette, C. (2005). *Theoretical and nursing practice implications of employment patterns and social exchange theory impact on the individual, organization and profession* (Ph.D. thesis). Toronto, Canada: Faculty of Nursing, University of Toronto.

Mansell, D. (2004). *Forging the future: A history of nursing in Canada.* Ann Arbor, MI: Tomas Press Publication.

Martinez, E., & García, A. (2000). *What is neo-liberalism.* Retrieved November 29, 2004, from http://www.globalexchange.org/campaigns/econ101/neoliberalDefined.html

Maslove, L., & Fooks, C. (2004). *Our health, our future: Creating quality workplaces for Canadian nurses; a progress report on implementing the final report of the Canadian Nursing Advisory Committee.* Ottawa, Canada: Canadian Policy Research Networks Inc.

McGillis-Hall, L., Doran, D., Ross-Baker, G., Pink, G. H., Sidan, S., O'Brien-Pallas, L. et al. (2003). Nursing staffing models as predictors of patient outcomes. *Medical Care, 4*(9), 1096-1109.

McGillis-Hall, L., Doran, D., & Pink, G. (2004). Nursing staffing models, nursing hours and patient safety outcomes. *Journal of Nursing Administration, 34*(1), 41-45.

McGillis-Hall, L. (Ed.). (2005). *Quality work environments for nurses and patient safety.* Sudbury, MA: Jones & Barlett.

McMichael, A. J. (2000). The urban environment and health in a world of increasing globalization: Issues for developing countries. *Bulletin of the World Health Organization, 78*(9), 1117-1126.

McMichael, A. J., Martens, P., Kovats, R. S., & Lele, S. (2000). Climate change and human health: Mapping and modeling potential impacts. In P. Elliott, J. S. Wakefield, N. G. Best, & D. J. Briggs (Eds.), *Spatial epidemiology: Methods and applications* (pp. 333-461). Oxford: Oxford University Press.

Meilicke, C. A., & Storch, J. L. (Eds.). (1980). *Perspectives on Canadian health and social services policy: History and emerging trends.* Ann Arbor, MI: Health Administrati Press.

Mussallem, H. (1960). *Spotlight on nursing education: The report of the pilot project of the evaluation of schools of nursing in Canada.* Ottawa, Ontario, Canada: Canadian Nurses Association.

Neuschler, E. (1998). Debate on U.S./Canada health expenditures—1. A: How well is Canada doing? In R. Chernomas & A. Sepehri (Eds.), *How to choose? A comparison of the U.S. and Canadian health care systems* (pp. 53-66). Amityville, NY: Baywood.

Nursing Sector Study Corporation. (2005). *Building the future: An integrated strategy for nursing human resources in Canada.* Ottawa, Canada: Author.

Oandasan, I., Baker, G. R., Baker, K., Bosco, C., D'Amour, D., Jones, L., et al. (2006). *Teamwork in health care: Promoting effective teamwork in health care in Canada.* Ottawa, Canada: Canadian Health Services Research Foundation.

O'Brien-Pallas, L., Alksnis, C., & Wang, S. (2003). *Bringing the future into focus: Projecting RN retirement in Canada.* Ottawa, Ontario, Canada: Canadian Institute of Health Information.

O'Brien-Pallas, L., Meyer, R., Alksnis, C., Tomblin-Murphy, G., Williams, S., Thomson, D., et al. (2002). *Nursing education data—Evaluation of strategy 7 of the nursing strategy for Canada* (report submitted to Health Canada). Toronto, Ontario, Canada: Nursing Effectiveness, Utilization, and Outcomes Research Unit, University of Toronto.

O'Brien-Pallas, L., Shamian, J., Thomson, D., Alksnis, C., Kochoorn, M., Kerr, M., et al. (2004). Work-related disability in Canadian nurses. *Journal of Nursing Scholarship, 36*(4), 352-356.

O'Brien-Pallas, L., Thomson, D., Alksnis, C., & Bruce, S. (2001). The economic impact of nurse staffing decisions: Time to turn down another road. *Hospital Quarterly* (Spring), 42-50.

O'Brien-Pallas, L., Thomson, D., McGill-Hall, L., Pink, G., Kerr, M., Wang, S., et al. (2004). *Evidence-based standards for measuring nurse staffing and performance.* Ottawa, Ontario, Canada: Canadian Health Services Research Foundation. Retrieved October 17, 2004, from http://www.fcrss.ca/final_research/ogc/pdf/obrien_final.pdf

Ogilvie, L., & Reutter, L. (2003). Primary health care: Complexities and possibilities from a nursing perspective. In J. C. Ross-Kerr & M. J. Wood (Eds.), *Canadian nursing: Issues and perspectives* (4th ed., pp. 441-465). Toronto, Ontario, Canada: Mosby.

O'Neil, J., Lemchuk-Favel, L., Allard, Y., & Postl, B. (1999). Community healing and Aboriginal self-government. In J. H. Hylton (Ed.), *Aboriginal self-government in Canada* (pp. 130-156). Saskatoon, SK: Purich.

Organisation for Economic Co-operation and Development [OECD]. (2004). *OECD Health Data 2004* (1st ed.). Retrieved November 30, 2004, from http://www.oecd.org/document/16/0,2340,en_2649_33929_2085200_1_1_1_1,00.html

Ostry, A. S. (2001). International trade regulation and publicly funded health care in Canada. *International Journal of Health Services, 31*(3), 475-580.

Picard, A. (2004a, June 24). Keep people healthy in the first place. *The Globe and Mail,* p. A15.

Picard, A. (2004b, October 14). Booming internet drug sales to Americans are a prescription for disaster in Canada. *The Globe and Mail,* p. A19.

Pierce, S. (2004). Clostridium difficile: No longer just a hospital problem? *Canadian Pharmaceutical Journal, 137*(6), 42.

Pooler, J. A. (2000). *Hierarchical organization in society: A Canadian perspective.* Aldershot, England: Ashgate.

Priest, A. (2006). *What's ailing our nurse? A discussion of the major issues affecting nursing human resources in Canada.* Ottawa, Canada: Canadian Health Services Research Foundation.

Pringle, D. (2005). In the beginning: Attrition from schools of nursing. In S. Devlin (Ed.), *The pulse of renewal* (pp. 19-20). Toronto: Longwoods Publishing Corporation.

Pringle, D. M., & Rowe, D. J. (1992). Voluntary community agencies: VON Canada as example. In A. J. Baumgart & J. Larsen (Eds.), *Canadian nursing faces the future* (2nd ed., pp. 611-618). Toronto, Ontario, Canada: Mosby.

Public Health Agency of Canada. (1997). *Leading causes of death and hospitalization in Canada.* Retrieved October 16, 2004, from http://www.phac-aspc.gc.ca/publicat/lcd-pcd97/mrt_mf_e.html#tab2

Public Health Agency of Canada. (2005a). *West Nile surveillance information.* Retrieved October 9, 2005, from http://dsol-smed.phac-aspc.gc.ca/wnv3/map_e.phtml?appname=human

Public Health Agency of Canada. (2005b). *HIV/AIDS: Epi updates.* Retrieved October 9, 2005 from, http://www.phac-aspc.gc.ca/publicat/epiu-aepi/epi-05/pdf/epi_05_e.pdf

Public Health Agency of Canada [PHAC]. (2004). *Leading causes of deaths and hospitalization in Canada.* Retrieved February 23, 2008, from http://www.phac-aspc.gc.ca/publicat/led-pcd97/index-eng.php

Ramsay, C., & Walker, M. (1998). Waiting your turn: Hospital waiting lists in Canada. In R. Chernomas & A. Sepehri (Eds.), *How to choose? A comparison of the US and Canadian health care systems* (pp. 153-175). Amityville, NY: Baywood.

Registered Nurses Association of Ontario (RNAO) & Registered Practical Nurses Association of Ontario (RPNAO). (2000). *Ensuring the care will be there: Report on nursing recruitment and retention in Ontario.* Toronto, Ontario, Canada: Author.

Rodger, G. L. (2003). Canadian Nurses Association. In M. McIntyre & E. Thomlinson (Eds.), *Realities of Canadian nursing: Professional, practice, and power issues* (pp. 125-142). New York: Lippincott Williams & Wilkins.

Romanow, R. (2002). *Health care and globalization* (Ch. 11). Ottawa, Ontario, Canada: Commission on the Future of Health Care in Canada. Retrieved October 17, 2004, from, http://www.hc-sc.gc.ca/english/pdf/romanow/pdfs/HCC_Chapter_11.pdf

Ross-Kerr, J. C. (2003a). Emergence of nursing unions as a social force in Canada. In J. C. Ross-Kerr & M. J. Wood (Eds.), *Canadian nursing: Issues and perspectives* (4th ed., pp. 280-300). Toronto, Ontario, Canada: Mosby.

Ross-Kerr, J. C. (2003b). Gender issues in nursing. In J. C. Ross-Kerr & M. J. Wood (Eds.), *Canadian nursing: Issues and perspectives* (4th ed., pp. 82-99). Toronto, Ontario, Canada: Mosby.

Ross-Kerr, J. C. (2003c). A historical approach to the evolution of university nursing in Canada. In J. C. Ross-Kerr & M. L. Wood (Eds.), *Canadian nursing: Issues and perspectives* (4th ed., pp. 350-367). Toronto, Ontario, Canada: Mosby.

Ross-Kerr, J. C. (2003d). The origins of nursing education in Canada: The emergence and growth of diploma programs. In J. Ross-Kerr & M. L. Wood (Eds.), *Canadian nursing: Issues and perspectives* (4th ed., pp. 330-331). Toronto, Ontario, Canada: Mosby.

Royal Commission on Aboriginal Peoples. (1996). *Report on the Royal Commission on Aboriginal Peoples (Vol. 3): Gathering strength.* Ottawa: Government of Canada.

Ryten, E. (2002). *Planning for the future: Nursing human resource projections.* Ottawa, Ontario, Canada: Canadian Nurses Association.

Sepehri, A., & Chernomas, R. (2004). Is the Canadian health care system fiscally sustainable? *International Journal of Health Services, 34*(2), 229-243.

Shamian, J., O'Brien-Pallas, L., Kerr, M., Koehoorn, M. W., Thomson, D., & Alksnis, C. (2001). *Effects of job strain, hospital organizational factors and individual characteristics on work related disability among nurses* (final report submitted to Workers' Safety Insurance Board). Ottawa, Ontario, Canada: Workers' Safety Insurance Board.

Shannon, V., & French, S. E. (2005). The impact of the re-engineered world of health-care in Canada on nursing and patient outcomes. *Nursing Inquiry, 12*(3), 231-239.

Shaw, J. (2004, Sept.-Oct.). From classroom to clinician: A glimpse of the evolution of nursing education through four centuries. *Registered Nurses Journal, 16*(5), 18-19. Toronto, ON: Registered Nurses Association of Ontario.

Sinclair, M. (2001). *Report of the Manitoba pediatric cardiac surgery inquest: An inquiry into 12 deaths of the Winnipeg Health Sciences Centre in 1994.* Associate Chief Justice Sinclair Commissioner. Winnipeg, Manitoba, Canada: Government of Manitoba.

Snowdon, A., Miller-Polgar, J., Potvin, J., & Follo, G. (2004). *Factors influencing child safety seat misuse.* Society of Automotive Engineering. World Congress, Report #04b-98.

Standing Senate Committee on Social Affairs, Science and Technology. (2002). *The health of Canadians—The federal role: Recommendations for reform* (Vol. 6) (first report on the State of the health care system in Canada, chaired by M. K. Kirby). Ottawa, Ontario, Canada: Queens Printer.

Statistics Canada. (1998). *The Daily: Monday, December 14th, 1999.* Retrieved February 23, 2008, from http://www.statcan.ca/Daily/English/981214/d981214.htm

Statistics Canada. (2003a). *Longitudinal Survey of Immigrants to Canada: Process, progress and prospects,* Statistics Canada Catalogue no. 89-611.

Statistics Canada. (2003b). *Deaths 2003.* Retrieved December 20, 2008, from http://www.statcan.gc.ca/pub/84f0211x/2003000/4067959_eng.htm

Statistics Canada. (2004). *Birth rate at all-time low.* Retrieved November 29, 2004, from http://www.statcan.ca/english/ads/11-002-XIE/2004/04/11804/11804_02p.htm

Statistics Canada. (2006). *The Daily: Monday, July 31st, 2006.* Retrieved February 22, 2008, from http://www.statcan.ca/Daily/English/060731/d060731b.htm

Statistics Canada. (2007a). *Portrait of the Canadian population in 2006: Highlights.* Retrieved February 22, 2008, from http://www12.statcan.ca/english/census06/analysis/popdwell/highlights.cfm

Statistics Canada. (2007b). *Portrait of the Canadian population in 2006, by age and sex: Highlights.* Retrieved February 22, 2008, from http://www12.statcan.ca/english/census06/analysis/agesex/highlights.cfm

Statistics Canada. (2007c). *Immigration in Canada: A portrait of the foreign-born population, 2006 census: Highlights.* Retrieved February 23, 2008, from http://www12.statcan.ca/english/census06/analysis/immcit/highlights.cfm

Statistics Canada. (2008a). *Aboriginal peoples in Canada in 2006: Inuit, Métis and First Nations, 2006 Census: Highlights.* Retrieved February 23, 2008, from http://www12.statcan.ca/english/census06/analysis/aboriginal/highlights.cfm

Statistics Canada. (2008b). *Gross domestic product, expenditure-based (quarterly).* Retrieved February 24, 2008, from http://www40.statcan.cal/101/cst01/gdpa02a.htm

Storch, J. (2003). The Canadian health care system and Canadian nurses. In M. McIntyre & E. Thomlinson (Eds.), *Realities of Canadian nursing: Professional, practice, and power issues* (pp. 35-59). New York: Lippincott Williams & Wilkins.

Torrance, G. (1998). Hospitals as health factories. In D. Coburn, C. D'Arcy, & G. M. Torrance (Eds.), *Health and Canadian society* (3rd ed., pp. 438-455). Toronto, Ontario, Canada: University of Toronto Press.

Toupin, G. (2002, July 21). La Suisse maraude les infirmières québécoises [The Swiss recruit Quebec nurses]. *La Presse.*

Tuohy, C. H. (1999). Dynamics of a changing health sphere: The United States, Britain and Canada. *Health Affairs, 18*(3), pp. 114-134.

Turner, B. (Ed.). (2004). *The Statesman's yearbook: The politics, cultures and economies of the world.* New York: Palgrave Macmillan.

Vancouver Coastal Health. (2004). Press release: *Vancouver supervised injection site saving lives.* Retrieved December 10, 2004, from http://www.vch.ca

Villeneuve, M., & MacDonald, J. (2006). *Toward 2020: Visions for nursing.* Ottawa, Canada: Canadian Nurses Association.

Waldram, J. B., Herring, D. A., & Young, T. K. (1995). *Aboriginal health in Canada: Historical, cultural, and epidemiological perspectives.* Toronto, Ontario, Canada: University of Toronto Press.

Wallace, E. (1980). The origin of the Social Welfare State in Canada, 1867-1900. In C. A. Meilicke & J. L. Storch (Eds.), *Perspectives on Canadian health and social services policy: History and emerging trends* (pp. 25-37). Ann Arbor, MI: Health Administration Press.

Wasekeesikaw, F. H. (2003). Challenges for the new millennium: nursing in First Nations communities. In M. McIntyre & E. Thomlinson (Eds.), *Realities of Canadian nursing: Professional, practice, and power issues* (pp. 447-469). Philadelphia, PA: Lippincott Williams & Wilkins.

Way, C., Baker, N., Chubbs, D., Davis, J., Barrett, B., & Parfay, P. (2001). *The impact of health care reforms on registered nurses* (final report). St. John's, Nfld: Department of Health and Community Services.

Weir, G. M. (1932). *Survey of nursing education in Canada.* Toronto, Ontario, Canada: University of Toronto Press.

West, J. (2004). *The USA and Canada 2004* (6th ed.). New York: Europa Publications.

White, P., Pringle, D., Doran, D., & McGillis-Hall, L. (2005). The nursing and health outcomes project. *Canadian Nurse, 101*(9), 15-18.

Williams, P. A., Deber, R., Baranek, P., & Gildiner, A. (2001). From medicare to home care: Globalization, state retrenchment, and the profitization of Canada's health-care system. In P. Armstrong, H. Armstrong, & D. Coburn (Eds.), *Unhealthy times: Political economy perspectives on health and care in Canada* (pp. 7-30). New York: Oxford University Press.

Wood, M. J. (2003). Entry to practice: Striving for the baccalaureate standard. In J. Ross-Kerr & M. L. Wood (Eds.), *Canadian nursing: Issues and perspectives* (4th ed., pp. 369-383). Toronto, Ontario, Canada: Mosby.

Wood, M. J., Giovannetti, P., & Ross-Kerr, J. C. (2004). *The Canadian Ph.D. in nursing: A discussion paper.* Ottawa, Ontario, Canada: Canadian Association of Schools of Nursing.

Wood, M. J., & Ross-Kerr, J. C. (2003a). The financing of nursing research in Canada. In J. C. Ross-Kerr & M. L. Wood (Eds.), *Canadian nursing: Issues and perspectives* (4th ed., pp. 158-176). Toronto, Ontario, Canada: Mosby.

Wood, M. J., & Ross-Kerr, J. (2003b). The growth of graduate education in nursing in Canada. In J. Ross-Kerr & M. L. Wood (Eds.), *Canadian nursing: Issues and perspectives* (4th ed., pp. 467-488). Toronto, Ontario, Canada: Mosby.

Woodward, D., Drager, N., Beaglehole, R., & Lipson, D. (2001). Globalization and health: A framework for analysis and action. *Bulletin of the World Health Organization, 79*(9), 875-881.

World Health Organization [WHO]. (1978). *Primary health care report of the International Conference on primary health care, Alma-Ata, USSR.* September 6-12, Geneva, Author.

World Health Organization [WHO]. (1986). Health and Welfare Canada and the Canadian Public Health Association *Ottawa charter for health promotion.* Ottawa, Ontario, Canada: Canadian Public Health Association.

Wotherspoon, T. (1994). Nursing education: Professionalism and control. In B. S. Bolaria & H. D. Dickinson (Eds.), *Health, illness and health care in Canada* (2nd ed., pp. 570-591). Toronto, Ontario, Canada: Hartcourt Brace and Company, Canada.

CHAPTER 8

Nursing in the United States

Karen Lucas Breda, Evelyn L. Barbee, and Maria Zadoroznyj

Today, the nearly 3 million nurses constitute the largest group of health care workers in the United States, and as such, one would expect them to have formidable influence both within the health care professions and over health care legislation (ANA, 2006). However, reality is not quite so simple and in this chapter, to analyze nursing in the United States, we need to focus on its situation within the global context and through the lenses of nursing's historical, social, and political economic dimensions. To do so, we also explore the evolution of modern nursing within the context of the U.S. political economy.

CONCEPTUALIZATION

The lens of critical political economy provides an innovative theoretical perspective by which to analyze the health care system and nursing care. It allows us to consider how the overarching political, economic, and cultural systems have influenced the real-life circumstances of nursing education and of nurses' work as well as to consider how the political economy and cultural systems have perpetuated the contradictions inherent in the health care system itself. Regrettably, our consideration in this chapter can only briefly highlight the major issues connected to the political economy of health care in the United States. Nevertheless, we attempt to elucidate the relationships among nursing, health care service, and health outcomes, and focus particularly on their impact on the development of nursing education systems and the role of the nurse.

As Merrill Singer points out in his 1986 article "Developing a Critical Perspective in Medical Anthropology," published in *Medical Anthropology Quarterly,* a central concern for critical social scientists is the explanation of the relationships among macro- and micro-levels of phenomena. In delineating the core propositions and research questions of critical medical anthropology, Singer (1986, pp. 128-129) identifies six key relationships:

1. location of the microcosm within the changing structure of global social relationships;
2. understanding the interrelationships between class and imperialism in the capitalistic world system;
3. investigation of the social origins of illness;
4. analysis of the nature of the health care system within the context of capitalism;
5. recognition of the power relationships within medicine; and
6. concern with the diversity and changing patterns of health and health related behaviors around the world.

In our examination of U.S. nursing, we address generally these propositions, and we use the concepts of social class, race, and gender to further expose imbedded patterns.

As we do so, we draw on the rich traditions in the critical political economy of health literature. Guiding our analysis are the works of Navarro (1979, 1986, 1990, 1999, 2003), Elling (1980, 1986, 1994, 2007), Waitzkin (1983), McKinlay (1984, 2002), Doyle (1979), Singer (1986, 1998), Singer & Baer (1995), and Baer, Singer, and Susser (2003). In addition, while research on U.S. nursing as a category of work is limited, several excellent studies conducted by critical theorists do exist (Brannon, 1990, 1994, 1996; Melosh, 1982; Packham, 1992; Reverby, 1987; Sacks, 1988; Wagner, 1980; Zadoroznyj, 1990). Finally, important English language critiques on nursing in Canada (Coburn, 1988), Australia (Street, 1992), South Africa (Marks, 1994, Rispel & Schneider, 1991), and Great Britain (Haywood & Fee, 1992) augment our analysis, though we recognize the uniqueness of political economy, cultural and ideological dimensions vary cross-nationally.

Economic globalization, misunderstood by many to be simply "the increasing connectedness of worldwide exchange," is, in reality, the growth of global capitalism. In the United States, economic globalization ignited neoliberal economic reforms in the 1980s, which in turn brought job restructuring and a new "lean" economy (Moody, 1997) with subsequent ramifications on all segments of society—including on the health care system in general and on nursing specifically. Thus, in order to understand today's reality in nursing and health care, it is essential to comprehend how nursing fits into the historical developments—including ideological, cultural, and structural—of the staunchly market-based capitalist health care system in the United States.

In brief, then, this chapter explores the historical political economy of nursing as an occupational category by considering the role of nursing leadership and the evolution of nursing educational systems, unions, and professional organizations. Also, we examine how the broad biomedical industrial complex, biomedical physicians, health administrators, and health systems interfaced with nursing to shape its trajectory. Finally, we consider how issues of social class, race, and gender intersect with each other as well as consider the current crisis in the supply of nurses and its implications for the future of nursing.

THE LAND AND PEOPLE OF THE UNITED STATES

The United States is geographically situated between the North Atlantic Ocean on the east and the North Pacific Ocean on the west and borders the countries of Canada to the north and Mexico to the south. It is the world's third most populated country, with more than 300 million people on one of the world's largest land masses. Compared with other countries in the Western Hemisphere, it is "about half the size of South America (or slightly larger than Brazil)" and smaller than Canada (World Fact Book, 2006). The United States was inhabited for over 15,000 years by indigenous people, and then European colonization began in earnest in the 1600s and continued for nearly 200 years. After the Revolutionary War, the United States declared independence from Great Britain in 1776 and ratified its constitution in 1788.

Although the subjugation of the U.S.'s indigenous inhabitants took place partly though warfare, murder, and enslavement, large percentages of the Native American population were lost to disease and epidemics from contact with European settlers. In fact, some estimates hold that up to 90 or 95% of some original population groups were devastated through contraction of a communicable disease (Whelchel, 2005), making the exploitation and subjugation of the remainder easy.

In addition to the colonization of indigenous groups, the United States had a 200-year-long history of brutal African slavery legalized through a substantial body of legislation enacted from the mid-1600s through the mid-1800s. The legislature not only made slavery a "permanent condition" for the African, but also ensured slavery's perpetuation by making all offspring of the female slave the property of the master. Additionally, slaves were denied all legal rights such as the right to own property or the right to be a part of any legal contract, even marriage (Becker, 1999). Slavery was a lucrative economic enterprise, and it fueled the profound racial bias that remains imbedded in U.S. society today allowing whites in America to retain a sense of superiority (Doane & Bonilla-Silva, 2003).

Although other waves of immigrants helped to create the racial and ethnic diversity and complexity of the present day United States, at various times, Congress established quotas to restrict the number of immigrants allowed entry to the United States from certain areas of the world. Both the Emergency Quota Act of 1921 and the Immigration Act of 1924, for example, effectively thwarted the influx of immigrants from sections of Europe and Asia. (Interestingly, those Acts placed no restrictions on immigration into the United States from Latin America including Mexico.) Ironically, many Europeans and Asians, restricted from migrating to the United States in the early part of the 20th century, chose instead to relocate to South America. These quotas on entry into the United States remained in place until the Immigration and Nationality Act of 1965 reopened U.S. borders to people from the previously restricted areas such as Southern and Eastern Europe.

Today, the U.S. population continues to grow and is increasingly diversified as a result of numerous migration waves. The 2000 census showed that people who consider themselves members of a racial or ethnic minority group make up about 30% of the population. By the year 2100, the U.S. Census Bureau estimates that those who consider themselves "non-Hispanic whites" will make up only 40% of the population. Non-Hispanic whites are defined as "people having origins in any of the original peoples of Europe, the Middle East, or North Africa" (Centers for Disease Control [CDC], 2006) and they have been historically referred to as the "majority."

This wide variety of population groups means that the need for nurses to understand diverse social and health care behaviors and attitudes is ever growing. Additionally, there are marked health inequities in the United States. People from ethnic and racial minority groups have health statistics that are significantly inferior to those of non-minorities. The U.S. Centers for Disease Control (CDC) reported that people in minority groups in the United States have a "disproportionate burden of preventable diseases, death, and disability compared with non-minorities" (2006). As a result, issues of health inequities (called health disparities in the United States) are an increasingly important public health issue.

In terms of government structure of the United States, there are 50 states, the District of Colombia, and a number of dependent areas such as Puerto Rico and the United States Virgin Islands. They are governed by a constitution-based federal republic with Washington, DC, as the nation's capital.

The U.S. benefits from large stores of natural resources such as coal, copper, and lead. It is also home to thousands of plant and tree species, including the largest and oldest-known trees in the world, the so-called "Redwoods" located in California. However, the United States is also the "largest single emitter of carbon dioxide from the burning of fossil fuels; water pollution from runoff of pesticides and fertilizers" (World Fact Book, 2006). While the United States has some history of land conservation and the creation of national parks and forests, its alarming deforestation, mining, and cattle ranching policies have taken a large toll on the environment. In fact, the U.S. record on health and environmental issues stands apart from many other industrialized countries. Its failure to ratify the popular Kyoto Protocol (Treaty) restricting greenhouse gas emissions is just one example.

The United States has an intensely market-oriented political economy; corporations, businesses, and wealthy private individuals make many of the decisions for the country. When compared to other countries (particularly Canada, Western Europe, Japan), U.S. companies, including health care corporations, have great leeway and autonomy in decision making pertaining to lay-offs, hiring and firing, product development, and facilities expansion. The U.S. labor market can be described as a "two-tier labor market" in which "those at the bottom lack the education and the professional/technical skills of those at the top and, more and more, fail to get comparable pay raises, health insurance coverage, and other benefits" (World Fact Book, 2006).

Wealth in the United States is increasingly concentrated in the top echelon of society. Even conservative former Federal Reserve Chairman Alan Greenspan admitted that the "rich-poor gap" in the United States has grown so quickly and is continuing to widen so much that it could have major effects on the nature of the U.S. economy (Greir, 2005). Certainly, it is the excessive and growing wealth at the top (particularly the top ½ to 1% of the population) combined with the shrinking incomes of the poor and working class shift the dynamics even more dramatically. The stark reality is that for over 30 years, privileged members of U.S. society have realized most of the economic gains, while the lower 80% of the population is actually worse economically (Economist, 2004). Most of the gains in GNP have been realized by a small percentage. The rest of the population is both worse economically and in health status than it was in the 1970s.

U.S. state-financed services such as welfare and universal health care commonly referred to as the "social safety net" are small, especially when the United States is compared to Canada, its neighbor immediately to the north. The rationale for a strong social safety net is to lessen overall poverty and to help prevent families and individuals from falling below the "poverty line." In the United States, those in support of a strong social safety net demonstrate that it improves the entire society's quality of life. On the other hand, conservatives argue that subsidizing business efforts will help all members of society when the economic benefits of business eventually "trickle down" to lower socio-economic groups. Despite the conservatives' reasoning, their scenarios have not played out. As already stated, a polarization of income concentrations has occurred and is more and more prominent among the U.S. workforce.

Finally, while English is spoken by the majority of the population, Spanish is the second most frequently spoken language and the percentage of Spanish speakers is increasing. Language and cultural diversity, lack of access to heath care, and issues associated with poverty all greatly affect health care and health outcomes.

THE POLITICAL ECONOMY OF U.S. HEALTH CARE

While the United States is one of the highest ranking industrial countries economically, its health care statistics fall well below the norm. Ironically, while the United States spends more on health care than any other industrialized country and its physicians earn more than anywhere else (Reinhardt, Hussey, & Anderson, 2002), the overall performance of the U.S. health care system and its ability to provide services to all of the population are inadequate. The World Health Organization (WHO, 2006) ranked the United States 72nd in the category of health system performance. In this ranking the United States placed below Chile (23rd), Canada (35th), Colombia (51st), Mexico (63rd), and even Argentina (71st). Of the case studies in this volume, only 78th place Brazil ranked lower than the United States in health system performance.

Population Health

The number of people over 65 in the United States is increasing faster than the population as a whole, placing an additional economic burden on the health care system. The burden is acute because U.S. health care is a system organized more toward costly treatment and intervention than it is toward less costly prevention measures. Interestingly, the "number of people in correctional institutions almost doubled (from 1.1 million to 2.0 million)" (National Center for Health Statistics, 2006, p. 18). Indeed, the overall rate of institutionalization in the United States saw a sharp rise to over 4 million persons. This increase occurred when the trend in most countries in the Americas is for deinstitutionalization. The rise in U.S. incarcerations rates is attributed to such policies as longer jail sentences and a more punitive climate for criminal offenses. Although often overlooked, the doubled number of incarcerated Americans poses unique challenges for the health care system in general and for nursing in particular.

As already noted, the number of people of color and ethnic minorities in the United States is also increasing. In recent polls almost "30% of adults and almost 40% of children identified themselves as Hispanic, Black, Asian, American Indian or Alaska Native, or Native Hawaiian or Other Pacific Islander" (National Center for Health Statistics, 2006, p. 20). Because the United States has a history of heath care inequities and disparities among different race and ethnic groups and is currently unable to reverse this trend, these data do not bore well for health projections.

Also public health issues, such as obesity, cost the U.S. public sector billions of dollars every year. For example, the chronic illness consequences of obesity, such as diabetes and heart disease, add to the ongoing cost of treating the U.S. population. A study from the Centers of Disease Control reported that US$75 billion is spent to treat obesity per year, about half of which (US$40 billion) is funded through public taxes. Yet, despite this burden to the population, the United States has blocked efforts by the World Health Organization to change the practices of fast food industries stating that "it [U.S.] does not accept that heavy marketing of high-calorie processed foods is causing obesity" (Jalil, 2004, p. 1).

The relationship between poverty and poor health is well documented. Poverty is one of the primary causes of disease (Fort, Mercer, & Gish, 2004, Labonte, 2003). Access to affordable, quality health care is associated with general well-being. Conversely, the lack of access negatively affects entire community systems. In the United States in particular, the lack of universal health care and adequate welfare is cited as one of the major indicators for decreasing quality of life for large segments of the population. In this regard, the United States is in stark contrast to other countries. It is one of the very few countries that does not have a publicly-funded universal health care system. Instead, the United States relies primarily on market-driven private health insurance plans that are historically connected to employment and partially paid for by employer contributions. Although some population groups in the United States are covered by government-sponsored health insurance plans, millions of people in the United States have no health insurance at all. In fact, the long-standing debate over government versus privately-sponsored health insurance plans is unresolved. Our analysis in this section touches on the major points of the debate and discusses how the debate relates to U.S. nursing.

U.S. Health Care Financing

The evolution of health care financing in the United States has a particularly unique trajectory shaped by its culture and political economy. The present-day record high costs of U.S. health care, the millions of people who lack health care insurance coverage, and the alarming inequities in health status among differing racial, ethnic, and class groups are complex social issues (Budrys, 2005; Erlen, 2005; Thomasson, 2007; U.S. Department of Health and Human Services, 2005).

By 1920 most industrialized countries (particularly in Europe, but also in Latin America) had adopted some form of a compulsory national health insurance which provided basic coverage to citizens for medical costs. Yet, a similar proposal in the United States during that period was strongly opposed by physician groups, pharmacists, and insurance companies who feared the loss of profits. Interestingly, the top U.S. labor leaders, although not the rank and file union members, also opposed nationalized health insurance (Starr, 1982). And so, the initial bill for compulsory health insurance failed to pass. Over the years the United States had repeated near successes in passing a mandatory, universal, government-sponsored health insurance bill, but each time powerful opponents successfully blocked the efforts. To offset the criticism for their part in blocking the legislation, insurance companies offered private policies to cover hospital costs, initially begrudgingly as they did not see it as a profitable endeavor. Ironically, the private health insurance business proved to have large profit margins.

Historical events also affected the development of U.S. health care financing. The economic collapse connected to the 1929 Stock Market Crash and the subsequent Great Depression years not only devastated the general economy, but also cut seriously into the viability of the budding health care industry. Hospital and physician income declined, nurses struggled to find employment, and the hospital and health care industry stagnated (Brannon, 1994). Between 1928 and 1935, over 300 U.S. hospitals closed their doors (Budrys, 2005). In this precarious economic climate, the need for hospitals to remain open and for health care providers to seek out a living forced them to find alternative methods of payment so as to assure themselves an income.

U.S. Health Insurance

Over the next several decades, health care insurance plans began offering hospitals a means of subsistence in the form of reimbursements. Some physicians and physician groups were able to negotiate reimbursement arrangements through health care insurance plans, thus regaining their economic independence. While the spread of these plans began slowly, in later years they expanded "at a phenomenal rate" (Kalisch & Kalisch, 1995, p. 305). Nurses, on the other hand, were unable to successfully negotiate reimbursement for their services through insurance plans. As a result of this failure, nurses lost their chance for economic and professional independence and autonomy, putting them in the precarious position of wage work, primarily in hospital settings (Ashley, 1976). Additionally, without the aid of collective organizations to negotiate wage packages, nurses were reduced to accepting grossly inferior wages and compensation.

Private Employer-Sponsored Health Care Insurance Plans

In lieu of compulsory national health insurance plans, the United States developed private employer-sponsored health care insurance plans that were offered as a benefit of employment. Initially, employers who were unable to pay competitive wages offered instead health care benefits to entice people to work for them. Eventually, private health care insurance plans offered through employers became the customary way for the U.S. population to access health care benefits. This system worked, in part, because the cost to employers for group health benefits was remarkably affordable.

One of the early grand initiatives was the privately owned and administered Blue Cross and Blue Shield. Also known as "The Blues," they were voluntary insurance agencies created by the medical profession and some hospitals in lieu of federally-sponsored mandatory insurance agencies. By the 1940s, just several decades after the inception of Blue Cross and Blue Shield plans, the "movement represented a major financing alternative, countering forces that had long lobbied politically for a form of national health insurance, a concept opposed vehemently by private medicine" (Sultz & Young, 2004, p. 233). Although no longer mutualized, Blue Cross and Blue Shield still exist as private entities in addition to the many other prepaid hospitalization and illness plans (Budrys, 2005; Sultz & Young, 2004).

The availability of private voluntary insurance plans in the United States decreased the perceived need for a mandatory, comprehensive, federally-funded health insurance program. These voluntary health insurance agencies did not infringe on the autonomy of the physician regarding the financial aspect of services, (that is, the concept of "fee for service" remained intact), and they reimbursed hospitals high rates for their services. So, while initially hesitant to support the plans, most physicians and hospitals became fully supportive because they retained a broad discretion over the parameters of the insurance plans and they gained economically. Thus began a long-standing, imbedded practice in the United States where the private health care insurance industry became intimately intertwined with the free market-dominated health care system. Consequently, both systems profited and have prevailed for many decades.

Over the subsequent years, a number of U.S. presidents and legislators tried unsuccessfully to pass legislation mandating a federally-funded, compulsory, national health insurance plan. In 1965, the combination of a Democratic president (Lyndon B. Johnson) and a liberal Democratic congress were able to pass legislation that at the least introduced an exceedingly modified health reform law. The "Medicare" and "Medicaid" plans established a solid role for the federal government in providing health care financing to specific (and, at that time, relatively small) portions of the population. Medicare provided funding for services to the elderly and Medicaid provided funding for services to the very poor. Yet, physician organizations, mainly the influential American Medical Association (AMA) and hospital groups, particularly the dominant American Hospital Association (AHA) opposed the Medicare and Medicaid plans and worked hard to limit their expansion and power. As a result of this, Medicare and Medicaid are not comprehensive programs and have severe limitations in coverage. Individuals who can afford to can make up the gap in coverage, sometimes called the "Medi-gap" by purchasing private insurance policies specifically designed for just that purpose (Budrys, 2005; Sultz & Young, 2004).

Despite Medicare and Medicaid, millions of Americans remain without any health insurance, and several million more are "underinsured" with insufficient coverage. Today, government-sponsored health care (Medicare, Medicaid, and health insurance for military personnel) cover a little more than 30% of those people who have health insurance.

However, the government-sponsored Medicare and Medicaid plans are more costly that originally intended and this, combined with record cost increases in private health insurance plans, have driven up the cost of U.S. health care in general. Another cause of the soaring cost of private and pubic health care is the so-called "medical industrial complex" which spurred the development of costly medical treatments that were reimbursable by the insurance plans. Under this system hospitals and physicians avoided non-reimbursable, though necessary, care such as preventative care. It is well known that when permitted, U.S. hospitals and physicians duplicated services based on profitability motives rather than on actual demographic and medical need. For example, the duplication of highly-profitable cardiac care surgical units within close geographical areas often took place. This phenomenon, combined with the lack of attention to prevention and primary care services and an overabundance of medical specialists, contributed greatly to the present day fragmentation of U.S. health care services (Favro, 2006).

In the United States, the debate over government-driven versus market-driven financing of health care intensified after the institution of Medicaid and Medicare. Increasing health care costs coupled with the growing numbers of working and middle class people with inadequate or no health care benefits are stark realities today. Medicare and Medicaid cover only the very poor and the elderly and are non-comprehensive and non-universal. Unfortunately, instead of being a comprehensive government-sponsored universal health care system where the entire population would have health insurance benefits, the Medicare and Medicaid programs were made available only to limited portions of the population, crippling their effectiveness. And then, rather than successfully expanding the programs, conservative analysts have blamed Medicare and Medicaid as the *cause* of health care cost increases and indirectly implicated them for fragmentation and failure of the entire U.S. health care system, instead of viewing U.S. Medicare and Medicaid systems as the *result* of a fragmented health care financing system. Indeed, the strong corporate push is to reform Medicare and Medicaid to move away from government-driven methods and toward market-driven methods (Families USA, 2006).

Conservative administrations have successfully passed so-called Medicare and Medicaid reforms that reduce the degree of government sponsorship and increased the degree of market sponsorship in the system. For example, in 2003, the U.S. Congress passed the Medicare Modernization Act (MMA) to hold down the cost of prescription drugs to senior citizens and people with disabilities. Paradoxically, since that time, costs have risen sharply with private insurance companies and the pharmaceutical industry realizing great profits.

Clinton Health Care Plan

A significant push for a universal nationalized health care system in the United States came in 1993 during the early years of Bill Clinton's first presidential administration. In response to popular pressure, President Clinton established the Task Force on National Health Care Reform soon after taking office and he put his wife Hillary Rodham Clinton in charge as director. The Clinton Health Care Plan proposed a mandate for all employers to provide health insurance coverage for all of their workers through a system of health maintenance organizations called HMOs. The complex, but universal plan would have covered the remaining citizens through state subsidized HMOs. In the process of the health care reform initiative, First Lady Hillary Rodham Clinton became a strong advocate for nursing. The health care reform she proposed envisioned a central role for nurses whom she viewed as essential to the delivery of primary care health services. While some nurses recognized Hillary Clinton as an ally, the relatively apolitical U.S. nursing workforce did not make a significant and concerted effort to rally around her or the President's plan.

Because many liberals backed the Clinton Health Care Plan and the Democratic Party, of which Clinton was a member, controlled both houses of congress (the House of Representative and the Senate), it appeared, at least initially, that the Clinton Health Care Plan would pass. Regrettably, a strong alliance among insurance companies and conservative groups countered the burgeoning health reform movement and the Clinton Health Plan did not pass. Instead, Congress expanded a system of "Managed Care" networks and Health Maintenance Organizations (HMOs) first conceptualized by President Richard Nixon in the 1970s and later developed by President Ronald Reagan in the 1980s. (Currently, welfare entitlements were significantly cut along with the partial dismantling of the so-called safety net for the poor and working class.)

Managed Care Era

Managed Care brought dramatic change to health care services in the United States with questionable effects on overall population health and an uncertain course for nursing. Since the 1990s when managed care networks and health maintenance organizations (HMOs) were extensively implemented into the U.S. health care system, significant changes have transpired for both providers and users.

U.S. Hospital Industry

To understand the evolution of nursing in the United States, it is essential to understand the historical trajectory of hospitals as the primary site of the health care delivery system. Hospitals hold significant ideological power themselves and are tied ideologically to other institutions of civil society (e.g., churches and schools) as well as to the institutions of political society (e.g., the legislature, the military, and state institutions) (Gramsci, 1991 [1930]; Hirst, 1979). Similarly, social relations and cultural practices associated with "medicine" are related to the social relations and cultural practices of priests, politicians, and professionals. In the well-known words of Rudolf Virchow, the 19th century physician and social advocate, "[p]olitics is medicine on a larger scale" (Elling, 1986). With the evolution of monopoly capitalism in the late 19th century, U.S. hospitals became even more connected to the market economy and to profit motives. Yet, at the same time, hospitals remained the location of cultural and social practices that have meaning and implications for U.S. society.

During the 19th and 20th centuries, hospitals took on a particularly powerful role and today continue to gain even more hegemony (Breda, 1992). U.S. hospitals, many of them privately owned, evolved within an active capitalist environment and, from the start, were shaped by that political economic environment. Today, hospitals are a part of the larger "biomedical industrial complex" and as such, are subject to the demands of global capitalism.

In the 19th century and earlier, the hospital was primarily housing for the sick, poor, and the insane: "hospitals had been primarily religious and charitable institutions for tending the sick, rather than medical institutions for their cure" (Starr, 1982, p. 143). As long as hospitals offered services primarily to the indigent, there was little need for them to maintain quality services for patients. But when hospitals began to seek paying patients, they transformed their services, creating the basis for health care as a new, lucrative industry. In brief, the modern hospital in the United States emerged to create an environment that would support paying patients and are now the central workplace and "workshop" for doctors and the biomedical establishment, even though "before the Civil War, an American doctor might contentedly spend an entire career in practice without setting foot on a hospital ward" (Starr, 1982, p. 146).

Early on, U.S. medical education was not affiliated with hospitals, and hospitals were not a primary nor even a secondary center of learning for physicians. Physicians learned their trade in apprenticeship arrangements. In fact, only a small percentage of the medical colleges offered academic content through formal university coursework. Ironically, it was not science that sparked the advancement of hospitals.

In the 19th century and earlier, when someone became ill, the families who could afford it, hired private physicians and trained or untrained nurses to provide care for the sick in the home. Servants and family members tended to the immediate needs of the sick. In families with economic means, the physician also routinely visited patients at home and nurses were hired.

At the time, U.S. hospitals were dirty, dreaded, and undesirable places. In order for paying customers to seek out hospital care, a major evolution was necessary. Hospitals needed to be converted into clean and functional facilities, respectable places of business with decent accommodations and reliable, efficient staff. In turn, the demand for staff who were skilled in meeting the needs of the sick in order to minister to the new hospital clientele prodded the creation of nursing training schools (Kalisch, 1986).

Why schools of nursing and their "students" became so integral to the budding U.S. hospital business is inextricably linked to the early phases of capitalism and the need for a reliable, dutiful, and obedient workforce from whom surplus value (in the form of labor) could be extracted. Since only a small percentage of hospitals and nurses were affiliated with religious organizations (unlike in Latin America), there were not sufficient numbers of religious sisters and nuns available to provide free labor in U.S. hospitals. So U.S. hospitals sought additional sources of free labor by opening their own schools of nursing and requiring their nursing students to provide the labor in the hospitals as part of their coursework.

U.S. Biomedicine

The 19th century was a period in the United States during which chiropractic, osteopathic, naturopathic, and homeopathic medical systems competed for survival with *allopathic* medicine, dominant today and often called regular medicine, biomedicine, or Western medicine. During the 19th century, numerous osteopathic, naturopathic, homeopathic, and chiropractic colleges of medicine offered solid programs of study, and in fact, they outnumbered colleges of allopathic medicine which had not yet gained a solid foothold in the U.S. economy (Baer, 2001).

Allopathic physicians (also now called "regular" physicians in many reports) not only competed with naturopathic, osteopathic, homeopathic, and chiropractic physicians, but also with indigenous healers, shaman, and healing priests. Doctors of allopathic medicine resisted the practices of those using other systems of healing and those who advocated a holistic, naturalistic, or even spiritualistic view of illness and health. Early on, allopathic medicine tried "to counteract or even combat the forces of nature" (Baer, 2001, p. 9) and it used invasive techniques such as bleeding, cupping, and inducing vomiting and diarrhea to rid the body of disease.

Later on, the discovery and dissemination of the so-called "germ theory" legitimized biology, human pathology, and situated biological determinism as the basis for allopathic medicine. Germ theory supported the idea that disease should be diagnosed by finding abnormalities in cells and that treatment should focus on reversing the abnormalities. This view privileged cell biology but ignored the social origins of disease. Consequently, and particularly after publication of the Flexner Report in 1910, germ theory facilitated allopathic physicians' claim of scientific superiority over other systems of medicine and healing (Baer, 2001).

The Flexner Report is important not only for the enormous impact it had on medicine and medical education, but also for the significance it had on nursing and nursing education. Abraham Flexner, under the auspices of the Carnegie Foundation, evaluated and rated colleges of medicine and training schools in the United States and Canada. He used the elite and financially solid Johns Hopkins Medical School as the gold standard against which he evaluated the other schools. The criteria he used to evaluate and grade the schools rewarded institutions with abundant financial resources and endowments and handicapped those with limited resources.

Also, the criteria he used favored allopathic medical schools with strong coursework in the sciences and curricula that mirrored that of Johns Hopkins. Not surprisingly, Flexner did not assign good scores to medical colleges that used apprenticeships to train physicians.

One consequence of the Flexner Report was that osteopathic, naturopathic, homeopathic, and chiropractic colleges of medicine as well as many small allopathic colleges of medicine lost funding and most were forced to close. Additionally, in the wake of the Flexner Report, large philanthropies such as the Rockefeller Foundation chose to support only those schools rated as superior, a rating Flexner gave only to well-positioned allopathic colleges of medicine. Ironically, homeopathy was John D. Rockefeller's preferred system of medicine (Baer, 2001). In fact, in earlier decades homeopathic physicians were the practitioners of choice among many wealthy families.

Another consequence of the Flexner Report was that "the doors (of medical education) were shut to blacks, to the majority of women and to poor white men" (Ehrenreich & English, 1972, p. 33) because only the most elite biomedical colleges remained open, and those were way out of the financial reach of all but the wealthiest students. Of the 186 schools Flexner surveyed between 1907 and 1909, 106 shut their doors, leaving only 80 in existence by the year 1920 (Budrys, 2005).

With the Flexner Report's sanctioning allopathic medicine, other forms of medicine and small allopathic colleges of medicine that catered to women, minorities, and people of modest means, lost power and prestige along with most of their public and private funding. The Flexner Report paved the way for allopathic medicine to ascend to absolute dominance in the U.S. health care market and it limited the applicant pool for medical school to affluent white males. After the Flexner Report, allopathic colleges of medicine and hospitals connected to elite institutions emerged as the dominant health system in the increasingly crowded and competitive health care marketplace. Thus, the biological sciences, including reductionism and positivism, dominated U.S. medicine and U.S. nursing. However, the stage had been set for several decades prior.

The philosophical underpinnings accompanying osteopathy, homeopathy, and other holistic healing systems posit the body as an integrated whole that cannot be fragmented or separated from the larger social context: in other words, the body is a seamless whole that is greater than the sum of its parts (Dossey, Keagan, & Guzzetta, 2005). On the other hand, allopathic medicine, or *biomedicine* as it later came to be called, adopts the principle of reductionism, viewing the body as a machine with parts that can be fixed or replaced. This perspective is compatible with the ideals of "self-reliance, rugged individualism, independence, pragmatism, [and] empiricism" (Baer, 2001, p. 35) that also represent the core values of capitalism and a capitalist way of thinking. Thus, biomedicine lent itself well to a capitalist political economic paradigm where hierarchical and patriarchal structures and institutions as well as standardization, efficiency, instrumentation, and specialization trumped a socialist paradigm where collaborative, democratic, and egalitarian social relations were primary. Baer comments on the irony of how "biomedicine":

... focused on pathogens as the cause of disease at a time when there was increasing labor unrest in the cities, populist sentiments were widespread among farmers and small-town people, and social medicine had recognized that many new illnesses had occupational and environmental underpinnings. (2001, p. 34)

In hindsight, biomedicine was the perfect partner for capitalism. The Flexner Report ensured biomedicine's position as the most accepted healing practice in the United States and its evolution as a powerful, elite, male-dominated, culturally-sterile institution. In the ensuing years, biomedicine easily gained cultural hegemony over other healing systems so that the ideas of biomedicine came to define the accepted view of health and medicine.

U.S. Biomedical Education

A market-driven economy shaped U.S. biomedical education. It evolved within an economic environment of industrialization, business, and small-scale corporations and was, from its early roots, capitalist in nature. As early as the late 1800s, physician training began to move away from informal, community-based apprenticeships with established doctors in private practice into formal education with professors in university-based schools of medicine. At the same time, the university as a social institution was undergoing a transformation comparable to that of the hospital. In the new climate of industrialization, both hospitals and universities focused increasingly on: (a) offering marketable services and (b) the production of new services. In the language of critical political economy, hospitals and universities focused on offering salable commodities.

Obviously, following the industrial model, an organized group of malleable workers was needed to provide services for the newly-conceptualized view of the hospital institution.

THE POLITICAL ECONOMY OF NURSING IN THE UNITED STATES

Before colonization, family and community members, including indigenous *healers* or *shaman,* tended to the health care needs of indigenous native people. *Shaman* used herbs and other natural remedies to heal the sick. Prayer and spirituality were integral elements of treatment. Traditional understandings of hot and cold, of energy and of a life force were part of the conceptual framework. The U.S. territory was vast, so natural regional differences existed among the scores of indigenous tribes and nations. While beliefs about sickness varied from group to group, cultural practices were all based on a holistic view of the world and of the person. North American native people lived in close proximity to the natural world and sought to have a complementary relationship with plants, animals, and the earth. Life was considered precious. But, little effort was made to prolong life as the person was viewed as a part of the greater whole.

Colonization and Slavery in the United States

Colonial rulers brought European traditions and thought to the new world, and within 300 years, colonial immigrants dominated both the native indigenous people and their land. Simultaneously, slavery added another dimension to the population. The enslavement of African tribal peoples added to the complexity of health belief systems by introducing African traditions and strategies for healing and care of the sick. Slavery also introduced a host of communicable infections and chronic diseases that were the product of colonization's and slavery's brutality and exploitation.

Both female and male members of North American slave communities carried out their own caring and healing practices. Often, slave trade broke up kinship networks and required members of different tribal groups to live and work side by side. As a result, U.S. slave communities shared a variety of resources and ideas about healing and care, creating new ways to treat illness and suffering as the slaves strove to adapt to the different climate and environment of North America. As they did so, they discovered American herbs and natural products to replace African ones.

Both indigenous North Americans and indigenous Africans provided extensive "lay nursing care." Certainly, within both groups, the line between healer and caregiver, between curer and companion is necessarily blurred. The presence of female healers and the role of women in caring for others are significant. Caregiver and healing roles in these groups were respected since survival of the entire group was dependent on the health and well-being of all of its members.

Obviously slaughter and forced resettlement of native peoples to reservations and the disintegration of their lifestyle had an enormous effect on their communities and on their cultural and healing practices. But even efforts to right these wrongs such as the dismantling of slavery in the United States (while withholding of civil rights to former slaves for a full century) had devastating consequences on the health and well-being of African Americans.

The Need for Nurses

After the American Civil War ended and U.S. slavery was abolished, the conditions of life changed dramatically for Americans. The war had devastated much of the farmland in the South. The demands of Northern industry required urban centers and a large industrial work force. Some former slaves migrated north for work, but segregation and restrictions on travel, housing, education, and other aspects of life in the North made survival for the former slaves extremely difficult.

At the same time, Caucasian immigrants from western Europe were welcomed and their migration grew at record rates. Civil institutions such as hospitals, clinics, schools, and churches were changing to meet the needs of this rapidly expanding population and the different political economy. There was no good plan to care for, house, and educate the mushrooming population. Racial prejudice, bigotry, segregation, and class strife came to define the social relations of the country.

Increases in the population occurred through immigration for over a century. The diversity and number of immigrants characterized the United States. New arrivals lived and worked alongside pre-existing populations with new immigrants arriving constantly. By the end of the 19th century, the United States was absorbing as many as 500,000 new immigrants each year (Mayer, in Baer, 1990). Of course, as the population swelled, so did the general health needs and, in particular, communicable diseases. Existing health care services were inundated with patients and unable to accommodate them.

An organized and prepared group of nurses appeared slowly in the United States during the middle to late 19th century. People willing to provide nursing care responded in increasing numbers to the needs of the population, first on an informal basis and later, as a consolidated group. The coastal cities of the northeastern part of the country were the sites of the first formal hospital-based programs of nursing. Less formal groups and programs also cropped up throughout the country, particularly in densely populated industrial areas (Dock, 1912; Kalisch & Kalisch, 2004).

Emergence of Modern Nursing in the United States

Several events in the 19th century spurred the development of an organized system of modern nursing in the United States:

1. Military conflicts such as the Civil War and the health care needs of soldiers on and off the battlefield demanded good nurses.
2. Early capitalist industry, technology, communications, and the simultaneous growth of urban areas reinforced society's desire for a formal nursing order.
3. The widespread prevalence of "communicable diseases, tuberculosis, smallpox, diphtheria, scarlet fever, yellow fever, cholera, and dysentery" (Dolan, 1969, p. 235) forced people to realize the need for nurses.

The threat of 1866 European cholera epidemic spreading to the United States and the New York City smallpox epidemic of 1874-1875 galvanized public opinion and the implementation of formal public health measures. When the worldwide influenza pandemic of 1918 that killed thousands in the United States occurred, the role of nursing in public health and the care of the sick was solidified.

Population pressure, the close proximity of living quarters in urban tenement buildings, poor sanitation, and the contamination of water spread illness in the cities. Nurses were seen as logical players to help reverse the unsanitary urban conditions and to teach the public about avoiding illness. In 1867, New York City Board of Health counsel Elisha Harris envisioned "nurses" becoming "our *missionaries of health*" (Dolan, 1969, p. 237). She saw that nurses could educate about cleanliness, disinfection, and disease prevention measures such as the isolation of the sick. Also, nurses could provide hands-on treatments that might decrease patients' suffering and enhance their comfort.

With the establishment of new hospitals arose the need for large numbers of nursing personnel to care for patients. In the rural United States, the shortage of physicians and the great distances from settlement to settlement necessitated the presence of a nurse in each community. Clearly, for nurses to function systematically and to understand the rationale for action, they needed formal education (Baer, 1990).

Capitalism Shapes Organized Nursing

Nineteenth century industrialization in Europe and the United States required an "organized corps of nurses" to staff the new health care facilities. With the advent of capitalist (market-driven) industrialization, a new ideal of nursing also appeared. Although the modern nurse first emerged because of military and religious organizations, industry and the consolidation of capital in the market economy necessitated the development of formal preparation and education for nurses. Thus, schools of nursing called "training schools" were founded to prepare nurses to work in hospital environments that catered to the needs of middle class and well-to-do families.

Some hospital-affiliated schools of nursing were connected to religious orders. In a number of cases, religious novitiates studied nursing as part of preparing for a religious order. Even in schools of nursing unaffiliated with a church, the living quarters for nursing students were located in proximity to hospitals and just as vigilantly supervised. Because of this, the students' families, particularly rural families of modest means, were often willing to permit their daughters to become nurses (Reverby, 1987).

Historically, nurses were socialized into a system that expected their adherence to rigid rules of comportment and action. Nurses were socialized to obey orders no matter how incongruent those orders were with their own needs and interests. While nurses could have organized into a formidable, unified, and vocal force, typically they did not. Ironically, nurses often aligned with their superiors rather than showing solidarity and allegiance to each other, a phenomenon labeled *cultural hegemony* by Antonio Gramsci (Femia, 1981).

In situations of unequal power relation, Gramsci's *cultural hegemony* describes how exploited groups (nurses in this case) uphold ideas propagated by dominant groups (hospital administrators and physicians) which are counter to their own interests. *Cultural hegemony* describes how dominant groups rule by consensus rather than by coercion and explains many of the contradictions that exist among social classes within a capitalist political economy (Breda, 1992; Gramsci, 1977).

Studies on nursing rarely underscore the fact that U.S. nursing grew up in the context of a capitalist political economy. Yet, not only did U.S. nursing emerge in this intensely market-driven system, but it functioned as an integral piece of labor within the capitalist political economy of health.

From the beginning of its modern period in the late 19th century, U.S. nursing repeatedly accommodated the labor market forces. When looking for work, nurses responded to changes in the private health care market by moving to new practice settings. These nurse movements were less about nurses' desires and more about where they could sell their labor.

For example, early 20th century nurses were forced to seek employment as so-called "private duty" nurses in wealthy homes because hospitals exclusively used "unpaid" student nurses to staff their wards. Nurses also accommodated the market system during the years of the Great Depression of 1929. Experienced graduate nurses, unable to find private duty work, flocked back to hospitals begging for work. Desperate financially, they worked for the minuscule wages hospitals offered them. During those difficult years, many nurses even worked in hospitals for no wages and accepted, in exchange, free room and board in the nurses' residence quarters (Ashley, 1976; Melosh, 1982; Reverby, 1987).

Historically, U.S. nursing labor was intricately tied to the rise of hospitals and the health care labor market, because hospitals owned and physically built the nursing schools next to their hospitals. These "hospital-based" apprentice-style schools of nursing fell under the hospital's jurisdiction, authority, influence, and power. When U.S. hospitals expanded or new ones were created as often happened (particularly between 1890 and 1920), almost every hospital opened its "own" school of nursing, sized proportionately to the dimension of the hospital. Thus, hospitals had a con- venient and cheap labor pool—the student nurses who, as part of their schooling, were required to work many hours per day, 6 or 7 days per week (Brannon, 1994). Additionally, hospitals occasionally "hired apprentices [students] out to private households to care for patients in their homes. The apprentice remained unpaid, but hospitals generated additional revenues through this practice" (Brannon, 1994, p. 63). At the turn of the 20th century it was so cost effective for hospitals to have schools of nursing that by 1928, there were 2,155 hospital-based schools of nursing (Melosh, 1982, p. 45) in the United States.

During that time, hospitals usually did not hire salaried teachers. Actual classroom education hours for apprentice student nurses were few and far between. When a classroom session did occur, it was often after the students had completed a long shift of work. Almost from their first day of *training* (not education), as it came to be called, student nurses were expected to staff the wards during the day and night in alternating shifts and carry out all responsibilities including those of charge nurses; in other words, student nurses assumed all the duties and responsibilities of a full-fledged graduate nurse. The curriculum of these early schools of nursing has been described as consisting of "two to three years of [hospital] ward work" (Melosh, 1982, p. 41).

Patriarchy, authoritarianism, and economic exploitation of nursing students proved to be a legacy difficult to reverse in the United States. Within the milieu of apprenticeship education, a few student nurses protested, but they were incapable of changing the system. Graduate nurses, usually outside the hospital hierarchy and devoid of power, were incapable of changing the market-based system which hospital administrators found convenient and highly profitable. Indeed, the model of hospital-based "nurses' training" was so advantageous to capitalist production that it was imbedded in modern U.S. nursing education and flourished for decades.

The concept of cultural hegemony explains how most nursing students and graduate nurses believed that the hospital-based "nurses' training" systems prepared them well and served their best interests and so through their cultural and social contexts, perpetuated the status quo. Eventually ideology shifted, and the "early nursing academics" aspired for formal university education, a method by which some nursing leaders used to resist exploitation. Simultaneously, and probably more importantly, by the mid-20th century hospitals were less interested in having nursing schools connected to their facilities as they were no longer economically profitable and in some cases, costly. Thus, nursing education slowly moved away from the hospital-based apprenticeship model and toward a university-based academic model. Subsequently, from the 1950s on, 2-year college associate degrees in nursing and numerous versions of baccalaureate degree and post-baccalaureate degree graduate programs (masters and doctoral level) proliferated.

Nursing Labor Process

No analysis of U.S. nursing is complete without addressing the work culture and the deep divisions within the nursing ranks. In *The Physician's Hand: Work, Culture, and Conflict in American Nursing,* Melosh (1982) dissected the divisions in nursing from a politico-historical perspective and found the "strength and character of nurses occupational culture, a tradition of pride in manual skills, of direct involvement with the sick, a respect for experience and often a concomitant mistrust for theory" (1982, p. 7).

Nursing chose professionalism as the route to legitimacy and as the main vehicle for developing the discipline. Nursing leaders sought status and respect for nursing by pursuing the same rights and privileges as those held by elite professions such as medicine and law. As part of the quest for professional status, nursing implemented licensing, regulations, and standardization criteria. Nursing, through its educational curriculum, aimed to identify a domain exclusive to nursing (Schwirian, 1998).

While nurses (e.g., floor duty, direct patient care, staff, and private duty nurses) came primarily from the laboring classes, nursing leaders (e.g., nursing school or hospital nursing superintendents) were long represented by an "articulate and self-conscious elite" (Melosh 1982, p. 3) that originated from the middle and even the upper middle classes. This cadre of elite nurses tried hard to recruit other nurses from the middle classes and to distance themselves from *uneducated* lay nurses who were predominantly from poor backgrounds. Historically, uneducated lay nurses provided the bulk of the labor in hospitals and other settings where sick people were found.

Taylorism

Frederick Winslow Taylor believed that employers should strive to separate the *head* or *intellectual* functions of work from the *body* or *physical* functions of work. Taylor inspired the *scientific management movement* of the late 19th century which called for managers to assume the intellectual functions of work and for front-line workers to carry out assigned duties. This division of labor was designed to create efficiency in the workplace.

Taylor based his theory of scientific management on three interrelated principles: (a) managers should separate the processes of work from the know-how of the workers; (b) managers should separate the concepts of the work from the people and places where the work is carried out; and (c) managers should use their "monopoly of knowledge" to control how the work is organized and completed. Ideally, these three principles allow owners and managers to control the processes of work to gain the greatest efficiencies and, thus, the greatest profits in a capitalist system (Braverman, 1998). By controlling the ideas and information related to the work and by maintaining full control over how the work is organized, managers could assign workers to tasks at will, substitute workers with other workers at will, and change the job duties at will. In sum, the theory of scientific management strips workers of their intellectual functions, decision-making opportunities, and autonomy on the job.

Today, *Taylorism*, as it is known, retains a solid footing. In the United States, despite the introduction of other schools of thought in industrial psychology, in human relations, and even in avant-guard management theory, the principles of scientific management remain the "bedrock of all work design" (Braverman, 1998, p. 60).

Nursing "Craft" versus "Routinized" Care

Craft is more than the ability merely to complete the task. As such, the nursing craft goes beyond the actual tasks nurses carry out and are observed completing (e.g., dispensing medications, carrying out treatments, providing personal care). Nursing craft, as any craft work, is "something stored up in the mind of the worker" (Braverman, 1998, p. 94).

This something "in the mind of the worker" involves not only hands-on skills, but also the expert, intuitive knowledge which evolves over time with experience. By separating the *head* work of nursing care from the *body* or physical work of nursing care, hospitals disregard much of the craft of nursing and use large percentages of less skilled workers to carry out many nursing functions. In the past, U.S. hospitals accomplished such separation by requiring *student* nurses to supply free labor during their apprenticeships. Presently, hospitals use auxiliary nurses (nurses' aides or patient care assistants) who have no formal nursing education to carry out much of nursing labor and they are paid wages far below nurses' wages.

The principles of Taylor's scientific management help explain why nursing labor was routinized, standardized, and stratified. Taylorism stripes "workers of craft knowledge and autonomous control and confront[s] them with a fully thought-out labor process in which they function as cogs and levers" (Braverman, 1998, p. 94). When the U.S. labor market implemented the principles of scientific management, almost anyone, even nursing students without experience or valuable skills in clinical judgment, could be used to carry out nursing functions, increasing, as previously noted, profits for hospitals and other health care facilities.

There was also more specialization so that only certain types of nurses could perform certain kinds of tasks. This specialization led to *piecemeal nursing care,* the antithesis of total patient care. Yet, piecemeal nursing care suits scientific management principles because nurses function in limited roles, believing that they are capable of doing only a small piece of the total nursing job.

Under the theory of scientific management, administrative nurses and physicians serve as intellectual fonts of information. Bolstering this concept, the apprenticeship model of nursing education in hospital-based schools kept nurses from making autonomous decisions about patient care. Instead, nurses followed orders and adhered to hospital rules and regulations.

One might ask how could "students" function in the role of the nurse before they completed their education? The answer lies in part because of scientific management, the intellectual and the physical work are separated, and the staff nurses in hospitals were expected to leave the intellectual work to the physician, the head nurse, and the nursing supervisor. In fact, biomedical physicians served as the brains of the nursing production process, together with supervisory nurses and head nurses who closely monitored the actions of ward nurses and visiting nurses. Highly-delineated hospital policies, procedures, and rigid hospital schedules provided the template for nurses to carry out nursing functions, many of which were task-oriented.

Thus, it was administrative (supervisory) nurses' responsibility to make sure staff nurses followed the biomedical physicians' orders as well as to curb and limit staff nurses' autonomy. By functioning as authoritarian figures, administrative nurses helped to maintain the status quo and the hegemony of the physician and the hospital administration.

U.S. Nursing and Scientific Management

Today, the environments in which actual hands-on nursing work takes place includes such environments as the hospital ward, the clinic, the nursing home, the school nurses' room, and the patient's home. These diverse settings are nursing's *shop floor*, the point of production for nurses and nursing labor (Packham, 1992).

Historically, "team nursing" was the dominant form of organization of U.S. nursing labor. Headed by registered nurses (RNs), who organized the assignments, the "teams" divided nursing functions hierarchically according to skill and level of education. Team nursing divided tasks into discrete units, thus it was easy to apply scientific management principles. However, such separation of the intellectual from the physical work of nursing is artificial, as nursing is a craft and the nurse is a craftsperson. In fact, during the 1970s, U.S. nursing resisted team nursing by philosophically opposing the breakup of its work into tasks that could be further subdivided and doled out as separate, exclusive units. The nursing profession argued that it is a total occupation and that nurses could provide cost effective comprehensive care to patients. They pushed for primary nursing (Brannon, 1990).

Introduced into U.S. hospitals in the 1970s, primary nursing has RNs assume all of the nursing care for their patients. It unifies nursing tasks, thus making the application of scientific management principles difficult, if not impossible. In the move to primary nursing, nurses succeeded briefly in dismantling the long tradition of "team nursing" where RNs worked in hierarchical teams with licensed practical nurses (LPNs) and auxiliary nurses (nurses' aides) providing care (Brannon, 1994). Unfortunately, primary nursing proved economically costly to health care systems and therefore was short-lived. Despite claims that primary nursing produced better health outcomes, in the 1990s, managed care systems replaced primary nursing with what were seen as more cost effective varieties of team nursing (Brannon, 1996).

Nurses and Physicians

For one unique historical and political economic moment during the early 1900s (Dolan, 1969; Kalisch & Kalisch, 2004), organized public health nurses in the United States reached critical mass and were able to mount remarkable disease and intervention programs. The public health and economic needs of poor people, largely, immigrant populations in urban areas and agricultural populations in rural areas, were overwhelming. But more importantly, the nurses succeeded because it was before biomedical physicians had consolidated control over health initiatives, and it was prior to the expansion of the biomedical industrial complex.

For their various disease prevention and intervention programs, the public health nurses worked autonomously to provide nursing services to large numbers of poor people and introduced sanitary measures to decrease the spread of communicable diseases. Also, public health nurses provided care in many communities and neighborhoods.

Unfortunately, the period was short-lived. Arguing that the nurses' actions were inspired by communist principles and values, the powerful American Medical Association (AMA) successfully lobbied the U.S. Congress to pass legislation limiting public health nursing and gutting the programs which funded them. Without funding, nurses were unable to continue their community pubic health work. The programs were slowly dismantled and public health nursing never again recovered the strength it held during that period. In the U.S. environment of general fear of communism, this scare tactic was remarkably successful in convincing many that the work of public health nurses should not be supported by government financing (Garey & Hott, 1988).

In sum, biomedical physicians used the same strategy that elite members used against all groups that infringed on their economic interests. Repeatedly, by aligning with powerful stakeholders such as board members of philanthropic institutions as well as with powerful political, corporate, and civic leaders, the biomedical physicians, a part of the ruling capitalist class, were able to restrict the practice of non-allopathic physicians and certainly of nurses. By maintaining dominance over other health care workers, biomedical physicians controlled medical knowledge, successfully monopolized practice, and gained a dominant position in the health care arena. Competition with other health care providers was essentially eliminated (Baer, 2001).

Historical Context of Class and Race in U.S. Nursing

Conditions of class and race determined who became nurses. Bias is particularly evident in the unequal treatment of people of color and minorities (Barbee, 1993).

In 2006 there were 2.9 million nurses in the United States. Although this number was an approximate 8% increase over the number of registered nurses in 2000 and despite the profession's avowed concern with increasing the number of minority nurses, there was no appreciable increase in the number of minorities in nursing. To understand why—despite a critical shortage of working professional nurses and a greater shortage of baccalaureate prepared nurses—the number of minorities in nursing is not increasing, we need to look at the history of U.S. nursing and nursing education (Barbee & Gibson, 2001).

In its formative years, nursing was a job done by two classes of white women, in two different environments. Middle and upper class white women turned to nursing when economic circumstances (that is, widowhood, divorce, abandonment) forced them to work (Reverby, 1987). These middle class nurses worked in white people's homes. As a result, their roles were vague and often it was difficult to determine whether they were servants or members of the family (Cheal, 1999; Reverby, 1987). On the other hand, lower class white women worked in the hospitals.

The first hospitals were established based on the philosophy that providing nursing care for the sick would improve their recovery and their return as productive members of society (Ashley, 1976; Cheal, 1999; Reverby, 1987). Although a New York City physician is credited with organizing the first comprehensive "training" courses for nurses in 1798, organized nurses training programs were not truly developed until after the Civil War (Kalisch & Kalisch, 1995). As Reverby (1987, p. 3) notes "the link between hospitals and nursing was forged in the context of post-Civil War social welfare reform." Indeed, prior to the first nurse's training programs, hospital nursing was a menial job done by lower-class white women (Kalisch & Kalisch, 1995; Reverby, 1987; Starr, 1982). The first hospital-based training programs were developed in 1873 by a reform movement among upper class women (Starr, 1982) who were concerned both with improving hospitals and, at the same time, providing respectable service work for middle class women (Reverby, 1987).

Yet, because these training programs provided the hospitals with cheap labor, conflict existed between nursing service and education (Reverby, 1987; Schuyler, 1978). Major reasons cited for the tension are: (a) the close involvement of physicians in nurses' training, (b) the development of hospitals themselves, and (c) the changes in U.S. physician practice and education (Reverby, 1987). Unfortunately, rarely noted in the literature is the capitalist context within which the tension existed and the fact that prestigious philanthropies and government showed repeated preferentiality to biomedical physicians.

Physicians were originally closely involved in nursing education and viewed nurses' training as hands-on at the patient's bedside rather than as learning theory in the classroom. Significantly, however, Starr points out that the physicians' primary objection against nurses receiving formal education was that "educated nurses would not do as they were told" (1982, p. 155). Similarly, Schuyler (1978) notes that although there was an attempt to model nurse training on the Nightingale program at Bellevue Hospital in New York City, the training was unsuccessful because the physicians *believed* that the theoretical and liberal education espoused by Nightingale was not important. Critical political economy suggests that more knowledge and autonomy for nurses would detract from biomedical hegemony and threaten the absolute patriarchy necessary for physicians to maintain control.

The relationships among the grand macro-level and the local micro-level phenomena, including local cultural and ideological relationships as well as grand structural level relationships illuminates that, as Cheal (1999, p. 58) notes "[t]he cultural education of nurses, which was an important aspect of Nightingale's philosophy of nursing education, was overtaken by schools' vocational orientation." In terms of race, class, and gender, although nurse reformers wanted to attract middle class white women to nursing, the bulk of the student population in hospital nurses training were from rural areas (Cheal, 1999). As Cheal (1999, p. 59) further points out, these early white nursing schools were analogous to the YMCAs that sought to "save" rural working girls that came to the city to work. The hospital diploma schools exercised affective and moral mandates over their students (Olesen & Whittaker, 1968). Indeed, very few professions controlled as large a portion of the individual's life as did the apprentice-type, residence-based schools of nursing. The images of what a nurse is, what a nurse does, and how one becomes a nurse were established in the hospital diploma schools and continued to pervade the image of nurses trained in university-based programs for many decades (Olesen & Whittaker, 1968).

The struggle to become a recognized profession led nursing leaders to call for standard curriculums, unified admission criteria, and a separation of ward service from nursing education. This last was critically important because, as we have seen, the economic ties between hospitals and their training programs were close and the educational budgets came from the hospitals. Thus, nursing leaders strove to move all education programs into institutions of higher learning (Melosh, 1982) to increase the professional status of nursing and resolve the service versus education conflict that framed nursing as a domestic task. Since 1896, the year the American Nurses' Association (ANA) was formed (Flanagan, 1976), white nurses have been engaged simultaneously in trying to upgrade the status of nursing and in trying to make the profession attractive to a higher social class. However, hospital administrators, many of whom were nurses themselves, resisted moving nursing education from hospitals to colleges because it differed from their ideas of "proper" training and drastically reduced their control (Melosh, 1982). As a result, student nurses continued to be used in hospital staff and supervisory positions until the 1950s (Melosh, 1982).

Internal Stratification in Nursing

Nursing in the United States has always been characterized by internal stratification, particularly along lines of social class (Melosh, 1982; Reverby, 1987). The successful 19th century ideological construction of nursing as a secular calling made it a respectable service for middle class "ladies." At the same time, its material benefits of providing training in a marketable skill, the small living allowance paid to student nurses, and room and board in an institution governed by moral guardianship made it an attractive occupational choice for women from lower and upwardly aspiring classes. The training school attended and subsequent occupational positions were indicative of an individual nurse's social strata.

At the turn of the 20th century, nursing was a women's occupation remarkable for its "self-conscious and articulate elite." This elite aspired to professionalize the occupation, yet from the outset, they met resistance from other nurses, many of whom "protested [the] leaders' strategies and criticized their professional ideology" (Melosh, 1982, pp. 4-5).

Racism in U.S. Nursing Education

From its beginnings, professional nursing in the United States had an institutional bias against blacks (Barbee, 1993; Hine, 1989). Early black nurses believed that if they proved their efficiency, they would be accepted by white nurses and their nurse establishment. Blacks erroneously concluded that being a nurse supplanted other differences between them and white nurses. Black nurses were either unaware or unwilling to acknowledge the unequal power relations that existed. Today the racial bias is evident in the small number of black registered nurses, the relatively low number of black nursing students, and the almost total absence of black nurses' contributions to nursing texts. As a result black nurses are marginalized. Brown's famous 1948 report "Nursing for the Future," still relevant today, pointed out that nursing, through racial discrimination, deprived the public of nursing care and perpetuated injustices to minorities (Brown, 1948).

Because of racism, racial quotas in white Northern schools and denial of admission to Southern ones (Hine, 1989), black schools of nursing developed separate, but parallel. In fact, 90 Black diploma programs existed between 1886 and 1982 (Carnegie, 1992). Additionally, the vast majority of the first generations of black nursing students were from working class backgrounds (Hine, 1989). For these black women, nursing promised upward mobility and a method by which they could address the myriad of health problems in the black communities. Yet the class origins and the overall social status of African American women, while making them easy recruits for nursing, exacerbated tensions with elite white nurse leaders who were laboring to distance the profession from any "taint of domestic servitude" (Hine, 1989), a job all too often associated with African American women. Undoubtedly, although nursing served as an important avenue of upward mobility for black women, black nurses had the added burden of being viewed as ambassadors for their race.

Thus, early black nursing leaders emphasized the genteel characteristics of black nurses and history is replete with references as to how black nurses should act. It would be a mistake to assume that this monitoring of conduct was limited to impressing white nurses. Because early black nurses felt obligated to "stand for the race," they themselves participated in molding the succeeding generations of black nursing students. Race relations provided yet another reason that both black and white nurses believed that they had to control the person who was becoming a nurse (Barbee, 1993).

In sum, originally the ranks of trained nurses were filled by white middle class women who needed respectable work and who accepted the ideology of nursing as female domestic work. But over time, this demographic was attracted to other fields opening up for women. Lower middle class and working class young women in search of a respectable occupation and upward mobility filled the void. Finally, in an attempt to gain professional status and respectability, nursing education moved from the hospital to academic settings.

Nurse Unionization Evolves in the United States

At the same time that nurses and nursing were becoming increasingly professionalized, a movement that was initially seen as its antithesis began taking hold and developing in strength and influence. The organization of nurses into unions grew rapidly between 1971, when only 3.1% of nurses were union members, and 1980 by which time the proportion had risen to 17.6% of nurses. The proportion of nurses who are union members has remained reasonably stable since, at around 16 or 17% (Hirsch & Macpherson, 2003). The collective organization of nurses into unions has been an important development in the shaping of contemporary nursing, and this section outlines some of the key features of the history of nurse unionization in the United States. This history is linked to larger political and economic issues, particularly those concerning the changing status of women and the changing character of family in the latter half of the 20th century. In addition, the unionization of workers in the United States is also subject to the legislative framework within which industrial relations are played out. Most importantly, though, the development of unionization and collective bargaining among registered nurses in the United States cannot be understood without close attention to the traditional spearhead of organized nursing in the United States, the American Nurses' Association (ANA), and its state affiliates, the State Nurses' Associations (SNAs). The history of the ANA's involvement in collective bargaining exemplifies the theoretical, ideological, and practical barriers and constraints on collective action by nurses. On a stage largely set by legislative framework, the ANA and its state affiliates undoubtedly constitute central actors.

Legislative Framework Influencing Unionization: The 1930s and 1940s

The National Labor Relations Act (NLRA) of 1935 (also called the Wagner Act) gave RNs, like most other employees in the United States, the right to bargain collectively with their employers. At this time, nurses were increasingly employed in hospitals rather than as private duty nurses, making feasible their organization into unions and collective bargaining units. However, the Board of Directors of the ANA strongly opposed nurse unionization as reported in the following Editorial:

> . . . The ANA does not at this time recommend nurse membership in unions . . . [because the board is convinced that] . . . in their professional organizations nurses have the instruments best fitted and equipped to improve every phase of their working and professional lives. . . . (*American Journal of Nursing* [*AJN*], 1937, p. 766)

Since the very beginning of collective bargaining in hospitals, then, the ANA has been claiming both its exclusive right to organize nurses and the distinctiveness of nursing from other occupations. The editorial went on to enumerate the professional advantages of membership in the ANA, which it was argued, already attended to nursing's professional and economic concerns. Opposition to unionization was even more strongly articulated a year later by a contributor to the ANAs journal, *AJN,* who claimed that "a nurses' union would be almost, if not quite as absurd as a mothers' union . . ." (Hart, 1938). These early comments in *AJN* reflect an ideological opposition to unionization and a view of collective bargaining as something associated with "unprofessional" blue collar unions. The use of the word "mother" highlights the gendered character of nursing and its assumed concomitant maternal attributes of altruism, subservience, and nurturance. The State Nurses' Associations (SNAs) were also generally unresponsive to the idea of collective bargaining to improve the working conditions of their members. The reasons were partly ideological, but also because three particular groups whose interests were not necessarily served by unionization dominated the SNAs: (a) nurse educators, who endorsed professionalization rather than unionization; (b) nurse administrators who had an allegiance to management; and (c) private duty nurses who obtained work through the registers kept by the SNAs. The membership numbers of private duty nurses were thus disproportionally higher and since private duty nurses were essentially self-employed, collective bargaining was not a strategy of particular relevance to them.

In the decade during which the Wagner Act opened up collective bargaining, there was also a significant transformation in the employment setting of registered nurses. In 1930, between 70 and 75% of nurses worked as private duty nurses. But by 1940, the majority of nurses were employed in hospitals. The effects of this transformation are complex; some have argued that it was because of the large scale employment of nurses in hospitals that Taylor's management principles could be applied wholesale to nursing work (Wagner, 1980, p. 272) making the nursing more "proletarianised." Others, such as Melosh (1982) argue that there was only a "partial and incomplete" application of Taylorism in nursing (1982, p. 173). And in fact, some nurses gained new power in hospital organizations and lost their direct dependence on doctors for employment. Thus, although by being hospital employees, nurses may have experienced economic proletarianization (insofar as they become employees rather than self-employed workers), they also stood to make some gains in terms of organizational authority and power.

The transition to hospital nursing was by no means followed by a rush of unionization; rather, unionization began slowly and occurred in only a few regions of the country, generally where there existed liberal labor laws and long histories of strong labor movements, such as California (in particular the Bay Area), certain parts of the northeast (such as New York City), and some midwestern states (most notably Minnesota) (Bullough, 1971). Even though quite small, the labor movement was sufficiently threatening that by 1944 the ANA Board discussed the appropriateness of collective bargaining by the association itself and deemed it to be theoretically feasible at the state but not the federal level. In 1945, a committee to study collective bargaining was established (Bullough, 1971, p. 278; Flanagan, 1986, p. 3). The Chair of this committee, Shirley Titus, the director of the California

SNA, and a committed, enthusiastic, and persuasive champion of collective bargaining for nurses was able to ". . . sell the idea in spite of the great hesitation . . . [of the ANA]" (Bullough, 1971, p. 278).

A year later the ANA successfully adopted an *economic security* program which allowed for the use of collective bargaining by SNAs for their members. The adoption of the strategy seems to be linked to the role of Titus herself, the nursing labor supply in the post-war period, and concerns that unless the ANA be seen to be prepared to act for nurses in collective bargaining, it would not be able to head off "a wide-scale movement of nurses into labor unions" (Bullough, 1971, p. 278). The ANA's economic security program precluded ANA members from membership in any other organization that could act as their bargaining agent (Bullough, 1971).

Still, the adoption of the program did not by any means signify a consensus about its appropriateness and acceptability. An *AJN* readership survey at the time indicated that a large proportion of respondents (41%) were so opposed that they thought it should be campaigned against (Bernays, 1946, p. 231). Some were opposed to unionism because they saw it as unprofessional, as indicated by such comments as "Unions are not for nurses. Nursing is a profession." Others cited professional ethics to highlight the disjunction between professionalism's call and unionism's strategy: "The weapon of trade unions is the strike; Ethically, nurses cannot strike, because lives would be endangered" (Bernays, 1946, p. 230).

Reflecting these wide-ranging views, the *AJN* pointed out that "(c)ollective bargaining is not to be confused with labor unionism" (*AJN,* 1946, p. 437). The cautionary language employed in this instance and for many years afterward is indicative of the ambivalence with which economic security program was approached. Perhaps the most important indicator of the ANA's profound ambivalence about the use of collective bargaining was the statement included in its 1946 economic security policy: "under no circumstances would a strike or use of any similar coercive device be countenanced" (*AJN,* 1946, pp. 728-746, cited in Bullough, 1971, p. 278).

1947 Taft-Hartley Amendments

Meanwhile, only 12 years after the passage of the Wagner Act, the 1947 Taft-Hartley amendments withdrew the right to collectively bargain from the majority of employees in the hospital industry (Zimmerman, 1975). In the wake of these amendments, an extraordinarily fragmented and complex array of collective bargaining systems emerged, determined by state legislation and the type of hospitals in which employees worked. Hospitals have historically been subject to different legislation over collective bargaining depending on whether they are publicly owned (and different legislation applies to federal and non-federal publicly owned hospitals) or, if privately owned, whether they operate for-profit or not-for-profit.

Private Sector Hospitals

Employees in non-profit hospitals in the private sector were excluded from National Labor Relations Board (NLRB) jurisdiction under the 1947 amendments on the grounds that "the hospital industry did not constitute interstate commerce . . ."

and therefore should not be included under the NLRA umbrella (Becker, Sloan, & Steinwald, 1982, p. 2). Approximately half of all hospitals in the United States at the time and two-thirds of the personnel for the entire hospital industry (Miller, 1980, p. 383) were thus excluded from the right of collective bargaining. While state-level legislation could have covered these employees, by 1974, only a dozen states had drawn up such legislation, leaving most employees within this sector without legal protection to unionize.

Technically, employees in for-profit, private sector hospitals were protected by the NLRB, but in practice the NLRB ". . . did not begin to exert jurisdiction over the for-profit hospitals until the late 1960s . . ." (Becker et al., 1982, p. 2).

SNA and Local Activity

Shortly after the passage of the Taft-Hartley amendments, a further constraint was imposed on nurses when the ANA's position regarding strike action was adopted as a no-strike pledge at the 1950 biennial conference of the ANA (Flanagan, 1986). Although the legal restrictions of the Taft-Hartley Act were geographically limited, they did, however, cover most of the states of the union. In combination with the ANA members' voluntary no-strike pledge, SNAs had very little power even where they could negotiate; they had, in the words of one analyst, "entered the game of collective bargaining only after voluntarily throwing away their trump card" (Bullough, 1971, p. 279). Mass resignations and work stoppages were used by nurses in this period, however, and by the mid-1960s the incidence of labor militancy among nurses increased exponentially. *AJN* reports indicate that work stoppages by nurses increased from two in 1962 to 34 in 1967 (Miller & Dodson, 1976, p. 42). Most of these work stoppages involved demonstrations and mass resignations in attempts to improve nurses' wages. For example in 1966, 1,500 RNs, or about half the RN employees of New York City's Department of Hospitals, threatened to resign if their salaries and work conditions were not improved. The result was substantial improvements in both areas.

Similar unrest occurred almost simultaneously in San Francisco, where nurses threatened to throw off the shackles of the ANA and its policies: many nurses left the California Nurses Association (CNA) to join larger, more militant labor unions such as the International Brotherhood of Teamsters (IBT, the "Teamsters") or the American Federation of Labor and Congress of Industrial Organizations (AFL-CIO.) Most stayed with the CNA, which engaged in rather "stormy and protracted" negotiations with Bay-area hospitals until the nurses established informational picketing and threatened mass resignations. As a result the CNA revoked its no-strike pledge and nurses finally negotiated an economically favorable contract (Bullough, 1971, p. 282). Similar incidents began occurring throughout the country, and gradually other states, such as Pennsylvania in 1966, also rescinded their no-strike pledge.

Tensions within the ANA resulted in significant restructuring of the organization. Three new commissions for collective action within nursing were established: (a) nursing services, (b) nursing education, and (c) economic and general welfare.

Labor militancy by registered nurses in the mid-1960s affected not only the organizational structure outlined above, but ANA policies. By 1969, the national ANA rescinded its no-strike pledge, a "belated ceremony" since many work stoppages had already occurred by the time the policy was rescinded, and several of the largest SNAs had already changed their official strike policies.

Other national organizational changes occurred: In 1968 the ANA's Economic and General Welfare Commission, under the leadership of another enthusiastic advocate of collective bargaining, Ann Zimmerman, adopted a so-called "new approach" to assisting the SNAs in their collective bargaining efforts. The basic philosophy and initial plans had first been approved by the ANA Board of Directors in September 1967. Six months later, Zimmerman stated that it had been developed to:

> . . . capitalize on today's favorable economic climate. Nurses in many parts of the country are doing better financially . . . as a result of the 1966 economic breakthrough which began in New York and California, but the momentum must continue and the gains must be broadened. . . . (*AJN,* 1968, p. 716)

The ANA hired mobile field staff to assist SNAs in organizing and representing nurses at their places of work. This program was paid for by ANA membership dues and matching funds from the SNAs. By 1970, 15 SNAs had received assistance, and in many of the states, the first-ever contracts between nurses and their employers were negotiated. Yet the ANA did not easily adopt this more aggressive collective bargaining. At the time the "new approach" was officially announced to the SNAs, an ANA director said: ". . . with the differences in views existing among the commissions, decisions such as that approving the new economic thrust have been made only after the most serious deliberations . . ." (*AJN,* 1968, p. 716).

It took more than 2 decades before the ANA's adoption of an "economic security" program in 1946 was implemented in a way with a potential for success to benefit the "rank and file" ANA membership. Obviously, the ANA's actions were defensive. It adopted the program but grew it incrementally. The tactics—first establishing a functional organizational unit, later adopting the "new approach," and finally rescinding the no-strike pledge—were belated responses of an organization primarily concerned with professionalization, not unionization.

Public Sector Hospitals

Employees in federal hospitals could not legally unionize or bargain until 1962, when President Kennedy's Executive Order 10988 was passed, giving 190,000 hospital workers these rights. Since then, the growth in the number of collective bargaining contracts in federal hospitals has been extraordinary. In 1961, there were none; by 1970, 52% of federal hospitals had such a contract, and by 1975 this figure had reached 75% (Becker et al., 1982, p. 3; Miller, 1980, p. 381).

Other Public Hospitals

Until 1959, there were no regulations at all covering collective bargaining for public sector workers—state or local. Wisconsin was the first state to implement legislation for collective bargaining rights covering employees in this sector, and gradually more states implemented such legislation, but by 1980 "only slightly more than half of the states . . . [had] . . . laws under which hospital workers [could] organize and bargain without question (Miller, 1980, p. 382). Still, despite the legislative complexities and the inter-state inconsistencies, there was a consistent growth in the rate of unionization for workers in this sector through the 1970s (Becker et al., 1982; Miller, 1980).

The 1974 Taft-Hartley Amendments

The 1947 Taft-Hartley Amendments (to the Wagner Act), which had restricted nurses from collective bargaining were themselves amended in 1974. Non-profit hospitals were once again (after a 27-year lapse in most states) brought under NLRA jurisdiction, thus giving their employees legal protection to unionize and opening the floodgates. In the first 8 months after passage of the 1974 amendments, there were 104 representation elections (an average of 15.5 a month) by professional/technical employees in the health care sector, of which 74.2% were won. This number compares to the nonprofessionals success rate of 52.5% and an overall 50.3% success rate in representation elections for all employees in all sectors (Rutsohn & Grimes, 1980). Obviously, the amendments caused a "one time jump in the pace of hospital unionization . . . [as well as] . . . a permanent speed up . . ." (Feldman, Hoffbeck, & Lee, 1981, p. 508).

The legislative changes of 1974 followed a decade-old grass roots movement by nurses, and finally opened the way for registered nurses to use the strategies commonly used by labor unions to improve their conditions. The threat of incursions by unions such as the AFL-CIO was undoubtedly another factor influencing the unionization of nurses. Since the 1940s this threat has become increasingly relevant as more and more nurses have indeed joined other unions for representation. By the 1960s, rank and file nurses themselves, sometimes through their SNAs and other times not, began using labor militancy to protest their conditions, economic and otherwise, and the ANA was forced to follow the leadership of its members.

"Professional Unionism" in U.S. Nursing

Since the 1930s when the labor relations legal framework first allowed for nurse collective bargaining, the ANA has volubly declared its unique suitability to function as nurses' representative in collective bargaining. This declaration became formalized in its adoption of the economic and general welfare program in 1946, but, it was well into the late 1960s and 1970s before an organizational framework and strike policy were implemented. Formal policy and organizational practice clashed in the ANA for over 2 decades. In the 1970s and 1980s, the ANA shifted toward support of the Economic and General Welfare Commission program and acceptance of the use of labor union strategies. In 1980, the president of the ANA declared the ANA to be a labor union, albeit a professional union, and finally by the 1980s the ANA's role as a labor union role was unequivocal. Nonetheless, its professional function in labor negotiations was vigorously emphasized and a hybrid of professionalization and unionization in nursing became fully developed. This hybrid continues to gain strength. By the mid-1980s, the ANA or its state affiliates represented more RNs in collective bargaining than any other organization or union: In fact, two-thirds of the nurses covered by a collective bargaining agreement were represented by their professional association.

The Changing Picture

Neoliberal economic reforms in health care started during the administrations of President Ronald Reagan in the 1980s. The 1980s introduction of market-based reforms in health care:

> . . . fundamentally changed the way health care is delivered in the United States . . . nurses who had experienced reform-related job restructuring held substantially more negative views of the climate for patient care. . . . Nurses concerned about a deteriorating climate for patient care indicated a desire for greater voice in the organization and staffing of hospitals and also indicated a greater readiness than other nurses to vote for a union. (Clark, Clar, Day, & Shea, 2001, p. 133)

As a result of the continued high cost of health care and the intensive privatization of care with Managed Care Corporations, nursing personnel shouldered the burden of cost containment measures that downsized and reallocated nurse patient ratios. Job restructuring, the further segmentation of nursing duties and heavier work and patient care loads contributed to nurses' increased job dissatisfaction. The inability to provide good patient care (a traditional hallmark of good nursing care) and relatively poor wages (particularly wage compression with years of service and experience) have been ongoing frustrations for U.S. nurses.

RNs view market-based health care reform negatively and express concerns about the "voice" they have in the organization, about staffing levels, and lack of administrative support. In addition, Clarke et al. (2001) found that ". . . a nurse's perception of the climate for patient care may . . . serve to 'trigger' interest in a union . . ." (p. 145). Consequently, interest in nurse unionization in the U.S. has increased since the 1980s. One study in a public hospital where there had been a strike asked nurses to rank what they perceived to be the causes of the strike. Results showed that "a majority of respondents considered heavy workloads (79%), difficulties in providing good quality of care (72%), low salaries (56%), patient overcrowding (55%), and poor working conditions (54%) to have been 'extremely important' causes. . . ." Even when asked to reflect on the underlying motives of fellow strikers, most believed the two things—"better salaries" (92%) and "improve the quality of care for patients" (92%) were evenly rated; then came working conditions (85%), protest against "uncaring attitudes of management" (72%) (Kravitz, Leake, & Zawacki, 1992, p. 650).

Breda (1997) showed that poor working conditions, not poor wages, were the main impetus for nurse unionization and that it was the lack of nurses' professional autonomy in an authoritarian medical system that spurred labor militancy. Nonetheless, while some RNs see unionization as a potential mechanism for enhancing professional practice and clinical decision making, "the majority of nurses have historically resisted positive identification with unionization" (Wilson, Hamilton, & Murphy, 1990, p. 35).

Perhaps the most noteworthy political economic action taken by RNs in the United States since 2000 has been the action of several progressive SNAs (California, Massachusetts, and Maine) to sever all ties with ANA and to initiate free-standing State Nurses Associations. One of the principle reasons was the ANA requirement that all SNAs join the United American Nurses (UAN), ANA's national union, thus giving over all rights to collective bargaining to the UAN and jeopardizing preexisting union contracts created by the SNAs.

Additionally, the disaffiliated SNAs contend that the ANA represents the interests of the nursing leadership rather than staff (bedside) nurses, and that even after 100 years in existence, it only has a low 7% membership rate of all U.S. nurses, thus failing to meet their broad needs. Furthermore, rank and file members have claimed for decades that the ANA leadership caters to a small wing of elite nurses and fails to adequately represent the agenda of the general membership. In light of the recent "health care crisis," the progressive disaffiliated SNAs maintain that the ANA failed to resist the "deskilling and substitution of nurses by unlicensed aides/techs" and that rather, it endorsed the intensely market-driven nature of managed care, urging instead its members to accept the new work designs and to "embrace change" (Massachusetts Nurses Association, 2001).

Since the disaffiliation, these SNAs have further championed progressive health issues such as single payer health insurance plans and guaranteed health care for all (Massachusetts Nurses Association, 2007). Additionally, in May 2007, the California Nurses Association (CAN), ostensibly the most progressive of the disaffiliated SNAs, together with its union arm the National Nurses Organizing Committee (NNOC) joined forces with the AFL-CIO, thus partnering 75,000 registered nurses with the 10 million member federation. Because the AFL-CIO is the largest federation of unions in the United States and functions as a national trade union center, it offers RNs the hope of garnering substantial collective strength. Furthermore, registered nurses from all 50 U.S. states are represented by the CNA/NNOC affiliation thus giving RNs a solid foothold in the national labor movement that extends beyond just nursing and other service workers.

Although progressive organizations like the California Nurses Association are making great strides in both protecting the rights of workers *and* striving for democratic health care, they currently represent a relatively small percentage of U.S. nurses. There is still a general lack of solidarity among U.S. nurses as an occupational category throughout the entire U.S. nursing workforce. Additionally, historic weak labor laws driven by capitalist interests and cultural hegemony help propagandize worker movements (as well as universal public health and social welfare provisions) with the tar of communism, a remnant of the *Red Scare* movements and *McCarthy Era* (Fried, 1990).

Nursing in the Contemporary U.S. Health Care Marketplace

Two historical events shaped the contemporary period in nursing: the Great Depression and Wartime.

The Effect of the Great Depression on U.S. Nursing

Prior to the economic crisis of 1929, large numbers of "graduate" nurses depended on private duty cases for work. In fact, in the year 1920, nearly three-quarters of all nurses (over 70%) were private duty nurses working either in private homes or in hospitals caring for private patients (Sultz & Young, 2004, p. 185). Private duty nurses found work through referrals to paying clients (usually wealthy) able to retain them. To get these all-important referrals, some nurses established alliances through their nursing school alumnae groups with the hospital boards where they trained and with local civic institutions (Baer, 1990, pp. 25-26). But, during the depression years, as hospitals closed and private caseloads dwindled, many private duty nurses were left without a means of income. Even the state-funded public health and visiting nurses who tended primarily to the poor suffered during this period when public funding was cut and some public health initiatives were abandoned. Unemployed and destitute nurses created a substantial nursing labor surplus. Financing for personnel and health care initiatives became a major issue. Schools of nursing and the development of the nursing educational system also languished during the Depression and in its aftermath.

Effects of Wartime on U.S. Nursing

Both World War I and II had a significant impact on nursing in the United States. With the acute care nature of battlefield injuries, hospitals along with the specialized nursing that characterized hospital care, took on increasing importance. While private duty and public health nursing typified U.S. nursing before World War I, the nursing care of hospitalized patients became a pattern after it. Wartime and the military also had an effect on the image of nursing in the United States. The image of the nurse in the early 20th century was one of an independent practitioner working in the community or in private homes. But after World War I the image of the nurse took on the hue of "patriotism, national sacrifice and efficiency" (Sultz & Young, 2004, p. 186). Visual images of nurses put forth by the media propagated the idea of nurses as "angels of mercy" and saviors. Dependence on the institution and on physician authority accompanied nurses' transition into hospital settings. Later, World War II created an increased interest in nursing and nursing education and provided for the allocation of more funds for nursing education (Sultz & Young, 2004, pp. 185-186).

Corporatization, Biomedicine, and Nursing

As is true in most advanced capitalist countries, the service sector is a large part of the economy. In the United States, it is nearly 75% of the workforce (Herzenberg, Alic, & Wial, 1998). Further, nurses and other health care workers make up a significant proportion of that 75%. Unlike manufacturing where improvements made in machinery and infrastructure can almost single-handedly result in productivity gains, in the service sector, productivity gains depend on the quality of the human workforce and the skill and expertise of the worker. In the health care service sector, investment in skilled nurses makes a significant difference in the quality of performance in the workplace and in the outcome for patients.

The U.S. service sector has relied almost exclusively on the theory of scientific management to organize its work practices and to structure the workforce. In this model, as mentioned previously, nursing responsibilities are broken up into observable tasks and discernable units and then subdivided among workers of varying skill sets. Today, professional nurses (RNs in the United States) are viewed as managers who delegate responsibilities and are "in charge of" workers with lower skill sets and less (or no) education. Subsequently, scientific management strategies calculate how many nurses are needed to staff a particular unit.

Yet, studies have shown a high percentage of nurses with high skill, autonomy, and "discretion over the planning and execution of their work" coupled with a smaller percentage of nurses or ancillary staff with low or minimal skills is a good fit for the service work needed in nursing care settings (Packham, 1992, p. 192). Packham suggests an analogy to manufacturing work where for nursing the product is "nursing care." Hospital "wards," ambulatory "clinics" and "community public health" settings are the shop floors of the production process for the nurse. The features and the quality of the product are then related to how the production process is organized on that nursing "shop floor" (p. 193). Packham concludes that the characteristic features of nursing services rely so heavily on the quality of the relationship between nurses and patients that new kinds of work organization are required (Packham, 1992).

Unfortunately, for decades the U.S. health care industry has instead focused heavily on levels of "nurse staffing" and the composition of the nursing workforce to measure the amount of nursing care needed by health care institutions. Driven by health care industry's historical link with the principles of Taylorism, Fordism, and the time-motion studies of nurses in the mid-20th century, the trend has been to decrease the number of high skill staff (RNs) and to increase the number of low-skill staff (auxiliary nurses—nursing aids or patient care assistants).

In recent years, managed care, downsizing, and the effects of advanced market forces initiated intensive reorganization of the U.S. health care delivery system and brought even more attention to nurse staffing (Jiang, Stocks, & Wong, 2006). Nursing scholars were drawn into the debate initiated by health policy scholars and economists by discussions around safe staffing issues and nurse patient ratios. Nurse scholars used the debate to introduce the discussion of measurements of good nursing care. Indeed, recent studies show important correlations between the quantity and the makeup of the nursing workforce with patient outcomes (Aiken, Clarke, Cheung, Sloane, & Silber, 2003; Aiken, Clarke, Sloane, Sochalski, & Silber, 2002; American Association of Critical Care Nurses, 2005; Buerhaus, 2001; Buerhaus, Staiger, & Auerback, 2000; Cho, 2001; Needleman, Buerhaus, Mattke, Stewart, & Zelevinsky, 2002).

Seeking Professionalism

Professionalism includes a "system of beliefs and behavior (concerning how things ought to be done) resulting from a dedicated commitment usually following a prolonged period of training" (McKinlay & Marceau, 2002, p. 381). Professionalism is best understood as a "social force" with its members welding power and status that is confirmed and upheld by the state through legal licenses and certification.

Professions historically were not subjected to intense ethical scrutiny from the outside. Rather, they were expected to police themselves. The ethical consciences of the professions were only intact when their members abided by the rules. The full-fledged professions such as medicine and law were cloaked by an air of unwavering public trust and thus protected from interference from outsiders (Cheal, 1999).

Some critical analysts argue that the traditional self-policing professionalism of U.S. physicians is on the decline in the neoliberal health care environment. Many factors, including but not limited to increased corporatization, may lead to the further breakdown. Some of the factors that challenge the U.S. medical profession are: (a) decreased protectionism of medicine by the State; (b) competition from other health care workers, including nurses; (c) increased globalization and informatics; (d) new views of the body and health; (e) decreased patient trust; (f) oversupply of physicians; and (g) fragmentation of labor and professional organizations for physicians (McKinlay & Marceau, 2002).

Perhaps the greatest influence, corporatization of U.S. health care, means not only that the financing of health care is increasingly and intensely led by market forces, but also that the work of health care practitioners including nurses, has a fundamentally different goal. While nursing continues to strive toward professional-ization, other health care professions, particularly medicine, have begun to abandon the professionalization model for a corporate one. Biomedicine's position of domi-nance in the health care arena is not as strong nor as monolithic as it was in the past. As the 21st century began and the era of U.S. managed care continued, medicine shifted its allegiance away from professionalism to include corporate strategies. The erosion of the physician's traditional role has implications for nursing as does the increased corporatization of health care as an industry.

Nursing Methods of Resistance: The Dialectic

Historically, in the absence of rigid bureaucratic structures, (e.g., public health settings) U.S. nursing assumed a substantial degree of independence and decision-making but in the rigid hospital bureaucracies, nursing was restricted, rule-driven, and lacked autonomy (Brannon, 1994). While the push to professionalize nursing came primarily from the nursing academics, the push to retain its working class status (proletarianization) came from the managers and administrators, some of whom were themselves physicians and nurses. In terms of nursing education, university-based nursing education programs supported the *professionalism model*. Hospital-based nursing education programs supported the *proletarianization model*. This *dialectic* has existed for many decades but has new relevancy under the gathering momentum of U.S. corporatization.

Since the 1950s and in some cases earlier, much of the U.S. nursing leadership believed that removing nursing schools from the control of hospitals would automatically allow nurses to gain more knowledge, autonomy, and professional status (as well as provide the elite members of the nursing profession with power and prestige) (Ashley, 1976; Wieczorek, 1985).

Hence, mid-20th century nursing leaders diligently helped to move schools of nursing out of the hospital-based apprenticeship programs and into the university-based associate, baccalaureate, masters, and doctoral degree programs. Nonetheless, U.S. nursing has been unable to mandate the baccalaureate degree as the minimum qualification for entry into professional practice. Simultaneously, the private health care industry has systematically sabotaged the professional nursing model.

To explain, since the 1950s, the nursing leadership delineated nurses' professional designation and responsibilities by creating levels of university degrees, licensure, and certification requirements (Brannon, 1994). However, in doing so, they inadvertently created an overly-intricate nursing hierarchy and division of labor. Today's nursing workforce is marked by so many levels of educational preparation, licensure, and certification that it is confusing for nurses and non-nurses alike. In part because of weak labor laws, an unconsolidated labor force and the free market structure of U.S. health care, it is fairly easy for the health care industry to ignore the designated levels of educational preparation for nurses and to employ workers that are less costly. While leaders in nursing attempted to raise the status of nursing from that of an occupation to that of a profession, hospital, and clinic administrators sought low-cost nursing labor. Because the nursing personnel budget was the largest segment of the overall personnel budget, hospital administrators continually sought to decrease those expenditures.

Administrators of health care agencies responded more to the economic constraints of the market than to the categories of nursing preparation. In fact, over the years health care administrators repeatedly reorganized nursing labor categories to fit the needs of their institutions based on economic and political necessity rather than on quality of client care or the advancement of nursing science. Consequently, a gap grew between the quest for an ideal nursing profession and the real life situations of nurses. This gap widened during the last half of the 20th century when the theoretical interests of nursing scholars deviated from the practical necessities and priorities of nurses in clinical practice.

Contemporary U.S. Nursing Education

Contributing to the confusion in U.S. nursing today are the many avenues by which nurses can receive basic preparation. There are three basic programs that qualify a student to take the registered nurse licensure examination: (a) a 2-year associate degree program, (b) a 3-year hospital based diploma program, and (c) a 4- to 5-year baccalaureate program. In addition, a number of master degree programs exist for those with degrees in other fields. There is at least one doctoral degree program that also prepares students for the licensure examination. Moreover, the 2-year associate degree program is a misnomer because, including all the perquisites, the programs are actually close to 3 years in length.

Nursing's trajectory in higher education parallels other U.S. health professions (pharmacy, physical therapy, medicine). After receiving licensure nurses can continue their education by pursuing masters or doctorate degrees in nursing or other fields. Notably, within academic circles, university schools with doctoral program have higher prestige. Originally a need for two types of doctoral programs in nursing was articulated: the academic and professional which would provide their graduates differential careers paths. Unfortunately, the pursuit of prestige via establishing a doctoral program can sometimes blind schools of nursing to the existence of other problems.

The titles of the professional nursing degrees include, in addition to the Ph.D.: doctor of nursing degrees (DN, ND) doctor of nursing science (DNSc, DNS), and the doctor of science in nursing (DSN). This plethora of professional doctoral degrees in nursing confuses both the public and the profession, and informally, some have questioned the proliferation of doctoral programs in nursing. The most recent addition is the Doctor of Nursing Practice (DNP). It is a terminal practice degree, endorsed by the American Association of Collegiate Schools of Nursing (AACN), and it is envisioned to replace the master's degree as the most advanced practice degree in nursing (AACN, 2004).

Although nursing education now occurs primarily in institutions of higher education, it may be erroneous to view this movement of educational venue as one of true change. As Bourdieu (1977) suggests, *reproduction* of models is more common than actual change. The dominant subordinate relationships seen in hospital-based training programs have often been reproduced wholesale in the university programs. As Melosh (1982) points out, hospital schools believed that nursing education was a moral initiation. They sought to shape a student's total personality.

Another aspect of hospital training reproduced within academic nursing is that of the rigid hospital hierarchy, which shaped the student's experiences of apprenticeship and initiated the student to both gender-based and non-gender-dominant subordinate social relations. Formality and distance were the hospital code (Melosh, 1982). Many schools rely on two-tiered faculty systems. "Clinical faculty" or adjunct part-time faculty who are not on the tenure track serve to reinforce the decreased emphasis on scholarship. Viewed in this light, the two-tiered system is yet another reproduction of the separation technical and professional nurses found within the hospital and encouraged by the ANA and other nursing organizations.

Because of the reproduction of the hospital social order into academic schools of nursing faculty are polarized into Taylor-like "provision of service" and "production of knowledge" groups. This polarization decreases the scholarly production in schools of nursing as well as nursing's reputation in academic institutions.

Specialization in Nursing

In recent decades, U.S. nursing specialized its services, mirroring the path of the biomedical specialties. Nursing sought funding for graduate programs focusing on medical specialties such as maternal child health, medical surgical nursing, and psychiatric mental health nursing. Yet, graduate nursing programs offering specialization in the non-medical areas (e.g., trans-cultural nursing and holistic nursing) struggled for economic support and failed to get their graduates adequately employed in their specialty areas.

Additionally, the trend in U.S. nursing for the biomedical specialties produced an overabundance of these graduate programs and a shortage of programs preparing nurses as advanced level generalists. Even today, higher salaries and greater value are afforded to nurses with specialty knowledge in high-tech and economically profitable specialties (e.g., cardiology) than to those with knowledge in other areas such as occupational health or community health nursing. U.S. nursing, intentionally or unintentionally, has facilitated the medical industrial complex by willingly educating and producing skilled workers to staff the specialty units while neglecting community, preventative, and general care nursing. Indeed, U.S. nurses have been slow to recognize the contradictions in biomedical care as well as in the political economy of health and hence they have been reluctant to advocate for change.

Implications for the 21st Century in U.S. Nursing

As U.S. nursing entered the new millennium, the supply of the nursing labor force was in flux. Enrollments in nursing education programs were down and practicing nurses were leaving the field in record numbers. Working conditions for nurses in hospitals, clinics, nursing homes, home care agencies, and other settings were, in the eyes of front line nurses, worse than ever (AACN, 2001, 2003, 2005; Coffey-Love, 2001; May, Bazzoli, & Gerland, 2006; Nagy, 2006; Yordy, 2006).

Nurses complained they could not give the nursing care their patients needed because of untenable work loads. Their patients were sicker and health care administrators were pushing patients through the system faster and faster. Nurses believed they were caught in the middle of a vicious circle of decreasing resources and increasing demands on their time. Additionally, mandatory documentation requirements took away precious minutes from their working day. The time nurses spent during their shift away from direct patient care grew each year.

Finally, ambitious, intelligent women from working-class and middle-class backgrounds were no longer funneled exclusively into the female-dominated "professions" of nursing, teaching, social work, and librarianship. With broader opportunities, women' career attitudes changed. Motivated women now choose their occupation from a number of non-nursing fields which provide more career mobility, as well as better working conditions and wages.

Yet, the ranks of U.S. nursing are still composed primarily of white, working-class, and middle-class women. Societal prejudices about nurses reinforce race, class, and gender categories for nurses, and nurses themselves adhere (albeit inadvertently) to imbedded societal prejudices. In the language, tone and style of recruitment campaigns, nurses try to recruit other women like themselves into nursing. Although it is common knowledge that nurses leave the field due to difficult work conditions, little autonomy, little career mobility, and relatively low wages, health care institutions are reluctant to lure nurses back into the job market by permanently improving wages, benefits, and working conditions. Institutions fear they will not be able to get rid of extra nurses once the supply problem is resolved. Typically, health care institutions introduce flexible working hours and monetary incentives to recruit new nurses instead of reversing poor working conditions. When the perceived crisis is over, the incentives are usually discontinued.

U.S. health care institutions offer one-time hiring bonuses for new nurses to attract them to their agencies, but often, the hiring package does not include a significant increase in the nurses' base pay. Typically, U.S. institutions do not reward experienced nurses for service or longevity with bonuses or other incentives, a practice that is demoralizing and disempowering to experienced nurses who perceive themselves as loyal to institutions.

Explaining the Current Nursing Shortage

Mainstream analysts view the nursing labor supply in terms of the shortage of nurses rather than in terms of supply. Because of this focus, the lack of nurses available to fill job vacancies periodically appears to reach crisis proportions.

Arguments related to the labor supply of nurses are often based on percentages of those entering nursing education programs, attrition rates from schools of nursing, graduation and licensing numbers, the average age of practicing nurses, and the projected number of nurses needed relative to projected illness rates. Rarely is the issue of nursing labor supply conceptualized in terms of the broad political economy. But by doing so, analysts could consider the nursing labor supply within the context of the medical industrial complex, the world capitalist system, the consolidation of capital and social class interests. Focusing on the larger issues would allow analysts to explore the dominance of certain beliefs and ideologies in society vis-à-vis nursing and biomedical hegemony, and perhaps solve the root causes of the periodic "labor shortages."

Nursing as an occupation periodically undergoes a significant dip in available workers. Each time this occurs, the general public is surprised and alarmed; nursing leaders rally for more funding for nursing initiatives, particularly nursing education programs, traineeship, and scholarships; nurses lobby for increased salaries; Rank and file nurses complain they are overworked and undervalued with little say in how their work is organized. Legislators look to beef up the supply of nurses quickly since they believe that the problem is acute. Treated as crisis proportions, the solutions proposed are instituted quickly and without long-range planning. All in all, the response is a bandage approach to remedy the problem of the nursing labor pool.

Solutions vary. For example, all programs in nursing (Associate Degree to RN) proliferated during one such shortage. Sometimes, the lack of nurses is perceived as an image problem, so campaigns are begun for nurses to visit children in middle and high schools to make the nursing career profile more visible and alluring. Often, funding is piped into nursing education programs to churn out new nurses quickly. Funding support and grant incentives to nursing educational programs are instituted when a nurse shortage is perceived and cut at the first sign of nurse abundance.

Critical analysts argue that instead of a "nursing shortage," different problems exist. There are large numbers of nurses not employed as nurses and many skilled nurses who leave nursing to take jobs in other fields. In fact, many skilled nurses abandon clinical practice because of conditions related to a poor work environment (e.g., job stress, job dissatisfaction, work overload, difficult schedules and shift work, relatively low salaries, little career mobility, flat wages, low status, little recognition, and high responsibility and accountability with little autonomy and authority, lack of respect for their work, and mandatory overtime).

Professional nursing and hospital associations such as the American Organization of Nurse Executives (AONE) and the American Health Care Association (AHCA) point to "changing workforce attitudes" and "increased opportunities for women" as the causes of decreased enrollments in nursing education programs and what they view as the "declining labor force supply for nursing services." They point to the fact that career choices for women have broadened dramatically since the 1970s and that some careers offer women more money and status than nursing. Consequently, they maintain that some women and men may be allured away from nursing and into other fields because of monetary and status concerns.

However, a contradiction exists in these arguments vis-à-vis the nurse shortage. For example, one intriguing question remains: How can an apparent labor force supply decline exist when the rates of unemployment are consistently increasing? And, while it is true that middle class and professional class women now have many more employment opportunities available, the AONE and the AHCA, sympathetic to management goals, rarely or never comment on the disastrous conditions of the nursing workplace nor do they institute measures to reverse it.

By conceptualizing the nurse shortage as a problem of "a dwindling workforce," management analysts frame the solution that merely convincing more people to become nurses will solve the nursing supply problem. And by viewing the shortage of nursing labor as a problem of numbers (decreasing enrollments and high attrition due to retirement of older nurses), U.S. society becomes fearful that the nursing supply will drop to record low numbers. The fear extends to the idea that nurses will not be available to care for the increasingly old and sick members of society and that hospitals are in danger of not having enough nurses. These emotional arguments take the attention away from the progressive degradation of nurses' work under advanced capitalism and do not focus on how the wider political economy of health impacts the field of nursing.

SUMMARY AND CONCLUSIONS

U.S. Nursing and Biomedicine

The evolution of nursing as a respectable form of work grew hand-in-hand with the evolution of biomedicine, the preparation of biomedical physicians, and the social development of the hospital as a civil institution. The advancement of nursing

and nursing education fit solidly in the capitalist transformation of hospital institutions and the industrialization of U.S. society. Physicians evolved from relatively
unsophisticated apprentices to university-prepared professionals. Nursing also had
to transform itself according to the demands of the labor market. Uneducated lay
nurses could no longer offer adequate nursing care in the new hospital industry.
Educated nurses were needed for the new hospitals in the industrialized market
driven U.S. health care system.

Nursing in the U.S. followed the development of capitalism from its competitive
beginnings into its monopolistic stages and finally into its current global phase.
Nursing in the U.S. grew up within a market-driven capitalist economic system that
fostered the growth of privatized health care.

Moreover, the rise and increased dominance of a market-driven economy fostered
a set of social classes that function in opposition to one another. Our analysis
revealed that both historically and contemporarily the nurse leaders' interests were
aligned with the power elite and not with the bedside staff nurses. Because nursing
leaders were often physically and emotionally removed from nurses who provided
day-to-day care, the leaders' aspirations for the budding profession were not well-
aligned with the real life experiences and possibilities of many regular nurses.
Nursing leaders developed formal academic preparation for nurses with educational credentials, licensure, and accreditation. In this, nursing mirrored the path of
biomedicine, which also had roots in allopathic apprenticeship programs before
entering academe.

As U.S. nursing entered the 21st century, it was shackled, so to speak, to the
vestiges of 20th century ideals of professionalism, while simultaneously faced with
the growing demands of 21st century advanced capitalism. Today, U.S. nursing
faces the extreme intensification and degradation of its work with the continued
rigid hierarchical control, coupled with relative low wages, limited power, status,
and autonomy. Even as nursing became more bureaucratized during the last half of
the 20th century, there was little indication that it attained the level of professional
status and autonomy its leaders desired. Thus far, the nursing establishment views
nursing in its ideal form without paying sufficient attention to how the political
economy of market systems places constraints on the daily work life of nurses.
Today, U.S. nursing is on a trajectory of creating an ever-widening gap between
nursing as it is practiced at the bedside on the frontlines and nursing as it is
represented in academe.

Nursing in the Neoliberal U.S. Health Care Marketplace

The introduction of market-based reforms and new corporate structures in health
care beginning in the 1980s dramatically changed how U.S. health care was
organized. Moreover, the growing influence of global capitalism in U.S. health care
has irrevocably altered the nature of work for nurses and other health care workers.
Permanent alterations in the nursing workplace are the result of a new corporate
influence in hospitals, medical centers, and other health care settings. The ability

of contemporary U.S. nursing to evolve within the new corporate and neoliberal climate requires radical new strategies and methods of education, research, and practice from both outside and within the discipline.

Critical political economic theory can further our understanding of the inter-relationships among classes under capitalism and how nursing fits into the formula. Our identification of capitalist health care and the role of the nurse in the production process will continue to help us unravel the persistent contradictions in U.S. nursing.

REFERENCES

Aiken, L. H., Clarke, S. P., Cheung, R. B., Sloane, D. M. & Silber, J. H. (2003). Education levels of hospital nurses and patient mortality. *Journal of American Medical Association, 290*(12), 1-8.

Aikin, L. H., Clarke, S. P., Sloane, D. M., Sochalski, J., & Silber, J. H. (2002). Hospital nurse staffing and patient mortality, nurse burnout, and job dissatisfaction. *Journal of American Medical Association, 288*(16), 1987-1993.

American Association of Colleges of Nursing. (2001). The baccalaureate degree in nursing as minimal preparation for professional practice. *Journal of Professional Nursing, 17*(5), 267-269.

American Association of Colleges of Nursing. (2003). *Faculty shortages in baccalaureate and graduate nursing programs: Scope of the problem and strategies for expanding the supply.* White paper. Retrieved June 10, 2006, from http://www.aacn.nche.edu/publications/whitepapers/facultyshortages.htm

American Association of Colleges of Nursing. (2004). *AACN position statement on the practice doctorate in nursing.* Retrieved June 9, 2006 from http://www.aacn.nche.edu/DNP/DNPPositionStatement.htm

American Association of Colleges of Nursing. (2005). *New data confirms shortage of nursing school faculty hinders efforts to address the nation's nursing shortage.* Retrieved June 29, 2006, from http://www.aacn.nche.edu/Media/NewsReleases/2005/Enrollments05.htm

American Association of Critical Care Nurses. (2005). *AACN's healthy work environment initiative.* Retrieved June 29, 2006, from http://www.aacn.org/aacn/pubpolcycy.nsf/vwdoc/workenv?opendocument

American Journal of Nursing [AJN]. (1937). Editorial, 37(7), 766.

American Journal of Nursing [AJN]. (1946). Editorial, 46(7), 437.

American Journal of Nursing [AJN]. (1968). Economics, 68(4), 716.

American Nurses Association. (2006, March 31). *Adequate nurse education funding, safe staffing and patient safety are among focuses of National Nurses Week 2006.* ANA press release 3-31-06. Retrieved March 31, 2006, from http://www.nursingworld.org/FunctionalMenuCategories/MediaResources/PressReleases/2006

Ashley, J. A. (1976). *Hospitals, paternalism & the role of the nurse.* New York: Teachers College Press.

Baer, E. (1990). *Editor's notes nursing in America: A history of social reform* (A Video Documentary). New York: National League for Nursing.

Baer, H. (2001). *Biomedicine and alternative healing systems in America: Issues of class, race, ethnicity and gender.* Madison, WI: University of Wisconsin.

Baer, H. (2003). The work of Andew Weil and Deepak Chopra: Two holistic health/New age gurus: A critique of the holistic health/New age movements. *Medical Anthropology Quarterly, 17*(2), 233-250.

Baer, H., Singer, M., & Susser, I. (2003). *Medical anthropology and the world system* (2nd ed.). Westport, CT: Praeger.

Barbee, E. L. (1993). Racism in U.S. nursing. *Medical Anthropological Quarterly, 7*(4), 346-362.

Barbee, E., & Gibson, S.(2001). Our dismal progress: The recruitment of non-Whites into nursing. *Journal of Nursing Education, 40*(6), 243-244.

Becker, E. (1999). *Chronology on the history of slavery.* Retrieved November 30, 2006, from http://innercity.org/holt/slavechron.html

Becker, E. R., Sloan, F. A., & Steinwald, B. (1982). Union activity in hospitals: Past, present and future. *Health Care Financing Review, 3,*(4): 1-13.

Bernays, E. L. (1946). Nurses and their professional organization. *AJN, 46*(7), 229-233.

Bourdieu, P. (1997). *Outline of a theory of practice.* London, UK: Cambridge University Press.

Brannon, R. (1990). The reorganization of the nursing labor process: From team to primary nursing. *International Journal of Health Services, 20*(3), 511-524.

Brannon, R. (1994). *Intensifying care: The hospital industry, professionalization, and the reorganization of the nursing labor process.* Amityville, NY: Baywood.

Brannon, R. (1996). Restructuring hospital nursing: Reversing the trend toward a professional work force. *International Journal of Health Services, 26*(4), 643-654.

Braverman, H. (1998). *Labor and monopoly capital: The degradation of work in the twentieth century.* New York: Monthly Review Press.

Breda, K. (1997). Professional nurses in unions: Working together pays off. *Journal of Professional Nursing, 13*(2), 99-109.

Breda, K. M. (1992). *Politics, culture and Gramscian hegemony in the Italian health service: A comparison of USLs.* Unpublished doctoral dissertation, University of Connecticut, Storrs.

Brown, E. L. (1948). *Nursing for the future: A report prepared for the national nursing council.* New York: Russell Sage Foundation.

Buchan, J., & Sochalski, J. (2003). The migration of nurses: Trends and policies. *Bulletin of the World Health Organization, 82*(8), 587-594.

Budrys, G. (2005). *Our unsystematic health care system* (2nd ed.). Lanham, MD: Rowman & Littlefield.

Buerhaus, P. (2001). Follow-up conversation with Lucien Leape on errors and adverse events in health care. *Nursing Outlook, 49*(2), 73-77.

Buerhaus, P., Staiger, D., & Auerback, D. (2000, June 14). Implications of an aging registered nurse workforce. *Journal of the American Medical Association, 283,* 2948-2954.

Bullough, B. (1971). The new militancy in nursing. *Nursing Forum, X,*(3), 273-288.

Carnegie M. E. (1992). Black nurses in the United States: 1879-1992. *Journal of National Black Nurses Association, 6*(1), 13-8.

Centers for Disease Control (CDC). (2006). *Office of minority health, racial and ethnic populations.* Retrieved December 13, 2006, from http://www.cdc.gov/omh/Populations/populations.htm

Cheal, N. (1999). *Medicine and nursing: Professions bound by gender, prescribed by society, an analysis of the Goldmark Report.* Unpublished doctoral dissertation, Georgia State University.

Chitty, K. K. (2001). *Professional nursing: Concepts and challenges* (3rd ed.). Philadelphia, PA: Saunders.

Cho, S. (2001). Nurse staffing and adverse patient outcomes: A systems approach. *Nursing Outlook, 49*(2), 78-85.

Clark, P. F, Clar, D., Day, D. V., & Shea, D. G. (2001). Health care reform & the workplace experience of nurses: Implications for patient care & unionizing. *Industrial and Labor Relations Review, 55*(1), 133-148.

Coburn, D. (1988). The development of Canadian nursing: Professionalization and proletarianization. *International Journal of Health Services, 18*(3), 437-456.

Coffey-Love, M. (2001). The nursing shortage: What is your role? *Nursing Forum, 36*(2), 29-35.

Doane, A. W., & Bonilla-Silva, E. (Ed.). (2003). *White out: The continuing significance of racism.* New York: Routledge.

Dock, L. (1912). *A history of nursing* (Vol. 3). New York: G. P. Putnam's Sons.

Dolan, J. (1969). *History of nursing* (12th ed). Philadelphia, PA: Saunders.

Dossey B. M., Keagan, L., & Guzzetta, C. E. (2005). *Holistic nursing: A handbook for practice* (4th ed). Boston, MA: Jones & Bartlett Publishers.

Doyal, L. (1979). *The political economy of health.* Boston, MA: South End Press.

Economist. (2004, December 29). *Mediocracy in America: Ever higher society, ever harder to ascend.* Retrieved November 30, 2006, from http://www. economist.com/world/na/displayStory.cfm?story id=3518560

Ehrenreich, B., & English, D. (1970). *Witches, nurses, midwives: A history of women healers.* Old Westbury, NY: Glass Mountain Pamphlets.

Elling, R. (1980). *Cross-national study of health systems: Political economies and health care.* New Brunswick, NJ: Transaction.

Elling, R. (1986). *The struggle for workers' health: A study of six industrialized countries.* Amityville, NY: Baywood.

Elling, R. (1994). Theory and method for the cross-national study of health systems. *International Journal of Health Services, 24*(2), 285-309.

Elling, R. (2007). Reflections on the health social sciences—Then and now. *International Journal of Health Services, 37*(4), 601-617.

Erlen, J. (2005). *History of American health insurance.* Retrieved January 3, 2007, from http://www.pitt.edu/~superl/lecture/lec20171/index.htm

Families USA. (2006, October). Medicare privatization: Windfall for the special interests. *Families USA Publication,* 06-105. Retrieved January 26, 2007, from http://www.familiesusa.org

Favro, T. (2006, August 29). *Nothing short of a complete overhaul will cure America's health care system.* City Mayor's Health Report. Retrieved July 7, 2007, from http://www.citymayors.com/health/health_usa.html

Femia, J. (1981). *Gramsci's political thought: Hegemony, consciousness, and the revolutionary Process.* Oxford, UK: Clarendon Press.

Feldman, R., Hoffbeck, R., & Lee, L. F. (1981). Hospital labor unions: Description and analysis. In N. Metzger (Ed.), *Handbook of health care human resources management* (pp. 505-528). Rockville, MD: Aspen.

Flanagan, L. (1976). *One strong voice: The story of the American Nurses' Association.* Kansas City, MO: American Nurses Association.

Flanagan, L. (1986). *Braving new frontiers: ANA's economic and general welfare program, 1946-1986.* Kansas City, MO: American Nurses Association.

Fried, R. M. (1990). *Nightmare in red: The McCarthy era in perspective.* New York: Oxford University Press.

Fort, M., Mercer, M. A., & Gish, O. (2004). *Sickness & wealth: The corporate attack on global Health.* Cambridge, MA: South End Press.

Garey, D., & Hott, L. (1988). *Sentimental women need not apply: A history of the American nurse* (VHS). New York: Florentine Films.

Gramsci, A. (1991) [1930]. *La questione meridionale* [The southern question]. Roma: Riuniti.

Gramsci, A. (1977). *Quarderni del carcere: L'edizione classica dei quaderni gramsciani interamente riveduta sul testo critico* [Prison notebooks: Classic edition of Gramsci's notebooks with full critique]. Roma: Editori Riuniti.

Grier, P. (2005, June 14). Rich-poor gap gaining attention. *Christian Science Monitor,* Retrieved November 30, 2006, from http://www.csmonitor.com/2005/0614/p01s03-usec.html

Hart, J. (1938). Economic security for nurses. *American Journal of Nursing, 38*(2), 391-395.

Haywood, S., & Fee, E. (1992). More in sorrow than in anger: The British nurses strike of 1988. *International Journal of Health Services, 22*(3), 397-415.

Herzenberg, S., Alic, J., & Wial, H. (1998). *Issues in Science and Technology.* Retrieved December 4, 2006, from http://www.issues.org/15.2/herzenberg.htm

Hine, D. C. (1989). *Black women in white: Racial conflict and cooperation in the nursing profession, 1890-1950.* Bloomington: Indiana University Press.

Hirsch, B. T., & Macpherson, D. A. (2003). Union membership and coverage database from the current population survey: Note" *Industrial and Labor Relations Review, 56*(2), 349-354.

Hirst, P. (1979). *On law and ideology.* Atlantic Highlands, NJ: Humanities.

Jalil, J. (2004, January 21). Obesity cost US $75bn, says study. *BBC News.* Retrieved November 30, 2006, from http://news.bbc.co.uk/go/pr/fr/2/hi/americas/3418603.stm

Jiang, J., Stocks, C., & Wong, C. (2006). Disparities between two common data sources on hospital nurse staffing. *Journal of Nursing Scholarship, 38*(2), 187-193.

Kalisch, P. A., & Kalish, B. J. (1986). *The advance of American nursing* (2nd ed.). Boston, MA: Little Brown & Company.

Kalisch, P., & Kalisch, B. (1995). *The advance of American nursing* (3rd ed.). Philadelphia, PA: Lippincott.

Kalisch, P., & Kalisch B. (2004). *American nursing: A history.* Philadelphia, PA: Lippincott.

Kingma, M. (2006). *Nurse on the move: Migration and the global health care economy.* Ithica, NY: Cornell University Press.

Kline, D. (2003). Push and pull factors in international nurse migration. *Journal of Nursing Scholarship, 35*(2), 107-111.

Kravitz, R. L., Leake, B., & Zawacki, B. (1992). Nurses' views of a public hospital strike. *Western Journal of Nursing Research, 14*(5), 645-661.

Labonte, R. (2003). *Dying for trade: Why globalization can be bad for our Health.* Toronto: The CSJ Foundation for Research and Education. Retrieved June 15, 2006, from http://www.sociasljustice.org/pdfs/dyingfortrade.pdf

Marks, S. (1994). *Divided sisterhood: Race, class and gender in the South African nursing profession.* New York: St. Martin's Press.

Massachusetts Nurses Association. (2001). *MNA disaffiliation from ANA..* Retrieved July 9, 2007, from www.massnurses.org/News/2001/disaff2/top10.htm

Massachusetts Nurses Association. (2007). *Single payer health care: A nurses' guide to single payer reform.* Retrieved April 12, 2007, from http://www.massnurses.org/singlepayer/singlepay.htm

May, J., Bazzoli, G., & Gerland, A. (2006, June 26). Hospitals' responses to nurses staffing shortages. *Health Affairs,* w316–w323. Retrieved June 28, 2006, from http://www.healthaffairs.org

McKinlay, J. (Ed.). (1984). *Issues in the political economy of health care.* New York: Tavistock.

McKinlay, J., & Marceau, L. (2002).The end of the golden age of doctoring. *International Journal of Health Services, 32*(2), 379-416.

Melosh, B. (1982). *The physician's hand" Work culture and conflict in American nursing.* Philadelphia, PA: Temple University Press.

Miller, M. H., & Dodson, L. (1976). Work stoppage amongst nurses. *Journal of Nursing Administration, 6*(10), 41-45.

Miller, R. U. (1980). Hospitals. In G. G. Somers (Ed.), *Collective bargaining: Contemporary American experience* (pp. 373-433). Madison, WI: Industrial Relations Research Association (IRRA) Series.

Moody, K. (1997). *Workers in a lean world: Unions in the international economy.* New York and London: Verso.

Nagy, A. (2006, June 26). Root cause of nursing shortage? No Class. *Connecticut Business News Journal.* Retrieved June 29, 2006, from http://www.contact.com/article_page.lasso?id=40055

National Center for Health Statistics. (2006). *Health, United States, 2006.* Retrieved November 28, 2006, from http://www.cdc.gov/nchs/data/hus/hus06.pdf

National Coalition on Health Care. (2004). *Health Insurance Cost.* Retrieved January 3, 2007, from http://www.nchc.org

Navarro, V. (1986). *Crisis, health, and medicine: A social critique.* New York: Tavistock.

Navarro, V. (1990). Race or class versus race and class: Mortality differentials in the United States. *Lancet, 336*(8725), 1238-1240.

Navarro, V. (1999). Health and equity in the world in the era of "globalization." *International Journal of Health Services, 29*(2), 215-226.

Navarro, V. (2003). The inhuman state of US healthcare. *Monthly Review, 55*(4). Retrieved January 9, 2007, from www.monthlyreview.org/0903navarro.htm

Navarro, V. (Ed.). (1979). *Imperialism, health and medicine.* Amityville, NY: Baywood.

Needleman, J., Buerhaus, P., Mattke, S., Stewart, M., & Zelevinsky, K. (2002). Nurse-staffing levels and the quality of care in hospitals. *New England Journal of Medicine, 346*(22), 1715-1722.

Olesen, V. L., & Whittaker E. W. (1968). *The silent dialogue.* San Francisco, CA: Jossey-Bass.

Packham, J. F. (1992). *The organization of work on the service-sector shop floor.* Unpublished doctoral dissertation, Johns Hopkins University.

Reinhardt, U., Hussey, P., & Anderson, G. (2002). Cross-national comparisons of health systems using OECD data, 1999. *Health Affairs, 21*(3), 169-181.

Reverby, S. M. (1987). *Ordered to care: The dilemma of American nursing, 1850-1945.* Cambridge, MA: Cambridge University Press.

Rispel, L., & Schneider, H. (1991). Professionalization of South African nursing: Who benefits? *International Journal of Health Services, 21*(1), 109-126.

Rutsohn, P. D., & Grimes, R. M. (1980). Nightingalism and negotiation—New attitudes of health professionals. In M. J. Levine, S. R. Zacur, & L. A. Horton (Eds.), *Professional issues in nursing: Challenges and opportunities* (pp. 277-285). Glen Ridge, NJ: Thomas Horton & Daughters.

Sacks, K. B. (1988). *Caring by the hour: Women, work, and organizing at duke medical center.* Urbana & Chicago: University of Illinois Press.

Schuyler, C. (1978). The Nightingale program for educating professional nurses and its initial interpretation in the United States. In M. L. Fitzpatrick (Ed.), *Historical studies in nursing* (pp. 31-54). New York: Teachers College Press.

Schwirian, P. (1998). *Professionalization of nursing: Current issues and trends* (3rd ed.). Philadelphia, PA: Lippincott.

Singer, M. (1986). Developing a critical perspective in medical anthropology. *Medical Anthropology Quarterly, 17,* 128-129.

Singer, M., & Baer, H. (1995). *Critical medical anthropology.* Amityville, NY: Baywood.

Singer, M. (Ed.). (1998). *The political economy of AIDS.* Amityville, NY: Baywood.

Starr, P. (1982). *The social transformation of American medicine.* New York: Basic Books, Inc.

Street, A. F. (1992). *Inside nursing: A critical ethnography of clinical nursing practice.* Albany, NY: State University of New York Press.

Sultz, H., & Young, K. (2004). *Health care USA* (4th ed.). Sudbury, MA: Jones & Bartlett.

Sweezy, P. (2004). Monopoly capitalism. *Monthly Review Press, 56*(5), 1-9. Retrieved June 26, 2007, from www.monthlyreview.org/1004pms2.htm

Thomasson, M. (2007). *Health Insurance in the USA.* Retrieved January 3, 2007, from http://eh.net/encyclopedia/article/thomasson.insurance.health.us

U.S. Department of Health and Human Services. (2005). *Overview of the uninsured in the United States: An analysis of the 2005 Current Population Survey.* Retrieved February 17, 2007, from http://aspe.hhs.gov/health/reports/05/uninsured-cps/index.htm

Wagner, D. (1980). The proletarianization of nursing in the United States, 1932-1946. *International Journal of Health Services, 10*(2), 271-290.

Waitzkin, H. (1983). *The second sickness: Contradictions of capitalist health care.* New York: The Free Press.

Whelchel, A. (2005). Review of the book *Plagues and peoples.*. Retrieved December 1, 2006, from http://worldhistoryconnected.press.uiuc.edu/3.1/br_whelchel.html

Wieczorek, R. R. (Ed.). (1985). *Power, politics, and policy in nursing.* New York: Springer.

Wilson, C. N., Hamilton C. L., & Murphy, E. (1990). Union dynamics in nursing. *Journal of Nursing Administration, 20*(2), 35-39.

World Fact Book. (2006). *United States.* Retrieved November 28, 2006, from http://www.cia.gov/cia/publications/factbook/geos.us.html#People

World Health Organization [WHO]. (2006). World Health Report. Retrieved November 30, 2006, from http://www.who.int/whr/2006/en/index/html

Yordy, K. (2006). *The nursing faculty shortage: A crisis for health care.* Retrieved, July 24, 2006, from http://www.rwjf.org/files/publications/other/NursingFacultyShortage071006.pdf

Zadoroznyj, M. (1990). *Paths of professionalization and unionization: The collective mobility projects of U.S. registered nurses, 1965-85.* Unpublished doctoral dissertation, University of Wisconsin-Madison.

Zimmerman, A. (1975). Taft-Hartley amended: Implications for nursing. *American Journal of Nursing, 75*(2), 284-296.

CHAPTER 9

Synthesis of Case Studies: Implications for Global Nursing and Health

Karen Lucas Breda

This volume provides a critical view of important socio-cultural and political economic issues by detailing the ebb and flow of nursing in different geo-political areas over time. This expanded cross-national case analysis of nursing is the result of a unique partnership of interdisciplinary scholars, educators, and practitioners. Each contributor is a content expert on nursing and on the country about which they write. The hope is that this work will spur others to further explore the historical connections among geo-political areas on the nature of health care systems, nursing, and nursing education.

The critical political economic perspective used throughout this volume reveals the relationships and contradictions between macro-level hemispheric and micro-level national phenomena. This approach explores, in part, the principles of pro-globalization versus pro-social justice as well as the concerns of neoliberalism, free trade agreements, the levels of capitalism, underdevelopment, corporatization, biomedicine, hegemony, resistance, division of labor, and social class. In addition to critical political economy, some case study contributors adopt supplementary models to augment their analyses. For example, Mexican authors draw on the concept of socialization to detail the topic of nursing status and the Brazilian authors use the Critical Holistic Paradigm to apply critical political economy to nursing. All of the authors view the capitalist world system as the basic unit of analysis.

In sum, this book shows how broad historical socio-cultural and political economic dimensions within nursing education and service helped to shape the field. The dynamics of globalization and neoliberal reforms are used as conceptual tools to explain current and persistent contradictions in nursing. Contributors to this volume see nursing as a form of social labor, including the organization of nursing and issues of production—topics rarely addressed in the literature.

THE IMPACT OF GLOBALIZATION AND NEOLIBERALISM
ON HEALTH AND NURSING

Twenty-first century economic globalization is characterized by the dominating presence of enormous transnational corporations. Corporations grow even larger through mergers, takeovers, and buyout, increasing in the concentration of capital to the point where transnational institutions dominate global markets, including health care system markets.

The history of present-day economic globalization is rooted in the colonialization of populations and in the industrialization of markets over the last 4 centuries. Colonial conquest and the slave trade throughout the Americas were main ingredients that allowed industry to prosper by providing it with free human labor. The toll on the health of populations throughout the period was enormous. The health consequences and repercussions particularly on vulnerable groups were appalling.

As the case study chapter authors corroborate, today more than ever contemporary globalization has shaped nursing and health care systems. Some of the dimensions of globalization include: (a) advancement in technology and telecommunications, (b) worldwide population expansion, (c) growth in trade among transnational corporations (TNCs), (d) the diminished power of the state and individuals vis-à-vis the increasing power of corporations, (e) strict transnational trade agreements with binding trade rules and multi-lateral institutions like the World Trade Organization, (f) the replacement of public education, health, and social services with private services, and (g) increased social inequalities leading to more poverty, strife, conflict, and violence (Labonte, 2003; McGregor, Doull, & Fisk, 2005).

While contemporary globalization had some positive aspects, particularly for the wealthy segments of society, its negative consequences are devastating to the quality of life and health status of billions of people worldwide. Even more disturbing is that the full extent of the harmful consequences of contemporary globalization for people and countries worldwide and specifically in the Americas is not yet realized (Labonte, 2003).

Contemporary globalization, driven by neoliberal ideals, is pervasive and is linked to extreme capitalism and to a global capitalist approach. The ideology of "neoliberal" globalization is hegemonic, insidious, and encompasses all aspects of society (Harvey, 2005). This ideological predominance, also referred to as the "cultural hegemony" of neoliberal globalization, is present in the institutions of civil society, that is, hospitals, schools, churches, as well as those of the political society, that is, the armed forces, law enforcement, the State (Breda, 1992).

Capitalism is a social economic system in which resources are privately owned and used in production that leads "to the accumulation of private wealth" (McGregor, 2001). Because capitalism is the prevailing economic system worldwide, its principles have inundated popular culture. Capitalism depends on the constant accumulation of profit without which capitalism cannot survive. And, as an economic system, capitalism has no place in its logic for the pure social welfare of the citizenry.

Contributors to this volume concur that neoliberal globalization fosters unfettered growth of extreme capitalism by creating an atmosphere that enhances the stockholders and increases the profit margins of multinational capitalist corporations by such mechanisms as: (a) the elimination of restrictions to commercial trade among countries and across borders; (b) an emphasis on individual, rather than collective rights and interests; (c) developing the infrastructure for global communication including information super highways; (d) the dominance and authority of financial centers; (e) and the formal negotiation and approval of international trade agreements (McGregor et al., 2005).

The Nursing Context

The world of nursing is usually hidden. It is mystified and obscured, as are the class relations imbedded in it. It remains, in the minds of some, the "dirty work" depicted by sociologist Everett Hughes (Hughes, Hughes, & Deutscher, 1958). In a 1951 article in the *American Journal of Nursing,* Hughes wrote that nursing is "among the many ancient arts that are now being turned into professions" (p. 294). Nursing across the Americas used professionalism as a development strategy with education as one major element for attaining professional status. Higher prestige is nearly always associated with "more schooling" (p. 295). Although professional nursing education moved into academic settings, the higher levels of preparation for nurses did not immediately translate into meaningful improvements for nurses in health care practice nor reverse the exploitative class relations for nurses in hierarchical health care systems.

Bedside care allows the nurse to be a cultural broker and to be what Hughes called a "shock absorber" between the patient and the institution, between the patient and other health care providers, and sometimes between the patient and the family. According to Hughes, who studied U.S. nurses in the 1950s, nurses made things happen and orchestrated the hospital drama. More than half a century later, Grace and Smith (2007) described Latin American nurses as the "glue" for the health care system (p. 295). While physicians in Latin America outnumber nurses by four to one and command much higher salaries, the few professional nurses there have great responsibility within primary health care networks. Grace and Smith (2007) cite an interesting contemporary example from a rural area in the outskirts of San Paolo, Brazil where:

> . . . [a] community health center made up of a clinic and a 100-bed hospital served as a hub of a system of smaller clinics in outlying villages and a third level of very small clinics in remote rural areas. The clinic in a small remote area was staffed by a lay midwife. The nurse within this system supervised patient care in the hospital and also in the clinics. She made weekly visits out to the rural areas and supervised the care, provided primarily by auxiliary nurses and nurse aids. The physicians came only to the hub, and the patients were referred in to them—physicians did not go out into the outlying communities. (p. 295)

This example nicely illustrates how nurses coordinate care and hold the system together. In the same example, Grace and Smith (2007) continue by explaining that:

> . . . [a]lthough they [physicians] were required to provide services in the clinic as "payback" for their medical education, most worked only a few hours per day, spending the rest of their time in their private practices. (p. 295)

Nursing, by absorbing physician responsibilities into its practice, significantly bolsters the earnings of doctors. Also, in doing so, nurses reinforce patriarchal relations. Some analysts might suggest that nursing is merely the *handmaiden* of the physician. However, in considering the social class position of nurses it is more accurate to conclude, in this case, that nursing is actually the *handmaiden* of the global capitalist system and that their accommodating actions reinforce class relations.

Supporting this view of nursing as handmaiden to extreme capitalism, Waitzkin adds an analysis of the Chilean health care system and the role of physicians in it. Despite Chile's long history of public health care and its adoption of a National Health Service in 1952, Chilean physicians and dentists have a long tradition of private practice and fee-for-service exploiting their relationship with the National Health Service facilities and services. Waitzkin writes:

> [p]hysicians tended to use SNS [Servicio Nacional de Salud, SNS] facilities while devoting a large part of their time to and energy to wealthier patients in private practice. Because they could join the SNS voluntarily and could work on a part-time basis, doctors gained access to SNS hospitals and clinics, where they maintained offices to see both SNS and private patients. Although private practitioners were expected to work a fixed proportion of time for the SNS, these hours were not enforced. (1983, p. 189)

The above example elucidates the class contradictions in the health care system and how it is impossible to separate health care from the wider political economic context. Historically, physicians retained autonomy and strict decision-making control over their duties and responsibilities, but nurses had little autonomy and decision-making control over theirs. The role of nurses in capitalist health care settings (regardless of public or private health care systems) was to accommodate the capitalist class.

As documented by the authors, physician associations (although not necessarily all physicians) throughout the Americas historically coveted their class interests and resisted threats, such as the advanced education of nurses, to their hegemony over the health system. Only the Canadian authors documented a measurable weakening of the physician hegemony with the strengthening of the National Health Service. Yet, this dip in the physician dominance may be temporary.

Nurse Formation

Systematic, formal studies of the work life of nurses are rare. For this reason an even closer look at nursing is in order. Because of the unique historical, political, and economic dimensions of nursing in the Americas, the lens of critical political economy is a particularly useful analytical tool. It includes the understanding of the dialectic which elucidates contradictions imbedded in social relations.

The authors comment that the varying levels of nursing educational preparation and nursing responsibility are a part of what makes nursing difficult to understand and bewildering for outsiders. To make matters worse, nurses themselves hold biases about the origin of the problems that afflict their field.

A case in point is that nursing programs preparing nurses at different educational levels often did not produce workers who could necessarily carry out different responsibilities. Across the Americas levels of nursing education were not always mutually exclusive, and hence, only in some instances were duties and responsibilities restricted, controlled, or limited to nurses with specific educational preparation. In fact, as several case study authors point out, even today nursing duties and responsibilities are often arbitrarily assigned to nurses without regard to their educational preparation.

Additionally, the complex and seemingly nonsensical array of nursing education programs and different levels of nursing practice, certification, and licensure across the Americas is also confusing both to nurses and non-nurses alike. Using critical political economy theory, we see the factors behind the confusing array. We see how the structure of nursing education and practice is intricately linked to the profit-driven interests of stakeholders who have held power over nursing for many decades (e.g., hospital administrators and trustees, physicians, nursing leaders, legislators, and health care institutions). Also, while nurses did not necessarily have direct input into the trajectory of the nursing field in practice settings, they unknowingly maintained the status quo, reproducing within nursing the same class, gender, and race relations that exist in the larger social context. Nonetheless, in academic settings, while nursing leaders in some cases designed educational programs to accommodate capitalist social relations (e.g., with strict biomedical curricula), in other cases they designed programs to resist capitalist social relations (e.g., see pro-social curricula examples from the Colombian chapter). The nursing curricula in Colombia and in other case examples in this volume promise to move nursing forward into a strong pro-social position.

Nurse Migration

Expert nursing knowledge is essential to the sustainability of local health care systems. The migration of large numbers of nurses to wealthier nations drains local resources and expertise. Nurses in developing countries are lured away from practice, research, and educational settings in their homeland to migrate to areas where salaries are higher and the quality of life is superior. Developing countries most in need of nurses functioning at the "expert" level are continually depleted of their rich human resources. To continually prepare new nurses and to mentor them until they function adequately is a time consuming and expensive proposition for developing countries. And for wealthier nations, importing lower cost nurses to fill a labor shortage is a short-sighted solution to fill a gap that could be reversed through other means.

The chronic cyclic shortage of nurses in the United States and Canada is attributed to a variety of issues from the graying of the nursing workforce, to poor working conditions, to the lack of nursing faculty. Historically, solutions to the nursing shortage in core capitalist countries have used a bandage approach or "patchwork" solutions ranging anywhere from hiring temporary staff and travel nurses, to sign-on bonuses, to flexing work shifts (May, Bazzoli, & Gerland, 2006; Nagy, 2006).

Private entrepreneurial firms and business ventures in industrialized nations such as the United States have created attractive opportunities for nurses in poor countries to migrate for work to wealthier countries. Recruiters from the entrepreneurial firms visit hospitals and other health care settings in different target countries to find experienced professionals willing to migrate to the United States (Kinsley, 2006). This recruitment occurs often without people in the developed world (especially the United States) having knowledge of the devastating effect the "brain drain" creates in poor countries. Additionally, nurses from the "destination" country and nurses from the "source" country are occasionally caught in adversarial relationships particularly when the migrating nurses are perceived as stealing jobs and opportunities.

Although discussion of the ethical issues associated with the ramifications of draining skilled workers from needy areas of the world began several years ago (Buchan & Sochalski, 2004; Chinn, 2006; Falk-Rafael, 2006) and although international health organizations are studying workforce issues among skilled health care workers including nurses (Buchan, Kingma, & Lorenzo, 2005), the representation of the issue in mainstream nursing magazines (not academic journals) in the United States is generally one-sided and reflects a biased micro-level view rather than a global macro-level perspective (Kinsley, 2006).

In sum, certainly, without treating the root cause of the lack of supply of nurses, the cyclic nursing shortages that have plagued health care institutions for decades will certainly reappear.

Signs of Resistance

Methods of resistance in nursing are worth considering here for they are well documented in the case study chapters. Nurses in different venues in the Americas resist unequal power relations and (to varying degrees) attempt to counter unfair hegemonic practices. Depending on the historical period and the local political economic context, nurses use a variety of means to resist oppressive work conditions and their general exploitation. Some of the methods nurses use to seek more tenable labor relations straddle the line between accommodation and resistance and may appear differently in varied contexts and time frames. What spurs nurses to resist are: patriarchal and hierarchal organizational structures; work intensification and fragmentation; wage compression; lack of recognition; and other unequal and oppressive relations. Nurses sometimes engage in what can be considered ineffective methods of resistance such nurse migration, avoidance, and distancing of patients and horizontal violence (infighting among nurses) as a way of lashing out against the system and mitigating to some extent untenable conditions.

Fortunately, productive resistance against exploitative systems is extensive. Some nursing groups use educational advancement and professionalism as a means of resistance; others used collectivization; still others use a combination of both. Canada is a model of how a group can use unionization and professionalization in tandem as a means of resistance. Consciousness raising, political and social action, community and public health activism, the development of participatory research methods and critical theoretical frameworks, praxis (the combination of theory and action), and striving for egalitarian professional organizations can be synergistic forms of resistance in nursing, particularly when combined with other methods of resistance such as collective action (unions) and movements to organize democratic health care services. Examples of all of these strategies appear in some form in the case study chapters.

Implications for Pro-Social Global Action

It is vital to use enhanced global communication in a positive and beneficial manner for the health of populations and the advancement of nursing. The ease of knowledge exchange through technology can aid in the prevention, screening, and treatment of diseases (Labonte, 2003). New knowledge and technology can prepare nurses and other health care professionals to use research evidence and conceptual frameworks to design locally-driven and culturally significant treatment protocols.

To create meaningful strategies for sustained health and quality of life, it is imperative that knowledge generation be a democratic and mutual exchange among wealthier nations and poorer nations and not a hierarchical, one-way flow. Indeed, much can be gained from local knowledge imbedded in history and culture, which is an essential ingredient in creating a formula for attaining and sustaining global health and well-being.

For example, local nursing knowledge can be used to help populations struggle for democratic health care and to understand and resist poverty, inequality, violence, and other negative dimensions of globalization. Nurses, as documented in the case studies in this volume are ideally positioned on the front lines of local health care delivery systems not only to educate and to deliver care, but also to be health activists and advocates for populations.

An initial step for nurses in the Americas is to better educate themselves about the negative ramifications of the underlying political economy of health and well-being and to formulate mechanisms for their own involvement in health policy and planning. Because the trend to privatize all health care services increases inequity and leads to the degradation of the quality of health care for the poor, nurses can voice crucial opposition to the dismantling of public health systems. Some nurses in the Americas already understand the social origins of illness and how oppression and poverty degrade the quality of life as well as increase disease and illness in communities. However, many more nurses can be taught how to lobby for well-funded, single-tiered, public health systems and learn concrete ways to actively oppose the rampant take-over of national public systems by for-profit private enterprises.

Poverty, inequity, and environmental degradation are the primary determinants of ill-health (Labonte, 2003). Nurses, as "the largest group of healthcare providers worldwide" (Falk-Rafael, 2006, p. 13) can develop a collective consciousness for social change. Nursing's history of class, gender, and racial oppression places it in a distinctive position and gives it a unique perspective for actualizing a new role for its members. The chapters in this volume (e.g., Mexico, Canada) deftly portray the human conditions and the relations of knowledge production for nurses.

Forging New Paths

Discontented with the effects of privatization, deregulation, and the ensuing growth in class inequities, segments of Latin American society are visibly and energetically resisting neoliberal models and shaping new local practices (Prashad & Ballve, 2006; Reygadas, 2006 in Hershberg & Rosen, 2006). More than mere isolated resistance movements, Latin America is now described as "on the offensive" and actively engaged in pro-social justice reform (Ballve, 2006, in Prashad & Ballve). Solid examples of initiatives opposing neoliberalism exist in a number of different countries in the region, explicitly Venezuela, Bolivia, Argentina, Mexico, Uruguay, Ecuador, Peru, Brazil, Guatemala, Paraguay, and Colombia (Prashad & Ballve, 2006). Latin America is fast becoming the hemisphere's leader in building counter-hegemonic actions as a new alternative to "privatization at all costs" and other forms of pro-globalization.

It thus behooves us to examine the structure of the pro-social justice movements in Latin America and to take note. While a few are isolated grassroots phenomena that have little chance of spreading regionally (e.g., some indigenous, peasant and worker movements), others are organized, solidly rooted across class lines and possessing significant national and state power (e.g., the Chavez administration in Venezuela). Nonetheless, all of them are important, because when considered in the aggregate, they lend credence to an obvious philosophical and cultural shift toward pro-social change.

Still, lest we get ahead of ourselves, important segments of Latin American society continue to steadfastly defend neoliberalism. Latin America houses large pockets of the "ultra rich" and the tendency toward the concentration of wealth has persisted over the decades. In fact, Latin America leads the world in the amount of income inequality as measured by the Gini coefficient (Reygadas, 2006, in Hershberg & Rosen, 2006). As a region the difference between the wealthiest segments of society and the rest of the population is greater than anywhere else. Debt structuring and the financial consequences of structural adjustment programs and free trade have grossly handicapped large segments of Latin Americans, including the middle class, and bolstered the wealth of privileged groups. On this point, Reygadas (2006) notes it is not by chance that "many of the great fortunes that have arisen in Latin America in recent years are tied to the financial sector." He continues by reminding us that "[m]any others who joined the ranks of the super-rich did so thanks to the privatization of public enterprises" (p. 130).

Health and education services are two of the public enterprises that were privatized. The neoliberal privatization of former state run systems generated new income inequalities and led even more to the concentration of wealth.

Myth of the North South Dichotomy

Critical health policy analysts remind us that it is misleading to view health policy and health status issues in terms of a rigid North South dichotomy. Such a view leads to inaccurate conclusions. The North South dichotomy thesis and early versions of the world system's approach argue somewhat deterministically that wealthy Northern countries and regions unilaterally extract surplus from poor Southern countries and regions leaving the South poorer and devoid of resources. This view has percolated into the ideology of international humanitarian organizations and is found in some of the literature of development organizations including the United Nations, the World Health Organization, and the Pan-American Health Organization. Yet, class analysis corrects this one-dimensional view and reveals the actual composition of classes as well as the presence of wealthy dominant classes, and poor subjugated classes in both the South and the North. Critical theorist Navarro (2004) reports that ". . . 20 percent of the richest persons in the world live in the South," and that the South has enough resources to care for itself (p. 2).

Instead, the crux of the issue of inequity and misdistribution of resources is connected to the alignment that exists in the North and in the South among wealthy, dominant groups where a massive concentration of power and wealth is present among a small percentage of the population. These wealthy dominant groups create policy and mechanisms that block the distribution of goods to those who need it. It is not in the interest of the dominant groups to redistribute wealth. Alliances exist among "the dominant classes and groups in the North and the dominant classes and groups in the South against a redistribution of resources that would adversely affect their interests" (Navarro, 2004, p. 2). Or as Harvey phrases it, the wealthy and the upper middle classes would strongly resist any reversal of the "privileges and power that have over the last thirty years been accumulating in the upper echelons of the capitalist class" (2005, p. 153).

Because the ideology of the dominant classes is present in the politics of the international health institutions that generate policy and programs, no realignment of resources or dilution of power has occurred in the recent past. In fact, it is precisely through the recent policies and programs of organizations such as the World Health Organization and the Pan-American Health Organization, that the capitalist world order is reproduced.

In a climate of market-driven solutions to all phenomena, complex multifaceted social and health issues do not fare well. In such an environment, "short-term results to satisfy stakeholders are justified at any cost" (Lerer & Matzopoulos, 2001, in Banerji, 2004, p. 24). Defining moments like the Alma-Ata Declaration on Primary

Health Care in 1978 inspired by the desire to make health a human "right for all" became secondary to private interests during the period of neoliberalism in the Americas. Consequently, health status and "almost all of the global indicators on health levels, life expectancy, infant mortality, and the like show losses rather than gains in well-being since the 1960s" (Harvey, 2005, p. 154).

One fear voiced by some critical analysts is that in the event of a financial capital crisis "a strong and powerful social democratic and working-class movement is in a better position to redeem capitalism than is capitalist class power itself" (Harvey 2005, p. 153), because it is the middle class and the poor who suffer the most during catastrophic economic events, they are the most keenly motivated to keep capital flowing through the system in order to meet their daily monetary needs. The wealthy have excellent mechanisms in place and at their disposal to protect themselves from financial ruin.

Social Justice and Nursing

Latin American nursing has had a particular historical focus on social justice issues and community-based public health care, in part because of Latin America's history of radical social change movements and nursing's link to initiatives rooted in this philosophical stance. Latin American nursing leadership, described at times as "revolutionary" (Grace & Smith, 2007, in Lynaugh et al., p. 304) stands in stark contrast to the U.S. nursing leadership that historically aligns with conservative members of the hospital and medical establishment and against progressive social change. Nursing in Latin America was particularly progressive during the Alma Ata years when nationalized health services were implemented in many Latin American countries. The vision for a people's health service with active citizen participation was admired and supported (see particularly chapters on Colombia and Argentina in this volume). During that time, Latin American nursing concentrated on broad population-based health care needs and "not on the nursing profession per se" (Grace & Smith, 2007, in Lynaugh et al., p. 304).

The concept of "citizen participation" is imbedded in the philosophy of a number of national health services as a mechanism to engender the input of community members and to link formal health care initiatives to local contexts, knowledge, and culture (Breda, 1992). While many of the national health services in Latin America have undergone significant structural changes over the last 2 decades, their original design was inspired by the principles of egalitarianism and universality of health services for the entire population.

The term "people's health service" is sometimes used to refer to a comprehensive national health service that provides universal and comprehensive care with a particular focus on prevention, health maintenance, and promotion and the elimination of healthcare inequities and egalitarian provision of services to all (Breda, 1992). A tenet of a people's health service is the notion of health care as a "right" rather than a "privilege" and is associated with socialist principles in the distribution and philosophy of all aspects of health care services. A fully implemented people's health service would be a single-tiered health care system where citizens would not need to purchase private health care services. It is safe to say that the national debates over the type of health care system (market-based vs. state-controlled national health care systems) was one of the major public discussions of the last decades with many European and Latin American countries implementing some type of "people's" national health care system in the second half of the 20th century.

Citizen participation, while ideologically sound and philosophically in sync with the spirit of a people's health service, has proved difficult to implement over long periods of time. The push for technological health care and to place professional, "technical" figures in decision-making positions conflicted with the notion of people's choice and people's voice in shaping an egalitarian national health service.

An example of successful citizen participation in the health care service emanates from Brazilian nursing in its locally-driven community health initiatives called "popular theater" and "health fairs." Nurses and other health workers mounted these initiatives in partnership with citizens as part of a series of innovative activities used to implement health promotion measures. A goal of nurses in the Brazilian National Health Service was to combine professional and local knowledge while putting into action the principle of citizen participation (see Brazilian chapter in this volume). As another form of resistance to the status quo, this praxis moves nursing actions to a higher level.

Although funding difficulties during neoliberal economic reforms in Brazil threatened these and other locally-driven projects, these innovative activities by Brazilian nursing championed meaningful health changes in the country. Ultimately, such initiatives lead to a more equitable health system while allowing nursing to make great strides in its evolution as a social practice.

Nursing in Canada has also been on the forefront of pro-social change through actions of resistance. Inspired by a social commitment to the well-being of the group, Canadian nurses took the lead from Canadians who defended collective rights over individual rights. These social values spurred the design of a social security system in Canada that included a nationalized health insurance plan rooted in the principles of public administration, universality, and portability of services from one province to another.

The Role of Philanthropic Institutions in Knowledge Production

Philanthropic institutions such as the Kellogg and the Rockefeller Foundations have a central role in forming the agenda for the social and behavioral sciences including nursing. These prominent foundations had a significant role in the development of modern nursing in each of the peripheral and semi-peripheral capitalist counties represented in this volume (see chapters on Brazil, Argentina, Mexico, Colombia, and Chile). While it is indisputable that funding from private foundations has positively affected the nature of nursing both as a discipline and as a profession, it has done so at a certain cost. While on one hand, funding from private foundations to conduct research and to advance "science" can be understood as helpful, even "miraculous" to a discipline, it has also historically "influenced the research agenda of those they supported financially" (Adams & Gorton, 2006, p. 450). The influence of private foundations for setting the agenda for the trajectory of scientific studies and educational programming cannot be overestimated. Such agenda setting is the case in nursing in Latin America as well as in non-Latin America.

The root of the issue does not rest with private philanthropic organizations. The extent to which the agendas of organizations like the United Nations, the World Health Organization, and the Pan-American Health Organization are influenced by ideological positions is also important to note.

The dilemma for nursing is that it has clearly benefited enormously from its connections to the above-mentioned organizations. These benefits are documented repeatedly in all seven case study chapters in this volume.

Yet, one example of Latin American nursing' resistance to hegemony and dominance was its refusal to accept an offer in 1987 by the Pan-American Health Organization to have the *American Journal of Nursing* (which was the official journal of the American Nurses Association) translated into Spanish and Portuguese. Instead, the Latin American nursing leadership requested a mechanism to have their local knowledge expanded and disseminated. They chose to have a Brazilian company that already offered computer-based information systems for physicians expand their project to fit the needs of nursing. Henceforth, the number of textbooks and other academic publications generated in Latin America has increased significantly in the last 2 decades (Grace & Smith, 2007, in Lynaugh et al.).

SUMMARY

This volume represents the application of critical theory to nursing in a cross-national case study. The primary focus is to explore how the political economy shapes nursing and nursing education over time in different geo-political contexts in the Americas. A corollary focus is to describe the segmentation of nursing in service organizations and how such segmentation affects the nursing workforce. Nurses are on the front lines of care and do much of the manual labor in health care facilities. Consequently, this critique appropriately addresses social class, as well as gender and race relations in nursing.

The intent is to pose questions that are rarely asked and to open lines of inquiry typically not treated in the academic literature. As the largest wage laborers in hospitals, extended care facilities, clinics, and community health agencies, nurses are enmeshed in the market-driven labor process. The hope is that this book will help health social scientists, health care professionals, and others understand how education is organized, how nursing labor is divided, and the role in it of profit and profitability in a market system.

In the same vein, many of the community-based public health nursing initiatives from Latin America derive from critical social and political economic theories. Much is to be learned from Latin America about these nursing-medicine-community partnerships (Grace & Smith, 2007, in Lynaugh et al.). Latin American nurses' involvement in the health for all initiatives spurred by Alma Ata are formidable.

Additionally, while university-based academic nursing programs in Latin America have been described as "amazingly similar to those in the United States" (Grace & Smith, 2007 in Lynaugh et al., p. 294), the context for clinical practice is dramatically different. One main difference is that the nurse physician ratio in most Latin American countries is one licensed nurse to five physicians (Malvarez & Agudelo, 2005). (The ratio of nurses to physicians in the United States and Canada is the opposite, that is, five nurses for every physician.) Consequently, the scope of responsibilities for many licensed nurses in Latin America is enormous. Also, while the length of university preparation for university-based nursing and medical education programs is similar, Latin America physicians earn four times more than nurses (Grace & Smith, 2007, in Lynaugh et al., p. 295).

Much has been written in this volume about the difficulties nurses face in the workplace: lack of status and respect, poor working conditions, long shift hours, and relatively low wages. Confusion exists across the Americas about the multiple levels of nursing preparation. While nurse educators struggle to produce increasing numbers of professional nurses, hospitals and other health care settings often fail to match nurses' level of education with their responsibilities on the job. In light of these issues, the supply and retention of a qualified, highly competent workforce in nursing is a concern that resurfaces repeatedly without an apparent or immediate resolution.

Nonetheless, nurses are ideally positioned to positively impact people's lives and to influence the structure of health care systems. Nurses offer essential services to families and communities when they are sick, in precarious uncertain health, and in the most vulnerable conditions. Although nursing has, in many cases, aligned itself with biomedicine, nursing has also compellingly demonstrated its resistance to the status quo in important ways. Nursing in the 21st century will increasingly assert itself as a holistic social practice. By doing so, nursing will focus more on prevention and community public health than do any of the other health professions. And nurses who function actively as social and health advocates will work to reshape the system.

The methodology for change is straightforward and the interventions are simple. First, nurses can more clearly grasp the influence of the global political economy on health status, on health care systems, and on the field of nursing. They can understand how the market-driven system and biomedicine jointly shaped the direction of nursing and the structure of health care systems. Second, nurses, particularly U.S. nurses, can redirect their advanced degree programs toward the critical social sciences. They can begin by partnering with Latin American and Canadian scholars who have more knowledge and experience with the critical social science perspective. Third, critical social scientists and nurses can partner to design theoretical applications of health care issues that nurses can apply to practice. Already, some groups of Latin American and Canadian nurses are actively corroborating to design community initiatives focusing on the well-being of communities and population groups.

Over the last several decades, neoliberalism has changed the face of health care markets, including labor markets, across the Americas in previously unimaginable ways. Because neoliberalism requires flexible and compliant labor, nurse migration, part-time work, temporary work contracts for nurses are necessary to support the profit goal. Almost every case study in this volume documents these labor practices and their enabling function to the neoliberal economic model. Indeed, some critical theorists fear that even countries with historically strong labor organizations are ill-prepared to reverse the current dynamic of imbedded neoliberalism tied to globalization (Harvey, 2005): Others (Collins & Wingard, 2000) predict it will be *communities* that "may become the new source of strength, replacing the old class conflicts and international labor organizations" (p. 2). If communities have the power to "become a countervailing force in this global system" (p. 2), then the role of nursing in this event is potentially enormous. In the final analysis, communities can be the promise of nursing and a truly egalitarian health system.

REFERENCES

Adams, J., & Gorton, D. (2006). The Mississippi Delta of Dollard and Powdermaker: A response to Anne Rose's commentary on "Southern Trauma." *American Anthropologist, 108*(2), 450-451.

Ballve, T. (2006). From resistance to offensive: NACLA and Latin America. In V. Prashad & T. Ballve (Eds.), *Dispatches from Latin America: On the frontlines against neoliberalism* (pp. 23-31). Boston, MA: South End Press.

Banerji, D. (2004). Reinventing mass communication: A World Health Organization tool for behavioral change to control disease. *International Journal of Health Services, 34*(1), 15-24.

Breda, K. M. (1992). *Politics, culture and Gramscian hegemony in the Italian health service: A comparison of USLs.* Unpublished doctoral dissertation, University of Connecticut, Storrs.

Buchan, J., Kingma, M., & Lorenzo, F. M. (2005). *International migration of nurses: Trends and policy implications.* Retrieved: July 6, 2006, from http://www.icn.ch/global/Issue5migration.pdf

Buchan, J., & Sochalski, J. (2004). The migration of nurses: Trends and policies. *Bulletin of the World Health Organization, 82*(8), 587-594.

Chinn, P. (2006). The global nurse shortage and healthcare. *Advances in Nursing Science, 29*(1), 1.

Collins, T. W., & Wingard, J. D. (2000). *Communities and capital: Local struggles against corporate power and privatization.* Athens, GA: University of Georgia Press.

Falk-Rafael, A. (2006). Globalization and global health: Toward nursing praxis in the global community. *Advances in Nursing Science, 29*(1), 2-14.

Grace, H., & Smith, G. (2007). Nursing in Latin America and the Caribbean. In J. Lynaugh, H. Grace, G. Smith, R. Sena, D. De Villalobos, & M. Hlalele (Eds.), *The W. K. Kellogg Foundation and the nursing profession: Shared values, shared legacy* (pp. 293-308). Indianapolis, IN: Sigma Theta Tau International.

Harvey, D. (2005). *A brief history of neoliberalism.* New York: Oxford.

Hershberg, E., & Rosen, F. (Eds.). (2006). *Latin America after neoliberalism: Turning the tide in the 21st century?* New York: The New Press.

Hughes, E. (1951). Studying the nurse's work. *American Journal of Nursing, 51,* 294-295.

Hughes, E., Hughes, H. M., & Deutscher, I. (1958). *Twenty thousand nurses tell their story.* Philadelphia, PA: Lippincott.

Kinsley, M. (2006, July 3). Coming to America: Foreign nurses find a home. *Nursing Spectrum, 10*(13), 12-13.

Labonte, R. (2003). *Dying for trade: Why globalization can be bad for our health.* Toronto: The CSJ Foundation for Research and Education. Retrieved June 15, 2006, from http://www.socialjustice.org/pdfs/dyingfortrade.pdf

Lynaugh, J., Grace, H., Smith, G., Sena, R., DeVillalobos, M., & Hlalele, M. (2007). *The W. K. Kellogg Foundation and the nursing profession: Shared values, shared legacy.* Indianapolis, IN: Sigma Theta Tau International.

Malvarez, S. M., & Agudelo, M. C. C. (2005). *Overview of the nursing workforce in Latin America.* Retrieved June 15, 2006, from International Council of Nursing Web Site: http://www.icn.ch/global/Issue6LatinAmerica.pdf

May, J., Bazzoli, G., & Gerland, A. (2006, June 26). Hospitals' responses to nurses staffing shortages. Health Affairs, w316-w323. Retrieved June 28, 2006, from http://www.healthaffairs.org

McGregor, S. (2001). Neoliberalism and health care: *International Journal of Consumer Studies. Special Edition on "Consumers and Health," 25*(2): 82-89. Retrieved June 16, 2006, from http://www.consultmcgregor.com/PDFs/research/neoliberalism.pdf

McGregor, S., Doull, J., & Fisk, L. (2005). *Neoliberalism, microbes, and peace: A human ecological perspective.* Retrieved June 17, 2006, from http://www.kon.org/archives/forum/14-1/McGregor.html

Nagy, A. (2006, June 26). Root cause of nursing shortage? No class. *Connecticut Business News Journal,* Retrieved June 29, 2006, from http://www.contact.com/article_page.lasso?id=40055

Navarro, V. (2004). Inequities are unhealthy. *Monthly Review, 56*(2). Retrieved January 9, 2006, from www.monthlyreview.org/0604navarro.htm

Prashad, V., & Ballve, T. (Eds.). (2006). *Dispatches from Latin America: On the frontlines against neoliberalism.* Boston, MA: South End Press.

Prashad, V. (2006). They rise from the earth: The promise of Latin America. In V. Prashad & T. Ballve (Eds.), *Dispatches from Latin America: On the frontlines against neoliberalism* (pp. 13-20). Boston, MA: South End Press.

Reygadas, L. (2006). Crime and citizen security in Latin America. In E. Hershberg & F. Rosen (Eds.), *Latin America after neoliberalism: Turning the tide in the 21st century?* (pp. 120-143). New York: The New Press.

APPENDICES

APPENDIX A
Abbreviations and Acronyms

AAN	American Academy of Nursing (USA)
AACN	American Association of Colleges of Nursing (USA)
ACEN	Academy of Chief Executives in Nursing (Canada)
ACHDHR	Advisory Committee on Health Delivery and Human Resources (Canada)
ACHIEEN	Asociación Chilena de Educación en Enfermería = Chilean Association for Nursing Education (Chile)
ACETRA	Asociación de Educación en Enfermería de Escuelas no Universitarias de la Argentina = Civic Association of Tertiary Schools of Nursing of the Argentinean Republic (Argentina)
ACOFAEN	Asociación Colombiana de Facultades de Enfermería = Colombian Association of Schools of Nursing (Colombia)
AEUERA	Asociación de Escuelas Universitarias de Enfermería de la República Argentina = Association of University Schools of Nursing of the Argentinean Republic (Argentina)
AFP	Administradora de Fondos de Pensiones = Pension Fund Administration (Chile)
AHA	American Hospital Association (USA)
AJN	American Journal of Nursing (AJN)
ALADEFE	Asociación Latinoamericana de Escuelas y Facultades de Enfermería = Latin America Association of Schools of Nursing (Latin America)
AMA	American Medical Association (USA)
AMEAS	Academia Mexicana de Enfermería en Antropología de la Salud (México)
AMENAC	Asociación Mexicana de Enfermeras en Nefrología, A.C. (México)
AMEPS	Asociación Mexicana de Escuelas de Salud Pública (México) Mexican Association of Schools of Public Health
AMFEM	Asociación Mexicana de Facultades y Escuelas de Medicina, A.C. (México)

ANA	American Nurses Association (USA)
ANAC	Aboriginal Nurses Association of Canada (Canada)
ANUIES	Asociación Nacional de Universidades e Instituciones de Educación Superior (México)
APS	Atención Primaria de Salud = Primary Health Care (Chile)
ARFEEC	Asociación Regional de Facultades y Escuelas de Enfermería Centro, A.C. (México)
ATSA	Asociación de Trabajadores de la Sanidad = Health Workers Association (Argentina)
BCG	Bacille Calmet-Guerin
BNA	Brazilian Nursing Association = ABEn Associação Brasileira de Enfermagem (Brazil)
CANARESSA	Catastri Nacional de Servicios y Recursos de Salud (Argentina) Inventory of Health Care Resources and Services
CANR	Canadian Association for Nursing Research (Canada)
CAPES	Coordenação de Aperfeiçoamento de Pessoal de Nível Superior = CFEGP Coordination for Further Education of Graduate Personnel (Brazil)
CASEN	Encuesta de Caracterización Económica = Economic Characterization Questionnaire (Chile)
CASN	Canadian Association of Schools of Nursing (Canada)
CAUSN	Canadian Association of University Schools of Nursing (Canada)
CBC	Canadian Broadcasting Corporation (Canada)
CDC	Centers for Disease Control (USA)
CIA	Central de Inteligencia Americana = Central Intelligence Agency (USA)
CENABAST	Central Nacional de Abastecimiento = National Supply Center (Chile)
CENEVAL	Centro Nacional de Evaluación (México)
CFN	Canadian Federation of Nurses (Canada)
CFNU	Canadian Federation of Nurses Unions (Canada)
CGT	Confederación General del Trabajo = General Confederation of Work (Argentina)

CHAP	Community Health Agents Program = PACS Programa de Agentes Comuniarios de Saúde (Brazil)
CICAD	Interamerican Drug Abuse Control Commission (USA) Comisión Interamericana para el Control del Abuso de Drogas (Latin America) Comissão Interamericana para o Contole do Abuso de Drogas (Brazil)
CIE	Consejo Internacional de Enfermería (Spanish) ICN International Council of Nurses
CIEES	Comités Interinstitucionales para la Evaluación de la Educación Superior (México)
CIFRHS	Comisión Interinstitucional para la Formación de Recursos Humanos en Salud (México)
CIHI	Canadian Institute for Health Information (Canada)
CLBC	Canadian Labour and Business Centre (Canada)
CMA	Canadian Medical Association (Canada)
CNA	Canadian Nursing Association (Canada)
CNA	California Nurses Association (USA)
CNAC	Canadian Nursing Advisory Committee (Canada)
CNAP	Comisión Nacional de Acreditación de Pregrado = National Commission for Accreditation of Undergraduate Programs (Chile)
CNATN	Canadian National Association of Trained Nurses (Canada)
CNE	Colegio Nacional de Enfermeras, A.C. (México)
CNF	Canadian Nurses Foundation (Canada)
CNI	Central Nacional de Inteligencia = National Central Intelligence (Chile)
CNPq	Conselho Nacional de Desenvolvimento Científico e Tecnológico = NCSTD National Council for Scientific and Technological Development (Brazil)
COIE	Comisión Interinstitucional de Enfermería (México)
COMACE	Consejo Mexicano de Acreditación y Certificación de Enfermería, A.C. (México)
COMEPO	Consejo Mexicano de Estudios de Posgrado (México)

COMIE	Consejo Mexicano de Investigación Educativa (México)
COMLE	Colegio Mexicano de Licenciados en Enfermería, A.C. (México)
COMPIE	Comité Mexicano para la Práctica Internacional de Enfermería (México)
COMRA	Confederación Médica de la República Argentina = Medical Confederation of the Argentinean Republic (Argentina)
CONAFE	Consejo Nacional de Fomento Educativo (México)
CONALEP	Colegio Nacional de Profesionales Técnicos (México)
CONAMED	Comisión Nacional de Arbitraje Médico (México)
CONAP	Comisión Nacional de Acreditación de Postgrado = Chilean National Commission for the Accreditation of Graduate Programs (Chile)
CONAVE	Comité Nacional de Vigilancia Epidemiológica (México)
CONEM	Colegio Nacional de Enfermeras Militares, A.C. (México)
COPAES	Consejo para la Acreditación de la Educación Superior (México)
CRC	Canadian Red Cross (Canada)
CUMEX	Consorcio de Universidades Mexicanas (México)
DANE	Departamento Administrativo Nacional de Estadística = National Administrative Department of Statistics (Colombia)
DC	Central District (Brazil)
DDS	Direct Disbursement System = SDD Sistema de Desembolso Direto (Brazil)
DMHLE	Department of Management in Health Labor and Education = DEGES Departamento de Gestão do Trabalho e da Educação na Saúde (Brazil)
DNHW	Department of National Health and Welfare (Canada)
DIF	Desarrollo Integral de la Familia (México)
ECAES	Exámenes de Estado de Calidad de la Educación Superior = State's Exams of Higher Education Quality (Colombia)
ESE	Empresas Sociales del Estado = State´s Social Enterprises (Colombia)
FAE	Federación Argentina de Enfermería = Argentinean Federation of Nursing (Argentina)

ENEP	Escuelas Nacionales de Estudios Profesionales (México)
ESEO	Escuela Superior de Enfermería y Obstetricia (México)
FCE	Federal Council of Education = CFE Consuelo Federal de Educação (Brazil)
FNC	Federal Nursing Council = COFEn Conselho Federal de Enfermagem (Brazil)
FEMAFEE	Federación Mexicana de Asociaciones de Facultades y Escuelas de Enfermería, A.C. (México)
FEMCAE	Federación Mexicana de Colegios y Asociaciones de Enfermería, A.C. (México)
FEPPEN	Federación Panamericana de Profesionales de Enfermería = Pan American Federation of Nursing Professionals
FID	Fondo Internacional de Desarrollo = International Monetary Fund
FONASA	Fondo Nacional de Salud = National Health Fund (Chile)
G8	Group of Eight
GATS	General Agreement on Trade in Services
GDP	Gross Domestic Product
HCWU	Hospital and Clinics Workers' Union = SEEHCS Sindicato dos Empregados de Hospitais e Casas de Saúde (Brazil)
HIV/AIDS	Human Immunodeficiency Virus/Acquired Immune Deficiency Syndrome
HPA	Hospitales Públicos de Autogestión = Self-Managed Public Hospitals (Argentina)
HPB	Health Protection Branch (Canada)
HPS	Hantavirus Pulmonary Síndrome
IADB	Inter American Development Bank
ICFES	Instituto Colombiano para el Fomento de la Educación Superior = Colombian Institute for the Promotion of the Higher Education (Colombia)
ICN	International Council of Nurses (Spanish) CIE
ICU	Intensive Care Unit
IHA	Integrated Health Actions = AIS Ações Integradas de Saúde (Brazil)

IMF	International Monetary Fund = FMI Fundo Monetário Internacional (Brazil)
IMR	Infant Mortality Rate
IMSS	Instituto Mexicano del Seguro Social (México)
INDEC	Instituto Nacional de Estadística y Censos de la República = National Institute for Statistics and Census (Argentina)
INEGI	Instituto Nacional de Estadística, Geografía e Informática (México)
IPEA	Instituto de Pesquisas Econômicas Aplicadas = IAER Institute of Applied Economics Research (Brazil)
IPN	Instituto Politécnico Nacional (México)
ISAPRE	Institución de Salud Previsional = Health (Forcast) Oversight Institution (Chile)
ISEM	Instituto de Salud del Estado de México (México)
ISP	Instituto de Salud Pública = Institute of Public Health (Chile)
ISSEMyM	Instituto de Seguridad Social del Estado de México y Municipios (México)
ISSSTE	Instituto de Seguridad Social al Servicio de los Trabajadores del Estado (México)
LPN	Licensed Practical Nurse (Canada & USA)
LOCE	Ley Orgánica Constitucional de Enseñanza = Higher Education Reform Law (Chile)
MCE	Ministry of Culture and Education = MEC Ministério da Educação e Cultura (Brazil)
MCE/DUA	Ministry of Education and Culture, Department for University Affairs = MEC/DAU Ministério da Educação, Departamento de Assuntos Universitários (Brazil)
ME	Ministry of Education = ME Ministério da Educação (Brazil)
ML	Ministry of Labor = MT Ministério do Trabalho (Brazil)
MERCOSUL	Mercado Comum do Sul = MERCOSUR Mercado Común del Sur = Common Market of the South = Área of Internal Free Trade and Common Commerce Policies among Latin American Countries: Argentina, Brasil, Paraguai, Uruguai, and Venezuela (Brazil)
MERCOSUR	Mercado Común del Sur = Common Market of the South (Argentina)

NAFTA	North American Free Trade Agreement
NATO	North Atlantic Treaty Organization
NCCE	National Confereration of Commerce Employees = CNTC Confederação Nacional dos Trabalhadores do Comércio (Brazil)
NHS	National Health System = SNS Sistema Nacional de Saúde (Brazil)
NINR	National Institute of Nursing Research (USA)
NLN	National League for Nursing (USA)
NLRB	National Labor Relations Board (USA)
NNAA	National Nursing Auxiliaries' Association = ANAE Associação Nacional de Auxiliares de Enfermagem (Brazil)
NNF	Nurses' National Federation = FNE Federação Nacional dos Enfermeiros (Brazil)
NNAU	National Nursing Auxiliaries Union = UNAE União Nacional dos Auxiliares de Enfermagem (Brazil)
NNOC	National Nurses Organizing Committee (USA)
NUNAT	National Union of Nursing Auxiliaries and Technicians = UNATE União Nacional dos Auxiliares e Técnicos de Enfermagem (Brazil)
OAS	Organization of American States = OEA Orgranização dos Estados Americanos (Brazil)
OCED	Organization for Economic Cooperation and Development
OEA	Organización de Estados Americanos = OAS Organization of American States
OFL	Orientations and Fundamentals Law = LDB Lei de Diretrizes e Bases (Brazil)
OIIQ	Ordre des infirmières et infirmiers du Québec (Canada)
ONP	Office of Nursing Policy (Canada)
OMS	Organización Mundial de la Salud (Spanish) (WHO) = Orgranização Mundial de Saúde (Brazil)
ONU	Organización de las Naciones Unidas (México)
OPN	Office of Nursing Policy (Canada)
OPV	Oral Polio Vaccine

PAE	Proceso de Atención de Enfermería (México)
PAHO	Pan American Health Organization (English) (OPS) = OPAS Orgarnização Panamericana de Saúde (Brazil)
PHC	Primary Health Care
PIB	Producto Interno Bruto (México)
PIFEM	Plan Integrador para el Fortalecimiento de la Enfermería Mexicana (México)
PMO	Presentación Médica Básica Obligatoria = Obligatory Basic Medical Service (Argentina)
PNE	Programa Nacional de Educación (México)
PNS	Plan Nacional de Salud (México)
PNUD	Programa de las Naciones Unidas para el Desarrollo = UNDP United Nations Development Program
PROCORHUS	Programa Colaborativo de Recursos Humanos en Salud (México)
PROMIN	Programa Materno Infantil = Maternal and Infant Program (Argentina)
PSMCS	Private Supplementary Medical Care System = SAMS Sistema de Atenção Médica Suplementar (Brazil)
PUEE	Plan Único de Especialización en Enfermería (México)
REAL	Red de Enfermería de América Latina = Latin American Web of Nursing
REMEDIAR	Program for the supply of ambulatory free medications (Argentina)
RN	Registered Nurse (Canada & USA)
RNs	Registered Nurses = Baccalaureate Nurses = Enfermeiras (Brazil)
RN-BS	Registered Nurses = Baccalaureate Nurses = Enfermeiras(os) (Brazil)
RNCs	Regional Nursing Councils = COREns Conselhos Regionais de Enfermagem (Brazil)
RNA	Registered Nursing Assistant (Canada)
RNAO	Registered Nurses Association of Ontario (Canada)
RPN	Registered Psychiatric Nurses (Canada)

RPNAO	Registered Practical Nurses Association of Ontario (Canada)
SAPU	Servicio Atención Primaria de Urgencia = Primary Emergency Health Care Services (Chile)
SARS	Severe Acute Respiratory Syndrome
SBPC	Sociedade Brasileira para o Progresso da Ciência = BSPS Brazilian Society for the Progress of Science (Brazil)
SCISP	Servicio Cooperativo Interamericano de Salud Pública = International Bureau of Public Health
SEP	Secretaría de Educación Pública = Minister of Public Education (México)
SEPLAN	Secretaria de Planejamento = PO Planning Office
SIARHE	Sistema de Información Administrativa de Recursos Humanos en Enfermería (México)
SNA	State Nurses Association (USA)
SNISS	Sistema Nacional Integrado de Servicios de Salud = Integrated National System of Health Services (Argentina)
SNEP	Superintendencia Nacional de Enseñanza Privada = National Supervision of Private Education (Argentina)
SNSS	Sistema Nacional de Servicios de Salud = National System of Health Care Services (Chile)
SPSFRS	São Paulo State Foundation of Research Support = FAPESP Fundação de Amparo à Pesquisa do Estado de São Paulo (Brazil)
SSA	Secretaría de Salud = Minister of Health (México)
TLC	Tratado de Libre Comercio (México) = Free Trade Agreement
TRIPS	Trade Related Intellectual Property Rights (Canada)
TSDF	Technical and Scientific Development Fund = FUNTEC Fundo do Desenvolvimento Técnico e Científico (Brazil)
UHS	Unified Health System = SUS Sistema Único de Saúde (Brazil)
UK	United Kingdom
UN	United Nations
UNAM	Universidad Nacional Autónoma de México (México) National Autonomous University of Mexico

UNESCO	United Nations Educational, Scientific and Cultural Organization
UNICEF	The United Nations Children's Fund
USAID	United States Agency for International Development = AEUDI Agência dos Estados Unidos de Desenvolvimento Internacional (Brazil)
VIH/SIDA	Virus Inmunodeficiencia Humano/ Síndrome de Inmunodeficiencia Adquirida HIV/AIDS
VON	Victorian Order of Nurses (Canada)
WB	World Bank = BM Banco Mundial (Brazil)
WHO	World Health Organization
WTO	World Trade Organization
WWII	World War II

APPENDIX B
Country Comparison of Nursing Titles and Educational Preparation

	Professional Nurse			
Country	Professional Nurse	Semesters or Years of Preparation	Post-Secondary School Yes/No	University Yes/No
Argentina	Licenciado en Enfermería	5 years	Yes	Yes 5 years
Brazil	All Registered Nurses in Brazil graduate from a BS program. The Portuguese word for RN-BS is Enfermeira(o).	8 to 10 semesters	Yes	Yes 4-year baccalaureate degree (university)
Canada	Registered Nurse RN	6-8 semesters 2, 3, or 4 years	Yes	4 year (3 years in Québec) baccalaureate degree (University) or 2-year Community College Diploma
Chile	Licenciado en Enfermería	10 semesters	Yes	Yes
Colombia	Enfermero-a (equivalent to Licenciado en Enfermería)	8 to 10 semesters	Yes	Yes
Mexico	Licenciado en Enfermería	4 years (8 semesters)	Yes	Yes 4-year
United States	Registered Nurse RN	4 years (8 semesters)	Yes	Yes 4-year baccalaureate degree (university)

APPENDIX B (Cont'd.)

Nursing Technician

Country	Nursing Technician	Semesters or Years of Preparation	Post-Secondary School Yes/No	University Yes/No
Argentina	Enfermería	3 years	Yes	Yes. The program is also offered by the Tertiary Schools of Nursing such as the Red Cross
Brazil	Nurse Technician = Técnico de Enfermagem	4 semesters	Yes	No
Canada	N/A	N/A	N/A	N/A
Chile	Técnico Nivel Superior en Enfermería	4 semesters	Yes	No
Colombia	Técnico en Enfermería	2 years	Yes	The program is offered by a university institution (smaller than universities) and the title is not university, but technical.
Mexico	Técnico en Enfermería	3 years	Yes	No
United States	Registered Nurse RN	2 years (4 or 5 semesters)	Yes	2-year associate degree (junior college)

APPENDIX B (Cont'd.)

Nursing Auxiliary

Country	Nursing Auxiliary	Semesters or Years of Preparation	Post-Secondary School Yes/No	University Yes/No
Argentina	Auxiliar de enfermería	9 months	No	No
Brazil	Nursing Auxiliar = Auxiliar de Enfermagem	2 semesters (New programs cannot be opened – operating programs must upgrade to nursing technicians)	Yes	No
Canada	Licensed Practical Nurse (LPN) or Registered Nursing Assistant (RNA)	1-2 years 2-4 semesters	Yes	No
Chile	Auxiliar de Enfermería	2 semesters	Yes	No
Colombia	Auxiliar de Enfermería	1 year of school plus 1 year of supervised work	Yes	No
Mexico	Auxiliar de Enfermería	2 years	Yes	No
United States	Licensed Practical Nurse (LPN)	10-12 months	Yes	No

APPENDIX B (Cont'd.)

Nursing Attendant/Aid

Country	Nursing Attendant/Aid	Semesters or Years of Preparation	Post-Secondary School Yes/No	University Yes/No
Argentina	—	It does not exist as a level of education. In some institutions there are not formally trainred staff who complete simple tasks such as helping or delivering mail.	—	—
Brazil	Nursing Attendant = Atendente de Enfermagem	1 semester (workers at this level are either retiring or they should further their education to qualify as nurse auxiliaries and then as nurse technicians)	No	No
Canada	Health Care Assistant	6-12 weeks	Yes	No
Chile	—	—	—	—
Colombia	N/A	N/A	N/A	N/A
Mexico	N/A	N/A	N/A	N/A
United States	Patient Care Assistant (PCA) or Nurse's Aid	2 to 6 weeks	Yes	No

APPENDIX B (Cont'd.)

Post-BSN Specialization Programs

Country	Post-Baccalaureate (1): Specialization	Semesters or Years of Preparation	Post-Secondary School Yes/No	University Yes/No
Argentina	Specialization	2 years	Yes	Yes
Brazil	Specialization/ Nurse Specialist (CNS)	2-3 senesters— 360 hours minimum and 600 hours maximum	Yes	Yes university graduate program *lato sensu* level
Canada	Specialization-PHC (Only)	1-1.5 years	Yes	Yes
Chile	Specialization	1 year	Yes	Yes
Colombia	Specialization	1-1½ years	Yes	Yes
Mexico	General Nursing	2 years	Yes	Yes
United States	Non-degree granting Certification programs		Yes	

Masters Programs

Country	Post-Baccalaureate (2): Masters	Semesters or Years of Preparation	Post-Secondary School Yes/No	University Yes/No
Argentina	Masters	2 years	Yes	Yes
Brazil	Masters	4 semesters	Yes	Yes university graduate program at *stricto sensu* level
Canada	Masters	4-8 semesters	Yes	Yes
Chile	Masters	4-6 semesters	Yes	Yes
Colombia	Masters	2 years	Yes	Yes
Mexico	Masters	4 semesters	Yes	Yes
United States	Masters	4 to 5 semesters	Yes	Yes

APPENDIX B (Cont'd.)

Doctoral Programs

Country	Post-Baccalaureate (3): Doctoral	Semesters or Years of Preparation	Post-Secondary School Yes/No	University Yes/No
Argentina	Doctoral program	4 years	Yes	Yes
Brazil	Doctoral program	6 semesters *or* 3 years	Yes	Yes university graduate program at *stricto sensu* level
	Post-doctoral program	2 semesters *or* 1 year	Yes	Yes university graduate program at *stricto sensu* level
Canada	Doctoral program	3-5 years	Yes	Yes
Chile	Doctoral program	3-5 years	Yes	Yes
Colombia	Doctoral program	3-5 years	Yes	Yes
Mexico	Doctoral program	2 years (4 semesters)	Yes	Yes
United States	Doctoral program	3-5 years	Yes	Yes

APPENDIX C

Questions for Discussion and Dialogue for Nursing and Globalization in the Americas: A Critical Perspective

Karen Lucas Breda

1. Describe the role of hospitals in the creation of hospital-based schools of nursing.
2. Why is nursing in the Americas made up mostly of women?
3. Compare and contrast the concepts of *proglobalization* and *prosocial justice*.
4. Explain the meaning of the term *neoliberalism*.
5. List two negative affects of *proglobalization*.
6. Why is it important to look at both macro-level (the big picture) and micro-level (the small picture) phenomena to understand health care and nursing?
7. Prestige is often associated with more schooling. Identify why higher levels of education for nurses is not always associated with more prestige for nursing.
8. Describe the socialization of female nurses in the Mexican case study.
9. Discuss what happened in Chile when nursing programs in private universities were allowed to proliferate.
10. Identify two national laws discussed in the Colombian and Argentinean chapters and illustrate how these laws have affected nursing in their respective countries.
11. Explain the differences between nurse unionization in the United States, Canada, and Latin America.
12. Describe the effects of increased privatization and deregulation on nursing practice and education in the Americas.
13. Discuss two methods of resistance used by nurses in Latin America.
14. Compare and contrast the population-focused nursing initiatives in Brazil, Colombia, and Canada. Explain why they are model programs to emulate.

15. Breda concludes that "nursing is the handmaiden of the global capitalist system." Discuss ways nursing has accommodated powerful and dominant figures.
16. Nurse migration, while appearing to benefit individual migrant nurses, is ultimately devastating for nursing, health care systems, and people in poor countries. Compare and contrast the benefits and drawbacks of nurse migration.
17. Illustrate and discuss the following: Analysts say that "nursing is the glue for the health care system."
18. Evaluate the ability of the case study countries to transform the future of nursing.
19. Envision several steps we can take to get more involved in prosocial global action for nursing in the Americas.
20. How has your reading of this book changed your understanding of nursing and globalization in the Americas?

From the Poem "Canto General" Written in 1950 by Pablo Neruda (Chile 1904-1974)

XVIII

AMÉRICA NO INVOCO TU NOMBRE EN VANO

AMÉRICA, no invoco tu nombre en vano.
Cuando sujeto al corazón la espada,
cuando aguanto en el alma la gotera,
cuando por las ventanas
un nuevo día tuyo me penetra,
soy y estoy en la luz que me produce,
vivo en la sombra que me determina,
duermo y despierto en tu esencial aurora:
dulce como las uvas, y terrible,
conductor del azúcar y el castigo,
empapado en esperma de tu especie,
amamantado en sangre de tu herencia.

XVIII

AMERICA I DO NOT INVOKE YOUR NAME IN VAIN

AMERICA, I do not invoke your name in vain.
When subject to the heart the sword,
when I hold in the soul the leak,
when by the windows
a new day yours penetrates to me,
I am and I am in the light that produces to me,
alive in the shade that determines to me,
I sleep and wide-awake in your essential aurora:
candy like the grapes, and terrible,
conductor of the sugar and the punishment,
soaked in sperm of your species,
nursed in blood of your inheritance.

Contributors

EDUARDO MIGUEL ARZANI is Dean of the School of Nursing at the Italian Institute College in Rosario, Argentina, and Titular Professor in its nursing management program. He was Titular Professor in nursing at the National University of *Rosario* in *Rosario*, Argentina until his retirement in 2004. He holds a master's degree in hospital management from the Autonomous University of Mexico (UNAM, 1982). He has had an extensive career as Dean and President of the Association of Argentinean Nursing Colleges and Schools. His research interests include nursing management, supply-demand service relationships, home health care, communications and coordination. Email: eduardomiguel.arzani@gmail.com

    EVELYN L. BARBEE earned a Ph.D. in anthropology from the University of Washington and masters and baccalaureate degrees in nursing from Teachers College, Columbia University, in New York, USA. Barbee is highly regarded for her seminal work on racism in U.S. nursing and for her research on depression among African American women. She held the rank of Professor at the Massachusetts College of Pharmacy and Health Sciences in Boston, Massachusetts until her retirement. Formerly, she held faculty positions at the University of Michigan and at the University of Wisconsin, Madison. She was the recipient of several honors and awards including the prestigious Bunting Fellowship at Harvard University in Cambridge, Massachusetts. She retains an active interest in the study of depression in African American women and in the area of racial health disparities. Email: eve1928@cox.net

    LUCILA CÁRDENAS BECERRIL holds a doctorate in education, a master's degree in Latin American studies and an undergraduate degree in nursing. She is a Professor in the School of Nursing and Obstetrics at the Autonomous University of the State of *México* in *Toluca, México* and the Past-President of the Mexican Federation of Colleges and Schools of Nursing. Dr. Cárdenas has authored over 12 books on nursing and co-authored 3 in the broader health care field. She lectures widely across Latin America, is an active researcher and a member of the Mexican National Research Group. Email: lucycabe62@yahoo.com

KAREN LUCAS BREDA is a tenured Associate Professor at the University of Hartford in West Hartford, Connecticut, USA. Breda holds a doctorate (Ph.D.) in anthropology from the University of Connecticut, in Storrs, Connecticut and a bachelor's degree (B.S.N.) and a master's degree (M.S.N.) from Boston University School of Nursing, in Boston, Massachusetts. First, as a Fulbright Scholar to Italy and later, as a fellow with the Giovanni Agnelli Foundation in Turin, Italy, Breda studied the political economy of health care in the Italian National Health System. Her interests in cross-national health care, globalization, and the world system have infused her scholarship and teaching for nearly two decades. Additionally, her specializations in critical political economy and cultural anthropology allow her to bring multidisciplinary analyses to her work. The volume "Nursing and Globalization in the Americas: A Critical Perspective" is an outcome of these efforts. Breda's clinical background is in pediatrics, mental health, and culturally-competent community nursing. Breda brings a critical and anthropological lens to her teaching and scholarship. Director of the grant-funded *Project Horizon*, a community service learning initiative at the University of Hartford, College of Education, Nursing and Health Professions, Breda works to link students, faculty and staff from across the university with community partners to co-create health, social and cultural advocacy initiatives. She is a local, national and international presenter, a successful grant writer, and an advocate for urban families and children living in poverty. She maintains her areas of expertise through reading, conference attendance and presentation, and professional networking, especially with colleagues from diverse professions and disciplines. Email: breda@hartford.edu

MARIA ALEJANDRA CHERVO is an Associate Professor of Nursing at the National University of *Rosario* in *Rosario*, Argentina. She graduated as a research methodology specialist from the National University of *Entre Ríos* in Argentina. She is completing a dual master's degree in nursing management and in higher education policy and management at the Center for Interdisciplinary Studies at the National University of *Rosario*. She directs undergraduate nursing research and graduate nursing research methodology as well as the community health nursing specialization program at the same university. Her research interests include nursing management and nursing education, especially curriculum and program development. Email: machervo@hotmail.com

PATRICIA JARA CONCHA is an Associate Professor at *Concepción* University in *Concepción*, Chile and is a doctoral candidate in the nursing doctoral program at the same university. Jara Concha received Master of Science degrees in nursing at the University of *Concepción* (1983 and 1994 respectively). As an adult intensive care clinical nurse specialist she functioned as a clinical perfusionist with the cardiac surgical team at the Regional Hospital of *Concepción* (1989 to 2002). She served as Dean of Nursing at the University of *Concepción* from 2002 to 2006. Presently, she is Director of the Commission for Assurance of Nursing Education Quality at the Chilean Association in Nursing Education and she is a research advisor to the Latin American Association of Colleges and Schools of Nursing (ALADEFE). Her main research interests include nursing practice, critical care nursing and nursing education. Email: pjara@udec.cl

HELENA MARIA SCHERLOWSKI LEAL DAVID is an Assistant Professor at the State University of *Rio de Janeiro*, Brazil. She received Ph.D. and Master's degrees in public health from the Oswaldo Cruz Foundation at the National School of Public Health in *Rio de Janeiro*. She teaches courses in research methodology, labor psychodynamics, public policy in health and education, and public health nursing. Her research focuses on working conditions and contemporaneous labor, drugs in the workplace, workers empowerment, and popular health education. David uses qualitative and participatory research methods. Email: helena.david@oi.com.br

JAQUELINE DA SILVA holds a Ph.D. in gerontological nursing from the University of California, San Francisco, USA and is a clinical nurse specialist, researcher, and faculty member of the Graduate Division of Anna Nery School of Nursing, Federal University of *Rio de Janeiro* in Brazil. She was a post-doctoral fellow in the "International research Capacity-Building Program to Study the Drug Phenomenon in Latin America and the Caribbean" co-sponsored by the Organization of American States/Inter-American Drug Abuse Control Commission–OAS/CICAD and the Center for Addiction and Mental Health–CAMH/Toronto/Canada. Her clinical expertise is caring for older adults. Her research areas include motivation to sustain self-care practices in chronic disease and the impact of illicit drug use on the drug users' family. Email: jackiedasilva@hotmail.com

GELSON LUIZ DE ALBUQUERQUE is a specialist in hospital and health care administration. He holds a master's degree in nursing science and a Ph.D. in nursing. An Associate Professor of nursing at the Federal University of Santa Catarina, in *Florianopolis, Santa Catarina*, Brazil, he teaches graduate and undergraduate courses. His 2002 book "The Struggle for Identity Training: Participation and Nursing." is informed by his research interests in health management, public health policy, health systems, and nursing organizations. De Albuqueque is the Past President of the *Santa Catarina* section of the Brazilian Nurses Association and Vice-President of the Pan-American Federation of Professional Nurses. Email: gelsonalbuquerque@yahoo.com.br

MARIA CECÍLIA PUNTEL DE ALMEIDA received her PhD in public health from the Oswaldo Cruz Foundation at the National School of Public Health in *Rio de Janeiro*, Brazil. Until her death in January 2009, she was a professor at the University of *São Paulo* at *Ribeirão Preto* College of Nursing in *São Paulo*, Brazil where she was on the graduate faculty in public health nursing. She served in many capacities: "Researcher 1B" in the Brazilian Council for Scientific and Techno-logical Development, Leader of the Research and Study Group on Collective Health, and Coordinator of the Technical Cooperation Agreements for Doctoral Education in Nursing between EERP-USP and the *Celaya* School of Nursing and Obstetrics at the University of *Guanajuato*, Mexico. Her research interests were in public health nursing, health practices, knowledge and policies. She authored two books: "Nursing Knowledge and its Practical Dimension" and "Nursing Work". To contact the University of *São Paulo at Ribeirão Preto*, email the Dean of the College of Nursing at: caroline@eerp.usp.br

MARÍA CLAUDIA DUQUE-PÁRAMO graduated with a Ph.D. in anthro-pology from the University of South Florida, in Tampa, Florida, USA in 2004. She received her bachelor's degree in nursing and her master's degree in community psychology from the *Pontificia Universidad Javeriana* in *Bogotá*, Colombia and she completed a specialization in pediatric nursing at the *Universidad Nacional Autónoma de México* in *México*. She is Full Professor at the School of Nursing in the *Pontificia Universidad Javeriana*. Throughout her academic career she has participated in working groups on nursing as a discipline, has given papers and has publications on topics related to nursing in Colombia. Her present research focuses on children and migration and child-centered research. Email: mcduque@javeriana.edu.co

JESSICA D. EMED holds a master's degree in nursing from McGill University in Montreal, Canada. She is a clinical nurse specialist in medicine and thrombosis at the Sir Mortimer B. Davis Jewish General Hospital and a nursing faculty Lecturer at McGill University. Emed's advocacy for individual and family health and empowerment shapes her clinical and scholarly work. She collaborates on the pan-Canadian "Safer Health Care Now!" campaign and serves on the Board of Directors of the community-based youth organization "Head and Hands." A published author, her research interests include evidence-based practice, illness prevention, patient and family coping, and staff development. Email:jemed@nurs.jgh.mcgill.ca

SUSAN FRENCH is Professor Emeritus, McMaster University and Professor (part-time) McGill University in Montreal, Canada. As a leader in the development of academic nursing in Canada, she played a pivotal role in the development of a national program of accreditation for undergraduate nursing education. Her extensive international experience focusing on the development of nursing and primary health care services provides her with a global perspective on nursing. For several decades her scholarship was in the area of career choices and the work environments of nurses as well as in community-based well elderly. She is a member of the philanthropic organization, The Newton Foundation, Montreal, dedicated to furthering the development of nursing in Montreal. Email: susan.french@mcgill.ca

MARICELA SÁNCHEZ GÁNDARA is a Professor in the School of Nursing at the University *Veracruzana* in *Veracruz*, *México*, and it's Past-Director. She has served as President of the Mexican Federation of Colleges and Schools of Nursing, of the Mexican Council for Accreditation and Certification of Nursing, and Director of the Port of *Veracruz* College of Nurses. Sánchez Gándara holds degrees in nursing, human development and thanatology. Her specialty areas are higher education and educational research. She has lectured in various educational and health venues both nationally and internationally. Email: mariwishga@yahoo.com.mx

BEATRIZ ARANA GÓMEZ holds a doctorate in nursing, a specialization in human development and a master's degree in peace studies and development. A Professor in the School of Nursing and Obstetrics at the Autonomous University of the State of *México* in *Toluca, México*, she teaches courses on research methodology and geriatrics, and advises masters and doctoral students in thesis preparation. She is an international consultant to the Board of Directors of the Anna Nery School of Nursing–Journal of Nursing, connected to the Federal University of *Rio de Janeiro* in Brazil. Her line of research includes evidence-based professional nursing care. Email: betyal8@yahoo.com.mx

MARTHA CECILIA LÓPEZ-MALDONADO is Full Professor and Director of Graduate Studies at the School of Nursing in the *Pontificia Universidad Javeriana* in *Bogotá,* Colombia. She received a master's degree in university administration and leadership from the *Universidad de los Andes,* and bachelor degrees in psychology and in nursing. She was Dean of the School of Nursing at the *Pontificia Universidad Javeriana* (1991-2001) and President of the Colombian Association of Schools of Nursing (1992-1998). She has conducted research on nursing and education. She has a research specialization on the phenomenon of drug use from the University of *São Paulo*. Her present research focuses on issues related to drug use and abuse. Email: mclopez@javeriana.edu.co

BEATRIZ CARMONA MEJÍA is a Professor at the National Autonomous University of Mexico in *Mexico City, México*. Beatriz Carmona Mejía holds degrees in nursing and specializations in holistic health and in nursing research. Currently, she is completing a Master's degree in business administration. She conducts research on complementary and holistic nursing interventions. She has held upper level administrative and leadership positions in Mexico and she is a member of the editorial board of the Journal of Nursing of the IMSS (the Mexican Institute of Social Security). She lectures in both national and international forums and is the co-author of several books. Email: bice61@yahoo.com.mx

TERESA ISABEL MICOZZI is a Professor of nursing at the National University of *Rosario* in *Rosario*, Argentina and Director of Research in the area of nursing education and multi-centric research studies. She holds a master's degree in nursing administration and an advanced specialization in epidemiology. She serves as official Spokesperson for the Education Section of the Latin American Association of Colleges and Schools of Nursing (ALADEFE), a part of the Latin American Union of Universities (UDUAL). Micozzi's background includes: Past-President of the Association of Argentinean Nursing Colleges and Schools, former Dean of Nursing and academic advisor in the graduate School of Medical Sciences at the University of *Rosario*, and former consultant to government organizations. She has numerous publications and awards. Email: teresamicozzi@hotmail.com

MARIA ITAYRA COELHO DE SOUZA PADILHA holds a Ph.D. in nursing from the Anna Nery School of Nursing at the Federal University of *Rio de Janeiro*, in Brazil and she completed post-doctoral studies at Lawrence Bloomberg School of Nursing, at the University of Toronto, in Ontario, Canada. Padilha is a Professor at the Federal University of *Santa Catarina*, in *Florianópolis*, Brazil and the former Vice-Coordinator of their graduate program in nursing. She is a member of Sigma Theta Tau, Rho Upsilon Chapter in Brazil and leader of the research group on nursing history in SC/Brazil. She has authored or edited over 100 articles, chapters, books, and monographs in Portuguese, English, and Spanish. Her research focuses on nursing history, especially teaching nursing history and professional identity. Email: padilha@nfr.ufsc.br

NESTOR ORTIZ REBOLLEDO is an Associate Professor at *Concepción* University in *Concepción*, Chile and is a doctoral candidate at the University of

Granada in Spain. He holds a graduate degree in psychotherapy and a master's degree in nursing from the University of *Concepción* (1993 and 1998 respectively). He completed a specialization in drug research at the University of *São Paulo* in Brazil and was awarded an Alpha Maristan Scholarship in community care through the European Community in 2001. His research interests are in the education of nurses in mental health and psychiatry. He has served as a Visiting Professor in international health at several other universities in Chile. Email: nortiz@udec.cl

MERRILL SINGER, a medical anthropologist, is a professor in the Department of Anthropology and senior research scientist at the Center for Health, Intervention and Prevention (University of Connecticut) and an affiliated scholar of the Center for Inter-disciplinary Research on AIDS (Yale University). He has published over 200 articles and book chapters and authored or edited 20 books. He is the recipient of the Rudolph Virchow Award, the George Foster Memorial Award for Practicing Anthropology, the AIDS and Anthropology Paper Prize and the Prize for Distinguished Achievement in the Critical Study of North America. Email: anthro8566@aol.com

SANDRA VALENZUELA SUAZO holds a doctorate in nursing from the University of *São Paulo*, in Brazil (1999). She is an Associate Professor at *Concepción* University in *Concepción*, Chile and was instrumental in creating Chile's first nursing doctoral program at the same university. She is Editor of the journal "Nursing Research Review" (*Ciencia y Enfermería*) and Director of the Chilean Association of Nursing Education. Her areas of research are gender and occupational health, women's health, and nursing care. She has served as a Visiting Professor at other universities in Chile and across Latin-America. Email: svalenzu@udec.cl

VERONICA BEHN THEUNE was Full Professor at the University of *Concepción* in *Concepción*, Chile, until her retirement in 2007 and she was Dean of Nursing at the same institution from 1994 to 1998. She is Past President of the Chilean Association of Nursing Education and served as Director of the Chilean Center of Development and Research for the International Classification for Nursing Practice (ICNP®). Presently, she advises for the Latin American Association of Colleges and Schools of Nursing (ALADEFE), is a member of the National Program of Accreditation for Undergraduate Nursing Education, and leads workshops related to ICNP®. Behn Theune holds a master's degree in nursing from the University of *Concepción*. Her areas of research are family nursing, health promotion and nursing education. Email: vbehn@udec.cl

MARIA DA GLORIA MIOTTO WRIGHT holds a Ph.D. in nursing, concentration in public health from the University of *São Paulo*, School of Nursing of *Ribeirão Preto*, SP/Brazil. She is the Coordinator of the Educational Development Program at the Demand Reduction Section of Inter-American Drug Abuse Control Commission–CICAD of the Organization of American States-OAS/US. She has occupied academic positions in Brazil, United States, Canada, and public positions at the Ministry of Education, and National Research Council–CNPq/Brazil. Her international leadership has advanced nursing graduate programs and research in Latin America and the Caribbean, as well as in the areas of public health and education. Her research interests include drugs and violence, international health;

nursing education and research. Her scientific papers have been published in Latin America, the United States, and Europe. Email: gwright@oas.org

MARIA ZADOROZNYJ holds a Ph.D. in sociology from the University of Wisconsin, Madison, USA. She holds the rank of Associate Professor in the Department of Sociology at Flinders University, Adelaide, Australia. Her doctoral thesis investigated the collective mobility strategies of registered nurses in the United States. Her research interests remain in the organization of work in the health sector, especially in the historical development of 'boundaries' around the knowledge and work of occupations such as medicine, midwifery, nursing and most recently of new classifications of paid care workers. She maintains an ongoing interest in the influence of structural factors such as gender and class on health and on the organization of health care work. Email: MariaZadoroznyj@flinders.edu.au

Index

San Vicente Hospital, 70
SARS, 238
"Schema for Nursing Research" (Gonzales,
    Jerez, Krebs & Royo), 88
Schools of nursing (free-standing),
    hospitals *vs.,* 2
Scientific management movement,
    293-294, 309
Shortage, nursing
  Argentina, 119
  Brazil, 148
  Canada, 248-249, 260
  globalization and neoliberalism, 328
  overview, 13-15
  United States, 314-315
Singer, Merrill, 275, 366
Sisters of Charity, 56
Slavery, 277, 289
Smallpox epidemic (1874-1875), 290
Social justice, 332-333
Social origins of disease, biomedicine
    taking attention away from, 3
Socio-economic development model, 99
Socioeconomic stratification, 48-49
Socio-political analysis, nursing as a ripe
    field for, 5
South America, 2
  See also individual countries
Soviet Union/Soviet, 80
Spain, 27, 55, 56, 100
State Nurses' Associations (SNAs),
    300-304
Status for nurses, low, 4
Stiepovich, Jasna, 90
Stock market crash (1929), 281
Structural adjustment programs (SAPs),
    9, 139
"Study of Chilean Human Resources and
    Nursing Needs" (Krebs), 71
Suazo, Sandra V., 366
Supply of nurses. *See* Shortage, nursing

Taylorism, 245, 293-294
Temporary work arrangements, 14
Theune, Veronica B., 366
Titus, Shirley, 301-302
Trade. *See* North American Free Trade
    Agreement

Transnational corporations, 58-59
  See also Globalization and neoliberalism
Tuberculosis, 238
20th century health care and
    regulation/allopathic medicine, 2-3
21st century, nursing challenges in the,
    259-263

Unions
  Argentina, 102-103, 110-111
  Brazil, 152-153
  Canada, 245-246
  Mexico, 213-214
United States, 300-308
United American Nurses (UAN), 307
United Kingdom, 107-108, 225-226,
    229-230
United Nations
  Children's Fund (UNICEF), 39, 71, 86
  Iraq, 93
  Program for Development (UNPD), 58,
    80, 103
  World Declaration on Higher Education
    for the Twenty First Century, 42
United Self-Defense Forces of Colombia
    (AUC), 24
United States
  biomedicine, 286-288, 315-316
  Canada, historical ties with, 225
  capitalism shapes organized nursing,
    291-293
  Chile, helping to overthrow Allende in,
    58
  class/race in nursing, historical context
    of, 296-300
  Clinton health care plan, 284
  Colombian health policies, influence on,
    35-37
  colonization and slavery, 277, 289
  core industrial first world country
    policies, 107-108
  corporatization/biomedicine, 309-310
  craft *vs.* routinized care, nursing,
    294-295
  cultural hegemony, 291-293
  demographics, 277-279
  Depression, The Great, 308
  divisions within the nursing ranks, 293,
    298-299